Building A New Asia

Building A New Asia

Edited by
Mahavir Singh

Maulana Abul Kalam Azad Institute of Asian Studies, Kolkata

SHIPRA

ISBN: 81-7541-241-0

First Published in India in 2005

Published by:
SHIPRA PUBLICATIONS
115-A, Vikas Marg, Shakarpur
Delhi-110092, INDIA
Phone: 91-11-55277210, 91-11-22500954
E-mail: info@shiprapublications.com
www.shiprapublications.com

Laser Typesetting by:
Sunshine Graphics
Delhi-110032

Printed at:
Chaudhary Offset Process
Delhi-110051

Contents

bilateral and multi-lateral cooperation in Asia and that this has been successful particularly in the field of security. However, the problem of security is closely connected with that of development and here he notes that globalisation based on neo-liberal theories has affected the capacity of many developing countries to carry on activities, which could help improve the condition of the poor. It is, therefore, important to present viable alternatives to the neo-liberal policies. Yurlov argues that globalisation is not the solution since it does not address issues of equitable distribution of resources. He concludes by emphasizing the need for evolving their own paradigm of development suitable for their socio-cultural framework by the Asian, Eurasian, African and Latin American countries. In the process they need to work out their own concept of globalisation.

In his paper C.P. Bhambhri who like Falix Yurlov examines the fall out of globalisation for development of a new Asia, raises a basic question, viz., is regionalism as a sub-system of global capitalism, an answer to the problems and difficulties faced by the newly industrializing countries or the late peripheral capitalist countries of the erstwhile decolonised world? The prevailing trend in Asia in the post Second World War period is, in Bhambhri's opinion, the adoption of the 'American model of market economy'. Under such conditions the path of regional associations of capitalist countries on the model of the European Union, the North-Atlantic Free Trade Association, the Association of East Asia and Asia-Pacific Rim countries, and G-7 countries in their search for security and development in the prevailing framework of new globalisation. Thus, the issue is according to Bhambhri "not to minimize the role of regional organizations but to understand that every region is following the capitalist path of development and the logic of capitalist development is such that it integrates regions and sub-regions in an unequal manner with one another, and with America, the sole imperialist military power in the 21st century."

But Bhambhri's scepticism about the chances of regionalism in Asia in the sphere of security and development without challenging the American "finance capital and market-led" neo-globalisation, is not shared by Xu Yongquan. In his paper Xu Yongquan makes the point that with the acceleration of globalisation and inter-dependence among economies certain trends are visible in Asian regional economic cooperation. First, the United State's attitude has changed from opposition to non-interference or acquiescence. Secondly Asian economies are no longer satisfied with the APEC model and have begun a stronger cooperation in some preferred sectors such as finance and information technology. And thirdly, China recognizes the importance of regional economic cooperation and is enthusiastic about exploring new possibilities of cooperation such as founding of a free trade zone on the basis of military and political cooperation within the Shanghai Cooperation organization.

The volumes include a number of papers related to the strategic triangle comprising China, India and Russia. In his contribution Chinese scholar Zhou Yuyun analyses both the favourable and the restricting conditions for promoting this trilateral cooperation. The fact that all the three powers stand for multi-polarisation of international relations, emphasize the need to strengthen the role of the U.N. and share a common stand in respect of fight against international terrorism, accounts for the favourable conditions for realizing this strategic triangle. The restricting conditions according to Zhou lie in the slow development of Sino-Indian relations as compared to Sino-Russian and Indo-Russian relations. Besides, China, India and Russia attach great importance to their respective relations with the United States and manifest a varied degree of eagerness towards trilateral cooperation. The development and strengthening of the mechanism for meeting in the United Nations and increased consultation and cooperation on regional issues of common concerns are considered practical steps of significance by him.

The paper by R.R. Subramanian contends that in the new unipolar world a major antidote to check the onward extension of the US led NATO to the regions of central Asia and South Asia would be cooperation between Russia, India and China. In his opinion Russia has an important role to play in bringing India and China closer in the evolution of a new Pan-Asian Security order. Hari Vasudevan in his contribution attempts to show that the notion of trilateral cooperation is not a sudden "arrival" in the Russian Ministry of Foreign Affairs. Rather, the idea of trilateral cooperation took shape during the last year of Soviet rule as "the formation of a Eurasian Zone of security and stability". The sharpness imparted to it by Primakov should not be seen merely as an attempt to create a greater space for Russian manouvre vis-à-vis the United States. It was a serious strategy for the post-cold war period.

R. R. Sharma's paper deals with the complex task of perceiving and defining the larger political, cultural and economic identity of Asia. Sharma is of the view that contemporary Asia is divided on several counts and reflects the continuing existence of several major identities, which hinders the prospects of a broader Asian Union and solidarity. Turning to the search for democratic culture and values in Asia he feels that a large number of Asian societies are politically dysfunctional where the ruling elite is invariably unresponsive and oppressive. Marked by poor governance, growing poverty and rampant corruption, there are no linkages between the political elite and the population. Sharma however, does not relate the fragile character of the democratic system in many Asian countries to their domestic politics alone, as forced democratization has been an important trend in these societies since the second would war. Many third world countries during this period were forced to accept the western model of democracy as a pre-condition for their acceptance in the international system. The outcome has been that these implanted democracies are half genuine, half imported – a situation, which has ultimately given rise to façade democratization. The solution in his opinion lies in creation of a healthy civil society, which alone will lead to creation of stable and accountable democracies.

Sharma concludes by emphasizing upon turbulent phase through which present day international relations are passing. Hence, the need of the hour is to take a holistic view of the sources of threat to peace and stability in Asia as whole and identify their real cause that lies in the new imperial urge, unilateralism, clash of civilizations, war against international terrorism which are nothing but new incarnation of the hegemonistic geopolitical ideas. The answer to the problem lies in establishing a network of genuine regional institutions to address issues like ethnic relations, cross border terrorism and environmental degradation etc. This is likely to stimulate the environmental degradation and stimulations.

If Sharma's paper makes a strong plea for setting up a network of regional security system as part of an overall global security system conceived in the spirit of the U.N. charter, Sharadindu Mukherji in his contribution rejects the feasibility of any regional cooperation in Asia particularly in the context of South Asia. For him "the quality of civil Society" is vital for country to enter into special relationship, which is not the case as he argues, with Pakistan and China. However, the civil society as a factor could take a back seat only when some urgent objective in the domain of external relations is to be achieved in a short time and the countries involved do not have a considerable common history and common international border.

Besides, the civil society factor which figures in a couple of papers as a facilitator in the development of regional cooperation among Asian countries in the domain of security and development, V. Suryanarayan reflects upon India's abiding influences in South east Asia and suggests their utilization for purposes of a benign cultural diplomacy. Analysing the impact of Ramanayana in Indonesia and the festival of Navrathri in Thailand, he however, urges a re-evaluation of the concept of greater India which denies the South Asian cultures autonomy of their own.

The volume also contains contributions by scholars advocating a closer cooperation between India, South Asia and Central Asia as neighbouring regions having close historical and cultural ties. Thus, in his papers Uzbek scholar diplomat F. G. Teshabaev brings out how Central Asia is becoming increasingly and deeply linked to the security issues of its southern and eastern neighbours. The new situation in his view has raised the importance of Central Asian and South Asian regional cooperation as a factor in geo-political stability of not only the region itself but of the whole world. The other Uzbek scholar diplomat Surat Mirkasymov in his paper emphasizes the significance of joint efforts to fight against common enemies such as terrorism, extremism and drug trafficking that are hindering the efforts to eliminate economic and social backwardness. In the absence of such joint efforts a new developed and secure Asia cannot be built.

Surendra Gopal's paper which discusses the development of India's relations with the Central Asian Republics in the post-Soviet period focuses on India's concerns about possible sources of instability in the region and on possibility of cooperation that could lead to stability. In his presentation Indian journalist D.R. Goyal recalls how Nehru's idea to rebuild the newly independent nations on the basis of cooperation rather than conflict and confrontation is still relevant in today's context though the would has changed today from bipolarity to unipolarity. Goyal finds fault with the present policies of the United States which do not reflect any sincere concern for democracy or earnestness about war against terrorism with the result that regional combinations are emerging in various parts of the globe to defend national sovereignty and arrest unilateralism increasingly evident in U.S. actions. He makes a plea for India which has considerable experience of mobilizing the protesting forces for a fair and just world order during the late 40s and 50s, to take steps to coordinate policies with countries of Southeast Asia, Africa and Latin America. No effort however is needed to build an anti-American block. Only the policy makers in Washington have to be persuaded to get out of the 'American interest first' syndrome.

P.L. Dash's paper highlight the emergence of Eurasia as a territorial entity following the disintegration of the Soviet Union and the rise of China and India as independent actors at regional and global levels. Within the Eurasian landmass the three Asias –West Asia, Central Asia and South Asia became important in the U.S. scheme of things. Dash emphasizes the centrality of Central Asia for India and points out the great potential of this region and Russia for transport and communication between southern and eastern parts of Asia and Europe. R.S. Yadav in his paper discusses the implications of Russia – India strategic partnership for the common security of Asia. The paper describes how in the post-cold war period the legacy of past relations among these countries along with multiple developments at global and regional levels have transformed Indo-Russian relations from bilateral "strategic cooperation" to "strategic partnership" with an aim not limited to bilateral defence cooperation but to regulate the regional and global developments in the interest of peace and stability in Asia and world as a whole. Both countries are making efforts to involve more countries of this region particularly China and Central Asian Republics in their pursuit of building a multi-polar world order.

Ajay Patnaik's paper dwells in detail on Indo-Central Asian cooperation particularly in the context of war against terrorism and of the future of this cooperation. It ends by mentioning various efforts towards evolving an Asian security and cooperation mechanism by OSCE, SICA, CIS Collective Security Treaty Organization and the SCO. Patnaik expresses the hope that China India and Iran will play crucial roles in the development of the security scenario in Central Asia. In her paper Vasundhara Mohan discusses how regional cooperation in Central Asia could go a long way in mitigating the effects of small domestic markets and extreme distances to industrialise markets. In her view such cooperation is not possible given the common historical and cultural experiences along with diversity and interdependence of their resource base. The Central Asian States have made only limited progress in achieving regional, political and economic objectives. If regional cooperation is to be increased it will require committed leadership from within and patient assistance from outside. Some individual papers included in this volume deal with the implications of developments in the middle east and south east Asia for evolution of mechanism of regional cooperation in the sphere of security and development in Asia. The paper by Chinese scholar Zhang Jianwei discuss the factors that influence the security and stability in the middle east, viz, the role of the United States, inter ethnic relations and religion. Unless the United Sates changes its Middle East policy of guaranteeing the absolute security of Israel, regional terrorism cannot be eradicated. In the Chinese scholars opinion the situation will only worsen once the United States implements its Great Middle – East Proposal. The Kurdish question will become a hot issue o the region while the contradictions between the Shiaite and Sunni Muslims will create trouble in Iraq leading to instability in the region.

S.P. Singh's paper discusses the threat to Southeast Asian security from the Al-Qaeda sponsored terrorism. Singh mentions the large-scale infiltration of the south east Asian countries by Islamists terrorist groups particularly the Philippines, Malaysia and Indonesia. The Islamist terrorists aim to replace the existing regimes with Islamic polity based on the tenets of the Shariat. The paper outlines the various bilateral and multilateral anti-terrorist measures undertaken by different countries in the region and the ASEAN to combat this menace. Singh also given details of assistance given by the United States to the South East Asian countries as an integral part of its global war against terrorism.

Shankari Sundararaman's paper has for its focus the changing dynamics of regionalism in South East Asia. She makes a case study of ASEAN regionalism, analyzing the problems faced by this regional organization. She examines critically the strategy devised by it to cope with the challenge of change. In her opinion ASEAN has survived through its resilience ad willingness to restructure itself according to the changing global environment. Its success has been attributed to the skilful combination of the two approaches – the legal-rational and social-cultural approach. The principle of consensus has served ASEAN well as it got support from a 'regional-cultural style'. Sundararaman in her paper discusses the impact of the 1997 financial crisis and the 9/11 terrorists attacks on the United States on South East Asian regionalism. The increasing economic ties of the ASEAN with India, China and the East Asian powers like Japan and South Korea have also been discussed in this paper. Besides, signing India-ASEAN free trade agreement and the China-ASEAN free trade agreement the ASEAN members have also signed agreements on economic cooperation on bilateral basis with several Asian countries.

Russian scholar Sergei Lounev underlines the importance of economic cooperation as the best way to achieve trust in the Asia-Pacific region. In his paper he emphasizes that comprehensive development of economic ties may overcome all political, military and cultural differences and help all the three Asian giants (China, Japan and India) to build mutual confidence with their neighbours. He argues that this cooperation can be best achieved in the sphere of energy in which Russia has vast resources. The Russian energy sector hold out prospects for a firm basis for regional inter-dependence and through its contribution to energy security serve as a barometer of regional integration. The prospects of strategic and inexpensive energy supply from its Siberian oil and gas fields by Russia to China-Japan and India provides a major opportunity for increased regional integration which reinforces the vision for a more integrated Asia.

Meena Singh Roy's paper argues for stronger linkages, more effective regional mechanisms of cooperation as Asia is more disunited than other continents where regional forums have been functioning activity. She examines an important initiative taken by the Central Asian Republic of Kazakhstan called the Conference on Interaction and Confidence Building Measures in Asia (CICA). This initiative aims at creating a regional mechanism of preventive measures in Asia and development of a new system of relations between the states of the vast Asian region.

The volume also includes country-specific papers related to Japan, Mongolia, Kyrgyzstan Tajikistan and Kazakhstan. Thus, Sanjana Joshi's paper brings out how the division of rolls envisaged by the U.S.-Japan security alliance has undergone "redefinition" over the years, with Japan assuming greater responsibility. This has however, not led to a complete "reassessment" of Japan's security ties with United States. It is therefore imperative that Japan's roll in Asia is assessed within the framework of the U.S.-Japan security alliance. From this it does not follow that in the efforts at Asian security cooperation the U.S. Japan alliance must be viewed in adversarial terms. But certainly Japan's activism in Asian security issues must be viewed in a more realistic and pragmatic manner. It is unlikely that Japan would be a reliable partner in forging Asian cooperation aimed at checkmating U.S. unilateralism. Kyrgyz scholar Ainur Elebaeva's paper underlines the fundamental political changes in the world and particularly in Asia following the disintegration of the Soviet Union and emergence of the newly independent states, active military involvement of the USA in Afghanistan in the wake of 9/11 terrorist attack on the USA and the U.S. invasion of Iraq in the present situation the national security of the Central Asian countries including Kyrgyzstan depends on how efficiently they manouvre through their foreign policy priorities and coordination with the most suitable partners in an effort to ensure comprehensive collective security and stability in this region as a whole. With its limited political economic and defense potential Kyrgyzstan had to maintain a balanced relationship with the three major players in the Asian political arena, mainly, Russia, China and the U.S.A.. Sharad K. Soni in his paper analyses Mongolia's security concerns in the post-cold war period on the basis of three key documents adopted by its government – "concept of national security of Mongolia", "concept of Mongolia's foreign policy" and "fundamentals of the military doctrine of Mongolia". These three documents are inter-linked so far as basic objectives are concerned which are geared to safe guarding the country's national interest and ensuring overall advancement of its people.

Tajik scholar Inom Sh. Normatov's paper analyses the complex nature of problems related to the use of water by the Central Asian Republics. The main use of water resources in the region is confined to energy generation and irrigation which in turn depends on the location of a particular country. The countries at the Upper stream are interested in use of water for generating energy, while those in the down stream in its use for irrigation. The problem further varies with the time of requirement of water for these purposes. For irrigation water is needed during the vegetation period i.e. from April to October. It is therefore necessary to fill a reservoir with water in winter to be used in summer whereas for power generation water is required during the coldest period of the year – October to April which demands filling the reservoir in summer for use in winter. From here the clash of interest begins. Since it is impossible to combine these two interests within one reservoir. Limited number of reservoirs in the areas where the river flow is greater further aggravates the problem. Such reservoirs are four in number – Nurek and Kayrakkum in Tajikistan, Toktogul in Kyrgyzstan and Andijan in Uzbekistan – out of which only Nurek and Toktogul can serve long-term purpose. Since they are situated in different states, lack of a developed and coordinated mechanism for their systematic operation is another problem. Altogether it has created an alarming situation in the Ural sea basin which faces an ecological disaster.

Another problem in the use of water resources is the existing water division which calls for reconsideration since the present limitation is not legally fixed. These limitations need to be fixed amicably by the Central Asian states through discussion, negotiation and working out of common principles of legal settlement. Finally, the paper suggests that the problems faced by the region in this sphere are neither due to insufficiency of water resources nor potentiality for sustainable development and nor due to present resource crunch of the Central Asian States, but because of the existing state of relations among them. The solution therefore depends on establishing good neighbourly mutually beneficial relations among the states of the region.

Indian scholar Hoshiar singh makes a comparison of the differences between the freedom movement of India which was peaceful and that of many a Asian countries who have to resort to armed struggle resulting in loss of human life and disruption in smooth flow of cultural traditions. As these nations won their independence through major military engagements, they inherited the military as a vital organ of the state after acquiring sovereignty. India on the contrary inherited the administrative steel frame from the British. However this borrowed administrative system had undergone many innovations during the last five decades. It is now almost a new institutional network performing a multiplicity of roles in an environment which is very different from the U.K. but has a lot in common with other countries in Asia. The Indian Administrative system has according to Singh handled "security" crisis as well as "development" challenges with considerable success even in difficult conditions, dominated by poverty, inequality and sharp diversities.

Kazakh scholar Askar Shomanov's paper focuses upon the multidimensional character of escalation of terrorist violence in particular regions of the world under the ideological influence of politicised Islam of the radical kind. During the last decade it has crossed the border of separate regions of the Muslim world and become a constant factor in the political life of many countries including the Western ones. This complex situation can, in Shomanov's view, only be tackled successfully through building a global system of security in a multipolar world order.

Drawing upon the cogent thinking on the subject developed by scholars in Russia and the Central Asian republics, Shomanov views the sprawling menace of terrorism fueled by religio-political extremism through the prism of history. Shomanov identifies the objective historical reasons behind this phenomenon and its significant social base. He also draws attention to exploitation of Islamic ideology by global centres of influence that promote their geo-political influence. The spread of religious extremism and its end-result — Islamist terrorism — is also examined in its aspect of opposition to neo-liberalism led globalisation.

In the last article of this volume Nalin Kumar Mohapatra has made an attempt to examine the regional security of Eurasian countries. He analyses the security threats– both traditional and non-traditional – to this region and role of Shanghai Cooperation Organisation in combating these threats. The paper also highlights the imperatives of economic cooperation among the SCO countries for strengthening peace and security in the region.

The editor would like to put on record his sincerest thanks to all the contributors of this volume for their cooperation. Thanks are also due to Prof. Devendra Kaushik, Chairman of the Executive Council of the Institute for his guidance and support and the Institute's Fellows – Anita Sengupta, Sanjana Joshi, Susmita Bhattacharya and Priya Singh for the editorial assistance rendered by them. It is our earnest hope that the volume will provide ample material to reflect upon to specialists and lay readers both and make its humble contribution to the churning of ideas on the vital problem of building a New Asia — peaceful, prosperous and stable.

1

Building a New Asian Security System through Regional Cooperation

Renewal of Bandung Spirit

DEVENDRA KAUSHIK

It is more than a decade since the Cold War ended. The changing scenario of inter-state relations on the Asian continent obviously calls for a new appraisal in view of the fact that the pessimistic prognosis made by Eurocentric Asian watchers, who forecast acute arms race and power rivalries among major Asian states resulting in bloody wars, has failed to materialise. In fact, there has not been any major war in Asia since the 1978-1979 China-Vietnam conflict. The festering Palestine-Israel conflict in West Asia and the Indo-Pak imbroglio over Kashmir would not have been there at least in such an acute form but for the abetment by outside powers, the United States in the first place. The ongoing bloodshed in Iraq is the direct result of the imperial course of unilateralism pursued by Washington. The recurrent threats in Taiwan and the Korean peninsula have also much to do with the course of policy followed by Washington. Surprisingly, there has been 'non-balancing' of Asian states against China, the lack of Japanese armament and five decades of 'non-invasion' by North Korea which only testifies to the growing maturity and statesmanship of the Asian states. [1]

From the above, however it does not follow that the developing nations in Asia do not face serious threats to security on their continent. The point to be emphasised is that the challenges to Asian security are, in the main, a byproduct of the aggressive course of unilaterialism pursued by the United States aimed at assuming control of the vast natural resources of the developing world. Beginning with the 70s of the last century, a powerful section of the US establishment has come to view the increasing consumption of the natural resources of the developing countries by their ever-growing population as a threat to the US security which must be counteracted by all possible means including the forcible ouster of the non-pliable regimes and seizure of their natural resources.

Asia, comprising China, India, Japan and a large part of Russia and containing half the world's population has not been a primary focus of international politics until recently. It is only during the last two decades that this continent has emerged as a region whose economic, military and diplomatic power has surpassed that of Europe. The most remarkable thing about Asian development is that the region has succeeded in avoiding both major and minor interstate conflicts. The dramatic power transition of the Asian giant China — the most populous nation of the world — which has evolved from a middle-ranking economy to the most vibrant economy in the world, already the second largest, has not evoked fears among the Asian countries. This has led many international analysts to speak of the Asian traditions of international relations as different from the Western traditions.

A prosperous and strong China has in fact become a sheet anchor of regional stability, showing little inclination towards becoming a revisionist or imperial power. In the recent past it has resolved territorial disputes with Afghanistan, Burma, Kazakhstan, Kyrgyzstan, Mongolia, Nepal, Pakistan and Russia. Beijing has also, more recently, settled border problems with Cambodia and Vietnam. Of course, unresolved disputes remain over Taiwan, with ASEAN over the Spartly Island and Japan over Senkaku Island. But then there remain unresolved disputes over the northern territories between Russia and Japan and over the Tokto Island between Japan and South Korea.Yet no war over territory has been waged in Asia, over the last two decades.

There are no signs of power rivalry between Japan and China. In fact, Japan has a 27 billion-trade deficit with China.[2] Forty thousand Taiwanese companies have investments in the PRC, employing 10 million people. The Taiwanese investment in the mainland is estimated between 40 to 50 billon dollars.[3] In 2001, 60 per cent of the Taiwanese direct foreign investment went to China.[4] Japan has not agreed to allow the USA the use of its military bases in the event of a conflict over Taiwan. The trade turnover between Japan and China increased 52 times since 1972 reaching 570 billion dollars in 1997. China is Japan's second largest trading partner and Japan ranks as China's largest trading partner. China's relations with Vietnam have also been quite cordial. In 1997 their trade amounted to 1.44 billion dollars. The Chinese investment in Vietnam was estimated at

102 million dollars. In 2000 Beijing, extended an assistance of 55 million dollars to modernize steel and other plants in Vietnam. The South East Asian countries — Malaysia, Singapore, Indonesia and the Philippines have excellent economic relations with China despite their military ties with the United States. In short, Asian countries do not fear China.

Recent developments in Asia have proved the pessimistic prognosis of Western publicists like Dick Wilson utterly wrong. Wilson who questioned the ability of Asians to live with peace among themselves and had predicted that "the wars of the coming decades, if there are to be any more, are likely to be between Asians, not between Europeans and Asians."[5] During the 1970s and 1980s it was quite trendy in the West to point out to the developing countries in Asia and Africa as the most serious threat to global security and stability. The much publicised British withdrawal in Asia from East of Suez was candidly described by a British analyst, Sir Esler Dening in 1968 in the following words: "We have felt obliged to withdraw our forces... in circumstances by no means favourable to us." Denying that the decision for military withdrawal from South East Asia and the Persian Gulf meant "that we consider ourselves as no longer having a role to play in Asia as a whole", Sir Dening declared that by adopting, for the time being "a low military profile" in Asia, the British were only looking forward to the "the recession of the wave of anti-colonialism in the hope that disillusioned Asian statesmen would then be willing to cooperate with the West."[6]

The hoped-for moment was misjudged to have arrived in May 2003 when Britain under Tony Blair tried to return to its former colony in Iraq riding Washington piggy-back as a coalition partner. The naked US-British aggression against Iraq, further intensification of the bloody suppression of the Palestinian people's right to national independence, the continued US threat of unilateral penal military action against the so-called "rogue" states in Asia, the beefed up US military presence in West Asia and the Gulf region, acquisition of military bases in Central Asia and Pakistan in the name of fighting international terrorism heralded the advent of the second wave of colonisation which poses a serious threat to security and stability on the Asian continent.

The first threat to peace, security and the development in Asia was posed during the 50s of the last century by the setting up of the military blocs — CENTO and SEATO — at the initiative of the US-led Western powers. This threat was sought to be countered by the non-aligned movement initiated by India under the leadership of Jawaharlal Nehru. Even before the attainment of independence the leadership of the Indian national movement visualised an active role for India in Asian affairs. It was conscious of the need for a wider Asian unity in building a new Asia after the overthrow of the colonial yoke. As early as 1920 Gandhi wrote about growing solidarity of Asian countries against Western colonialism. At the 1922 annual session of the Indian National Congress C.R. Das urged Indian participation in an Asian federation which he regarded as inevitable. The talk about Asian federation was again heard at the Congress sessions in 1926 and 1928.[7]

After the attainment of freedom, India under the leadership of Nehru began to address itself more concretely to the task facing the emerging countries of Asia and to work out a common approach to ensuring peace and security on the continent. India's geostrategic location as the meeting point between West and South East Asia and its cultural ties even with the more remote East Asia predetermined a major role for it in the affairs of Asia. The fact that it was among the first few Asian countries to throw off the colonial yoke also placed it in the vanguard of the struggle for other Asian countries' freedom.

At the Asian Relations Conference held in Delhi, on the eve of independence, Nehru gave a call for faith in Asia. The Conference stressed the need for Asian unity and announced the arrival of Asia on the world stage. China and the Central Asian Republics then forming parts of the USSR participated in the Conference. Later, addressing the UN General Assembly in Paris in 1948 Nehru declared: "... the world is something bigger than Europe. ... Asia counts in world affairs. Tomorrow it will count much more than today."[8]

India's notable contribution to peace and security in Asia and the world lies in evolving the principles of Nonalignment and the concept of an area of peace in reply to the military bloc politics of the Western powers in the post-war years. Not international communism but poverty and backwardness of Asian peoples posed a threat to their security. As tension began to travel from Europe to Asia in 1952-1955 with the Western project to set up a Middle East Command, the Northern tier strategy, the US military assistance to Pakistan, the creation of SEATO and the Baghdad pact, India tried to meet this challenge by evolving the concept of peace area. To the Dullesean strategy of collective security through military pacts Nehru counterposed the concept of collective peace which was a further elaboration of his concept of area of peace. Together with China, India formulated the strategy of ensuring security through cooperation based on the *Panchshila* or the five principles of peaceful coexistence, embodied in the Sino-Indian agreement on Tibet in 1954. The *Panchsila* approach to security relied on peaceful cooperation, rather than military competition, among nations for preservation of peace. It sought to raise a structure of peace in Asia based on mutual assurance by the states to conduct their relations on the basis of mutual respect for sovereignty and territorial integrity, non-interference in internal affairs, settlement of disputes through peaceful means, peaceful co-existence and mutually beneficial cooperation. The Bandung conference of Afro-Asian states held in 1955 adopted this approach to security jointly evolved by India and China.

In a way, the espousal in June 1969 by the Soviet leader Leonid Brezhnev of the idea of a system of collective security in Asia was a continuation of the Sino-Indian joint approach of security through peaceful cooperation and not through military means. It was, however, misconstrued as directed at isolating China under conditions of sharp ideological differences between the Soviet Union and China mainly related to the character of the process of social transformation going on in the countries of the third world and the policy of non-alignment. Brezhnev's proposal for discussion on the idea of collective security in Asia which came in the wake of the initiative already taken towards European security referred to the proposed system as the "best replacement for the existing military groupings".[9] Yet in the atmosphere vitiated by Sino-Soviet rift it was conveniently ignored. Commenting on the proposal of Brezhnev, the French weekly *Le Monde* wrote in its issue of 16 July 1969: "The system Russians envisage would be a very open one ... it would not be directed against anyone and in suitable circumstance, non-Asian powers might participate.... The suggestion is for a pact that would neither be anti-Chinese nor anti-American."

In fact, Berzhnev's proposal was a combination of the old Soviet thinking on collective security from the early 30s of the last century. At the meeting of the Political Commission of the Conference on the Reduction and Limitation of Armaments (Geneva 1933) the Soviet delegation, by way of amendment to the draft of the European Declaration on the non-use of force, proposed that the sphere of action of this principle be extended beyond Europe.[10] At the 17th session of the League of Nations (28 September 1936) the Soviet Foreign Minister, M. Litvinov, thus outlined the Soviet idea of collective security at the regional level: "The principal idea contained in its (Soviet government's) suggestion is of regional and, if necessary, bilateral pacts of mutual assistance. We have in mind regions of various geographical sizes and shapes including even entire *continents* (emphasis added), since larger the region covered by the pact, the greater the guarantees of security."[11]

After a long pause, the drive towards Asian security received a shot in arm with the emergence of the Shanghai Five. The process began in 1989 with negotiations on Confidence Building Measures on the Soviet-Chinese border to help the talks already under way between the two countries to settle their border problems. These negotiations were later transformed into talks on confidence building measures and reduction of armed forces between Russia, Kazakhstan, Kyrgyzstan and Tajikistan on one hand and China on the other, following the disintegration of the USSR in 1991. These talks which started in 1989 at the bilateral level between the then USSR and the PRC acquired in 1993 the character of a multilateral dialogue between Russia, China and the three bordering Central Asian states of Kazakhstan, Kyrgyzstan and Tajikistan. On 26 April 1996 the Presidents of the five border states met in

Shanghai to sign a package of 14 agreements on border issues, confidence building measures and reduction of armed forces deployed in the border regions. The Shanghai Five, renamed the Shanghai Forum after Uzbekistan joined it as an observer at its Dushanbe summit in July 2000, evolved into a Eurasian regional organisation to cope with the challenges of political normalisation in the Central Asian region.

The Shanghai Five reflected the commonality of the national interests of the two great powers — Russia and China — in Central Asia. China's commitment to Shanghai Five began out of its desire to counter the challenge of Islamic secessionism in Xinjiang. It was also concerned about getting branded as an anti-Muslim state before the adjoining Central Asian states where it had important economic stakes. The Russian initiative was motivated by the domestic political environment and the threat to its security, due to breakdown of law and order in the northern and southern Caucasian region, having wider repercussions on the Central Asian scene. As the principal successor state Russia claimed responsibility for the containment of intra-regional conflicts in the former Soviet space where it had vital economic and security interests of the region.

The Shanghai Five agreements on confidence building measures in 1996 helped reduce tension and initiated demilitarization along the borders of the member states. After significant success in border delimitation and demilitarization the Shanghai Five shifted its attention to elimination of religious militancy in the region. At the August 1999 summit in Bishkek an agreement was reached on practical measures in this direction. In 2001, with Uzbekistan joining the group at a meeting of the heads of the state and government held in Shanghai, it was decided to set up an anti-terrorism centre in Bishkek and also to raise a rapid deployment force. The Shanghai Five mechanism was upgraded as the Shanghai Cooperation Organisation (SCO), the first regional cooperation organisation in the Eurasian region. The Shanghai Convention against Terrorism, Separatism and Extremism was signed by the six state leaders on 15 June 2001. Already at the Dushanbe summit in July 2000 (with the Uzbekistan President as observer) it was decided to widen inter-state cooperation in diplomatic, commercial, military and technological and other fields for reinforcing regional security and stability. The leaders committed themselves to cooperation in combating traffic in drugs and arms, in fighting terrorism, religious extremism and separatism as also in resolving disputes over trans-border resources such as water, energy and transport infrastructure. At a meeting of the Foreign Ministers of the SCO, held in Beijing in January 2002, documents for fostering cooperation in the fields of maintaining regional security and stability and combating threats from terrorism, separatism and religious extremism were adopted. It was announced that peace and stability must be ensured through the motto "security through cooperation".

The main spirit behind the SCO is the growing realization among the Eurasian powers that regional security cannot be ensured through overseas security structures located far from the territory. For this it is necessary that a group of neighbouring states in a region recognise themselves as a community in which their national identity is complementary rather than adversial to their neighbours. Regular meetings and personal contacts among leadership lead to an *esprit de corps* and help defuse the crisis. The SCO has particular focus on non-traditional security issues such as the environment protection, water management and cooperation in development of energy and transport, prevention of drugs and arms trafficking, organised crimes as also in dealing with migration and refugees. The SCO is engaged in economic cooperation with an understanding that economic development is conducive to the security of the region.

Viewed in the above perspective, the criticism of the SCO by some Western analysts like Stephen Blank that the organisation has failed as a "security provider "and only added to "a long line of abortive attempts to reorganise Central Asia under Russian leadership" is misplaced and unfair.[12] To say that the SCO has played no role in the war against terrorism in Afghanistan and Central Asia is also wide of the mark. The joint declaration of war on terrorism and religious extremism by the six SCO states has certainly contributed to the development of an atmosphere necessary to ensure the success of the fight against international terrorism in Afghanistan and Central Asia. The SCO has not just contributed to creation of an atmosphere for launching a successful struggle against terrorism in Central Asia, it has also made a tangible contribution in 2002 to this struggle by conducting Sino-Kyrgyz joint anti-terror exercises and joint military manoeuvres in Kazakhstan in August, 2002 with the participation of five members of the organisation (with the sole exception of Uzbekistan). After his recent talks with President Putin the President of Uzbekistan has also shown his eagerness for cooperation in setting up a SCO anti-terrorist centre in Tashkent.

The SCO summit, held in June 2002, in St. Petersburg adopted the Charter of the SCO and Declaration of Heads of States of Members of the SCO. Coming in the wake of Russo-American agreement in Moscow for reduction of nuclear arms and the Rome Declaration setting up the Russia-NATO Joint Council, the signing of these documents in St. Petersburg was of great significance for they imparted a legal status to the SCO as an international organisation. From a confidence building mechanism the SCO has evolved into a collective security system as an Asian alternative to the system of US-led liberal world order based on unilateral military action against terrorism and tyranny bypassing the UN.

If there were any doubts and misgivings about Russia's westward tilt, these were cleared by President Putin himself during his meeting with President Bush in St. Petersburg when he seized the opportune moment to stress the important role of the SCO. Putin also emphasised, before the press after his talks with the President of Finland Tarja Halonen, that Russia continues to have "major interests in the East" and China was one of "Russia's critical partners". The foreign policy of Russia under Putin is geared to the goal of providing strategic stability in the world, by establishment of a new global security system through permanent dialogue with the United States. Putin has also advanced the concept of a "stable arc" which aims to set up a buffer zone along the NATO in the West to be formed by the CIS Collective Security Treaty Organisation in the middle and the SCO in the East with Russia's participation in both. On the eve of the St. Petersburg summit the Russian media aired the view that Russia adopts a complementary policy towards Europe, the United States, China and Central Asia in order to deal with current challenges and pressures.

The SCO Declaration at its 2002 St. Petersburg summit emphasised that "to maintain global strategic balance and stability under the present international circumstances is of special significance". It also stated that "the organisation hopes to strengthen cooperation among its member states and with other nations as well. It also hopes to explore and eliminate some possible side effects and risks in the process of globalization, maintain diversification in economic, social and cultural fields. The international community likes to see a new concept of security on the basis of mutual trust, mutual benefit, equality and assistance. This helps to get rid of the factors and sources detrimental to the world security".

Some analysts in the West who are yet to overcome the old cold war mindset have viewed the SCO as the NATO of the East — an alliance of Russia, China and Central Asian states to checkmate American influence in Central Asia. The origin, development and gradual refinement of the "Shanghai Spirit" has demonstrated to the world community that a system of regional security can be created on the basis of cooperation resulting in a "win-win" situation for all. It has put an end to the military confrontation on the Eurasian borders that lasted for over three decades. Chinese scholar Lu Zhong-wei has aptly summed up the "Shanghai spirit" as the five 'C's of "confidence, communication, co-operation, co-existence and common interest".

To sum up, the SCO originated just seven years back in April 1996 as the Shanghai Five grouping on the basis of confidence building agreements signed at its first summit in Shanghai. In 1997, at its second summit in Moscow, the leaders of the five powers went ahead to conclude an agreement on mutual reduction of armed forces across the former Soviet-Chinese border. The summit meeting at Almaty in 1998 demonstrated that they could reach agreement both in political sphere (to contain and beat back attacks by Islamist extremists and terrorists in Central Asia) as well as in trade and economic affairs. On June 15, 2001 the Shanghai Five again met in Shanghai, admitted Uzbekistan as the sixth member and institutionalized their grouping as the Shanghai Cooperation Organisation (SCO). Finally at the summit held in St. Petersburg in July 2002, the SCO adopted its Declaration and Charter. At the next summit held in May 2003 in Moscow the SCO members adopted documents on the operation of the permanent SCO agencies — the Secretariat and the Executive Committee of the regional Anti-Terrorist structure in Bishkek. The flag and the emblem of the SCO was adopted and Zhang Deguang, Ambassador of China to Russia was appointed to the post of SCO Executive Secretary. The Moscow summit decided to take up the development of the North-South Transport Corridor which is being constructed to ensure continuous transit of containers cargoes from Asia to Europe. The SCO has finalised agreements on clearing up consequences of emergency situations, transport cooperation projects, contacts between prosecutors' offices and border departments. The Defence Ministers and Foreign Ministers of the six states meet regularly to discuss cooperation to ensure regional security and fight terrorism, drugs and arms trafficking, organised crime, etc. There has also been a SCO Prime Ministers meet in Shanghai in September 2003.

The SCO is not a closed organisation and is open for new participants as full-fledged members or observers. Mongolia, India, Iran, Pakistan and even the USA have expressed interest in interaction with the SCO. At the time of adoption of the basic documents of the organisation at St. Petersburg in 2003 President Putin stated that India was exploring the possibilities of participating in a wide range of SCO activities through Foreign Minister channels. India's the then Foreign Minister Yashwant Sinha is reported to have said, "India believes that the SCO fulfills important tasks, especially in the struggle against the threat of terrorism. India is interested in joining the SCO and has notified Russia and other member states of her intentions. Our membership in the SCO does not depend on whether any other country is or is not going to join this structure. We believe that India can contribute considerably to the SCO activities. However, we realise as well that at the present moment its admission regulations make it difficult to become a new member. Nevertheless, we watch its activities attentively".[13] The Indian Foreign Minister Sinha's statement on India's willingness to forge cooperation with the SCO was a positive response to the declaration by the SCO Prime Ministers at their meet in Beijing, in September 2003, that their organisation "adopts an opening up policy and is willing to carry out various dialogues and cooperation with other countries and international organisations according to the UN charter".[14]

Cooperation among the Eurasian powers is going apace in economic, political and security affairs. The Eurasian Economic Community, the Collective Security Treaty Organisation of the six CIS states, the six members SCO and the Almaty Conferences on Interaction and Confidence Building Measures, convened at the initiative of President Nazarbayev of Kazakhstan, form the contours of the emerging security structure in Asia. As one of the key actors on the Asian scene India has to formulate its energetic response to this evolving architecture of Asian security and regional cooperation. However, to assume its legitimate place in this set-up India has first to deepen its strategic understanding with China. The India-China relationship has to be raised to a strategic level to match the Indo-Russian strategic partnership. A strengthened Eurasian trilateral relationship alone can lay the strong foundation for an edifice of peace and cooperation in Asia. The principles for building Asian security and regional cooperation are anchored in the historical experience of resurgent Asia. These are the time-tested principles of peaceful coexistence, equality of states, mutually beneficial cooperation among them based on respect for their sovereignty and territorial integrity and non-interference in their domestic affairs. These principles were jointly propounded by India and China in the 50s of the last century and reaffirmed by the Bandung Afro-Asian Conference. The ill-fated Soviet proposal for Asian security was based on the same inclusive approach of ensuring security through cooperation and non-military means, in conformity with the principles enshrined in the UN Charter and based on the international law. The SCO has once again reinvented them.

The alternative is to have a global security system run by America not as a mere superpower or hegemon but a full-blown empire in the Roman and British sense. Calling for the military occupation of Afghanistan and Iraq (who knows which will be next!) Max Boot the editor of the *Wall Street Journal* ridiculed the title of Patrick Buchanan's last book *America: A Republic not an Empire*. He wrote: "This analysis is exactly backward. September 11 attack was a result of insufficient American involvement and ambition; the solution is to be more expansive in our goals and more assertive in their implementation." Demanding military occupation of Afghanistan and Iraq, Boot cited the stabilizing effect of the 19 th century British role in the region. "Afghanistan and other troubled lands today cry out for the sort of enlightened foreign administration provided by self confident Englishmen in Jodhpurs and pith helmets."

Unfortunately experts close to security policy makers in India (and the top security architect himself) seem to be blissfully ignorant of the grave nature of the threat to peace emanating in Asia and elsewhere from this new imperial approach and are recommending to India to work for retaining in Central Asia a "useful and constructive balance of forces." that ensures "greater autonomy and strategic space to the Central Asian countries themselves". [15] More or less in a somewhat similar vein the National Security Adviser is cited by an Indo-American scholar as favouring a "cooperative security order, rooted in pluralism" Such an order in his view "has to be inclusive, but inclusive in a flexible manner for all countries cannot contribute equally or... be equally ready to participate in such an exercise".[16]

The China visit of the then Prime Minister Atal Bihari Vajpayee was widely hailed as a ground-breaking exercise which cleared the way for successful development of multi faceted relations between the two Asian giants, in all fields including the strategic. Vajpayee's remark, after the signing of the joint declaration with the Chinese Prime Minister Wen Jiabao, that "we should focus on the simple truth that there is no objective reason for discord between us, and neither of us is a threat to the other", should be a warning to those who still persist with their reservations on the "Chinese dominated SCO" justifying them by the present favourable situation offering "flexibility and resilience" partly because of the so called "US-Russian understanding on specific issue". The argument usually advanced against fostering strategic cooperation between the key Eurasian powers-Russia, China and India-that it is a pipedream in view of the pre-occupation of each of these three states with improving its relations with the world's strongest military and economic power, the United States, (Russia looking for investment capital, China's vested interest in US market yielding 50 billion dollars of trade surplus annually and India's expectations on paradigm shift in the US South-Asia policy) is rather a superficial one.

The case for increased strategic cooperation, between the three Eurasian powers, is not based on their disinterestedness in relations with the world's most powerful nations. Naturally all the three states are vitally interested in expanding their economic ties and political and security dialogues with the United States. But as an American scholar Julie M. Rahm wrote in *Parameters* (Winter, 2001-2002), "it is a fact that each of these states (Russia, China and India) is involved in a similar dynamics. Each is consolidating its relationship with the others, while also expanding its relations with the United States. In terms of strategic pay offs, this partnership could yield them, at a minimum, enhanced benefits of bilateral cooperation with each other and, at a maximum, it can serve to circumscribe US influence."And it is precisely to circumscribe the new imperial onslaught of the United States that the strengthening of strategic and economic cooperation between the three great Eurasian powers is the need of the hour. The Eurasian triangle of peace and cooperation, which is in the process of formation, has become the sheet anchor of Asian and global security.

The China visit of Prime Minister Vajpayee in June 2003 took place following the US invasion of Iraq in defiance of the UN and world public opinion. It became evident to both China and India that the world has become a dangerous place as the United States, which was earlier a paragon of economic development and bastion of social stability, has turned unpredictable. This has happened because of its transformation into an Empire under compulsions generated by the international financial and economic crisis resulting from the relentless pursuit of monetarist policy followed by it under dictation from speculative finance capital.

Before his departure Vajpayee told the press that in view of the dramatic changes of the world during recent years "two of the worlds largest and most populous developing countries, India and China, should remain in close touch on global issues of concern to developing countries"[17] Vajpayee also stated, "our dialogue now addresses not only the various areas in which we can improve bilateral cooperation, but also international issues such as terrorism, security, environmental sustainable development and multilateral economic regimes".

Vajpayee's meetings with the Chinese leaders during his June 2003 China visit was the third meeting of top Indian and Chinese leader within a month's time. Earlier Vajpayee had met the Chinese President Hu Jintao in St. Petersburg in Russia and Evian in France in the month of May. During his visit Vajpayee succeeded in developing a deep personal rapport with the top Chinese leadership. Prime Minister Wen Jiabao greeted Vajpayee as a "man of peace who is seeking to resolve the long lasting conflict with Pakistan."

The remark made by the Chinese Prime Minister, while receiving earlier in April the Indian Defence Minister George Fernandes, that; "our big countries should always be friendly with each other from generation to generation. I think during then past 2200 years, about 99.9 per cent of the time, we have devoted to friendly cooperation...the two countries have had a long history of interaction and misunderstandings form only 0.1 per cent of the time", was subsequently repeatedly echoed by George Fernandes in India after returning from China. The joint declaration issued at the end of Vajpayee's visit affirmed the commitment of both the countries "to qualitatively enhancing bilateral relationship at all levels and in all areas while addressing differences through peaceful means in a fair reasonable and mutually acceptable manner". It also stated that "differences should not be allowed to affect the overall development of bilateral relations". The Declaration also reiterated the agreement of the two sides to "maintain peace and stability regionally", "strengthen multipolarity at the international level, and promote a long term constructive and cooperative partnership on the basis of principles of *Panchshila*, mutual respect and sensitivity for each other's concerns and equality".

The Declaration also underlined that "as two major developing countries, India and China have a broad mutual interest in the maintenance of peace, stability and prosperity in Asia and the world and a mutual desire in developing wider and closer cooperation and understanding in regional and international affairs". Reiterating that the "common interests of the two sides outweigh their differences" and that "the two are not a threat to each other", it also stated that "neither sides shall use or threaten to use force against the other". The Joint Declaration also stated that the two sides "viewed positively each other's participation in regional and sub-regional multilateral cooperation processes in Asia". It also acknowledged the "vital importance of the role of the UN in world peace, stability and development".[18]

Vajpayee's China visit highlighted economic cooperation as key to India-China relations. Growing at the rate of 30 per cent annually, the target of 10 billion dollar worth of bilateral trade has long been attained. It was decided to form a joint study group to raise economic cooperation to greater heights and work out an agreement on India-China Free Trade Area. A decision was taken to open border trade through Nathu La pass in Sikkim, which has been subsequently shown as a part of India in the Chinese map on an internet website. The greatest achievement of the Vajpayee visit was the agreement between the two sides to appoint a special representative from each to "explore from the political perspective of the overall bilateral relationship, the framework of a boundary settlement." Since the objective of talks by special representatives, National Security Adviser Brajesh Mishra and Senior Chinese Vice-Minister Dai Dingguo was to explore a "framework" and not the delimitation of the border, it will be desirable if the talks between the special representatives do not take a long time to reach a consensus on a framework for resolving the border dispute which has acted as a roadblock in improving bilateral ties for more than two decades. It is also necessary to take the opposition into confidence which, however, has not been done. This factor along with omission to indicate a deadline has raised some misgivings about this exercise.

Closer India-China relations to which Vajpayee's visit made a significant contribution have been held by Russia as a chance to strengthen ties in the Moscow-Delhi-Beijing triangle. An official spokesman for the Russian Foreign Ministry, Alexander Yakovenko, was reported to have said that Russia was happy with India and China signing a Declaration on the principles of friendly relations and comprehensive cooperation. "The signing of the document", Yakovenko stated, "will not only promote good relations between Beijing and New Delhi but also facilitate trilateral ties with Russia". He further added, "cooperation in the triangular format is undoubtedly instrumental for strengthening peace and security in the region in the context of new threat and challenges in the era of globalization." The Press Trust of India (PTI) quoted a senior Chinese Foreign Ministry official saying on June 30, 2003 that "China, Russia and India share many common interests in promoting a democratic international relationship and safeguarding international security and stability and development. The official said that the countries have many identical positions and concerns and noted their joint discussions on trilateral cooperation. In the past according to this official the proposed strategic triangle failed to take off mainly due to lack of trust between New Delhi and Beijing.

But with their bilateral relations having entered a new phase, trilateral ties "offer immense scope for them to cooperate, maintain regional and global peace and stability."[19]

In the grim situation facing the world today, when the United States has turned into a new imperial power by unleashing a war on Iraq to gain control of its oil wealth, the Eurasian vision of cooperation is the only hope for humanity to overcome the crisis into which it has been plunged by the international speculative finance capital in a unipolar world order. The creation of Russia-China-India Strategic Triangle of Cooperation for executing mega projects of infrastructural development of railroad and gas pipelines, for constructing a landbridge across Eurasia alone has the potential to extricate the world economy from depression. Japan, the Far East and China if joined with Rotterdam in Europe by two routes, one the Siberian and the other the so-called Silk Road would greatly help the revival of world economy through cheap overland transport of goods and creation of development corridors along the railway lines joining Europe with Asia.

The Eurasian perspective of ensuring security through intensified peaceful cooperation among India, China, Russia and the Central Asian republics offers a viable paradigm for building a system of Asian security. The forging of the Eurasian trilateral cooperation on the basis of peaceful coexistence and strategic partnership is directed at restoring the missing equilibrium in the present international security environment which has been vitiated of late on account of the aberrant behaviour of the United States, which is hell-bent on attaining its objective unilaterally, bypassing the UN and riding roughshod, not only over world public opinion but also the opinion of its alliance partners. In such a situation the deepening of tripartite Eurasian Cooperation is both timely and opportune. Such a formation will only help the United States in becoming a normal law-abiding member of the international community by shedding its hyperpower complex and adapting itself to what Russian scholar N.A. Simonia charecterises as the ongoing transition from superpower status to the status of an ordinary great power, albeit, still "the first one, the major one, the richest one", yet nevertheless an ordinary great power. By 2015 its share of world gross product will amount to 18.6 per cent, the same as that of India and China put together.[20] The United States will only be serving its own interests in the first place by having mutually beneficial cooperation with each of the three countries forming the Eurasian triangle.

The developments, currently taking place in Asia, in the direction of growth of regional economic cooperation augur well for the emergence of a new Asian security system as a counterweight to a unilateral system of global security sought to be sustained by the United States of America, as the so-called hyper power through its military might. The three great Asian powers, Japan, China and India, have taken important steps towards forging free-trade linkages with the ASEAN. The joint statement of the First ASEAN-India joint summit at Phnom Penh in November 2002 affirmed that the Charter of the United Nations, the Treaty of Amity and Cooperation in South-East Asia, the five principles of peaceful co-existence and other universally recognised principles of international law should serve as basic norms governing their relations. The meeting also reaffirmed the common interest of India-ASEAN powers in developing the programme of action for the Mekong-Ganga cooperation focussing on important areas of cooperation such as tourism, culture, education and transport and communication. India also attached importance and agreed to look into possible participation in regional and sub-regional development programmes, such as ASEAN-Mekong Basin Development Cooperation (AMBDC) and the Greater Mekong-Sub-Region (GMS).

India's declaration of its intention to participate in the Greater Mekong Cooperation Project sets at rest speculation about India trying to counter China in this region through the Ganga-Mekong project, involving India, Thailand, Vietnam, Laos, Cambodia and Myanmar. Apart from Mekong-Ganga project, India has since 1998 also taken an active interest in a free trade zone comprising Bangladesh, Myanmar, Sri Lanka and Thailand. The five countries decided at the second ministerial meeting in April to set-up the Free Trade Zone and in February 2004 they signed (except Bangladesh) the framework agreement on Free Trade Area. Bhutan and Nepal have also joined this group, recently. These countries will establish linkages through the south corridor of the Trans-Asian Railway and the Asian Highway. Some progress has also been made in the direction of upgrading SAARC into SAFTA early 2003 at the SAARC summit in Pakistan. Bilateral cooperation between China and Myanmar has also been growing, of late. However, the Kunming initiative for cooperation between China, India, Myanmar and Bangladesh, which began in August 1999, has not made the expected progress on account of India's concern over existing problems in northeastern states. The restoration of the old Burma road from Kunming to Ledo to connect with the Indian railway network and national highway will lead to the establishment of a landbridge between the Pacific and Indian Ocean and enable the two great Asian powers to work jointly for Asian prosperity.

In December 2003, Japan took initiative in convening a meeting to celebrate 30 years of economic and political relations with the ASEAN. The meeting resulted in the signing of the Tokyo Declaration for dynamic and enduring Japanese-ASEAN Partnership in the new millennium. Japanese Prime Minister Koizumi pledged $3 billion for projects in S.E. Asia, over next three years, which includes $1.5 billion for human resources development programme including 40,000 student and technical expert exchanges and another $1.5 billion for the development of the Greater Mekong and assistance to the Brunei-Indonesia-Malaysia-Philippines, East Asia Growth Area (BIMP-EAGA). Prime Minister Koizumi and President Megawati explained, at a press conference in Tokyo, that the initiative was not a "counter China move". A week later the South Korean President hosted the inaugural meeting of East Asian Forum including the 10 ASEAN member states and their partners-China, Japan and South Korea, along with 50 government representatives and scholars for strengthening cooperation among Asian countries.

Simultaneously, on 16 December 2003 in Bangkok the Thai Foreign Minister hosted a brief meeting of the Ministers and senior officials from ten Asian and European countries to discuss a plan for peace and national reconciliation in neighbouring Myanmar, termed as the "Bangkok process". The Myanmar Foreign Minister Min Aung outlined a plan to convene a national convention in 2004 that would draft a constitution with the participation of all eight groups including the opposition, the National League for Democracy, led by Mrs. Aung-San Suu Kyi. Participants in the meeting included the representative of the UN Secretary General and representatives from China, India, Japan, Austria, France, Italy and ASEAN.

To sum up, progress in the direction of regional cooperation starting from the Shanghai Cooperation Organisation to Eurasian Economic Community, Central Asian Cooperation Organisation, SAARC, BIMSTEC, ASEAN and East Asia Growth Area (EAGA) alongwith the on-going work on Greater-Mekong sub-Regional Cooperation, building of roads and railway lines in Myanmar and Thailand, Iranian initiative for a Dialogue of Cultures, North-South Transport Corridor, construction of gas pipelines in the Eurasian region and connection of the Asia-Pacific coast with Europe, through the already functioning 8 railway lines, alongwith the Kazakh President's initiative of Conference on Interaction and Confidence Building Measures in Asia (CICMA) at Almaty, and the Uzbek President's initiative for organising permanent seminar on Asian Security in Tashkent, a structure of peace and security in Asia in the Bandung spirit through cooperation and non-military means is gradually coming up. As the world celebrates the 50th anniversary of the Bandung conference in 2005, it is important to keep alive this spirit to ensure peace and progress on the world's largest populated continent which is home to half of mankind.

REFERENCES

1. David C. Kang, "Getting Asia Wrong", *International Security,* Vol. 27, No. 4, Spring, 2003, pp. 57-85.
2. David Krager and Ichiko Fuyuno " Innovate or Die: Reinventing Japan", *Far Eastern Economic Review*, 25 April 2002.

3. The actual figures may be higher for the 40-50 billion dollars figure relate to approved investment only, *Far Eastern Economic Review*, 5 July 2001, p. 56.
4. David C. Kang, *op. cit*, p. 70.
5. Dick Wilson, *Asia Awakes—A Continent in Transition*, London, 1970, p. 3.
6. Sir Esler Dening, "A New Look at Asia,", *Journal of the Royal Central Asian Society*, Vol. IV, Part II, June 1968, pp. 136-39.
7. Bimal Prasad, *Origins of Indian Foreign Policy*, Calcutta, 1960, pp. 72-77.
8. *Jawaharlal Nehru's Speeches: 1947-1949*, New Delhi, 1949, p. 299.
9. *Pravda*, 8 June 1969.
10. *League of Nations, Records of the Conference for the Reduction and Limitation of Armaments: Minutes of the Political Commission*, Series D, Vol. 5, Geneva, pp. 12-13.
11. *League of Nations Assembly, 77th Verbatim Record of the 17th Ordinanry Session of the Assembly of the League of Nations 8th Plenary Meeting*, 28 September 1936, p. 7.
12. Stephen Blank, "The Shanghai Cooperation Organisation: A Post Mortem", *Nordic Newsletter of Asian Studies*, No. 3, 2002.
13. *Vremya novesti*, 19 February, 2003.
14. http://www.chinadaily.com. 23 September, 2003.
15. Obviously endorsing such a course S.D.Muni cites a note prepared in 1999 for Indian policy guidelines in Central Asia at the instance of Defence Minister George Fernandes, see S.D. Muni, "India and Central Asia: Towards a Cooperative Future" in Nirmala Joshi (ed.), *Central Asia: The Great Game Replayed*, Delhi, 2003, pp. 124-25.
16. Ibid, cited by Muthiah Alagappa "Constructive Security Order in Asia: Conceptions and Issues" in Muthiah Alagappa (ed.), *Asian Security Order: Asian Security Order and Normative Features*, Stanford University Press, 2003 as quoted by S.D. Muni.
17. Cited by Ramtanu Maitra, "Vajpayee's Historic Trip Strengthen India-China Ties", *EIR*, (Washington) 4 July 2003, Vol. 30, No. 26, p. 42.
18. For full text of the Joint Declaration see *Hindu*, 25 June 2003.
19. Cited by Mary Burdman, "Indian Prime Minister in China: A Good Beginning", *EIR*, Vol. 30, No. 27, 11 July 2003, pp. 40-42.
20. Cited by Mikhail Titarenko, "Russia-China-India: Tripartite Cooperation and the US Factor", *China Report*, vol. 39, no. 3, 2003, pp. 343-45.

2

Security and Cooperation in Asia

Favourable Conditions and Adverse Factors

Du Yanling

THE POSITIVE CHANGES OF ASIAN SECURITY

Since the beginning of the century, some new changes took place in Asian security. Generally speaking, those changes moved towards a good direction. The main reasons that cause the trend are:

First, after "9/11", the United States adjusted its policy in Asia-Pacific region. Under the banner of joint anti-terrorism, Sino-US relations have improved a lot. The improvement of Sino-US relations has brought good influence on the security of Asia-Pacific region. The Asia-Pacific security has entered a relatively stable stage.

Second, China initiated the idea of marching towards peaceful development. It pushes forward its Asian policies of "building good relationships and partnerships with the neighbours" and "creating a good environment of peace and security with the neighbours to achieve common development". We believe that the prosperity and development of China's economy will contribute to the prosperity and development of Asian economy and Asian regional security and stability. China's development has become one of the most important factors that guarantee the stability of Asian security.

Third, the rapid development of the economic globalization and integrity of the economy of the Asia-Pacific region has strengthened the economic relations and interdependence among Asian countries. All countries have gradually realized that only by strengthening the economic cooperation among Asian countries, can the self-development of Asian countries be faster. It has become the inner factor that promotes the stability of Asian security.

Fourth, India and Pakistan have taken important steps towards reconciliation, which has made great contributions to the stability, not only in South Asia but also in Asia as a whole.

THE RAPID DEVELOPMENT OF ASIAN COOPERATION

Under the good momentum that the Asian security develops towards stability, the Asian cooperation has gained a more relaxed environment of development and has developed rapidly.

First, Ninth ASEAN Summit held on Oct. 8, 2003 *Declaration of ASEAN Concord II* (*Bali Concord II*) was issued. In the declaration, the ASEAN countries expressed the joint demand of building a more coherent association like European Union, after its 36-year growth and development. It called for building ASEAN Security Community, ASEAN Economic Community and ASEAN Social-Cultural Community. Further more, it initiated the roadmap to complete the establishment of an ASEAN Community in the year 2020, which indicated that ASEAN has turned from a loose regional association, with economic cooperation as the main part, to a more cohesive and integrated regional organization. The summit may be regarded as an important mile stone in the history of the development of ASEAN as well as the history of the cooperation and development of Asia.

Second, Northeast Asia, China, Japan and Republic of Korea (ROK) jointly signed and issued the *Joint Declaration on the Promotion of Tripartite Cooperation among the People's Republic of China, Japan and the Republic of Korea* on October 7th, 2003, in Bali, Indonesia. It is the first document jointly issued by the leaders of China, Japan and ROK. It stipulated the framework and principles of tripartite cooperation. The Chinese side put forward the suggestions of continuing the study of establishing tripartite free trade zone, convening the seminar of rejuvenating China's North East and Northeast Asian Cooperation in China and setting up the system of logistics cooperation, to which Japan and ROK have given positive response. The comprehensive cooperation of China, Japan and ROK will bring more stable driving forces for the regional cooperation in Northeast Asia and which is conducive to the development of the regional economic cooperation

Third, the cooperation among ASEAN, China, Japan, ROK and India has achieved new progress. In October 2003, the Chinese government declared to formally join the Treaty of Amity and Cooperation in Southeast Asia and signed the joint declaration to build strategic partnership with ASEAN oriented principles of peace and prosperity. It symbolized that the bilateral relations between China and ASEAN have stepped to a new stage. In fact, China has always played an important role in Asian regional cooperation. In November 2001, the leaders of ASEAN and China held a meeting in Brunei. Both sides agreed to build China-ASEAN free trade zone in the coming 10 years. In November 2002, the ASEAN and China Summit was held in Phnom Phnh. The two sides signed the Framework Agreement on ASEAN-China Economic Cooperation, which started the process of the free trade. Under China's effort, Japan, ROK and India have all expressed their will of strengthening the comprehensive cooperation with ASEAN and China and to vigorously push forward the development of Asian free trade zone. In December 2003, Japan and ASEAN held a special summit and the Japanese government declared to join the Treaty of Amity and Cooperation in Southeast Asia and signed the ASEAN agreement on building Japan-ASEAN free trade zone in 2012. India also took part in the Treaty of Amity and Cooperation in Southeast Asia.

Fourth, the reconciliation between Pakistan and India brings new energy to the development of the South Asian Association for Regional Cooperation (SAARC). The Twelfth SAARC Summit issued Islamabad Declaration for strengthening of economic cooperation, as the main content. The leaders of the 7 countries, that attended the summit, signed many documents, including the Agreement on South Asian Free Trade Area, which became the dividing line of restarting the South Asian regional cooperation.

Fifth, the countries in Asia actively carried out the regional cooperation of anti-terrorism, SARS prevention and treatment, bird-flu prevention, and so on. The secretariat of Shanghai Cooperation Organization has been set up. China, India and Pakistan separately held maritime joint military manoeuvre. Some countries in Asia held summit meetings to discuss cracking down on terrorism and preventing and treating SARS and bird-flu.

SOME GRAVE CHALLENGES IN ASIAN SECURITY AND COOPERATION

First, the non-traditional security threats like terrorism still lie ahead of Asian countries in the field of security and cooperation. After "9/11", the United States launched a war against international terrorism. Under the support of the international community, the terrorism has undergone serious attacks. However, the war gave rise to the reaction of terrorism. The struggle between the international terrorism and the anti-terrorism forces becomes increasingly intensified. The struggle between the United States and the terrorism relates to the complicated national and religious background. Some Asian countries are involved in the struggle though unwillingly, which have formed serious challenges to the situation of Asian security.

Second, the situation of Northeast Asian security is pregnant with grim possibilities. As long as the nuclear issue of DPRK is not solved, real peace will not be there in Asia, the regional cooperation will not be developed fully and comprehensively. With the vigorous efforts of parties concerned, the settlement of the nuclear issue of DPRK is on the correct path. The second six-party talks, not only enables the people recognize the complexity of the problem and the difficulty of solving the problem, but also lets the world see the bright prospect. Both the two sides have the good wishes to push forward the settlement of the issue in a peaceful way.

Third, it is undeniable that Taiwan question is China's domestic affair. Nevertheless, due to the historical and practical reasons, the question is still an important and uncertain factor that affects Asian security.

Fourth, the national contradictions, the religious conflicts, the boundary disputes and the seeking of resources within a country, among countries and regions are the serious challenges that exist in the situation of Asian security and cooperation. The utility of water resources in Central Asian countries, as well as the national problems and the delimitation of boundary lines left by former USSR gravely affect the development of normal exchanges and cooperation among those countries and form threats on the stability of Central Asia. The security and stability in South Asia are closely linked with the development of Pakistan-India relations. We are fully confident about the ongoing reconciliation process between the leaders of Pakistan and India. We believe that they have enough wisdom to bring the people of the two countries to peaceful times without war. China's northwest border also faces the threats of extremism, separatism and terrorism.

In the final analysis, after entering the new century, the Asian countries need a good situation of vigorous development in the fields of regional security and cooperation. But at the same time, they also face the serious and practical challenges. Most valuably, the leaders of all countries have shown their spirit of pragmatism and cooperation. Next year is the 50th anniversary of the convocation of Bandung Conference, which originated in Asia and reflects the spirit of Five Principles of Peaceful Co-existence. We believe that our Asian people will surely be able to carry forward the Bandung Spirit and jointly build a peaceful, prosperous and progressive Asia.

3

New Asia
Development and Globalisation

FELIX N. YURLOV

At the beginning of the 21st century we entered a new stage of development Every country—big and small — is in search of its own place in the new international setting, a search for not only a new foreign policy, but for a more fundamental change in the very strategy of development We have no choice but to reconsider many of the old values of international and domestic developments.

In the new political environment, where the struggle between the two systems — capitalist and socialist — has been relegated to history, real problems facing the world begin to emerge in their genuine garb. No more are they distorted and deformed by the ideological struggle of the two superpowers. Though they are the same old problems of freedom, democracy, equality and inequality, poverty and abundance, social justice, the role of the state in a market economy, etc. — they appear in a more undisguised form than was the case before.

After the downfall of the USSR, the former socialist countries dreamt of a miraculous establishment of a "society of abundance". But this idea has not worked, even in the framework of Western values, to say nothing of the poorer countries. More so when a very substantial part of the population of the planet lives in poverty and deprivation. Therefore, the idea "the society of abundance" is not the road to stability, but rather to destabilisation, not to peace, but to conflicts.

In spite of the plurality of ideas regarding developmental models in the post-cold war period most of them can be grouped into two sections. While the proponents of the first group are convinced that mankind will adopt the model of development proposed by the "winners" of the cold war, which is liberal democracy, the second group argues that many countries of the former second world and the third world will have to search for their own new ways of development, taking into account their cultural and civilisational peculiarities.

One of the ramifications of global development, luring the years after World War II, was a tremendous growth of social and economic inequality on the planet The "golden billion" people, living mostly in the affluent countries of the North, are getting alienated from the majority of the five billion people in the developing world. The crucial question is: will it be possible to ensure material prosperity and dignified life to this silent majority in the 21st century? If so, then what are the resources and how can they acquire them?

The answer to this fundamental question cannot be obtained by substituting the dogma of a socialist paradise by the dogma of the unlimited freedom of a market economy. The last few years have proved that we have to search for an answer from the history, of both the developed and developing societies, and from the latest experiences of each and every country. The destruction of the previous system of international relations has resulted in the strengthening of the positions of the Western states, "the winners" in the cold war. But this victorious euphoria is fast fading away. The new world order has still to emerge. It is sheer oversimplification to declare that the new order would be dominated by one ideology or a single paradigm of development. One of the reasons why it cannot be so is the remarkable progress achieved by the former colonial countries. Their independent role in international relations is growing with every passing year. The centre of the world economic and political activities is gradually shifting to the Asia Pacific region.

Today, more than ever before, the developing countries deserve the thorough attention of politicians and scholars; more so when we discuss issues relating to such giants as China and India. India's experiment during the last fifty years is of special interest. It has been trying to solve large-scale, complex problems within the framework of political democracy which is one of the most important elements of modernisation of Indian society. In spite of the many challenges to Indian democracy, including poverty and illiteracy, its present achievements give hope that, in the not too distant future, it will be able to advance to a position of one of the major economic powers of the world.

We can now register the start of an age in which New Asia will acquire the economic, political and military power equal to that of the USA and Western Europe. It will enable the Asian countries to exert influence, not only in their own region, but in the world. Asians will be able to have an equal say in writing the rules for the world. The next few decades will see the rise of the new and vigorous Asia which will be able to break the monopoly of the West, as world power. The signs of this trend are already there. This economic strength is a driving force in New Asia. The Asians have succeeded in accomplishing an industrial revolution in 50 years that took the West 200 years. Nowadays Asian economies are growing much faster compared with Western Europe and the United States.

At the same time most Western politicians consider that the West is now at an extraordinary peak of power in relation to the other civilisations. It dominates international, political and security institutions (and with Japan — international economic institutions). Global, political security and economic issues are effectively settled by a directorate, headed by the United States.

But things are changing fast. The last few years are marked by positive developments in bilateral and multisided cooperation in Asia. One of them was the creation, in 2001, of the Shanghai Cooperation Organisation with Russia, China, Kazakhstan. Kirghizia, Tajikistan and Uzbekistan, as its participants. This organisation embraces more than 1.5 billion people and has huge resources, human, financial and technological potential.

The Shanghai Cooperation Organisation has been created not as an instrument of confrontation with any other country, but as an organisation which aims at ensuring mutual security at regional and global levels. India expressed its willingness to join the organisation. It will be a very positive development for the future of Asia.

Basically the same are the aims of the Collective Security Treaty Organisation of Russia and the CIS countries.

Efforts of the Asian countries to work out a collective approach towards strengthening security, mutual trust and confidence in Asia were manifested at the Asian Conference on Confidence Building Measures held in June 2002 in Almaty, where 16 Asian states, including Russia, India, Pakistan, Iran, Israel, Palestine and others, signed a document, which creates framework for moving in this direction.

Thus, we can say that in addition to the already functioning organisations like ASEAN, SAARC, we now have other important mechanisms of fostering cooperation in Asia.

The main problem of course is not only the creation of such organisations and organising different fora, but their effectiveness and enlargement. They should not work in isolation, but attract more and more states to share their activities.

So we can note with satisfaction some positive developments in the Asian region as far as the problems of security are concerned.

The national interests of Russia demand special attention towards the Asian continent. During the last two decades these countries demonstrated their ability to dynamically develop their economies, especially high-tech and IT industries.

Today the Asian countries share 25 per cent of the world GDP, a quarter of the world export, more than 40 per cent of the world foreign exchange reserves (that is 1 trillion dollars out of 2 trillion dollars). More than 40 per cent of the world's investments find their way to the Asian countries. Evidently Asia is being fast transformed into one of the leading economic and political centres of the world.

At the same time we can't avoid mentioning that a number of Asian countries are facing many fundamental problems and challenges which stand on the way of their future development.

The problem of development is very closely connected with that of security. A poor and underdeveloped country can hardly carry on such policies which ensure its security.

The present stage of globalisation, based on so called new liberal agenda, has clear international ramifications, as it leads to the increased global inequality, greater inequities within countries and slower rates of poverty reduction. Globalisation based on neo-liberal policies has undermined the capacity of many developing countries to carry on strategies which would help improve the conditions of the poor.

The experience of such countries as Bangladesh and Combodia shows that neo-liberal trade and macro policies with some aid inflows have rendered domestic economy uncompetitive. These countries experience huge losses in terms of foregone income in return for little aid.

In case of large countries, such as China, India and Russia, growth has to be more focused on domestic efforts, if they want to solve their own problems of social protection.

Unilateralism remains the most significant instrument in carrying globalisation in its present form. By using this instrument the US forces huge concessions from developing countries and provides protection for its own large companies.

Some experts also note that countries that have experienced huge trade losses and deindustrialisation are also being affected by the systematic manipulation of markets by large multinational companies.

Therefore, it is important to present viable alternatives to the neo-liberal policies, to present new paradigms of development, which will change the lives of the people in the developing world for the better.

The present problems of the dotcom bust and the stock market bubble were recently manifested in the US measures of curbing offshore outsourcing. And that was in spite of much proclaimed slogans of globalisation.

In the last decade private sector in the developed countries looked for ways to develop facilities in low-cost countries, such as India, Russia, China, Brazil and others. Prior to that, many manufacturing jobs were shifted to China and South-East Asia, where local workers worked for a tenth of the wages of the workers in the developed countries. The result was — bigger profits for the big international companies, creation of some jobs in developing countries, and loss of jobs in the rich countries. In the period of "jobless growth" this also resulted in a series of protectionist measures in the US and other developed countries.

At the same time it should be noted that globalisation has become one of the most important factors of development. There was an immense growth of contacts and ties among peoples and countries in economy, technology and culture in the second half of the twentieth century. During the last 50 years, per capita income in the world has triplled. The world GDP has increased tenfold — from $ 3 trillion to $ 30 trillion. In the last quarter of the twentieth century, there has been a 10 per cent increase of the number of people with a medium level of well-being.

Today, globalisation seems to be embracing everything and everybody and winning everywhere. But the impact of globalisation on the socio-economic processes and the situation in different countries and regions is multidimensional and contradictory. The above average numbers hide the huge inequality between people, countries and regions. Besides, poverty, unemployment, and illiteracy remain the main challenges faced by humanity.

Though theoretically globalisation provides opportunity to all countries, in practice it is the countries, which are most industrialized, advanced, rich and competitive, that take advantage of the enhanced market opportunities to further strengthen their positions and to prosper. That is why the divergence of global income became a reality. Today, the rich countries account for about 60 per cent of the world GDP but only for 15 per cent of the worid population. About 70 per cent of foreign direct investment goes from one rich country to another, eight developing countries receive 20 per cent, and the remainder is divided among more than 100 poor nations.

Globalisation, seemingly, has only economic goals on its agenda. But in reality some of its results may bring social and political upheavals caused by the inequality between people and countries. In the inter depending world. which is based only on market relations, the winner is always the strongest. Economic and social Darwinism forces tough competition upon everybody, as well as the need to adapt to the conditions of struggle, which are often alien and not apprehensible by many people. Market defends only the chosen ones and pays no heed to the interests of common men.

There are very few politicians, public figures and scholars in the world who would oppose the integration of efforts of all the countries in commerce, finance and technologies. However, it is not the problem of integration but rather of market fund'amentalism, which cannot meet all the challenges, more so of social, moral and ethical, based on the idea that all people are born equal in their rights and opportunities.

The present globalisation does not offer equal conditions to all the participants. Instead, it offers such integration of the worid, which does not take into account the interests of all the countries and peoples. Basically, it corresponds to the interests of the West. The world is not being globalised, it is being Americanized. In many industries the United States accounts for almost 50 per cent of the world market. More than half of any business activity is controlled, or at least influenced, from the United States. About two thirds of advertising and marketing services are concentrated in the USA. Investment banking industry is also dominated by the US franchises. But if history is any indication, US political and economic hegemony will eventually wane. The example of Great Britain is there. What will come next? Perhaps we should look to the East for a new reason to name the era.

Theoretically, globalisation should have helped faster growth, rise in living standards, opening new vistas for all people of the world. But in practice it happens differently. Globalisation benefits mostly big private companies and rich countries.

It is no surprise that a backlash has begun. It is happening, because the benefits of globalisation are unevenly distributed; because the global market is not yet underpinned by rules based on shared social objectives; and because, if all of tomorrow's poor follow the same path that brought today's rich to prosperity, the earth's resources will soon be exhausted. Thus, the central challenge we face today is to ensure that globalisation becomes a positive force for all the world's people, instead of leaving billions of them behind, in squalor.

But how should this be done? How to eliminate the growing inequality? Obviously, only the developing countries, specially the poorest of them, cannot successfully shoulder this responsibility. It is necessary to create conditions under which they will become equal participants of the process of development, so that the market relations would stop being a one-way road — in the direction and to the benefit of only the rich countries. Other important measures are necessary, particularly, liberation of the poorest countries of their debts. Unfortunately, there is not much progress in this. Many years ago the rich countries of the Organization for Economic Cooperation and Development (OECD) committed themselves to give 0.7 per cent of their GDP in development aid. Yet, very few have lived up to that promise.

Thus, globalisation divides countries by winners and losers, by those who benefit from it and those who lose as a result of it.

After the collapse of the USSR, protagonists of the idea of global liberalisation appeared in big numbers in the West and elsewhere. Some of them proclaimed that this model of development may happen to be the final point of the ideological development of humanity, the final form of human governance. Supporters of this concept even declared that we had reached the end of history. According to them, the ideal of liberal democracy could not be improved.

The appearance of these prophets, in their different garbs, was aimed at declaring the end of any alternative development, as well as at making people believe that there was only one way of development in the world, that is neo-liberalism.

Politicians and scholars of this school of thought failed to discuss some fundamental problems facing the bigger part of the humanity, such as hunger, poverty, unemployment, illiteracy, discrimination of minorities, mass emigration, spread of diseases, ecological degradation and other social problems.

Neo-liberal ideology also does not give an answer to other important questions. Today, we are witnessing attempts to create a new world order led by a single superpower. We are witnessing many bloody conflicts in different regions of the world in which developed countries play not an insignificant role, and often not a very noble one. More than 10 years after the fall of the Berlin Wall, we see the erection of even higher and stronger walls of tariffs and visas. The rich countries are sparing no effort to safeguard their prosperity.

According to the loudly declared principles of neo-liberalism, there should be an unrestricted freedom of movement of people across the borders, including the international flow of labour. But it does not happen this way. The same applies to high trade barriers in agriculture, built by many developed countries to protect their farmers' profits.

The huge gap in income and standard of life of different countries and social groups, as well as such global problems as pollution and degradation of ecosystems undermine the very foundation of the sustainable development of the humanity. Gaps in income between the poorest and the richest people and countries have continued to widen. In 1960, the 20 per cent of world's population in the richest countries had 30 times the income of the poorest 20 per cent In 1997 it was 74 times. Actually, this has been the trend for nearly two centuries. In the nineteenth century, disparity between the rich and the poor though increased substantially, but not in such proportion as in the twentieth century. The gap between the richest and the poorest country was about 3 to 1 in 1820, and 11 to 1 in 1913.

The majority of the developing countries cannot accept the present neo-liberal paradigm of development as it does not give opportunity to satisfy even the basic needs of a huge mass of people. As per the UN poverty index, 1.2 billion people in the developing countries have no basic conditions, which would allow them to live longer than 40 years, to have education and an adequate dwelling place. About 1.3 billion people have no access to safe water. One out of every seven school age children does not attend school. 1.3 billion people live on less than a dollar a day.

Today, it is evident that the over consumption of the minority of the earth's population has come into a sharp contradiction with hunger, abysmal poverty and human degradation in many countries of Asia, Africa and Latin America. According to the World Bank, during the last 15 years, per capita income decreased in more than 100 countries; in 60 of them per capita consumption decreased 1 per cent annually. The problem of consumption is becoming one of the biggest challenges of the twenty-first century. The poor countries are desperately in need of its growth to satisfy their basic requirements or even to simply survive. But it is not going to be an easy task to accomplish, as the socio-economic and ecological situation in the world is quite unfavourable.

The experience, of both the developed and the developing countries, shows that the market economy cannot by itself solve the problems of rising polarization or poverty and richness, control over natural resources and increasing ecological degradation. It also shows that super consumption and prosperity are confined to the minority, both in the West and in the East.

And new problems have appeared in their full strength, not less dangerous than the old ones. Among them are international terrorism, rising number of military conflicts, spread of AIDS, etc.

Thus, the humanity entered the twenty-first century with a host of unresolved problems, old and new. Many of them are caused by an uneven and inequitable development of different regions and different social groups in the poor and the rich countries. The enormousness of these problems and the inability of the world community to resolve them during many decades and even centuries give little hope for their quick solution in the twenty-first century. The market economy, declared as a panacea for treating all economic and social ills and evils, does not take into account many global factors, including the cost of the natural resources.

Inequality has deeply penetrated not only in the sphere of material life, but also in the culture — mass media, literature, music. It has become one of the important features of present globalisation.

The stream of this cultural production flows mainly in one direction — from the rich countries to the poor ones. The quality of this production raises doubts and objections in many countries. In this context it is befitting to remind of Mahatma Gandhi's words: "I do not want my house to be walled on all sides and my windows to be stuffed. I want the cultures of all the lands to be blown about my house as freely as possible. But I refuse to be blown off my feet by any."

Inequality in the world is closely tied to ecological problems. One of the main results of the twentieth century was the decimation of natural environment and drawing down the non-renewable resources of the earth. Prof. Edward O. Wilson of Harvard University said that the ecological footprint — the average amount of productive land and sea appropriated by each person in bits and pieces from around the world for food, water, housing, energy, transportation, commerce, and waste absorption — is roughly one hectare in developing nations but 10 hectares in the United States. The footprint for the total human population is just 2.2 hectares. It means that to reach the present US level of consumption for every person in the world, we would need at least four more planet Earths.

The conservation of energy, and anti-pollution technologies must be supplemented by measures aimed to arrest population growth in the developing world, as well as excessive consummerism in rich countries. The majority of the world population cannot be denied certain minimum of civilized facilities if we adhere to the tenets of social justice, equality and democratic rights. One of the main ideas of Mahatma Gandhi was that the world had enough for everybody's need, but not for everybody's greed. "If by advance, he said, you mean everyone having plenty to eat and drink and to clothe himself with, to keep his mind trained and educated, I should be satisfied. But I would not like to pack more stuffs into my belly that I can digest and have more things than I can usefully use... The satisfaction of one's physical needs, even the intellectual needs of one's narrow self, must come at a certain point to a dead stop before it degenerates into physical and intellectual voluptuousness."

The Washington consensus, the universality of the rich-country model is both simplistic and self-serving. What the world needs is a country-by-country approach. Developing nations should do what corresponds to their national interests. The external economic aid must conform to each country's unique political and social context.

The experience of other countries may be useful, but to successfully carry out reforms, a country should also take into account its own specific features, cultural and historical traditions, and the mentality of its people.

The challenges faced by humanity at the beginning of the twenty-first century, to a great extent are the result of the wasteful Western economy, which is not proving itself as viable not only for the whole world, but in the long run even for the West itself, because it destroys supporting ecosystems, and undermines prospects of global partnership of developed and developing nations. A vision of socio-economic, political and environmental justice based on perceptions of both the rich and the poor countries is required. The thesis that there is an alternative to neoliberalism should be widely discussed along with such problems as equality, human development, sovereignty, independence and freedom of the peoples all over the world.

Ultimately the rich countries will be forced to pay more attention to the fate of the underprivileged — if only to enjoy their own safety. But in the meantime, there should be a consistent effort to build a new economy, which would be able to ensure better standards of life for all the people. There is an urgent need to change the global direction of previous historic trends. We have to create such constructive and non-confrontational models of development, which will take into account specific features, traditions, and values of every country and will be based on broad international cooperation.

It is important to judge globalisation from different angles. Globalisation means different things to different people. It can hardly be considered a blessing to the socially disadvantaged, including rural poor in the developing countries. It benefits the rich rather than addressing the needs of the poor. It often means widening the gap between the rich and the poor. Expansion of globalisation is being followed by increasing competition, which in turn results in shrinking opportunities for the poor. If a large section of the society is left behind, then development can't be called development The growth may be acceptable to all sections of society, if it increases jobs, ensures future development, takes care for everybody, especially underpriviledged and the vulnerable groups.

Prof. Jan Bremen of Amsterdam School of Social Science Research argues: "As the globalisation progresses, the world is getting structured into a hierarchical mode. Inequality is evident. Globalisation leaves the impression of being colonialism of the past... In the present context globalisation is leading to democratic imperialism. The globalised world has created a hierarchy... The mainstream society will have to promptly address the issues of capital redistribution; employment creation, job security, provision of social welfare in terms of health, house and education".

The United Nations Millennium Development Goals (MDG) aim to satisfy the basic human needs, by 2015. However some experts say that these objectives are so limited that MDG ought to stand for the Minimum Development Goals. But even these goals are not being implemented property.

Nevertheless, some politicians and experts in the developed countries express their concern for the future of rich and wealthy in case there is a rapid economic development in the developing countries. Some even call it "a development nightmare". Kenneth Rogoff, Professor of Economics and director of the Centre for International Development at Harvard University and former chief economist and director of research at the International Monitory Fund. raises a question: "What if 1.3 billion Chinese and 1.1 billion Indians suddenly all had cars and began churning out automobile exhaust at prodigious US rates?.. Absent huge new discoveries or brilliant new inventions, oil could easily reach $ 200 per barrel, as consumption and depletion rates accellerate. The mighty US dollar would become a boutique currency and the euro experiment a sideshow. Investors would clamour for Chinese yuan and Indian rupees. The world's youth would grow up thinking that "Hollywood" must be a wordplay on "Bollywood", and McDonald's humbergers would be viewed a minor ethnic cuisine... Such rapid economic development offers a clear upside for today's rich countries". Rogoff speaks of "latent insecurities in rich countries", of "underlying fears", which must be addressed. And he finds an answer on how to deal with this problem. "Rich countries. — he writes, — could easily afford to triple their aid budgets (which is about 2 per cent of their state budgets) without running the remotest risk of the "nightmare" scenario coming true... with little danger of any rapid catch up". And he adds: "... some day. world income distribution will be radically different than it is today, but not anytime soon".

This is one of the modes, some Western politicians and experts express their concern, about the future of the rich and wealthy. But very unfortunately, they seem to have little concern for the large sections of the poor and underprivileged in the developing countries.

It is becoming clearer with every passing day that Asian, Eurasian, Latin American and African countries have to evolve their own indigenous paradigms of development, suitable for their socio- cultural framework. They have to work out their own concepts of globalisation. They have to thoroughly analyse and reconsider the role of the state and market and work out mechanism, both for the state and the market failures.

All these require comprehensive analytical research and public discussion, and unity of actions in this endeavour.

4

Imperialism — The Building of a New Asia

C.P. Bhambhri

The European Union, the North Atlantic Free Trade Association, the Association of East Asia and Asia Pacific Rim countries, and G-7 countries like United States, Canada, Italy, Germany, France, England, Japan (now including New Russia) have emerged as 'clubs' or 'regional associations' of capitalist countries with a view to coordinate their activities in the field of global trade, and finance. Not only this, the European Union and 54 years old North Atlantic Treaty Organization for Defence are set to expand with the addition of new countries like Slovenia, Estonia, Latvia, Lithuania, Romania and Bulgaria. What is the significance of these regional economic and defence associations in the twenty first century? If on the one hand, it has been proclaimed that trans-national regional associations and organizations are a product of the new logic of centralization-cum-globalization of capital, on the other, regionalisation of advanced and Newly Industrialized Countries (NIC) of East Asia have been seen as 'advantageous' to western capitalist countries because of the 'uneven levels' of development of East Asia. Mexico in NAFTA, or Indonesia in ASEAN can benefit if a capitalist grant, like the United States and Japan, is ready to lead and provide a helping hand to a little less developed capitalist country in the neighborhood. Mexican crisis brought United States immediately in a rescue mission because Mexico was part of NAFTA and during the financial crisis of 1997, Thailand, Indonesia, South Korea looked towards Japan, their capitalist leader, to bail them out of such a crisis. Regional Associations like EU or NAFTA or ASEAN are considered beneficial both in normal times and also during any 'crisis period', because the logic of 'unequal development of capitalism' has found a great corrective in regional cooperation and interdependence. Golman Sacks, an American investment bank, predicted, in October 2003, that the future growth-centres are Brazil, Russia, China and India and if this is the future direction of development, both India and China are trying their best to become 'active' partners in the ASEAN and Asia-Pacific Rim Association. India, Brazil and South Africa, three developing capitalist countries are also evolving a common front to achieve their goals in a cooperative manner. The question : Is regionalism as a sub-system of global capitalism an answer to the problems and difficulties faced by the newly industrializing countries or the late peripheral capitalist countries of the erstwhile decolonized world? The European Union and North Atlantic Free Trade Association has been sold to every region and sub-region as the model of cooperative capitalism based on the advantages of the scale of economy and the beneficial results of the acceptance of classical David Ricardo Law of Comparative Advantages. It has been argued that in the age of new globalization, which began in 1989, with the historic collapse of the Wall of Berlin and the unification of Germany, tariff walls and protectionist barriers have outlived their utility and 'free trade' among the nations and 'market determined economic transactions' have shown the path to prosperity. The state-led economic growth of the Warsaw Pact countries had built 'barriers' for trade and capital flow and the outflow and this model collapsed in the 1990s, giving place to the so-called time tested model of free market economy which is neither defensible on the basis of any theory or empirical reality.

A little digression is essential here to bring into sharp focus the relationship between State/Government and Market in economic affairs of society and that it is historically wrong or false to state that state-led planned model of economic growth was practiced only by the communists or newly liberated countries of Asia, Africa and Latin America. It was the decade of Reagan-Thatcher economic ideology that sold to everyone the practices of market fundamentalism. Joseph E. Stightz is no Marxist when he writes: 'There has been a battle of ideas between those who advocate a minimalist role for the state and those who see the government as playing an important yet limited role, not only in correcting failures and limitations of the market but also in working toward greater social justice.'[1]

What Lenin had said in the beginning of the twentieth century, many economists, including Stiglitz tell us about the capitalism of 1990s. This was the decade in which finance reigned supreme; Central Banks, composed mainly of experts from the financial community, were to be left alone to set monetary policy, their steady hand ensuring stable growth without inflation.'[2] The decade of 1990s had witnessed the emergence of capitalists, ideology completely determined and controlled by 'Global Finance Capital' which burried Keynesian Welfare economics and it has Stiglitz to state: What happened in the nineties was that a set of long-standing checks and balances — a balance between Wall Street, Main Street (or High Street, as it is called in the United Kingdom) and labour, between Old Industry and New Technology, Government — and the market was upset, in some essential ways, by the new ascendancy of finance. Everyone deified to its judgement. Countries including the United States, were told to accept the discipline of the market. Longstanding wisdom, that there were alternative policies, that different policies affected different groups differently, that there were trade-offs, that politics provided the arena through which the trade-offs were evaluated and choices were made, was shunted aside.'[3]

It is not only that finance capital became 'supreme factor' the American model of 'market economy' for the management of economies' was recommend to be 'adopted throughout the world', and we have the testimony of Stiglitz : 'Those countries which did not voluntarily mimic America, in the hope that their economy too would experience a boom, including those that thought America had not gotten the balance right, were cajoled, badgered, and, in the case of developing countries dependent on assistance from the International Monetary Fund, effectively forced to go along what was described as the sweep of history.'[4]

Hence the only issue is of not regarding Regional Association of Asia. The central issue is that the context in which every capitalist country is operating is determined by the commanding position of finance capital and Americans, who have become a pre-eminent actor in the present global phase of capitalism, and are selling a market-led model of capitalism. While in history, many models like British classical model of capitalism was different from the Tsarist Russian state capitalism or German system of so-called 'social market' capitalism and Japanese system of Developmental Capitalism were practiced on the basis of historical specificites and experiences of different societies, the decade of 1990s wants to roll back the history of capitalism by steam rolling the only model of American market-led capitalism.

TIGER ECONOMIES TO CRONY CAPITALISM OF EAST ASIA

East Asia's capitalist economic development in post-world II phase was highly acclaimed and it was also suggested that the East Asians had some indigenous cultural advantages which contributed to the East Asian miracle says the World Development Report 1991.[5]

MEIJI JAPAN'S PENCHANT FOR EDUCATION

Countries with a longstanding commitment to educating their populations have the most advanced economies today. The policy changes associated with the restoration of the Meiji emperor in Japan in 1868 are a case in point. Japan had been isolated from global technological developmets for more than two centuries, and was agricultural and largely feudal. In the mid-1890s, it came under the intense pressure from European and US traders to open its ports and, more generally, to match the economic and military prowess of the West. A revolution brought a new, technocratic governent to power. The government's initiative to import technology is by now legendary: missions were sent abroad to learn about science, technology, and administrative machinery was imported; legions of foreign advisers were hired; and model factories were established in textiles, glass, cement making, and machine tools. The salaries of hired foreigners, who accompanied imported new machinery between 1870 and 1885, averaged 42 per cent of the total annual expenditures of the Ministry of Industrial Affairs. Engineers and technicians accounted for 40 per cent of all foreigners employed by the government and private firms.

What is less well-known, but probably more important for Japan's sustained success, is that extra ordinary changes were made in the educational system. At the beginning of the Meiji era, literacy was only 15 per cent, but by 1872 a universal and compulsory system of elementary education had been introduced and the foundations for secondary education had been laid. On the basis of careful investigation, the education system was patterned on the French system of school districts; the university system was patterned on that of the United States. Primary school attendance rates grew from less than 30 per cent in 1873 to more than 90 per cent in 1907. The number of secondary schools expanded tenfold during the period 1885-1915. Japan became one of the world's most educated and most education-conscious nations. Achieving this required a strong commitment. Japan consistently expended a greater share of its real domestic product on education than any European or other Asian nation.

Robert Gilpin highlights some specific Japanese attitudes and strategies which made Japan to occupy equal status with G-7 countries. He highlights, specially the Japan's real goal since the Meiji Restoration (1868), for 'making the economy self-sufficient' and 'catching up with the West.' Further, Gilpin refers to two other salient features of Japan like the role of 'developmental state capitalism' and 'cultural uniqueness' Gilpin observes: 'These political goals have resulted in a national economic policy for Japan best characterized as neo-mercantilism; it involves state assistance, regulation, and protection of specific industrial sectors in order to increase their international competitiveness and attain the 'commanding heights' of the global economy'. Further, Gilpin states that a later developer had 'Another very important source of this powerful economic derive is the Japanese people's overwhelming belief in their uniqueness, in the superiority of their culture, and in their manifest destiny to become a great power.'[6] Gilpin concludes that 'In many ways, the Japanese state created today's Japanese society.'[7] What happened to the East Asian Miracle? Why is Japan facing deep economic recession for the last fourteen years without any hope of recovery? Japan is not the only model of 'developmental capitalist state'. Yamamoto Tadashi and Kim Gould Ashizawan observe: 'In the post war period, Korea and Thailand sought economic growth through.... a reliance on authoritarian and interventionist states, which was predicated on the passivity of their citizens, in both the social and political areas. As these developmental states have transformed themselves into industrial states, the so-called Asian growth model based on 'Asian values' has been called into serious question.'[8]

The Asian financial crisis of 1997 led the intellectuals to re-examine the model of East Asian Capitalist development and provided a golden opportunity to the International Monetary Fund to dictate American model of market-economy to Thailand, South Korea et al which approached the IMF for succour and support in the period of financial crisis. The East Asians forgot that IMF has failed stories and Argentina is standing always in the queu before the IMF for rescue operation. The IMF and World Bank sold the American model to the crisis ridden East Asia and Gilpin tells us that 'the American model, like the neo-classical model rests on the assumption that markets are competitive..."[9] and market-led and not state-led development can achieve capitalist growth Writing on East Asian crisis, including the strongest of them Japan, Ross Garmant states "..... Japan...a country that had been having its own, slow-burning financial problems for some years before the East Asian crisis began, in which some of the same contributory factors are evident-such as a boom-and-burst cycle in asset markets, and weakness in the financial system and its regulatory regime.'[10]

And further, 'the Japanese case is important, moreover, because Japan's dominant role in regional trade and capital flows meant that its own slow growth and currency weakness helped it to trigger the East Asian crisis, and now adds to the difficulty of recovery in the region.'[11]

It is clear that Japan is a part of the problem of East Asia and regional association of ASEAN to bail out any member country out from the crisis. The World Bank was also very appreciative of East Asia then what happened? Why crisis?[12]

While rejecting the traditional explanations about East Asian Miracle like state intervention, or technological progress or 'Asian Culture', the Report found the success story as a 'decisive vindication of neo-liberal emphasis on the central role of the market in economic development.[13] This testimonial of World Bank, given in 1993, burst in 1997 with serious financial crisis alongwith a general economic crisis of East Asia. And 'crony capitalism' became a standard explanation for the crisis and..... 'the East Asian developmental state contained the seeds of its own destruction.'[14] The so-called greatness of ASEAN has been exposed by Stiglitz when he says that at the start of East Asian crisis, Japan suggested the creation of an 'Asia Monetary Fund' with a promised grant of US$ 100 billion to bail out the fraternity of East Asia. The United States did not encourage this idea because if Japan was given a leading role, it would erode American global hegemony. Stiglitz brings out clearly Japan versus America's role in 'regional crisis' of 1999. He informs us, 'America had become a strong advocate of regional trade agreements, especially those, like NAFTA, in which we (Americans) would play a dominant role. But the Asia Monetary Fund, with the ample resources supplied by Japan, would limit America's ability to dictate policy in the region. The US Treasury knew that, and was willing to risk the region's downturn becoming worse without the aid.'[15]

Indonesia, South Korea and Thailand went to IMF and its dictations for the bail out of the crisis and Japan remained a spectator before a real imperialist hegemonic.

NATIONAL INTEREST VS. REGIONAL ASSOCIATION

It deserves to be stated clearly that 'The crisis in East Asia and the recent recessions in Latin America show that premature capital market liberalisation can result in enormous economic volatility, increasing poverty and destruction of the middle class.'[16] The real villian of the piece is the US, because the terms and conditions of globalization, whether capital market liberalisation or Intellectual Property Provisions (TRIPSs) are being set by the sole hyper power in the present unipolar world. Speculators like George Soros and others made full use of the myth created by the Americans that 'Capital Market controls' lead to economic inefficiency and capital market liberalization is a must for the flow of 'capital' irrespective of the fact that a country may not need 'capital form abroad'.

The essential character of contemporary (post-1990s) globalization is found in pax-Americana and historically it is different from all earlier phases of global capitalism because 'balance of power' and inter-imperialist competition and wars of the past have been replaced by 'unipolar hyper super hegemony of American capitalism' over all other regional or sub-regional capitalist associations and organizations. The central question about Asian Regional Association is: Is Asia part of an American unipolar New International Economic Order or it is a road block to uniploarism of America? The Russian

President Putin on his election, on March 16, 2004, spelt out his foreign policy by stating that Russia is part of Europe and along with Europe, he (Putin) will like to establish a triangular relationship with Russia, China and India. Is it a road towards 'multipolarism'? The ASEAN or SAARC or Asia Pacific Rim countries have not shown any capacity to challenge American hegemony and on the drop of the hat, Indonesia, Thailand and South Korea rushed to IMF, World Bank in 1997 and Malaysia followed its own path to deal with the financial crisis of 1997.

In summation it may be stated that every region and sub-region in Asia is searching for solutions to the challenges of capitalist development and neither China nor Japan separately or in unity can pose any challenge to American capitalist hegemony. It is for the first time in post-World War II history that Japan has sent the so-called 'peace keeping force in Iraq' to bail out occupying American forces in that country. Not only this. Having accepted US 'Dollar' as exchange currency instead of the earlier Gold Standard System, every newly developing capitalist country has integrated its economy, market and monetary system with America. The issue is not to minimise the role of regional organizations but to understand that every region is following the capitalist path of development and the logic of capitalist development is such that it integrates regions and sub-regions in an unequal manner with one another, and with America, the sole imperialist military power in the Twenty First Century. Is there a way out from unipolar to multipolar democratic world order?

REFERENCES

1. Joseph Stiglitz, *The Roaring Nineties: Seeds of Destruction*' Penguin Books, London, 2003, p. XI
2. *Ibid.*, p. XIII
3. Stiglitz, *Ibid.*, p. XIV
4. Stiglitz, *Ibid.*, p. XXI
5. *World Development Report 1991*, The Challenge of Development, New Delhi, Oxford University Press, 1991, p. 58.
6. Robert Gilpin, *Global Political Economy: Understanding the International Economic Order,* Princeton, Princeton University Press, 2001, p. 157-58.
7. Gilpin, *Ibid.*, p. 159, p.156-68.
8. Yamamoto Tadashi (Ed.), *Governance and Civil Society in a Global Age,* Washington, Brookings Institution Press, 2001, p. 14.
9. Ross H. McLeod and Ross Garmaet.
10. *East Asia in Crisis: From being a Miracle to needing one?*, London Routledge P., 1998, p. 5.
11. Ross Garmant, *Ibid.*

12. World Bank, *The East Asian Miracle: Economic Growth and Public Policy,* New Delhi, Oxford University Press, 1993.
13. Quoted by Gilpin, *op. cit.,* p. 325.
14. Gilpin *op. cit.,* p. 330.
15. Joseph Stiglitz, *The Roaring Nineties: Seeds of Destruction,* London, Penguin Books, 2003, p. 228.
16. Joseph E. Stiglitz, 'Social Dimensions of Globalization', *The Economic Times,* New Delhi, 15 March 2004, p. 8. Also see Joseph Stiglitz, *Globalization Its Discontents,* Penguin Books, New Delhi, 2000, pp. 89-112.

5

A Preliminary Analysis of the Development of the Asian Regional Economic Cooperation

Xu Yongquan

21st century is the one of economic globalization. The economic globalization directly pushes the free flow of goods, services, capital, technology and personnel in the world. At the same time, it also indirectly influences the combination and mutual absorbing of the laws, politics and culture of different economies. Therefore, the economic cooperation among different economies has continuously emerged and developed and more and more free trade zones, communities and tariff unions can be seen day by day. With the intensification of the economic globalization, the success of the European and North America regional economic cooperation and the absence of Asian regional economic cooperation, strengthening Asian economic cooperation has become a strong voice.

THE MAIN FACTORS THAT CAUSE THE DIFFICULTIES AND COMPLICATIONS OF ASIAN REGIONAL COOPERATION

The Asian regional cooperation starts late and develops slowly. The difficulties and complications in the process had made Asia and the world dissatisfied and disappointed. The main factors that cause the form of that situation are as follows.

Internal Factors

The uneven development of Asian economy has been caused by the unfavourable conditions for the regional cooperation. Since the middle of last century, Asian economy had never played a role of a black horse. The emergence of the four Asian dragons, the rapid advancement of Japanese economy and the fast development of ASEAN economy, as well as the achievements, that China had scored in the past 20 years of reform and opening up have all attracted the attention of the world. However, the development of Asian economy is imbanlanced. Because of the differences and uneven development of the economic level, most of the rich countries like Japan and Republic of Korea (ROK) would like to cooperate with the European and American clubs far away. The poor countries like Pakistan and Democratic People's Republic of Korea (DPRK) have to work hard to shake off the poverty. They have no needs or demands with each other and hardly find the way and, content with the cooperation are that is acceptable to each other.

The variety of the political systems and law systems is the important factors that restrain the Asian regional economic cooperation. Although the countries have no doubt on the guiding principle of giving priority to the development of economic and trade relations under the spirit of developing side by side by seeking common ground while shelving differences, the influence of the political and law systems on the development of economic and trade relations is still undeniable. Sometimes, it is of ultra importance. As to the development of building close economic relations, the obstacles of politics and laws are more prominent. In economy, most of the Asian countries choose the system of market economy. Yet in politics, some countries set up the system of western style, while some newly emerging market-economy countries are in the process of improving and developing their political systems. Under the situation of the existence of different political systems, the regional economic cooperation has been restrained to a great degree.

The suspicions and jealousy in politics and military have done great harm to the Asian regional economic cooperation. Unlike the situation of West Europe and North America, there is lack of mutual trust among Asian countries and regions. The suspicions and jealousy in politics and military are evident. Although there are no large-scale military conflicts in Asia, the prospects of Nuclear Issues of DPRK are not clear, the disputes along the Southeast coastal line come up time to time and the historical problems of Japan have not been solved completely. All those have left the region with lack of unity in politics and trust in military and sometimes even with frictions. Under such a situation, the regional economic cooperation is short of basic requirements.

The similarity of culture's with different essence is another important obstacle of Asian regional economic cooperation. Asia is a region with variable nationalities, including big nationalities like Hun, Japanese, Korean and Mongolian. It is also one of the regions with the most complicated situation of nationalities in the world. All nationalities in the region have formed different cultural and psychological characteristics in the past. The nationalities in Asia have obvious differences, not only in languages, religious beliefs, national characteristics and traditions, but also in ethics, value concepts, codes of conduct, the ways of thinking and culture. The complications and pluralism of the national culture and psychology leads to the relations of discrimination and are loosly organized, which lacks centripetal force.

The External Reasons

The relations between the United States and Japan have excessively restrained the strength of Japan and its development in Asia. After the World War II, the United States ensured the right to keep its military presence in Japan; through the Treaty of Japan-US Security. On the other hand, the United States safeguarded its military status and political influence in Japan and the whole of East Asia and Asia-Pacific region by adopting series of measures of supporting the development of the Japanese economy. The United States hopes to strengthen the Japan-US strategic alliance, so that it can further protect its economic, military and political interests in Asia. Therefore, the United States does its utmost to oppose Japan's action of taking part in other organizations, which will weaken the Japan-US relations and do harm to the existed structure. From the view of the Japanese side, Japan hopes to maintain the special relations with its biggest trade partners. At the same time, because of its isolated and awkward political status in Asia, Japan has to do things cautiously and within limits.

The contradictions between the United States and Southeast Asian countries constitute a serious constraint on the self-determination of Southeast Asian countries. Due to the fact that Southeast Asian countries are huge markets with growing importance, America is not willing to relinquish such favourable interests. According to America's strategy, an important point of occupying and safeguarding the market is to oppose an Asian economic organization not involving America, especially one dominated by China, Japan and South Korea which may possibly replace the status of America in Asia. Although Southeast Asian countries are somewhat dependent on their Asian neighbours like China, Japan and South Korea, they also compete with them, which reflects a tendency to view the regional economic cooperation negatively. On the other hand, because of their strong reliance on American economy and the all-round influence of

America, Southeast Asian countries cannot get away from the influence and pressure from America, which is to say they have to listen to America most of the times.

The features of the APEC Forum disturb the thorough development of regional economic cooperation of Asia. Since its establishment in 1989, APEC has held 11 non-official summits, attended by ministers of trade, foreign affairs, finance and telecommunication etc, and have released guiding documents like Bogor Declaration — Shanghai Declaration and scored some achievements. However, APEC is no more than a regional forum, with serious constraints due to the absence of fixed organization and feasible mechanism of cooperation and the fact that its declarations and action guidelines have no binding power on its members.

THE LATEST UPDATES AND ANALYSIS OF ASIAN REGIONAL COOPERATION

To develop Asian regional cooperation is a long and winding process. However as the process of globalization accelerating and inter-dependence among economies deepens, the voice of Asian regional economic cooperation become louder and relevant and countries make more efforts on it, which leads to some new eye-catching trends. The reasons for these trends are as follows:

1. US attitude toward Asian regional economic cooperation changed from opposition to non-interference or acquiescence, which constitutes a new compelling factor for Asian regional economic cooperation. As considering its own national interest and its global strategy, the United States has always been wary of Asian regional economic cooperation, and intervened directly or indirectly. In recent years, as economic globalization and integration of regional economies go deep, an obvious turn of American attitude regarding Asian regional economic cooperation has taken place. The United States believes that the regional cooperation as in Europe and North America is unlikely to take shape in Asia in the near future. As long as the United States participates positively and continues to exert influence, its interests will be maintained. As a result, the United States begins to acquiesce in Asian regional economic cooperation, or at least does not to interfere.
2. APEC has strengthened its functions in terms of promoting regional economic cooperation. As a regional forum, it is developing a new mode of growing pragmatism. Conferences of all kinds and levels along with forums are held every year, such as APEC informal summit meeting, meeting of foreign ministers and trade ministers, meeting of finance

ministers, meeting of information ministers and meeting of ministers of small and medium-size enterprises etc. These meetings have produced consistent and normative guiding documents in terms of manifesto and action plan of the common objective, which help promote the continuous development of regional trade and investment. Apparently economies are no longer satisfied with the mode of APEC Forum. Instead they begin to seek stronger cooperation, particularly in some preferred sectors such as finance and information.

3. China recognizes the importance of regional economic cooperation organizations, and starts vigorously to study and explore possibilities of participation. As the economic globalization presses ahead, China is continuously seeking various forms of economic cooperation modes and begins to bring new content to it. The outstanding points are: (1) to vigorously develop economic cooperation with ASEAN, and speed up the pace to establish a free trade zone by way of "counting-down"; (2) to positively promote substantial talks in forums like APEC and BOAO Forum to form a "win-win" situation; (3) to actively respond to and guide the domestic regional economic cooperation with Hong Kong, Macao and Taiwan, and implement CEPA; (4) to actively study the cooperative relationship with Japan and ROK, and be disposed to set up a free trade zone of the three countries of "10+3". In the meantime, China is enthusiastic about developing economic and trade relations with the Commonwealth of Independent States, and further promoting the founding of a free trade zone on the basis of military and political cooperation established by the Shanghai Cooperation Organization.

6

Strategic Triangle of China, India and Russia

Ideal and Reality

ZHOU YUYUN

FAVOURABLE CONDITIONS FOR PROMOTING TRILATERAL COOPERATION AMONG CHINA, INDIA AND RUSSIA

1. China, India and Russia all stand for world multi-polarization and oppose unilateralism in international relations, which is the international background for strengthening cooperation among the three countries.

Being a developing country, China has always advocated world multi-polarization, which is fairly consistent with the views of India and Russia. For instance, an India scholar has mentioned in "A Triangle Family in Europe-Asia Continent Begins to Live" that a multi-polar global system will emerge in the 21st century, in which the US, the EU, China, Russia, Japan, the ASEAN and India will be the main factors in the international economic and political system. China, India and Russia will play more important roles in world affairs, so as to make the world change from the current unipolar state to a multi-polar or multi-centered one.

Because of advocating world multi-polarization, all three countries emphasize the necessity to strengthen the role of the UN. A Russian scholar believes the role of the UN should be strengthened to resist the form of a unipolar world. Exploiting the potential of cooperation among Russia, China and India is not only of great significance to safeguarding national interests of the three countries, but also probably becomes a global moral and political element that contributes to the establishment of a fair world order, unharmful to the interests of all countries, no matter big or small. A Russian scholar, in his paper Civilizational Alliance of Russia, China, India and Iran, discusses the meaning and value of the world multi-polarization proceeding from the prospect of the differences between east civilization and that of the west. He believes that compared with west civilization that seeks hegemony, the east one attaches more importance to the subsistence of human beings, pays close attention to the interpersonal relations, and provides guidance on how to live in harmony with others. The peaceful development of international community should absorb the historical civilization and experience of the east. The human beings need a new living pattern and a new world structure, which distinguishes the Europe-centralism and globalism imposed upon others.

In current world, the economic strength and military superiority of the United States have reached an unparalleled level, especially the military advantage. The US inputs merely 3.5 per cent of its GDP to realize its exclusively dominating position. American scholars affirm that in fields of utmost importance, there is no powerful rival against America, so far. The characteristics of the American hegemony is that it is a kind of hegemony in system, which is supported not only by material forces such as military and economic strength, but also by some soft forces like a vast amount of thoughts and culture. Some scholars assert that if the trend of unipolarization is reinforced, then the relations among Russia, China and India will inevitably be closer.

2. China, India and Russia have common voices in respect of international anti-terrorism, and share a great deal of joint points on the interests of the geopolitical strategy, which will push forward the trilateral cooperation to some extent.

The war in Afghanistan led to significant changes in the geopolitical structure of Central Asia. China, Russia, India and the Central-Asia Republic of former USSR are in the same geopolitical region, therefore their national interests are closely related. One factor that promotes the cooperation among China, India and Russia is the rise of Islamic Fundamentalism. The Muslims are distributed over the extensive regions from West Asia and North Africa to Southeast Asia. South Asia will probably become the center of the confrontations between Islamic Fundamentalism and International community. It has been years that Russia, China and India are all threatened by terrorism. For example, armed forces being entrenched along the border between India and Pakistan continuously cross the border and engage in terrorism; terrorists in Chechnya of Russia directly threatens the security and stability in North Caucasia and the central part of Russia; since external Islamic Fundamentalists support separatists in Sinkiang of China, which seriously threatens territorial integrity of China, so that China has to close down the border. Thus China, India and Russia are natural geopolitical alliances against regional terrorism. Terrorism carried out by the Islamic extremists can be restrained and eradicated based only on cooperation of the international community including China, India and Russia.

Secondly, there are some similar objective conditions for the cooperation among China, India and Russia.

In terms of geography, territories of China, India and Russia are linked by mountains and rivers. The total territory covers 30 million square kilometers, exceeding the sum of the US, Japan and Europe. The total amount of population of the three countries is about 2.5 billion, which nearly accounts for 35 per cent of the world population. Close cooperation among the three countries will be conducive to the peace and stability of the world.

In view of history, both China and India have the history of thousands of years civilization. The friendship between the two peoples dates back to ancient times. The common experience of anti-colonialism and anti-imperialism makes two peoples come closer. At that time, the former USSR not only supported and helped independence and liberation activities of the Chinese and Indian people, but also provided guidance and assistance for their future construction and development, after independence. Social systems of China and India are also emulated some extent. The three countries had been aiding and supporting each other, which has led to the historical friendship deeply rooted among the masses.

With regard to the reality, China, India and Russia are all lagging behind relatively, and facing arduous tasks of assuring a sustainable growth of national economy and keeping up with the developing trend of the world. Given this situation, all the three countries regard surrounding security and stability as the precondition for economic development. Meanwhile, there exists huge potential for the economic and trade cooperation among China, Russia and India.

RESTRICTING CONDITIONS FOR PROMOTING TRILATERAL COOPERATION AMONG CHINA, INDIA AND RUSSIA

1. The development of Sino-Indian relations hasn't maturated enough compared with that of Sino-Russian and Indian-Russian temporarily, which to a large extent restrains the intensity and scope of trilateral cooperation.

At present, the relations between China, Russia and India do not form an equilateral triangle. An Indian scholar holds that the triangle relationship among China, India and Russia looks like an isosceles triangle, whose two sides—Sino-Russian side and Indian-Russian side are equal, but the third side, Sino—Indian side, is a little bit shorter. In other words, although Russia has intimate relations with both China and India, yet China and India in this triangle are not so close. China and Russia established "strategic cooperative partnership" in April 1996, China and India established "constructive cooperative partnership" in November 1996, and India and Russia established strategic partnership. In contrast, Sino-Russian side and India-Russian side have better relations, and Sino-India side lags behind relatively, which is the main factor that influences the trilateral cooperation.

2. China, India and Russia attach great importance to their respective relations with the US. If trilateral relationship among the three is based upon anti-Americanism, it does not conform to their national interests. Additionally, the US frequently creates obstacles among China, India and Russia.

Economy and trade are weatherglass of international relations. The volume of Sino-Indian trade amounts to $6 billion, the volume of Indian-Russian trade amounts to $1.2 billion and the volume of Sino-Russian trade amounts to $15.8 billion. However, the trade volume between any country of the three with the US greatly exceeds that of the mutual trade among them. The volume of Sino-American trade is more than $12.63 billion with more than $50 billion trade surplus of China, the volume of Russian-American trade is $6.9 billion, and the volume of Indo-American trade is $26 billion.

In addition, the US keeps high alert on the development of relations among China, India and Russia, and adopts relative preventive measures. American scholars propose to implement "big-powers balance strategy" in Asia, so as to prevent countries in this region from forming alliances. In recent years, the United States improves its relations with India on its own and intensifies the diplomatic relations with India. In the report on "Asia in 2025", the Department of Defence of the US pointed out that the constantly rising China will be the biggest regional threat to the US. Moreover, if the US wants to retain its crucial role in Asia-Pacific region, it must build the advance base of campaign in South Asia and Southeast Asia, in which India has rising strategic potential. The US must prepare to pay any price to prevent this form of alliance between China and India.

Concerning the US-Russian relations, bilateral reciprocal effect has appeared from time to time. The US plays up that the rapidly rising China is a latent threat to Russia. US media claims that China has the ambition of expansion on the Far East Siberia area, and will ultimately be the chief opponent of Russia. The US intends to instigate the feelings of estrangement on the "strategic cooperative partnership" between Russia and China. The position and measures adopted by US on the US-Indian and US-Russian relations cast shadows on potential trilateral cooperation among China, India and Russia.

3. China, India and Russia hold different standpoints and show varied extent of eagerness towards trilateral cooperation. All of them are developing relations

with the third countries according to their own schedule, but do not consider relations among the three as a whole.

Russia is an active advocate of the trilateral cooperation. President Putin, in his first term, took China and India as the corner stone of Russia's diplomatic policy in Asia. In October 2000, for the first time in public, President Putin mentioned the issue of establishing relations among Russia, China and India before he visited India: "If it is admitted that India, China, and Russia have some common interests as Asian countries, then we would like to safeguard the interests together. I cannot see any particularity and dangers in it, as long as the suggestions on bilateral and multilateral cooperation are public, transparent and reasonable to all partners. In November, 2001, Mr. Ivanov, Russian Foreign Minister, expressed that Russia, China and India are shouldering increasingly heavy responsibilities on building global security and stability system. Coordinating their respective standpoints and reaching common understandings will undoubtedly contribute to the stability of the Asia-Pacific region and the world as a whole.

In contrast, China and India seem to be more cautious about the strategic alliance. China definitely expresses its foreign policy of non-alignment, and will not ally with any big power or group of countries. During his visit to Russia in March 1999, Chinese Premier expressed that, "establishing and maintaining good relations among Russia, China and South Asian countries will contribute to the peace and stability of South Asia and the whole world". In his expression, the word "strategic triangle" was not used. Before he visited China, the Indian Foreign Minister indicated that although India, Russia and China have common interests and strategic objectives in regional and global affairs, but denies that the similarity will lead to an alliance of the three countries.

CONCLUSIONS

1. There haven't been sufficient conditions for the establishment of strategic triangle among China, Indian and Russia so far, so the cooperative relations of the three will not head for strategic triangle. Developing and strengthening the meeting mechanism in the UN among foreign ministers of the three countries, and enhancing consultation and cooperation on international and regional issues of common concerns will be a practical choice.
2. Even the slow and cautious trilateral cooperation is of realistic significance to promote world multi-polarization, prevent unilateralism, improve bilateral relations among the three, and strengthen international cooperation of anti-terrorism.

7

Russia-India-China

Strategic Cooperation and a Pan Asian Order

R.R. Subramanian

In the new world disorder, that manifests itself through terrorism and unipolarity of the lone superpower—the United States and its hegemonistic pursuits in Iraq after September 11, 2001, an antidote becomes a necessity. One major antidote to check the onward extension of a US led NATO into areas of Central Asia and South Asia would be strategic cooperation between Russia, China and India. This has become all the more relevant because of the decision of the Bush Administration to upgrade the status of Pakistan to a non-NATO ally *a la* Israel, Japan, Philippines and Australia.

US Secretary of State Gen. Colin Powell, has indicated in no uncertain terms in Islamabad, that the new status of Pakistan is being contemplated in order to facilitate easy transfer of American weapons to a nuclearised Pakistan. China, which has engaged in strategic cooperation with Pakistan since 1965 and provided nuclear assistance to Dr. A.Q. Khan since the 1990s has reasons to be concerned with the pro-American stance of its ally. Since the all-weather 3,000 kms Karokoran highway connects Urungi in Xinjiang province with Gilgit in Pakistan occupied Kashmir, Beijing must contemplate the consequences of an increased American involvement in the areas in proximity to China as also for its interests in Central Asia. China's engagement with India is a trend that facilitates further strategic cooperation in a triangular framework.

The strategic relationship between India, China and Russia has a dynamics of its own. The then Russian, President Yevgeny Primakoff, promoted the idea of a strategic triangle in December 1998 during a visit to New Delhi. All the three sides of the triangle face a threat from Islamic terrorism; be it in Chechnya, Kashmir or Xinjiang. The US attempts to fight Islamic terrorism globally seems purely to further own interests.

There is another major confluence of interests between the troika that relates to ballistic missile defence.[1] After the attacks on the WTO, in New York on September 11, 2001 the United States has stepped up efforts to evolve a notional missile defence (NMD) by investing billions in order to blunt possible missile attacks by China and Russia on the continental United States (CONUS).[2] In order to protect its non-NATO allies, like Japan and Australia, it is proposed to deploy a Theatre Missile Defence (TMD) at the regional level. If indeed Pakistan were to be incorporated as a non-NATO all one would have to ascertain whether Washington intends to deploy a TMD to blunt the missile attacks by India in retaliation to attack by Pakistan.

China has to view with concern the increased access of US military to the bases in Pakistan. Beijing has a major stake in the development of the Gwadar port in Baluchistan. The US in its attempts to wage war on terrorism in the Middle East and thereby to secure its oil interests may increase its naval presence say at Karachi port. Pakistan may be compared to Israel in regard to the ambiguity of its possession of nuclear weapons. Also the US turns a blind eye to Pakistan's procurement of nuclear weapons in so far as it perceives it to be of lesser consequence than fighting the Al-Qaida in Iraq and Afghanistan.

As far as Russia and China are concerned the presence of Osama Bin Laden, in the tribal areas of Afghanistan bordering Pakistan, can prove to be a source of concern be it for aiding Chechen militants or Uighir irredentist's claims in Xinjiang. These concerns should cause China to further the constructive engagement it has started with India. After the May 1998 explosions of nuclear devices by India, China adopted a negative posture towards New Delhi by becoming Chairman of the five permanent members committee of the Security Council and adopting resolution 1972, in June 1998. This resolution called on India and Pakistan to immediately halt nuclear testing, sign the CTBT and give up nuclear weapons. Subsequently the NDA government with Jaswant Singh as the Exteral Affairs Minister, began a series of interactions with China and assuaged Beijing's concerns about India targeting China with ballistic missiles.

Since April 1974 China had employed intermediate range and medium range ballistic missiles (IRBMs and MRBMs) in the mountainous caves and valley of the Tibet Autonomous Region (TAR), bordering Qinghai. These missiles had been deployed to target the Soviet Far East, so as to deter the SS-20 missiles that Moscow had deployed at the height of its rivalry with Beijing, All that has changed now, with Sino-Russian relation reaching a trade volume of over $10bn.

One important milestone in the evolution of Russia-India relations was the signing of the Declaration on Strategic Partnership between Moscow and Delhi, in October 2000. In November 2001 Vladimir Putin, the Russian President and the Indian Prime Minister Atal Bihari Vajpayee stressed that "it would be inappropriate to talk about attempts by three countries to form a new axis or pole of opposition to other international groups. Coordinating efforts among Russia, India and China is aimed exclusively at developing adequate responses to the new challenges posed by extremism and terrorism"[3].

Russian and Chinese relations of "equal trusting partnership and strategic cooperation" do not envisage Russia and China as entering into any kind of alliance against any third country. This approach can be discerned in the construction of Indian foreign policy, as is reflected in treaties, agreements and joint statements by Russia, the People's Republic of China and India"[4]; for example, in Article 8 of the Treaty of Good Neighbourliness, Friendship and Cooperation between the Russian Federation (RF) and the People's Republic of China (PRC) concluded in Moscow on July 16, 2001 and in the Joint Declaration between the PRC and the RF, signed on December 2, 2002 in Beijing. In this Declaration President Putin and PRC Chairman Jiang Zemin emphasised that "friendly relations between the two countries are a new type of interstate relations not built on entering an alliance, not espousing confrotnation and not directed against third countries"[5].

However, it needs to be stressed that in spite of the American military hegemonistic designs in Iraq in West Asia and Afghanistan in South Asia, the three members of the triangle do not want to be drawn into an alliance. At best it remains a cooperation among nations interested in preserving a Pan Asian security Order. It needs stressing, however, that were the US to extend NATO's military activities beyond the continent of Europe into Central, West, East and South Asia the triangle must redefine its present posture.

How far China, under the new dispensation of Hu Jin Tao, goes to *redefine* its military relationship, with Pakistan (in view of the latter's increasing relevance in Washington's strategic force planning in a non-polycentric world) would greatly determine the evolution of a Russia-China-India cooperation. The Sino-Indian boundary issue will continue to bedevil the triangular relationship. but then a cue should be taken from the manner in which Beijing and Moscow have gone about trying to solve their boundary problems.

It also needs to be stressed that as far as China is concerned there cannot be 'two tigers in a mountain". The Himalayan mountain ranges divide the two tigers as far as their territoriality is concerned. But it is for the Russian bear to act as the intermediary/antidote and emphasis the importance of the evolution of a new Pan Asian Security Order.

India's participation in the Shangai Cooperation Organisation (SCO) could constitute a first step towards the creation of some sort of alliance between Russia, China and India. It would upset "the new geopolitical game plan of Washington to create a balance of power favouring the continuation of a unipolar world under the soft hegemony of the United States".[6]

The recent initiative of Gen Colin Powell as US Secretary of State further reflects the above contention. Will the US hegemony eventually spill over into the western regions of China? The Uighir militancy may be encouraged to foment the creation of an eastern Turkestan that has oil fields of the Tarim Basin. How far the US force planning in this direction can be sustained if the neocons of the Bush Administration are defeated by the Democratic Party of Senator John Kerry is to be seen.

India's Russia and China have a common interest in building a multipolar world order as does France in the European Union. The three countries in Asia share similar concerns in regard to national sovereignty and opposing unilaterist actions by a US-led NATO extending beyond Europe into Central Asia and South Asia. Multipolarity would be a rejection of American hegemony. It also reflects the different situations of the concerned States.[7]

For Russia it means prevention of a further loss of face whilst for India and China, a desire to become major actors in the global scene. The Chinese scholar Huang Zhengji has observed "multipolrity just refers to the multiple forces in the international community that are possessed of certain strength and representatives of certain interest".[8]

To be a pole, a country must be powerful, both economically and militarily. At present it remains unclear how the asymmetries, as the rivalries between India and China, can be managed to further strategic cooperation in a triangle. For example how does China, unlike Russia, view India's role in a multiplier world.

No doubt Beijing has re-evaluated India's capacity as a pole after the nuclear tests of May 1998 as also its economic growth since 1991. Whilst Russia supports India's quest for a permanent seat in the Security Council, it remains unclear as to how China views this issue. China perceives itself as a global power whilst confining India within South Asia.

India must get herself out of the confines of South Asia and play a more significant strategic role in the Asia and Pacific Region. The navies of Russia, China and India must exercise jointly in the areas contiguous to the Andaman and Nicobar islands. These three navies should ensure that the Asia-Pacific region remains one of peace. Russia, India and China participate in the ASEAN Regional Forum (ARF), an annual exercise that enables these large neighbours to participate in strategic dialogue with the ASEAN countries and can thus coordinate their stands.

The US-Japan strategic relationship might militate against the formation of a Russia-India-China triangulation of interests aimed at fostering a Pan Asian Security Organisation. Chinese scholar and advisor to the China Institute of International Studies pointed out in a conference held at the Institute of Far Eastern Studies, Moscow in September 2001: "All the three countries are firmly opposed to unilateralism. All the three countries are in favour of maintaining global strategic alliance and stability; and can hold consultations on relevant question such as BMD."[9]

REFERENCES

1. Swaran Singh, 'Strategic Triangle and Ballistic Missile Defence' *India, China, Russia: Intricacies of an Asian Tringle.* Edited by Boquerat and Fredric Gare; Indian Research Press, New Delhi.
2. R.R. Subramanian, *India China and Pakistan: Defence and Nuclear Tangle in Asia,* ABC Press, New Delhi, 1990.
3. *Nezavisimaya Gazetta* 20 November 2001.
4. Galina Yaskina, 'Russia-China-India: Prospects for Trilateral Co-operation' *Far Eastern Affairs* Vol. 31, No. 1, 2003, pp. 6-17.
5. Renmin Ribao, Beijing, December 3, 2002.
6. Devendra Kaushik, 'The New Geopolitics of Central Asia: Russia, China and India in J.K. Ray, *Asia Annual 2000,* Shipra Publications, Delhi, 2000, p. 181.
7. Fredric Gare, 'India, China and Russia: Strategic Partnership or Strategic Competition'.
8. Hung Zhengji, 'The Irresistible Multipolarity Trend of the World' *International Strategic Studies* 4/1997 VI-5. p. 3.
9. Cheng Ruisheng, 'Areas of Possible Co-operation between China-Russia and India in the New Century', *China Report,* Vol. 38, No. 1, Jan.-March, 2002, p. 86.

8

Russia-India-China Cooperation
The Shaping of a Notion in Russian Foreign Policy

Hari Vasudevan

In the recent past, the "triangle" of consultation and cooperation between the Russian Federation, India and the People's Republic of China has been part of strategic thinking and foreign policy discussions in the world politics. A general literature has begun to evolve on the subject even as "track two diplomacy" has focused on arranging meetings between representatives of the three states to strengthen interaction. How far "alliances" or coordination of policies can be a phenomenon of the future has been a focus of enquiry.

In this, almost all accounts of India-Russia-China cooperation deal with general issues, setting out to measure the potential of cooperation, avoiding focus on any one area of a possible triangular relationship. Neither trilateral trading links, nor the significance of overlap of the military production establishments charting out feasible paths of cooperation have been explored to any great extent. Nor has there been a careful study of crucial times when positions coincide/diverge-as in the case of the run up to the Iraq crisis of 2003. Either leading actors treat the notion of cooperation as far-fetched merely a gambit to be played to contain the expansion of US authority. Or it is acknowledged that these are relationships still in the making—positions that do not bear assertion until they are tried in various forums and circumstances. This in itself demands some perspective as to why the notion came into existence at all on the Russian side, when E.M. Primakov asserted the importance of such cooperation in December 1998 in New Delhi. Where does it figure in the policy assumptions of major actors in the Russian Federation?

In looking closely at this problem in this study it is seen that at a crucial level of policy making in the Russian Federation—the Ministry of Foreign Affairs—the notion was no sudden "arrival". The importance of Russian cooperation with China and India was a standard motif of statements engendered by the Soviet as well as the Russian Ministry. The sharpness given to it by E.M. Primakov was a consequence of his own rejection of unipolarity. Overall, the notion has existed in an uncertain state, ad the effect of the perspectives on the enunciation of policy has violently oscillated.

The presentation shows the varying fate of the notion of India-Russia-China cooperation in the Ministry over the period 1991-2003. It begins with the shape the notion took during the Shevarnadze Ministry during the last years of Soviet rule. And then proceeds to look at how the idea receded in significance under Andrei Kozyrev, First Minister of Foreign Affairs of the Russian Federation. The study then examines the position taken by E.M. Primakov.

No claims are made that such a picture reflects the course of Russian foreign policy wholly. Given the strength of Presidential power for the making of such a policy, no account of Ministerial concerns can be the final word on the way Russia takes its stand in world affairs. However, given the uncertainty, also in Presidential behaviour and the influence of lobbies in diverting attention at crucial times, the pivotal location of the Ministry vis foreign policy makes it a force that cannot be ignored.

THE SIGNIFICANCE OF THE MINISTRY OF FOREIGN AFFAIRS IN FOREIGN POLICY MAKING IN THE RUSSIAN FEDERATION

The General Perspective

Most commentators on Russian foreign policy agree that its course was shaped after the events of December 1991, by a variety of circumstances. Factors that were significant were the force of Presidential authority in the Federation, the priorities of the Ministry of Foreign Affairs or the specific desires of any one of the many lobbies that were concerned with policy, including ad hoc parliamentary coalitions. The constitutional authority of the Presidential office and the very character of Russian politics placed the President in an exceptional position. This followed directly from initiatives taken by Boris Yeltsin. These included his reinforcement of the institution in 1991[1], the exceptional powers given to the institution by Parliament, following the August putsch of 1991 and the disintegration of the USSR in December 1991[2], and the terms of the 1993 Constitution[3], when the Russian Executive ceased to be responsible to Parliament in any serious manner. Elsewhere, Russian politics, involved the fragility of party politics[4] and the failure of Parliamentary institutions to form their imprint on policy. Regional bodies that had been unusually active outside the Soviet Union and those that had been exceptionally independent of Mosow in the later years of prestroika (such as members of the Siberian Agreement and the Far Eastern Agreement) were faced with revenue constraints during the post-disintegration economic crisis that prevented their assertion of authority, as they had done in the past. The very nature of the President, however, and his refusal to guide everyday policy in a regular manner, made insignificant the influence of the various institutions set up to give him vigorous control over government.

Such a situation determined that when Presidential authority asserted itself, it could be decisive. Otherwise, individual locations of power could be of exceptional significance. These "locations" could vary from important oligarchs (such as Boris Berezovskii), exceptionally influential individuals such as Anatolii Chubais, or important bodies of government—such as the Ministry of Foreign Affairs or the Ministry of Defence. Though almost all these actors had to bear in mind the various deep structural factors that were crucial to Russia's external relations that took shape in the way Russian economic and political life developed. The significance of such factors transcended (or subsumed) oscillations in the policy-making establishment between "Atlanticists" (who were pro-NATO) and "Eurasianists" (who called for an independent Russian course in the global affairs). Here, while pulls and counter-pulls cancelled, leaving the Russian Presidency as the prime agent of manoeuvre, where the President chose not to exert himself, other bodies or individuals could be of supreme importance. Crucial among such structural factors were:

(i) The network of ties that linked the Russian Federation with the superpower status of the Soviet Union pacts, agreements and a new international presence for the new Russian state—associated with START and SALT, the OSCE summits discussions.

(ii) The energy complex and the system of exports of oil and natural gas. A major source of official revenues, and the energy sector came to be dominated by major state corporations—Rosneft, Lukoil, Surguftneftgaz—over of the 90s.

(ii) The network of interests that handled the country's debt—so crucial to a country with a debt of 144.4 bn. Roubles (1st April 2001)—65 per cent of GNP.

(iii) The network of interests that handles Russia's dealings with the CIS.

(iv) The interests that deal with the Federation's integration into the global market and into Europe. The integration of the Russian Federation with the global economy has revolved partly around the energy complex and partly around special regions and regional associations. In the latter case, 30 per cent of exports are said to come from 10 Russian regions.

The Standing and Nature of the Russian Ministry

In such circumstances, the Russian Foreign Ministry initially had weaknesses in impressing itself on foreign policy. Major interests drew the new country in different directions.

In the Ministry itself, substantial reorganisation and chaos followed from the integration of the Union Ministry after 1991 with the Ministry of Foreign affairs of the RSFSR. Contemporaries sensed a major shake up that led to objections and resentment. Changes included the sudden promotion in influence of a number of personalities. Andrei Kolosovskii, and a team of recent graduates from MGIMO, who joined the Russian Ministry in preference over the Union Ministry; Fedor Shelova Kovedyaev—a specialist on the ancient world; Georgii Kunadze—head of a Department of IMEMO and a Japan specialist of standing; Boris Kolokolov—Deputy Ministry of Foreign Affairs of the Russian Federation since 1981; and Georgii Mamedov—Head of the Section of the USSR Ministry dealing with the USA and Canada, who came to the Russian Ministry after the Minsk agreement. Established figures of the Union Ministry were sidelined; Anatolii Adamishin, Alexei Obukhov, Viktor Komplektov, Valentin Falin and Julius Kvitsinkii.[6] A running tussle took place between the Ministry and the Parliament, despite the prevailing ban on the old Communist party. The "democrat" Vladimir Lukin clearly had major point of disagreement with his erstwhile protege, the Minister Andrei Kozyrev. This placed major strains on the working of the Ministry, which faced a problem of personnel owing to the decline in interest among young Russians in diplomatic careers in the aftermath of the disintegration, when banking and business careers came to have a premium.

Major advantages, though, still remained with Smolenskaia Ploshchad. The Ministry controlled the major "men on the spot", and the expertise on the Russian establishments abroad. Close relations between the first Russian Foreign Minister, Andrei Kozyrev, and the Russian President, Boris Yeltsin, ensured that the Ministry influenced the first appointments to major positions in the last months of 1991. Post 1995, following the appointment of E.M. Primakov as Minister, further reinforced authority. Primakov was not merely close to President Yeltsin. He had considerable influence with the Foreign Intelligence Service, which he headed during 1991-95, and close links with various factions in the Russian Parliament.

THE MINISTRY OF FOREIGN AFFAIRS AND "TRIANGULAR COOPERATION" UNDER ANDREI KOZYREV

The General Perspective

It was against such a background that Russia's first Foreign Minister, Andrei Kozyrev, established the significance of Asia for the Russia's foreign policy. He was banking on Soviet Foreign Minister, Eduard Shevernadze's sense of the "the unique opportunities the Soviet Union had for the formation of a Eurasian zone of security and stability, bringing together West and East, Europe and Asia". His focus, though was the more narrow interests of the Russian Federation, and the responsibilities it inherited from the Soviet Union. The factors that he had to balance were:

The admiration of his NATO counterparts: he was clear also that he did not intend to allow the Federation to be caught up in the CIS at the cost of Russia's interests. While maintaining cordial relations with Russia's "near abroad", and monitoring this region closely, he worked to strengthen the country's relations with the United States and members of NATO, setting no direct goal for the Federation other than the development of "democracy", a "free economy" and adequate security. He was also determined to use the good offices of the CSCE (OSCE), or tri-partite discussions, involving a non-CIS member, to solve disputes between CIS states and Russia.

Despite latter' statements to the contrary, Kozyrev (and many "democrats"), had a distinct sense of Russia as a special European power, whose main interests lay with how she oriented herself around the European Union, the Council of Europe the CSCE and "Europe" and the main partner, United States. The difference between this attitude and the notions which guided Soviet statesmen at Helsinki (1976) and M.S. Gorbachev when he spoke of "a common European home" in which the USSR had a stake, was that here the relationship with "the West" was considered the lodestone of the Federation's foreign policy.

The United States provided the Federation with support in the Camp David Declaration of Ist February 1992. The Federation Support Act of 1992 extended this commitment to assistance for the Russian Federation still further. James Baker and George Bush gave great attention to the provision for the mobilization "of the executive branch, the Congress and the private sector to support democracy and free markets in Russia and Eurasia". Symbolic of Support for the new Russia, and Washington's nod to Russia's European orientation, was the Washington Charter on American-Russian Partnership and Friendship of June 17, 1992, which seemed to project a special relationship between the US and Russia in global politics, centering on Europe. Kozyrev pursued this engagement with the

US to its logical conclusion in his negotiations over the START treaty in December/January 1992/93[7].

Moving East

While Kozyrev's policy provided back-up to the Yeltsin reforms, the Minister himself came under increasing pressure for his pro-Western stance from 1994, both in the media and in the Russian Parliament[8]. Moreover, with time, the US expressed criticism of Russia's forward policy in the Caucasus in 1993 (when Georgia was well nigh compelled to join the CIS security pact due to Russian support for Akhazian militants). The consequence was the slow focus on Kozyrev's part on Asia policy. This evolved to the point were, just before the President dropped him as Minister in 1995, he was able to make a series of statements that stressed the significance of "Eastern policy" to both himself and the Russian Federation.

Significantly, though, in his 1995 memoirs, Kozyrev is careful to stress that the "move to the East" will be in terms of specific Russian national interest. There is no mention of any special benefits that would accrue to Russia except peace. Kozyrev is also quite specific that the opportunities that have been made available to Russia in the Asia-Pacific Region, to come to terms with China and Japan, are linked to the new relationship with the United States post 1991. Kozhyrev was also decided that the main agenda in developing relations with "Asia" should be a somewhat unspecific "peace", and the resolution of border disputes (especially with China and Japan). This he sees as the path to economic improvements in Asiatic Russia.[9]

Hence, Kozyrev—see the "new approach" to Asia (he is clear that it is "new") as part of a grand strategy, as Shevarnadze did. Nor was he willing to look at the engagement with expectations that it would significantly alter Russioa's international standing in the prevailing global context. What was really "new" for Kozyrev was the detente with "the West". Distinctive also was the stress in Kozyrev's "credo" that the RF should avoid an "either or" position when it came to its relations in Asia: that pure and simple she should focus on national interest. This was a distinct break with the Soviet traditions and provided the opportunity to view India and China together, when cooperation was conceived.

In principle, therefore, Kozyrev argued:

> "Our main strategic interest in Southern and Western Asia—the preservation of stability—directed us to a corresponding logic for the way we developed our relations with the countries of the region. Russia broke with the Soviet practice of seeking geopolitical alliances with some states against other states. Relations with each of them represented for us considerable significance on its own terms."

Kozyrev used the case of India to prove his point.

> "This affects first and foremost our traditional cooperation with a great Asiatic country—India, As distinct from the Soviet period, cooperation now is shorn of elements of counterbalance and counterweight vis a vis China, Pakistan and the USA in South Asia. Such attempts at counterbalance in the past led to a one-sided aspect of Soviet foreign policy, and limited the opportunities for the development of relations with other important countries of the region, turning them into possible opponents of our country".[10]

E.M. PRIMAKOV AND TRIANGULAR COOPERATION

General Perspectives

E.M. Primakov's vision of foreign affairs represented a distinct break from the concerns and perspective that characterized Kozyrev. In his memoirs, the former PM has made this quite clear. He has not only made digs at Kozyrev's incapacity to understand the real interests of the Russian state he has gone on to assert that the post-Cold War scenario was more of a level playing field than many commentators understood and that Kozyrev comprehended. This, he regarded as the main reason for the necessity to avoid a sense in policy making circles in Russia that Russia had (as part of the Soviet Union) "lost" the Cold War and must act accordingly. Hence, according to Primakov[11]:

> "It is not right to regard a powerful US as identical with a single center in global affairs—a center around which and at the dictates of which all meaningful processes and events in the international arena take shape. Such an approach would wholly ignore the great tendency towards a transition from a confrontations bi-polar world to a multipolar world. This was a tendency that had already appeared some time before the end of the Cold War in the form of inequalities in economic development of different sections of the world. But it was a tendency that became lost among the demands of the two sides and the parameters of ubiquitous confrontations.... This in itself did not contradict the very real fact that after the end of the cold war, the Soviet Union, a superpower, ceased to exist. Formally, a situation took shape where it was possible to say that in international affairs there remained only one superpower. However, "...this was only formally speaking. It is worth remembering that the very notion of a superpower was an attribute of the Cold War. no one can doubt that in the post-confrontations period, the USA the most powerful state in the world—in military, economic and financial terms. But it is emerged as not a power that is called upon to lead others and subordinate them to itself for an indefinite period of time."

The critique of a "westward learning" position was quite clear.

> "The protagonists of accommodation with the "civilised West" at any cost proceed from the idea that the alternative to this, given what has transpired, is an unavoidable drift towards confrontation. This is not so. Russia can and ought to work towards equitable relations of partnership with everyone, search out threads where interests coincide and weave these with others..... There are those who think that today Russia is not up to an active foreign policy. That she should focus on internal affairs, resurrect her economy, carry thorough military reforms and only then appear in international affairs as a player on the international stage. Such a point of view will not stand up to critical examination. First, because, for Russia it would be difficult without an active foreign policy, to implement fundamental internal reforms, and preserve the unity of her territory. Russia cannot be indifferent to how and in what capacity she should enter the world economy—as a supplier of raw materials that has to put up with discrimination or as an equal participant. The answer to this question also is a function of the foreign policy.
>
> And if Russia is to continue to act in the international arena as one of its basic subjects, then it must follow a multifaceted policy..... to be active everywhere. In the case of the USA, Europe, China, Japan, India, the Near East, the Asia Pacific region, and Latin America and Africa."

According to Primakov, the assertion of independence had an important domestic component.

> "The defeatist line", either in internal or external affairs, will not allow and has not allowed that distance that we require from that part (part not whole) of the USSR's legacy that is unacceptable to Russia. The struggle for democratisation of social life and for reform will be more successful the less we persuade ourselves and those around us that everything is in fine, stale and just among them and we only have to follow their example and thereafter fall behind them in their policies."

And Primakov asserted the capacity of the state to carry through such a course:

> "Does she [Russia] have the strength? Of course, it is difficult to use somewhat depleted reserves to proceed in all directions. But, if we were to conduct an objective stock-taking of political influence accumulated over time, an exceptional geopolitical position, a frontal presence in the world nuclear club, and the standing of a permanent member of the Security Council of the UN, potential economic capacity, an advanced level of military production that

establishes conditions for military-technical cooperation with a number of foreign countries, the huge intellectual and scientific and technical potential of the country... we can say with confidence that there exists a sound foundation for a multifaceted foreign policy for Russia."

A rider to the assertion of the need for independence led almost ineluctably to notions such as "triangular cooperation":

"A further stimulus for such a policy is the incontestable opposition of the vast majority of states to acceptance of a world order regulated by one power...."

Towards the Notion of Triangular Cooperation

From the following Primakov's final move towards the development of the notion of triangular cooperation there can be no doubt that he accorded, both India and China, a special role in his overall view of global politics, and writing of his experiences of both countries in his memoirs, Primakov expressed his admiration for them. The idea that he was putting forward in Delhi in December 1998, though, went further than mere admiration or Kozyrev's limited notion of Russian interest. At issue was the search for partners to create a greater space for Russian manoeuvre. The seriousness of this was to be stressed. The *demarche* to these countries could not be seen merely as part of a game, to armtwist the US it was a strategy for the post-Cold War period.

Implicitly speaking of the present, even as he discussed the past, and the development under Gorbachev of close relations with India and China Primakov made the "strategy" clear.

"Did this mean that we were playing with so-called "Indian" or "Chinese" card? I have already written that such a view was widely circulated in the US. It is just crude, and it comes from the hubris of Americocentrism (the notion that everything revolves around the US and no more). The notion is doubly crude since it does not take account of the concern of the USSR (later Russia) in active development of relations with these fast growing Asiatic giants, the population of which constitute half of humanity. Also, we could not and cannot disregard the fact that a diversification of links unconditionally strengthens our role as a great world power, even as regards the US....."

REFERENCES

1. The country's Executive Presidency was created in 1991 and the first elections to the position took place in March 1991.
2. See H.S. Vasudevan, *Russia's Presidency,* in *Economic and Political Weekly,* 1994.

3. For the terms of the Constitution of 1993, see the official website of the Russian Government. When consulted on 16/3/03, this dealt with the authority of the Presidency in Section 4 (on the Presidency itself) and also in Section 5 (on the Federal Assembly), Section 6 on the Government of the Russian Federation which indicates clearly that the Cabinet is not responsible to parliament strictly, and that the President has exceptional control over it), and the Section 7 on the Judiciary (e.g. Artitcle 125-9 on the Constitutional Court indicates the dependency of the body on the Presidency).
4. For the political system and politics, see the most recent contributions in Michael McFaul, *Russia's Revolution,* (Cornell University Press, 2002) and Archie Brown and Lilia Shevtsova (eds.) *Gorbachev, Yeltsin, Putin, Political Leadership in Russia's Transition* (Carnegie, Washington, 2002). Also see H.S. Vasudevan, *Party formation and the Russian Political System,* in M.K. Palat and Geeti Sen (ed.) *Rethinking Russia* (New Delhi 1994) and the more recent work of Joel Ostrow on the character of the Russian political system.
5. See A.M. Salmin, *Iznanaka Vneshnei Politiki* in Rossiiskaia Politiia (Politeia, Moscow, 2001). Undoubtedly the finest and most comprehensive essay on the Russian foreign policy establishment that has been written to date. Salmin, however, fails to see the exceptional authority that the Presidency has come to occupy in all the "sub-systems" and institutions that make up the "seamy side" of foreign policy. Like many scholars, he assumes that Presidential authority is temporary at best, failing to see its unusal force where many institutions run against each other. For the institutions of control that reinforce this authority under Vladimir Putin see also A.A. Mukhin, *Kto est' Mister Putin I Kto s nim prishel* (Gnom I.D., Moscow, 2002).
6. Vitalii Survilli, *MID Rossi. Nebosreb v razreze. Nezavisimaya Gazeta,* 20 May 1992.
7. Camp David Declaration on New Relations by President Bush and President Yeltsin, February 1, 1992. Freedom Support Act 1992: White House Fact Sheet. Washington Charter for American-Russian Partnership and Friendship of 17 June 1992. USIA Report.
8. Most disturbing to the United States was that much of the criticism of Kozyrev did not come from Communists of Russian nationalists. And it is worth noting that throughout the history of post-1991 Russia, a "democratic" critique of Kozyrev's policies was not wanting. Hence, in "democratic" circles, in the April 1992 Congress of People's Deputies, and in the preparation of the December Congress, there was a regular critique of Russia's lack of sense of its own interests. Among those who took a position hostile to Kozyrev were Vladimir Lukin, then Ambassador in Washington. Peter Aven's officials at the Ministry of Foreign Economic Affairs as well as the Americophile Galina Starovoytova, President Yeltsin's advisor on nationalities' policy. Elsewhere, Kozyrev earned the deep hostility of the political scientist and commentator Andrannik Migranyan, whose acute analyses of the problems of Russian political transition had won him a powerful position n the media and who was also respected for his views in the Presidential apparatus. Migranyan had attracted attention in the Soviet Union and the USA for his views, and his article published in 1989, on the "Long Road to our European Home", had accurately warned of many of the nationalities' complications the USSR would face.

See P. Aven, Vneshneekonomicheskie svyazi Rossii, kakimi im byt? IMEMO 1992: Izvestiia 1992. Deklaratsiya Prav cheloveka dolzhna poluchit's garantii of vsekh stran; A Migranyan, Rossiya i blizhnee zarubezhe, in Nezavisimaya Gazeta 18 January 1994.

9. Andrei Kozyre, *Preobrazheniia*, Moscow, 1995, pp. 237 ff.
10. Kozyrev, *op. cit.*, pp. 248-49.
11. Evgenii Primakov, *Gody v bol'shoi politike*, Moscow, 1999, pp. 207 ff.

9

Stabilizing Asia

Regional and Global Challenges

R.R. Sharma

The geographical spread of Asia is indicative of its importance in world affairs. Asia occupies a little more than one-third of the landmass of our earth. It is populated by more than half of world's homo sapiens. The continent has within it a diverse variety of political and economic structures. The resource endowement of Asia is indeed extraordinarily rich. More significantly, a very large area of Asia falls within the vast landmass of Eurasia, and is thus closely connected with Eurasian strategic environment. However, how do we perceive and define the larger political, cultural, economic identity of Asia? This is a complex task, which poses several problems. Jawaharlal Nehru, the first Prime Minister of India, was probably the first political leader of the emerging Asia to grapple with the complexities of Asian identity, development and security. It is not that he found all the appropriate answers. Nevertheless his innovative mind came out with a vision, and an appropriate response to the emerging challenges in Asia. Now, when the paramount issue of Asian security and stability has emerged as a leading issue in global politics, it is worthwhile to recall Nehru's pioneering effort to project and articulate the concept of "collective Asian Security", which could be, as he felt, a significant input into the maintenance of world order.

It also serves a purpose to recall the first Asian Relations Conference held in Delhi in March 1947 at the instance of Nehru, who passionately articulated the vision of Asian unity, solidarity and identity. In his inaugural address, Nehru said:

> "We stand at the end of an era and on the threshold of a new period of history.... we can look back on our long past, and look forward to the future that is taking shape before our eyes.... the time has come for us, peoples of Asia, to meet together, to hold together and to advance together. It was not only a vague desire, but a compulsion..."[1]

With a considerable clarity, he pinpointed the strategic role of Asia in global politics in, what he called, the 'atomic age': "In this atomic age Asia will have to function effectively.... Indeed, there can be no peace unless Asia plays her part. There is today conflict in many countries, and all of us in Asia are full of our own problems. Nevertheless, the emergence of Asia in world affairs could be a powerful influence for world peace."[2]

Nehru therefore pleaded for a "close Union of countries bordering on the Indian Ocean, both for defence and trade purposes", a system of defence, stretching from the West to South East Asia in which "India because of her intrinsic importance and her strategic position was to play a significant role. He desired that "the coordination of various countries in Middle East, India and the South East Asia is not only possible, but undoubtedly certain in the future." He indicated that the question of "Asiatic Federation" was necessary, both for defence and trade purposes."

Frankly, the practical outcome of the historic Asian Relations Conference was minimal. The political impact was likewise limited, though not altogether insignificant. The conference did not give birth to any effective mechanism for multilateral cooperation and coordination among the Asian nations. What survived was the vision of Asian solidarity and message of conference — multilateralism. The conference pushed Asia to the outside community of nations as a continental policy factor.

EMERGING ASIAN IDENTITY

While the search for Asian identity continues, it faces a serious challenge of political turbulence and destabilization. It has been, and continues to be, an arena of acute conflict. Asia has several reasons to address itself to the problem of security and the problems of peace and tranquility in its vast region. The prevalent insecurity is tied up with the state of instability, which, however, flows out of the internal identity crises in several Asian countries. This is amply reflected in the fact that now internal conflicts have a preponderance over the international wars and conflicts in the region. One has, therefore, to examine the several dimensions of the problem of identity. In spite of these problems, modern Asia is changing, and in many ways, it is quite different from that which previously existed in the early part of the second half of the last century. Asia is incomparably far more developed than at any other stage of its development. In fact, Asia has been lauded for its fast economic progress and growth over the past decades. Both China and India are displaying tremendous growth momentum. Over and above, there is a greater regional economic integration. Thus, the new transformation is indeed significant. It now enjoys unparalleled prospects of growth and economic development. The nature of new Asia however remains somewhat ambiguous. Its mode of governance is far from satisfactory. The existing disjunctures are easily traceable to earlier period, and thus underline the contemporary Asian dilemmas.

A geographical Asia is not difficult to define in broad terms. But Asia is not just a "geographical expression". Asia is therefore defined in several ways and more particularly, not just what it is, but also what it has been in the past — a nursery, a home of great civilizations. Nevertheless, a cogent idea of progress associated with the mainstream of Asian development has by now come to prevail over the cultural elitism implied by the emphasis on civilization. The plan to refashion Asia, or create it anew has not really taken off substantially. It remains fragmented because there is no consensus as to what Asia stands for. Practically, most people in Asian countries seldom see themselves as Asians, as for example, the Europeans do. They primarily identify themselves as citizens of the appropriate nation state. It is not far fetched to conclude that, as of now, most Asians do not acknowledge any Asian identity. It is only in the political discourse that the issue of identity figures as a desirable value and a long-term objective. Thus, the contemporary Asia is, as in earlier times, divided on several counts and reflects the continuing existence of several major identities. Invariably, groups of people have several overlapping or nested identities at the same time. And apparently, there is hierarchy of different identities, with privileged groups having preferential access to the resources, and others largely excluded from them. This, and quite a few other factors, leave the prospect of broader Asian Union and solidarity as a distant and far off project. However, the regional economic integration as a strategy of development is generating synergies, which could be helpful in the long run.

SEARCHING FOR DEMOCRATIC CULTURE AND VALUES

Many Asian states are searching for domestic tranquility, which remains more as a hope than reality. It is largely due to fact that a large number of these societies are, by and large, politically dysfunctional. An overwhelming number of people feel that they are often left at the margins and excluded. The governing political elite is invariably unresponsive and oppressive. The missing link is the sense of participation. The failure of the leadership is most marked at least in two key areas, namely, governance and the economy. The governance is, of course, poor. Over and above, the political elites in several countries of Asia have opted for a kind of façade (authoritarian) democracies, wherein a systematic effort is made to prevent the expression of popular will through institutionalized pluralism. In the area of the economy, there is deepening poverty, an extensive unemployment, stifling corruption, a patronage system, designed to benefit a small "self-absorbed elite." There is a general lack of desired linkages between the political elite and the population. In a variety of cases, the cooperation of the people is sought through coercive means. This obviously leads to a large-scale popular discontent, which in turn, gets channeled into destabilizing movements.

The fragile character of democratic systems in many countries of Asia is not entirely due to the domestic politics and its socio-economic dynamics. It needs to be emphasized that democracy is not just an internal, domestic issue in Asia. It is transnational. The emergence and acceptance of democracy is first of all, the function of the international system. After the Second World War, forced democratization has invariably been a governing trend. Because of their structural and conjunctural weakness, the Third World countries were forced "to accept the model of western democracy that has been the fundamental precondition for their acceptance in the international system."[3]

The role of US in the first wave of forced democratization has been cogently argued by Samuel Huntington: "The single biggest extension of democratic liberties in the history of world came at the end of the World War II, when stable democratic regimes were inaugurated in defeated Axis countries: Germany, Japan, Italy, Austria.... The imposition of democracy on these countries was almost entirely the work of the United States.... As a result of American determination and power, the former axis countries were 'forced to be free" Huntington quotes here the book of John D. Montgomery, *Forced to be Free: The Artificial Revolution in Germany and Japan.*[4] The same treatment was meted out to the so-called "penetrated societies" of southern Europe and later on to Asian and other Third World countries.

The Post War forced democratization or "imposed democracies" were accepted by the Asian countries. However, they acted in accordance with their respective historical traditions and idiosyncrasies. The political outcome has been a mixed-one. The implanted democracies have turned out to be "half genuine, half imported". The political actors have put on their masks, which bear the "imprint of forced democratization and cover the real, domestic nature of politics".[5] The forced democratization in many parts of Asia has ultimately led to facade-democratization, in which case the external patron accepts a pseudo or superficial democratization". There are several examples of this.

The process of forcing democracies on other countries has not come to an end, but has acquired a new content in the contemporary global politics. And US is at the forefront of this. Consider the following:

"While the hegemonists in Bush administration were united in dismissing Powell's views, they disagreed among themselves over a key question: To what extent should the United States use its power to promote America's ideals? A minority, led by Wolfowitz and Richard Perle was, what the Press often referred to as neoconservatives, but they might be more accurately called democratic imperialists, argued that the US should actively deploy its overwhelming military, economic and political might to remake the world in its image.... They were less worried about the dangers of nation-building, and more willing to commit the nation's resources ... to creating democracies in their wake."[6] We also learn that the so-called "democratic imperialists" and "assertive nationalists" — Rice and Cheney — are deeply skeptical of nation building, and "scornful that American Power should create what others were unable to build for themselves." Rice in fact explained: "America's pursuit of the national interest will create conditions that promote freedom, markets and peace. The pursuit of national interests after World War II led to more prosperous and democratic world."[7] Obviously, the façade democracies which were forced on the Third World were in pursuit of the national interests of the US.

Façade democracies have been instituted in accordance with the minimal principles of democracy, or its "most fragile features", namely, the so-called "free elections". Consequently, several variants of facade democracy have taken roots in the political culture of Asian countries. Forced democratization in many countries of Asia has led to façade democratization where the "external patron" grants legitimacy to pseudo or superficial democratization by building "an external façade for the given polity", which has an apparent look of democratic structure from outside. This façade democracy is "static and fragile, and in most cases it brings instability and insecurity" for itself and most of all for its neighbours.[8] L. Whitehead suggests that the European definitions of democracy "seem to give more stress on social and economic participation, whereas Americans give almost exclusive emphasis to electoral aspect."[9] Let us have a searching look at the different variants of democracies in the Asian countries.

In political discourse, democracy is invariably projected as the foremost universal value. There are in fact two democratic values, which stand as "*twin pillars*" in the democratic value system: "*Competition* and *Participation*". The noted political scientist, Robert Dahl, categorizes them as the "two theoretical dimensions of democratization". He discusses the historical precedents and deviations of democratization as the lack of these combined values namely, "competitive oligarchies, closed hegemonies, and inclusive hegemonies."[10] By competition, he means, 'competition of elites' and participation refers to the "participation of whole population in the political processes". Dahl argues that participation and competition as basic democratic values have been invariably incorporated in the constitutions and institution of all democratic countries. However, there is a "huge gap between the declared democratic values of the constitutions and socio-political realities" in many countries. Now, if we extend Dahl's twin model of democratic values to Asian countries, we get the following "ideal type" of democratic system in Asia:

1. *Formalist Democracies*: In this type of democracies, there is no actual counter elite in the form of an organized and institutionalized opposition that could offer a fundamentally different political alternative. Consequently, the "misinformed or often intimidated electorate freely re-elect the same ruling elite, may be with large pseudo participation". (Pakistan is a typical example of this type and falls into the category of façade democracy).
2. *Elitist Democracies*: In these types of democracies, there do exist some competitive elites. However, they are comparatively small and share power alternatively among themselves. They invariably exclude the mass of the people from real political activities as well as the decision-making processes. Therefore, it leads to a political situation where politics turns into "a remote realm" for the common man. (A large chunk of Asian countries falls in this category. India is haltingly moving away from this model into a substantive democracy).
3. *Partyist Democracies*: This is the type in which political parties are the foremost political actors. They invariably seek to exclude other political and social actors from political life by monopolizing the decision-making process on the parliamentary level. Implicitly, "high politics becomes a chamber-dream of the party oligarchy" (Japan fits into this category).
4. *Tyrannical Democracies*: These are the clever distortions of majorty type democracies. The tiny political elite obtains parliamentary majority and refers to it for their electoral legitimation. The elites invariably act as tyrants and refuse the necessary compromise in political and social life. They refuse to establish "consensual democracy for the purpose of fundamental change". Some analysts have characterized them as an "infantile disorder". (All Central and West Asian countries easily fall into this type. They are the best examples of a façade democracy).[11]

From the above-mentioned broad typology of democracies in the Asian countries, it is obvious that there is great deal of "democracy deficit" in these countries. Quite a few of them have had military regimes, which are devoid of legitimacy as well as long-term vision. While some Asian countries are totally façade democracies, the others are at the halfway point between the façade and real, substantial democracies. Significantly, this has serious implications for regional and sub-regional security and stability. It has also limited the efficiency and efficacy of the political structures. The lack of elite-mass linkages and socio-political dialogue — as "a dialogue of the deaf" — not only retards socio-economic development, but also encourages traditionalist-conservative formations. It certainly pushes back the formation of a healthy civil society. In order to create stable and accountable democracies, we have to enable civil society to grow and flourish. Democratic development is invariably linked to a vibrant civil society. If we are thinking in terms of creating a valid security order in Asia, we must in that case move in the direction of substantial democratization, in the first place. The substantial threat for security and stability does not come from without, but from the 'nature of things', i.e., from within.

QUEST FOR SECURITY

1989 was the year of 20th century. Some hail it as the "year of miracles". This was the year, which witnessed the collapse of socialism, and the whole bipolar world. More significantly, this was the year when the Old World Order (OWO) collapsed, and "whole logic of the previous world system turned upside down". The "pacted peace" with mutually stable alliance systems and "enemy images" was central to OWO.

In a certain sense the Old World Order was well organized and regulated. It took care of the international security matters. The New World Order (NWO) which seeks to replace the OWO is in its formative and hazy stage. What, however, is certain is that it is logically aligned to globalization. From this specific standpoint, NWO has to be based on the "concept of widest meaning of economic, political, cultural and communicational security in an uncertain global system. It is almost unquantifiable as an aggregate of many factors, so is the behaviour of great number of smaller and bigger, global, national and sub-national actors."[12] The NWO is conceptually explained within the parameters of "Chaos Theory", which deals essentially with the concept of "order within disorder." The 'world of chaos' will increasingly transform a number of Asian countries to manage a kind of permanent internal crisis due, at least partly, to their increasingly unfavourable conditions in the global polity and economy.

This is largely because of the emerging globalization, which has enhanced the role of nation states, which seek to secure external and internal condition of economic growth. Now each state strives to create a favourable external economic environment and maintain it against all kind of odds and changes in world economy. In this effort, all the advantage rests with the developed western countries, particularly with the US. In fact, efforts to establish American hegemony would eventually mean an "American globalization" in the world economy, politics, security and culture in contrast to "global globalization". The US policy of hegemony and its implications for Asia at a later stage is discussed now. For now, it suffices to point out that globalization poses a major threat to Asian states, which are increasingly marginalized by globalization. There is a growing recognition that the "globalization has shown to be unresponsive and oppressive to human needs and equity of participation. Interdependence suggests that security is connected to new ways of relating to our global community based on inclusion, participation and access to meeting basic needs.[13]

The concepts of security have been in the melting pot for nearly two decades. The events of 11 September 2001, however, brought about a lasting change in the perception of security. The Europeans have been preoccupied for over a decade with the new concept of security, within the framework of NATO, pointing out that the narrow military meaning of security has become outdated. The traditional understanding of security had been tied to the idea of defending the sovereignty of the nation states. The danger to the security of a country was assumed to emanate from across the border by the invading "enemy". The enemy within the country did not enter into our perception of threats. Towards that end of 1980s, it was pointed out that our security concerns must also include not only military security, but also political, economic and the social security. The sources of insecurity are indeed many dimensional. Therefore, there is an obvious need to identify the deeper sources of insecurity.

The political security signifies that the state makes every effort to raise the basic strength of its society with a view to protecting it from extremist factors. Likewise, economic security implies that a country has unhindered access, without outside coercion to its need of raw materials, energy, by means of free trade etc. Social security obviously refers to the availability of required welfare schemes in a given country so as to maintain a degree of social peace. Obviously, the new dimensions of security are not easily available in the context of Asia for various reasons, which include both domestic as well as international compulsions and constraints. As pointed out above, in the aftermath of 11 September 2001, it became even more obvious that bigger and more powerful weapons do not necessarily create greater security. Security was no longer tied to weapons alone. It is aptly argued that social, political and economic exclusion of people are the "soils where insecurity is bred..." Security is closely associated with religious and ethnic harmony. The various ethnic and religious groups have to respect each other through a spirit of coexistence, and the state on its part has to ensure the protection of minority rights.

A host of security problems can be obviated by promoting multilateral and regional regimes. Undoubtedly, multilateralism and regionalism constitute a practical and viable foundation of security in Asia. In recent years, multilateral regional arrangements have found favour with several Asian countries. The multilateral regimes such as APEC, ASEAN, ARF, SCO illustrate this trend. Both India and China have come out openly in support of multilateral cooperation.

DOCTRINES OF HEGEMONY AND PREEMPTION

The global order is becoming increasingly uncertain and unregulated. It is a 'World of Chaos'. Of course, beholders of "Chaos Theory" argue that there is an "order within disorder." However, much of the contemporary international system is crumbling beneath the burden of unregulated global mechanisms, and the emerging institutions, which are programmed and regulated by the global powers and their projected values. Significantly, while democracy is projected as a cherished value, there is, however, a global democracy deficit. There is enormous concentration of power, from the economic realm to the cultural sphere. There is no worthwhile mechanism to counterbalance these globally. Decidedly, this has given rise to huge dissatisfaction in the world public opinion.

Taking note of the contemporary anarchy in international relations, political analysts seek to introduce the notion of "hegemon" as a stabilizing factor. Quite a few, in fact, are inclined to argue that the US has finally emerged as "the ultimate hegemon" in the global system. Throughout the recent history of international relations the US has played broadly three different kind of strategic roles: limited partner, security manager, hegemon.

Of these, what role should the United States play invariably depends on its perception of national interest in a region or country? Both in Europe and in Asia US has a clearly defined footprint, which is maintained through a web of alliance relationships. Through its political involvement and military presence, it has acquired the requisite muscle to plant its flag in Asia. The American administration took a conscious decision at the dawn of twenty-first century to shift US security policy away from the collective security order to a unilateral policy, which apparently is focused on a more bellicose military posture. Consequently, the Asian security order, already under stress, is entering into a period of turbulent change and more instability.

Evidently, unilateralism has its roots in "a strain of political thinking best labeled hegemonist". The strategy of hegemony has passed through several phases of its realization. And finally, it has arrived as a dangerous doctrine. The hegemonist strain of thinking had always argued, "America's immense power and the willingness to wield it ... is the key to securing America's interests in the world." The idea is by no means new. "The worldview that drove it existed long before jet planes plowed into the Twin Towers and the Pentagon ... what September 11 provided was the rationale and opportunity to carry out his revolution."[14] Hegemonist arguments were updated in the early 1990s after the demise of the Soviet Union.

An initial contribution was a 1992 Pentagon study prepared by Dick Cheney and Paul Wolfowitz. It maintained that US national security policy after the cold war should seek to "transform the unipolar moment into a unipolar era" by precluding the emergence of any potential future global competitor.

The US policy of hegomonism rests on a few major propositions. The foremost is that power, especially military power, "matters". If "power matters, great powers matter most of all", argued Rice.[15] Therefore, the US primacy was "both real and usable." However, it is not just capability, but also "the will" to use the power that must become a part of the new policy. The power must be "exercised solely in terms of American interests." Rice was sufficiently critical of those who advocated, "that the United States is exercising power legitimately only when it is doing so on behalf of someone or something else."[16]

Another leading assumption underlying the new hegemonist worldview states that multilateral agreements and institutions are neither essential nor necessarily conducive to American interests. President Bush and his advisors articulated "a distinctly instrumental view of formal multilateral efforts — they were fine, if they served immediate and concrete American interests."[17] It is worthwhile to recall that the 1992 draft Pentagon planning document argued that the US "should be postured to act independently", because "future coalitions would be ad hoc assemblies often not lasting beyond the crises being confronted, and in many cases carrying only general agreement over the objectives to be accomplished."[18] If the Asian nations were to follow the above proposition or the reasoning, their security and stability would be totally and permanently compromised.

More significantly, the hegemonists in Bush administration held on to the belief that the US is a "unique power and others see it as such". In fact, practically most Americans, who have come to believe that this is self-evident, hold this kind of view extensively. President Bush and his advisors "accepted this billiard ball view of the world where the United States was the biggest (and most virtuous) ball on the table and could move every other ball when and where it wanted.

The only exception was Collin Powell..."[19] Rice put it across without mincing words. "America's pursuit of national interests will create conditions that promote freedom, markets and peace. Its pursuit of national interests after World War II led to more prosperous and democratic world. This can happen again."[20] Since the US possessed unrivalled power, it therefore had the right to set the international agenda.

In the new national security strategy of the United States, previous policies, which were designed to promote multilateralism howsoever limited, have been rejected in favour of pre-emptive strikes and offensive counter-proliferation strategies. More specifically, the US is now planning to "restore nuclear weapons to the Centre stage of national security policy."[21] The US Nuclear Policy Review (2002) identifies seven countries against which nuclear weapons may be used in the national interest in certain circumstances. Significantly, six of these namely, China, Iran, Iraq, Libya, North Korea and Syria, are Asian powers. The remaining country, Russia, is a Eurasian power. The question which is frequently asked is after Afghanistan and Iraq, "who is the next". There are still two remaining members of the axis of evil — Iran and North Korea. Additionally, there are a few other so-called "rogue states", which were described by John Bolton, US Under-Secretary of State, as the "junior varsity axis of evil". These were identified as Syria, Libya and Cuba. It was proclaimed that they would be confronted. Richard Perle declared that the US would like to "deliver a short message, a two word message; you are next."[22] After the Iraq war, this message has in fact been delivered to Syria, North Korea and Iran. Iran has already emerged as the next focus of US concerns.

The point being argued is because of a major paradigm shift in the US foreign policy, the region of Asia is in an imminent danger of becoming more unstable and less secure. Since the US is potentially the most influential power in Asia, its policies have transformed the strategic environment. It will not be out of context to examine the US "doctrine of preemption" and its strategic likely impact on Asia.

It was, in fact, President Bush who clarified that the US has a "new doctrine called preemption", which signified a major departure for US foreign policy. The doctrine was explained at length in the National Security Strategy document released by the While House on September 20, 2002. It argued that the US "will consistently strive to enlist the support of international community, we will not hesitate to act alone, if necessary, to exercise our right of self-defense by acting pre-emptively."[23] Evidently, President Bush was of the firm view that preemption was not a mere option, but what Michael Gordon of New York Times called "a cardinal principle of his foreign policy.[24] Logically, preemption is the twin sister of hegemonism. Central to both is the belief in America's unprecedented power, which has to be used to "remake the world in America's image."

Preemption strategy does not imply only the use of power against terrorists and tyrants who were determined to seek technologies of mass destruction. It also signified the use of force to remove "obstacles and threats to liberty and freedom that existed throughout the world." Therefore, the US has the right as well as the power "to change the *status quo*." This may be achieved by bringing about, if required, a regime change in the so-called rouge or undesirable states. The US policy of toppling other governments, particularly in Asia, is not new. It has propped up dictators, or human right abusing corrupt regimes. However, it has never been an openly declared option of US policy. "It is not clear to me what advantage there is in declaring it publicly.... By making it public, we also tend to add to the world's perception that we are arrogant and unilateral", lamented Brent Scowcroft, a former Security Advisor to first Bush Administration.[25] Unilateralism is of course both the stated and unstated principle of the American policy. In a short while after assuming office, President Bush withdrew from five major multilateral international agreements including, the ABM Treaty, the Kyoto Protocol, and the Treaty establishing International Criminal Court. In the light of the available evidence, it is quite obvious that the regime change was "the gist of both the Afghanistan and Iraq wars."[26]

The preemption doctrine, as expected, has had a demonstration effect. India assumed that it was a universal doctrine. The then Finance Minister of India, Mr. Jaswant Singh, publicly declared during his visit to US that "every nation has that right.... It is not the prerogative of any one country. Preemption is the right of any nation to prevent injury to itself." Russia, likewise, incorporated it in its latest military doctrine of 2003.[27] The doctrine appears attractive to several other countries. However, it stands to reason that it, as Henry Kissinger aptly asserted, "cannot be in either the American national interest or the world's interest to develop principles that grant every nation an unfettered right to preemption against its own definition of threats to its security."[28] There is, obviously, a very thin line, which separates preemption from unlawful aggression. Any endeavour to legitimize the doctrine/strategy of preemption in the unstable environment of Asia is shortsighted and fraught with exceedingly dangerous consequences.

DOCTRINE OF WAR ON TERROR AND ASIA

The 'Doctrine of the War on Terror' was proclaimed by President Bush in the wake of events of September 11, 2001. This doctrine has a genetical affinity with the doctrines of hegemony and preemption. In a certain sense, it is a logical extension of these, and is equally pernicious. Moreover, the so-called doctrine of the war on terror is more directly relevant to Asia because the arena of war on terror is Asia. As stated earlier, the entire Asia from West Asia to North East Asia has now emerged as the "theatre of war". It started with Afghanistan and Central Asia with immediate consequences for South Asia. Subsequently, there was the so-called "second front" in Philippines in South East Asia. The ongoing intensified wars in West Asia/Middle East are as much part of the war on terror. While these wars are regional, they are however, global in scope. Consequently, there is resurgence of military factor both in Asian as well as international relations.

The war on terror was declared as a "civilization's fight". It was deemed as an attack on freedom, and any nation not joining the war on the side of US was supporting the terrorists — "either you are with US, or you are with the terrorists", argued President Bush. There was no choice for a nation. It was almost like directive, a command. However, it was never made clear as to what was the nature of the war? And the so-called war is directed precisely towards whom. That is why Stanley Hoffman asked: "Whom are we fighting? ....To proclaim a war on terrorism in general.... is ambition, indeed, for we need to distinguish among types of terrorists? A determined project of ridding the world of all rogues and terrorists is a dream that would be seen abroad as a demonstration of rabid imperialism."[29]

In his State of the Union address on January 29, 2002, President Bush referred to expansion of war on terror: "While the most visible military action is in Afghanistan, America is acting elsewhere. We have troops in Philippines. Our soldiers are working with the Bosnian government. Our Navy is patrolling the coast of Africa." If one were to read this along with his famous declaration of war against the "axis of evil", then the whole of Asian region from West Asia to North East Asia, through Central, South and South East Asia would obviously be converted into the theatre of US war on terror. The war on terror (or terrorism) is not only, as Raphael Pearl put it, "a misnomer", but "an open-ended war", which is extremely dangerous, and a continuing threat to global and particularly Asian peace.

SOUTH EAST ASIA

The so-called "second front" of war on terror was disproportionate to the evidence on terrorism in South East Asia. There is little doubt that there are some Islamic fundamentalist groups, which are fairly active in Malaysia, Singapore, Philippines and Indonesia. They are apparently well organized and armed. However, there is no convincing evidence to suggest that they are definitely linked to international terrorism, to Al Queda, etc. In fact, *Far Eastern Economic Review* reported: "Many people in the region are now saying that US efforts to combat global terrorism in the region are in danger of doing as much harm as good."[30]

It is no secret that US has considerable strategic interest in South East Asia. There are at least three major studies undertaken in the recent past by US Council on Foreign Relations, RAND, and Heritage Foundation, which have pointed to the region's strategic geopolitical significance to US interests, and how these should be addressed. The reports invariably point out that the region "sets aside some of the world's most critical sea lanes." More than 1.5 trillion worth merchandise trade passed through the Straits of Malacca in the year 2000, which was nearly half of world's trade, including crucial oil supplies from the Persian Gulf to Japan, China and South Korea. Any dislocation of energy supplies would have an immediate and "devastating impact on the economies of East Asia, and would have significant secondary effects on the US economy as well." Highlighting the vast significance of Malacca Strait, Bodansky, the Director of the US Congressional Task Force on Terrorism argues: "The global strategic growth and expansion of aspiring powers can be contained and regulated through the mere control over the movement of their naval forces through the Strait of Malacca."[31]

Obviously, the three reports mentioned above suggested that "the highest American priority should be assigned to maintaining regional security through the prevention of intra-regional conflict and domination by an outside power or coalition." Therefore, the US administration should preserve a credible military presence...." It is indeed imperative to ensure regional security. However, the very idea of its domination by an outside power — "the US which should have a credible military presence" — has a negating consequence. Significantly, the Heritage Foundation study had no compunction in asserting that the War on terror would "ultimately be pursued in South East Asia with or without the express approval of local governments."[32] On the face of it, the US policy is more indicative of reinforcing its expansive military presence in the region than dealing with the problem of terrorism, and many other major regional issues.

Despite the constraints of global politics, multilateralism in South East Asia has grown and picked up remarkable speed through regional and extra regional cooperation. ASEAN has shown a commendable political flexibility by including extra regional countries with which "complementarities based on shared geography" are evident in a variety of areas, including security, economic and cultural fields. There is well considered effort to develop land and cross border connectivity through infrastructure development both within and across with neighbours. More significantly, ASEAN, and ARF are working on a policy design to create multilateral regimes. In fact, there are several schemes of economic integration which are taking shape in Asia at the regional level. China, India and Japan are engaged in a comprehensive economic cooperation pact with several ASEAN countries. Likewise, SCO is critically important for the region of Central

Asia. This has the potential to generate a greater cohesion among Asian countries, and maintain the security of sea-lanes in the region.

CENTRAL ASIA

Unlike south East Asia, there are several critical questions about Central Asia. The Central Asia is fairly important because of its proximity to Afghanistan and South Asia. The Russian withdrawal from Central Asia after the break up of the Soviet Union gave rise to a variety of security problems. The region was left without a security manager. Intra regional feuds and rivalries eroded the possibilities of region-wide cooperation and consolidation. The "commonwealth of Independent States" did not live up to its expectations for a number of reasons. The Central Asian republics had therefore to content with domestic insurgencies, cross-border terrorism, growth of militant Islam, drug and gun running, etc. The republics witnessed the emergence of authoritarian regimes, poor governance and extensive corruption. Because of political and security vacuum, the region has gradually emerged as a hotbed of factional and big power rivalries.

In 1997, the Deputy Secretary of State, Strobe Talbot, gave a major address outlining the US approach to Central Asia. He argued that the US has no compelling interest in the region. The region was in no way of critical, strategic importance to the US: "It has been fashionable to proclaim, or at least predict, a replay of 'great game' in Caucasus and Central Asia. The implication of course is that the driving dynamics of the region, fuelled and lubricated by oil, will be the competition of the great powers. Our goal is to avoid and actively discourage...." However, if "internal and cross border conflicts simmer and flare, the region could become a breeding ground of terrorism, hotbed of religious and political extremism and battleground for outright war."[33] Strobe Talbot was, however, telling only a half-truth.

The strategic importance of the region grew manifold after September 11. Central Asia which was for some American analysts "a strategic quicksand" or a "mission too far" became mission immediate and urgent. To begin with, the US decided to be "Central Asia's security manager".[34] However, Eugene Rumer makes a bold observation, which is at the heart of the issue. He says: "In the aftermath of September 11, though it would be shortsighted to define US interests in Central Asia merely in terms of operational counter terrorism requirements and ongoing military operations in Afghanistan. The tragedy of the terrorist attacks has given a new and very different meaning to the notion first articulated by US policy makers in 1990s.... the absence of geopolitical competition..."[35]

This was officially confirmed by Elizabeth Jones, Assistant Secretary of State for Eurasian Affairs in a testimony before the US Senate Sub-Committee in

December 2001. Jones testified that US had no intention of abandoning Central Asia after the Afghan War. She outlined four US priorities in the region: *Combating Terrorism, reform, the rule of law,* and *Caspian Sea energy resources.* Collin Powel also confirmed that Kazakhstan's oil was of "critical importance" to the US. Military presence is essential for the US to control Caspian Sea and Caspian energy resources. Apparently, this is a "sub-text of the war" in Afghanistan.

The US cannot however maintain its footprint in Central Asia without the active cooperation of most important regional powers, namely, Russia, China and Iran. Each of these nations has a huge stake in the region. These nations have offered their cooperation so far in the interest of regional stability and security. However, their concern for stability and security does not "outweigh fears of US preponderance". Tensions are bound to rise, and resolving the growing tensions obviously would be a formidable task. The former Russian Defense Minister, Sergei Iranov, in fact, reminded the US that it had promised to close down military bases in Uzbekistan and Kyrgyzstan after the completion of its military operation in Afghanistan. "We did not object to the basis, but set a condition that they operate only as long as it takes to stabilize the situation in Afghanistan", Iranov informed a NATO Conference in Colorado Springs. He went on to assert that the "CIS is an extremely important security zone for Russia ... we have boosted and will further boost our presence in the Commonwealth of Independent States." Russia is thus showing a new assertiveness towards the CIS as a part of a broader revision of its "defense doctrine post-9/11." There is thus a clear signal to the US to accept Russia's dominant role in Central Asia.

While sharply disagreeing with the US on its policy of unilateralism and a host of other issues, President Putin has been steadily expanding the cooperative agenda with the US. Therefore, he will have to walk the razor's edge in promoting Russia's national interests, particularly in Central Asia. He has thus come out with what apparently is useful concept of building an "arch of stability" stretching from Europe through the Caucasus and Central Asia to China and South East Asia. This is a kind of a counter paradigm to "the arch of instability", which the US argued extends from the Caribbean Basin through Africa to South and Central Asia and across to North Korea. This justified the role of the US as a global hegemon. President Putin clarified that the arch of stability must be based on "entwined regional security arrangements" that should preclude domination either by the US or China.[36] Russia has thus worked out both military alliances as well as bilateral and multilateral agreements with the Central Asian States and China. Russia is also actively pursuing the project of Moscow-Delhi-Beijing triangle, which in its perception could emerge as a pillar of stability in Asia.

Looking globally, international relations are passing through a turbulent phase. There exists a worldview which seeks to undermine the credibility of important multilateral institutions, globally as well as at the regional level. Efforts are being made to erode the well-meaning patterns of cooperation. Fareed Zakaria aptly summed up the situation in his Newsweek Column: "At this crucial moment in world history, the influential hardliners in the Bush administration stand in theological opposition to the very idea of international cooperation. Even when the administration comes to multilateralism... it does so grudgingly and half-heartedly. President Bush's excellent Television address....is quickly countered by Vice-President Dick Cheney's combative and dishonest performance."

The security and political landscape in Asia has been changed largely by the US policies, more particularly in the post 11 September period. The war on terror has "accelerated the process of militarization of Asia". There is now an intensified arms race in Asia. "In a way during the past decade after the end of Cold War, the Asian region did not witness an arms race worth mentioning. Now all countries big and small across Asia including China, India, Pakistan Indonesia, Philippines, Singapore, and Malaysia are... acquiring weapons"[37], argues Ninan Koshy. The US war on terror has, in fact, resulted in further escalation of conflicts in Eurasia, in West Asia, South Asia and South East Asian countries such as Philippines and Indonesia. It is estimated that "eight of twenty-three high intensity conflicts are located in the Asian region, which caused over the years death of at least 25,000 people. The total death toll of the eight conflicts in the Asian region amount to 1,64,700 people."[38]

Thus to conclude, under the new dispensation of things, one finds vast areas of the Asian continent extending from the Caspian Sea and the Persian Gulf to the Malacca Straits including the whole of South Asia in the middle, face a serious challenge of political turbulence and destabilization. The ouster of the Taliban from power in Afghanistan and the establishment of an internationally supported Karzai government in Kabul, the overthrow of the Saddam regime in Iraq have not brought peace and stability to West and South West Asia. The war in Iraq and Afghanistan has turned into counter insurgency operation.

The spillover effect of developments in Afghanistan has had its impact on the stability of regimes in Pakistan and Central Asian republics. The instability in regions directly neighbouring China is likely to affect the situation in the Xinjiang and the Tibetan region. The situation in India — the hub of South Asian sub-continent — has also not remained unaffected by the disquieting developments that have taken place in Pakistan, Nepal, Sri Lank and Bangladesh. The two neighbouring states of India — Nepal in the North and Sri Lanka in the South — are presently facing a grave challenge to their territorial integrity and stability.

The need of the hour is to take a holistic view of the sources of threat to peace and stability in the West Asian, Central Asian and South Asian regions as a whole and identify their real cause that lies in the 'new imperial' urge behind keeping the present iniquitous and unjust international order intact without seriously addressing the basic faults in the outdated and unworkable international financial, economic and security system. Unilateralism, "clash of civilizations", war against international terrorism are but a new incarnations of the hegemonistic geopolitical ideas.

Time has come to reject totally these outdated, deleterious concepts and take a new look at the problem of meeting the challenges of destabilization lurking before Asia in general and South and South East, West and Central Asia in particular. In a situation when the South Asian subcontinent and the areas adjacent to it in West Asia and Central Asia are facing a serious threat of destabilization, it is all the more important to strengthen in every possible manner the bilateral and regional initiatives to meet this new threat to the Asian states. Both India and China, the two most important Asian powers, for mediation, must come forward with creative initiatives to build an effective structure of Asian peace and stability in the spirit of UN charter, which endorses regional security system as part of an overall global security system. It is imperative to establish a network of regional institutions to address issue like ethnic relations, cross-border terrorism, reconciliation, transnational crime and illicit trade, environmental degradation, etc. This is likely to stimulate the environment of security and regional integration. The outside powers, the US in the first place, are welcome to such a regional security system as observers and guarantors.

REFERENCES

1. *The Indian Annual Register* (IAR), Vol. 1, New Delhi, Jan-June, 1947, p. 273.
2. *Ibid.*, p. 275.
3. Attila Agh, "Basic Democratic Values and Political Realities", *Budapest Papers on Democratic Transition*, No. 70, p. 10, 1993.
4. S.P. Huntington, *American Politics and Promise of Disharmony*, Cambridge, Mass, 1981, p. 249.
5. Attila Agh, *op. cit.*, p. 11.
6. I.H. Daalder and James M. Lindsay, "*America Unbound: The Bush Revolution in Foreign Policy*", Brookings Institute Press, Washington, 2003, pp. 46-47.
7. *Ibid.*, p. 47.

8. Attila Agh, *op. cit.*, p. 17.
9. Laurence Whitehead, 'Internal Aspects of Democratization', in G.O. Donnell, *et al, Transition from Authoritarian Rule, Comparative Perspectives*, Baltimore & London, John Hopkins Univ. Press, pp. 17-18.
10. Robert Dahl, *Oligarchy, Participation and Opposition*, New Heaven & London, Yale University Press, 1971, p. 7.
11. Attila Agh has applied Dahl's Conceptual model to analyze the political situation in Eastern and Central Europe. See, *Budapest papers on Democratic Transition, op.cit.* (no. 70), 1993.
12. Attila Agh, *op.cit.*, p. 5.
13. Monique Makenkamp, P.V. Tongeren, and H.V.D. Veen (eds.), in "Searching for Peace in Central and South Asia", Lynne Rienner Publishers, London, p. 12.
14. I.H. Daalder and James Lindsay, *America Unbound, op.cit.*, p. 13.
15. Condoleezza Rice, cited in *Ibid.*, p. 43.
16. C. Rice, "Promoting the National Interest", *Foreign Affairs*, Vol. 79, 2000, p. 62.
17. Daalder and Lindsay, *op. cit.*, p. 44.
18. Quoted in Daalder and Lindsay, *Ibid.*, p. 45.
19. *Ibid.*
20. C. Rice, "Promoting the National Interest", *op.cit.*, p. 47.
21. Susan Willett, *Costs of Disarmament — Disarming the costs*, UNIDIR, Geneva, 2003, p. 2.
22. R. Perle, Quoted in Daalder and Lindsay, *op.cit.*, p. 173.
23. G.W. Bush quoted in David Sanger, "Bush to Outline Doctrine of Striking Foes First", *New York Times*, September 20, 2002, AI.
24. Mick R. Gordon, "Serving Notice of a New US, Poised to Hit first and Alone", *New York Times*, January 27, 2003, p. A1.
25. Brent Scowcroft quoted in Daalder and Lindsay, *op. cit.*, 126.
26. Daalder and Lindsay, *op. cit.*, p. 14. There are two other important analysts, who arrived at a similar conclusion. See Bob Woodward, "Plan of Attack", Simon & Schuster, London, 2004, Richard Clarke, "Against All Enemies", Free Press, New York, 2004.
27. Russian Defence Minister, Ivanov, Proclaimed that Russia could deliver preemptive strikes not only if threatened militarily, but also if faced with attempts "to limit-Russia access to regions that are essential for its survival, or those that are important from economic or financial point of view, see *The Hindu*, November 4, 2003.
28. Henry Kissinger, "Consult and Control: By Words for Battling the New Enemy" in *Washington Post*, September 16, 2002.
29. Stanley Hoffman, *The New York Review of Books*, November 1, 2001.
30. *Far Eastern Economic Review*, January 18. 2003.
31. Yossef Bondansky quoted in Ninan Koshy, *The War on Terror;* Leftward Books, New Delhi, 2003, p. 147.
32. Dana Dillian and Paola Pasicolan, "South East Asian and War Against Terrorism", Heritage Foundation, October 2001, cited in Ninan Koshy, *op. cit.*, p. 153.

33. S. Talbot quoted in Strategic *Forum,* no. 195, December 2002, p. 2, and Ninan Koshy, *op. cit.,* (no. 31), p. 102.
34. Eugene Rumer, "Flashman's Revenge: Central Asia After September 11" in *Strategic Forum, op. cit.,* p. 2.
35. *Ibid.*
36. Putin quoted by Vladimir Radyuhin, "Rebuilding Russia's Global Role", *The Hindu,* 27 July 2003.
37. Ninan Koshy, *op. cit.*, p. 165.
38. Monique Mekenkamp, *et. al., op. cit.*, p. 19.

10

Status Quo or Big Leap Forward

Domestic Constraints and Civil Society in Contemporary Asia

SARADINDU MUKHERJI

Enduring and meaningful relationships between nations are not built in a day and diplomacy, oblivious of domestic factors as prevailing in the countries being sought to be so linked, can not be sustained in a positive direction for long. Substantive partnerships between countries having a history of strained, indifferent or awkward relationships call for deeper understanding and emphasis on the underlying factors of discord which are inherent in a nation's ethos and embedded in its collective consciousness[1] A dynamic relationship can blossom into joint efforts in tackling various problems and much more if there is a tacit acceptance of the existing hiatus, a sensitivity to each other's bonafide grievances and the necessary will to rectify the fault-lines. Prime Minister Atal Bihari Vajpayee had repeatedly underlined a change in mindset for undertaking and pursuing any peace process.[2]

In the diplomatic aperture, contemporary Asia is being increasingly seen as a volatile area. Despite Buddha and Gandhi, other saints and seers, non-violence has always been a determining factor in its variegated society and complex politics, as in other continents. There were other sources of thought and action which had grown and survived on discord and disaffection and perhaps they were more effective being of a negative or destructive nature. Invasions and wanton violence, which had been endemic over the last millennium or so, and often, went unchallenged, are being countered effectively in recent times and it is feared in

Western capitals that this might lead to nuclear holocaust of unimaginable proportions. It is also a strong apprehension that after 11th September 2001, the strongest and safest countries in the Western hemisphere are unsafe and likely to be the targets of rogue nations or similar elements who may use nukes as mere toys upon them and wreck a havoc of unimaginable proportions.

The object of this study is to identify the major fault-lines which hinder genuine understanding between countries of Asia and suggest an approach that might help attain better grasp over the essentials of the situation.[3] Amidst all talks of a rapid progress towards a global village and the campaign of peaceniks, there has also occurred what Mike Davies calls, "the globalization of fear". As Philip Bobbit says with much candour:

"No less than the market and law courts, with which it is inextricably interwined, war is a creative act of the civilized man, with important consequences for the rest of human culture"[4]

HISTORICAL BACKGROUND

History offers many examples of countries of diverse, sometimes of diametrically different nature with different objectives in external relations often entering into special relationships based on some immediate economic or strategic considerations. While some of these diplomatic arrangements have been successful others ended in abysmal failures. Without going far back in time, one may just cite some examples of these two principal categories. The League of Three Emperors was ultimately left with two; as the Czarist Russia withdrew because its interest in the Balkans came in conflict with that of the Habsburgs. Hence it gravitated to the other camp though the Russian state was different in character from the two. This was also the time when the English Lion was locked in a duel with the Russian Bear over their respective sphere of influence. The combination of Axis Powers against Western democracies similarly demonstrate a solidarity based on a comparable polity and mindset as well as similar foreign policy aims. In more recent times, the NATO, Warsaw Pact, CENTO, SEATO show the viability of regional blocs with constituents from diverse socio-political backgrounds, based on a shared understanding of the ideological imperatives (in many, though not all cases) and the apprehension of the impending conflict with the 'other'. It was however, moulded ultimately by the enormous military superiority of the undisputed leader of the team enabling it in controlling the client states to preserve its supremacy by various means at its disposal-including a very generous give and take policy.

The point here is not to stress either the very fragility of each and every diplomatic club or an inherent opportunism in all grouping of nations but the overriding relevance of similarities in aims and objectives of the countries entering into special arrangements with one another. Mere setting up of various foras in the international chess-board of diplomacy, without any relevance to the domestic epicenter of decision-making, may not lead anywhere. Thus similarities in political culture and mindset help in forging closer diplomatic ties that generally succeed in weeding out the irritants in the existing relationship and gear it towards a combined effort to face the bigger challenge which confront the parties involved.[5]

Bandung experiment and the Hindi-Chini Bhai Bhai slogans ended pathetically on the snowy heights of Bomdilla and Aksai Chin, despite Nehru's spirited campaign for China's entry to the UNO and all the numbo-jumbo of third world solidarity and Pan Asian fraternity. Ideological incompatibility was not the cause of disaster but irreconciliable conception of national interest based on an understanding of the past. Pandit Nehru, obsessed with fighting European imperialism since the salad days of Brussels Congress (1927), had failed to notice other impulses and emerging theatres of imperialism even after three decades in the era of European decolonization which Bipin Chandra Pal did not miss out fifty years earlier.[6] The disaster and humiliation of 1962 was perhaps avoidable if our Foreign Office had read Pal and then taken due note of the then I.B. Chief Indu Bhushan Mallick's detailed dispatches on China's road building project in Aksai Chin. The obvious lesson from this and similar episodes is the primacy of geo-strategic factors among other things in formulating external relations and defence preparedness.

Attitude of Soviet Russia as well as US during the Indo-Pakistan war of 1971, also called the Bangladesh war of independence, exemplified both the geo-strategic factors as well as the compulsions of cold war. Building on the traditional friendship between New Delhi and Moscow, despite dissimilar socio-political systems, it went on to mature and fructify in the tumultuous days of 1971. As for support from other Asian countries for the Indian stand, only Bhutan had cared while "traditional friends" in the Arab world looked elsewhere. Thus there are various other factors at work in contemporary Asia which are built on different perceptions.

CONFLICTING TENDENCIES AND TRENDS

Recently, there have been attempts at one level, such as ASEAN, Almaity Conclave etc to carry forward the task initiated at Bandung. But there are also other attempts in different directions. Besides Bali bombing, there are also efforts, such as the one made by Gerakan Mujahideen Islam Pattani (GMIP), also known as the Pattani Islamic Mujahidden Movement operating in southernmost provinces in Thailand. According to intelligence agencies this group is likely to emerge as a household name very soon. Some people are talking of a pan-regional Islamic State comprising southern Thailand, the southern Philipines, Malaysia and Indonesia. It may be noted that these ideas have come out from the more established Jemaah Islamiyah (Indonesia) and Kumpulan Mujahideen Malaysia who have mooted the idea of amalgamating Indonesia, Malaysia and the southern Philipines into a regional Islamic State [7]

We see similar forces at work elsewhere in Asia including India's neighbourhood and their ramifications within India. It is rightly believed that except for whatever is meant by "Asian values" in terms of family ties etc, Asia is more divided because of the heterogeneity of its polities. Despite many deficiencies, the perception is that India has more in common with the Western democracies than some, if not most of the countries of Asia. As the French Foreign Minister Dominique De Villepin put it recently:

> "India is already at the heart of the new international system which is taking shape. —our two countries share a common vision, that of a multipolar world in which the rule of law and the strength of multilateral institutions are essential. — India's affirmation on the international scene is for France, a sign of hope— I formulate the wish that France, Europe and India, true to their fight for liberty, continue to fight for liberty, continue to strive for a world free of fear and oppression"[8]

POLITY AND CROSS-BORDER TERRORISM

Of late Benazir Bhutto, the former Pakistan Prime Minister while visiting India had often criticized President Musharaff for his undemocratic rule and called for his ouster. It may be borne in mind that though as an elected Prime Minister, she had never fought shy of using the religious factor and terrorism while dealing with India. As Raman puts it:

> "Benazir, who returned to power in 1993 did cooperate with Washington in acting against the narcotics barons and terrorists in whom the US was interested, but went back on her assurances to the White House to stop the ISI's support to terrorism in India and other countries. — Extremist elements from Kashmir and other parts of India continued going to the training camps in Afghan territory and the infiltration of Pakistani and other mercenaries into Kashmir was intensified"[9]

He adds further, "In an intervention in the House of Representatives on June 22,1994, Bill McCollum drew attention to Benazir going back on her words. He said, "I rise today to bring to the attention of the House a very important matter. The role of Pakistan in aiding and abetting terrorism in Kashmir is well documented, so much so that the administration almost placed the Pakistani regime on the 1993 list of State-sponsors of terrorism. However, the administration did not take such action because it was assured by Pakistan that Islamabad was taking credible steps to dissociate itself from the militants in Kashmir" McCollum also pointed out that, "Recent reports, however, suggest that Pakistan never stopped its aid to the terrorists in Kashmir. A report in the Washington Post, dated May 16, 1994, titled, "Pakistan Aiding Rebels in Kashmir. Muslims Reportedly Armed and Trained" by John Ward Anderson, datelined Muzaffarabad, gives a first-hand account of such assistance by Pakistan to terrorists in Kashmir.[10]

These passages are cited to confirm two basic ideas germane to the discussion we are engaged in. That all elected governments are not exactly paragons of virtue and there are few differences between such democratic governments and dictatorial regimes which might have preceded them or succeeded them in a familiar political musical chair game, where an appeal to the primordial sentiments is the constant factor. [11] A section of Indian media also thinks in such terms. They continue to believe that a democratically elected Bhutto and Nawaz Sheriff would inaugurate an unprecedented entente between the two embattled nations.[12]

In expecting, as some Western democracies still do, that restoration of democratic rule would transform Pakistan instantaneously they are oversimplifying. It is a fact, as Bertrand Russell once pointed out, that democracies rarely fight among themselves and also achieve victories in combat over the authoritarian states. The Commonwealth Secretary General Don McKinnon has talked of lifting Pakistan's suspension from the world body if Gen. Musharaff restores democratic rule. He further reiterated that, "Our judgement is made on the basis of country's democratic credentials and value of its democratic institutions"[13]

Secondly the nature and extent of terrorist related violence in Kashmir, which goes on even now, on a reduced scale and intensity according to some, must be accepted as a reality and countered. Earlier too, Pakistan had promised to desist from carrying out terrorist attack against India but relented on it. Addressing the Army Day parade on 15th January, the then Chief of the Army Staff, Gen.Vij had said that the not only were terrorist camps in Pakistan-Occupied Kashmir active but the terrorists on both sides of the border had exchanged as many as 15,000 messages a day"[14] It is absurd to expect that Islamabad would easily give it up.

President Musaharaff's much publicized speech on the 18th February to the Muslim clergymen was hailed by the Indian media and the political class as the enunciation of a moderate policy, since he had talked about the necessity of curbing religious fundamentalism and control the role of madrasas and mosques there. He had also asked the foreign militants based in Pakistan to go back. The fact of Musharaff talking of "the freedom struggle in Kashmir", which was offensive to India, was perhaps deliberately sought to be ignored by all. Despite this incendiary statement, the Pakistani President was eulogized for his "conciliatory tone" which was to pave the way for Indo-Pakistani friendship. We will revert to an analysis of this statement later but the question which arises here is that as long as Pakistan takes a stand that what is happening in Kashmir is a "freedom struggle" that amounts to its approval and abetment of terrorism and thus against India's basic stance.

Again, after four weeks Gen. Musharaff, in his satellite address to the India Today Conclave had repeatedly stressed that Kashmir was the core issue and the uncertain value of confidence-building measures: In a terse message he said that, "Let us be pragmatic. Let us learn to accept the harsh facts. Kashmir has to be settled in equitable way acceptable to India, Pakistan and Kashmiris. India and Pakistan must bury the past and chart a new roadmap for peace—". He said Kashmir was the source of disunity in South Asia" and because of this SAARC was on the "periphery of impotence" that Indian MEA reminded Islamabad that any unilateral interpretation of the 6th January Joint Press Statement will not be conducive to building trust or taking the process forward and there was no such "central or core issue". Our MEA also reminded that "public rhetoric" is "contrary to the understanding and restraints" observed since January. India also criticized General's "double standards" in describing the violent attack on him as terrorism, whereas the activities in J&K were part of a "freedom struggle". MEA took the stand that the peace process has created a "vast goodwill" which is being consolidated upon through confidence-building measures. It said further, that "reality needs to be acknowledged and built upon. Contrary efforts would not be in keeping with the sentiments of the people in both the countries."[15]

NON-STATE ACTORS

A related issue may be examined here. The category of so called "non-state actors"—used in reference to some terrorists and mercenaries are generally seen as those unrestrained elements who are supposed to be working on their own and who are ever ready to spoil the party i.e., the understanding assiduously achieved between embattled nations. But the term itself sounds problematic. This author has said earlier that:

> "Even while being non-state types, they represent fairly well-known organizations. In most cases, however, they are directly sponsored by states such as Pakistan or Saudi Arabia. That is how they can operate smoothly through

> foreign territories such as Nepal and Bangladesh. It is also true that some of them have been financed and encouraged at some stage by few advanced democracies. That is what the USA had done in Afghanistan to check the Russians. Bin Laden is a very glaring example of that gross miscalculation."[16]

What perhaps needs to be borne in mind is that quite a few of these non-state organizations actually enjoy active support from the governments, both material and moral, since they pursue the goals which their sponsors are not in a position to undertake openly, for the time being. This however, does not exclude the existence of a few genuine non-state actors. A recent media report suggests that fifty per cent of the militants killed in 2004 in Kashmir were of foreign origin (eighty in last two months). The report further says that the "overwhelming majority of the foreigner terrorists were from Pakistan, quite a few of them came from Afghanistan showing continuing effort of the fundamentalist seminaries to find recruits for the alleged jihad"[17] While one may concede the fact that because of the nature of prevailing situation in Afghanistan, the non-state actors originating from there may be really without any support and their whereabouts might be unknown to the authorities. But in case of the terrorists of Pakistani origin, it would be rather incredible to believe that Islamabad would be unaware of all of them.

It is quite a task to ask what inference must one draw when Indian armymen are routinely killed in our Jammu and Kashmir by alleged "militants". Two jawans and a woman were killed following a five-hour long encounter with the militants in Phulwana district on 11 March 2003. Subsequently, the Jaish-e-Mohammad owned responsibility for that (HT 12 March 04). Next day four jawans were again killed and three armymen including a major were injured when an army patrol was ambushed. In another incident one woman and six other civilians were killed by militants in Poonch district.[18] As I was writing this there came another report of the killing of our jawans.[19]

The question to ponder is are they really without the support of any state? And how does one respond to such attacks on our armed forces who are also being accused of human-rights violation by all and sundry. Surely there is a way out.

CONFIDENCE BUILDING MEASURES?

Problems are perhaps bound to crop up if confidence building measures are not reciprocated. It is not just the speech of the General which some would tend to project as a mere verbal ruse to keep the domestic constituency happy (as if India does not have a domestic opinion to cater to) but also more visible manifestations, which might very legitimately be taken as confidence shattering measure. It was reported that Pakistan was building bunkers along the LOC and "stockpiling them with heavy weaponry and ammunition". Citing army sources, it said that these "bunkers and posts all along the sensitive LOC provided covering fire to the infiltrators. The retaliatory fire by Indian forces had damaged these posts and Pakistan was now taking advantage of the ceasefire, which came about in November last year, to turn these posts into concrete bunkers to withstand Indian fire. It concluded that this meant that Pakistan was not sincere about its much publicised pledge to stop aiding infiltrators.[20]

The Pakistani test fire of Nuclear capable ballistic missile Shaheen-II on (9 March 2004), with a reported range of 2000 km, does no exactly fit into the category of a confidence building measure. As Francois Gautier, observed, "If Musharaff was serious about peace and amity, he would have waited for the end of the present cricket series, to test the long range missiles, Shaheen, which can bring a nuclear warhead upon any city in India"[21]. Even the US administration criticized the timing of the Pakistani test.

The question needs to be asked is whether Pakistan, or any society for that matter, can transform itself so suddenly. As The Pioneer put it, "The thaw in Indo-Pakistan relations has not curbed the designs of the ISI to keep terrorism going in Jammu and Kashmir. The agency has now asked Hizbul Mujahideen chief Syed Salahuddin to change his code and also the communication base in Pakistan, in order to avoid interception by the Indian security agencies"[22] As Bernard-Henri Levy described Pakistan recently, "the biggest rogue of all rogue states of today— What is taking form there between Islamabad and Karachi is a blackhole compared to which Saddam Hussein's Baghdad was an obsolete weapons dump"[23] What continues to create doubt are developments such as these. The Jaish-e-Mohammad activists allegedly behind the assassination attempt on Gen. Musharaff have been released. Moreover, Lashkar-e-Toiba is also reported to have started both fund-raising and recruitment[24].

Friendship can not blossom suddenly; as some people tend to believe so fervently. The idea of Indo-Pak-Iran Oil pipe line is fine but the minimum that we expect from Islamabad before that is an extension of the most-favoured nation status which the latter is bound, overdue as it is, to provide to India under WTO norms.[25] Earlier during the hey-days of Gujral doctrine, there was an orchestrated campaign that Pakistan was about to provide India with electricity and sugar and so we must open up our doors with relaxed visa rules etc. Ultimately nothing emerged.

Similarly, there is very little to cheer up on the Indo-Bangladesh borders, too. The Statesman report observed, "though SAARC nations during their Islamabad summit vowed to crack down on terrorism, there is no let up in the activities of fundamentalist groups along the border with Bangladesh". It further observed that "the authorities here are worried over the manner in which certain diehard Islamic groups have been misusing religious units along international border for their purpose. The region's state governments have already been asked by the Union Home Ministry to take proper action against misuse of religious institutions by interested quarters in areas along the frontier line."[26] Bangladesh, moreover remains adamant in refusing natural gas to India and denying transit route, just to spite it.

And Dhaka's attitude has to be seen in the larger perspective of its socio-religious fabric. Thus what is perhaps more important in such cases is that assumption of power by military or any other undemocratic government need not necessarily bring about a change in its policy of espousing cross-border terrorism especially when Pakistan deals with India.

As for Bangladesh, it is little different in the sense that while not being so much directly involved in cross-border terrorism against India, it happens to be a safe sanctuary for anti-India terrorist groups who besides the patronage of Bangladeshi government also enjoy the support from Pakistani agencies. As we know Bangladesh having alternated between democratic and military regime over the years has a democratically elected government which is closely tied with the Islamic fundamentalists but persists with harbouring numerous anti-India terrorist groups.

Dhaka's dogged refusal to act against them as the exemplary conduct of the Royal Bhutanese Army is a further confirmation of the importance it accords to sheltering the anti-India insurgent groups on its soil. Thus what is crucial for Dhaka in determining Indo-Bangladesh Relations is the maintenance of these militants' camps as a tool of its foreign policy irrespective of the complexion and character of the government and covert arrangement it has with non-Bangladeshi organizations who are united in their hostility and antagonism towards India.

ROLE OF CIVIL SOCIETY

Ultimately, it is the civil society which explains why a particular society/ polity behaves the way it does. The Japanese concept of kokutai (the fundamental character of state) may help us understand the organic constituents of a State system and its societal roots. Civil society's role becomes crucial in India's relationship with Pakistan/Bangladesh where religious-cultural factors tend to shape the politics and the resultant mindset. It may be reiterated that "The primacy accorded to cultural issues in the evolution of international relationships assumes particular relevance in societies where primordial loyalties, far from abating, are generally increasing."[27]

In fact, Islamabad itself causes such suspicion, by its indiscreet act-deliberate or otherwise. One Indian T.V. channel reported on 4th March that Pakistan had asked India to desist from "human right violations" and thus prepare for a more conducive environment for the future talks. (NDTV, 4 March). Incidentally, same day there was a news-item emanating that the visiting Pakistani Chairman Joint Chief of Staff. Gen Muhammad Aziz Khan had offered Nigeria "unspecified military assistance and nuclear power". Khan was further reported to have told his counterpart in Abuja that, "Pakistan had to take its destiny into its hands to become a nuclear state because of the regular threats posed by hostile neighbours". (Rediff, 4 March). The early part of the statement was retracted after a few hours but not the latter part. While this is easily explained in the immediate aftermath of la affaire Qadir Khan, the remainder of the statement was very much in the mould of the traditional statement of the Pakistan Foreign Office. None revealed even an iota of the SAARC spirit (January 2004).

RELIGIOUS MINORITIES

Perhaps a more fundamental criterion for judging a nation's character and ethos is its treatment of various sections of its society, i.e, the minorities. It is this strand, more than anything else, which lays bare the real character of the society and the principles of administration. No amount of talks, seminars and examples of "people to people" contact can smother the treatment of minorities that can provide us about that society's ethos. To cut a big story short, one may take note of the fact as to how the religious minorities in Pakistan-23 per cent in 1947 have been reduced to 2 per cent and in Bangladesh 29 per cent in 1947 have been reduced to 10 per cent or so (much less according to many).[28] More than fifty years after partition, the harassed and persecuted minorities are still coming over to India.[29] Is it not queer, that all the talk of people-to people contact and economic/cultural and sporting relationships are ignoring the existing state of relationships between the peoples of the same country?

Thus at the very base is the quality of civil society of the countries entering into special relationship. That becomes of paramount importance when foreign policy objectives are dissimilar (even partly) even if not confrontationist. Civil society as a factor takes a back seat only when some overriding and urgent objective in the domain of external relations is to be achieved in a short time by the countries involved and these countries do not have a considerable common history and common international border. One may explain it like this. India's relationship with countries such as Philipines or Malayasia and any special diplomatic understanding between them may blossom and achieve great success irrespective of the role of civil society.

TOWARDS A CONCLUSION

Despite such roadblocks the roadmap is clear: to survive and prosper all nations have to keep trying to forge entente and alliances. G. Parthasarathy commends the Indian initiative in signing a framework agreement for establishing SAFTA. But then he also says that "when one goes through the fine print of the SAFTA, there is cause of concern. We have provided an unprecedented, open-ended commitment to compensate Bangladesh for revenue losses in import duties". He further comments that, "New Delhi evidently failed to realize, even during the Kathmandu Summit that such an open-ended provision is unprecedented and, in the long-term, unworkable. New Delhi's mistake in agreeing to the Bangladesh demand for compensation soon became evident when ASEAN countries, like Myanmar and Thailand, flatly turned down a Bangladesh proposal for such compensation when negotiations were held recently in Thailand to conclude a free trade agreement between Bhutan, Nepal and the members of the BIMSTEC Grouping: Bangladesh, India, Myanamar, Thailand and Sri Lanka. Bangladesh may well find itself excluded from this free trade agreement if it persists with its demand.[30]

It is a sign of maturity that our sense of pan-Asian solidarity should not prevent us from looking elsewhere. The first trilateral meeting between India, Brazil and South Africa (IBSA forum) held in early March in New Delhi may be pointer to the alternative being kept open by the South Block As M.P.M.Menon a former Ambassador to Brazil argued, "The success of the IBSA Dialogue Forum will depend upon how much importance each country attaches to this initiative and the subsequent actions they take to strengthen this forum.If properly nurtured, it could boost the interests of developing countries. The Group of 77 is eagerly tracking the birth and growth of this new organization". Minister of External Affairs correctly put it that this would South-South cooperation will be significantly enlarged.

The latest memorandum, signed (January 2004) between China and ASEAN, to combat non-traditional security threats such as terrorism, drug trafficking, sea piracy and economic crime has a lesson for all in Asia. In August 2002, the US and ASEAN had signed a cooperation declaration to combat international terrorism as well as announcing ASEAN Cooperation Plan which aims to combat drug and human trafficking, They also expect to make southeast Asia a drug-free zone by 2015 and curb terrorism and sea piracy. The January meeting between China, ASEAN countries, Japan and Korea happened to be the first meeting to discuss transnational crime. India and other countries in Asia may take up such issues before seeking to tackle other issues i.e. conventional causes of discord and war.

The grant of "major non-NATO ally" status to Pakistan by the US has once again raised a big question mark over the viability of cooperative venture by the Asian countries. Are they really interested in forging meaningful ties with their estranged enemies ? Clearly our foreign policy makers have a challenging job ahead.[31]

REFERENCES

1. Saradindu Mukherji, *Subjects Citizens and Refugees: Tragedy in the Chittagong Hill Tracts 1947-1998* (Voice of India, Delhi 2000) explains the roots of intolerance which leads to a breakdown of civil society, causing among others, forced migration of the unwanted. Also see, Saradindu Mukherji, Nationalism is the Cornerstone of BJP"s Foreign Policy", BJP Website (written on the eve of the general elections of 1998).
2. *The Times of India* 2 January 2004.
3. Saradindu Mukherji, Potentialities Of Cultural Cooperation Between Neighbouring Countries: A Case Study of Indo-Bangladesh Relations" in B.K. Jahangir and Jayanta Ray (ed), *India-Bangladesh Cooperation Broadening Measures* (K.P. Bagchi, Kolkata 1997). Hereafter Indo-Bangladesh.
4. Philip Bobbit, Shield of Achilles. Foreword By Michael Howard (Knoff, New York 2003), p. 6.
5. Anglo-American relationship over the years is a classic example of the roots of enduring bond between nations.
6. Bipin Chandra Pal, *Nationality and Empire: A Running Study of Some Current Indian Problems* (Thacker and Spink, Calcutta, Simla, 1916).
7. *The Statesman*, 10 January 2004 quoting The Nation,
8. *The Indian Express* 14 February 2004.
9. B. Raman, "Pakistani Sponsorship of Terrorism" in M.L.Sondhi, (ed), *Terrorism and Political Violence* (ICSSR, Har Anand, New Delhi, 2000) pp. 63-64.
10. *Ibid.*
11. Saradindu Mukherji, "The Horror Story of Pakistan's Minorities" in *The Times of India*, 14 March 1995.
12. Vir Sanghvi, "Musharraf and the Peace Process" in *Sunday Hindustan Times*, 21, March 2004.
13. *The Pioneer*, 20 March 2004.
14. *The Pioneer*, 17 March 2004.
15. The Statesman, 15 March 2004, *The Hindustan Times* 15 March 2004, *The Pioneer* 15 March 2004.
16. Saradindu Mukherji, unpublished manuscript likely to be published soon. p. 237.
17. *The Times of India*.
18. *The Deccan Herald*, 15 March 2004; *Dainik Jagaran* 15 March 2004.
19. *The Hindustan Times*, 21 March 2004; *The Indian Express* 21 March 2004.
20. *The Pioneer*, 15 March 2004.

21. *The Pioneer,* 17 March 2004.
22. *The Pioneer,* 3 March 2004.
23. Claude Arpi in *The Pioneer,* 9 March 2004.
24. *The Hindu,* 13 March 2004. (Editorial).
25. Saradindu Mukherji.
26. *The Statesman,* 11 January 2004.
27. Saradindu Mukherji, Culture, *op. cit.* 93.
28. Jayanta Ray, Democracy and Nationalismon Trial: A Study of East Pakistan (Simla, 1968): Bangladesh Hindu Buddhist Christain Unity Council, Communal Discrimination in Bangladesh: Facts and Documents (Chittagong 1993). K.Callard, Pakistan, A Political Study (London 1958) pp. 232-65. S.K. Bhattacharya, Genocide in East Pakistan/Bangladesh (A.Ghosh, Houston,1987): Saradindu Mukherji. Genocide of Hindus Must Stop, *The Pioneer* 27 Dec 1971: "Are the Minorities in Bangladesh Endangered"? *The Pioneer* 22 Oct 1993. "The Minorities Trauma in Bangladesh" *The Indian Express,*15 june 1995: Pakistan is Not a Modern State" The Pioneer 31 March 1995. "The Plight of Minorities in Pakistan", *The Indian Express* 8 June 1995. There is a long list of other publications which provide a detailed description of this tragedy but for some time now Human Rights Congress for Bangladesh Minorities (HRCBM) has been providing a very authentic information. Achinta Gupta, Mohit Ray and Tapan Ghosh, Five Decades of Ongoing Ethnic Cleansing: A Report On Atrocities on Minorities in Bangladesh (Campaign Against Atrocities on Minorities in Bangladesh (CAAMB, Kolkata, 2004) Taslima Nasreen, *Lajja* (Dhaka,1993).
29. Saradindu Mukherji, "Exodus From Bangladesh and Indian Response" Paper presented at 4th IRAP Oxford 1994: "Vested or Enemy Property Act and the Mnorities in Bangladesh" paper presented at 8th World Conference of International Society of Family Laws, Cardiff, June-July 1994: "Immigrants Legal and Illegal" *The Hindustan Times,* 30 May 1995. Koenraad Elst, *The Demographic Siege* (Voice of India, New Delhi,1998). B.P. Saha, "Trans-Border Migration" in Indo-Bangladesh. *op. cit.*
30. *The Pioneer* 11 March 2004. Doubts persists over this issue. See Saradindu Mukherji, "Safta Can Never Take Off" *The Pioneer* 8 Sept. 1995.
31. Jaswant Singh, *Defending India* (Macmillan India, Bangalore 1999). This offers a competent and analytical survey of the dimensions of external relations and related defence issues.

11

Reflections on India's Cultural Relations with South-East Asia

V. SURYANARAYAN

For civilizational states like India and China no epoch in history is complete in itself; it is both a continuation and a beginning. Narasimha Rao, former Prime Minister, underlined this basic reality in his famous speech, *India and the Asia-Pacific — Forging A New Relationship* in October 1994, at the Institute of Southeast Asian Studies in Singapore. Narasimha Rao rightly highlighted that the closer relationship, which India seeks to build with its Southeast Asian and Asia-Pacific neighbours, has to be fashioned on twin foundations — the benign interaction of the past and mutuality of interests that exist at present.

In this study efforts are made to reflect upon one of these facets; India's abiding cultural influences in Southeast Asia and how this significant feature can be utilized to fashion a benign cultural diplomacy. In its relations with Southeast Asian countries, India has several plus points. Historically Burma, Thailand, Cambodia, Laos, Malaysia and Indonesia have been deeply influenced by Indian political ideas, religion, art and language. The spread of Indian cultural influences, leading to the cultural enrichment of Southeast Asian countries, constitutes a glorious chapter in Indian and Southeast Asian history, alike. The famous lines of Rabindranath Tagore, who visited Java in 1927, comes to my mind:

> In a dim distant unrecorded age
> we had met, thou and I

> when my speech became tangled in thine
> and my life in thy life ...
>
> From the heavens spoke to me two mighty voices
> the one that sung of Rama's glory of sorrow
> and the other Arjuna's triumphant arm
> urging me to bear along the waves
> this epic lines to the eastern islands;
> and the heart of my land murmured to me its hope
> that it might build its nest of love
> in a far away land of its dream

Indianised kingdoms like Funan, Sri Kshetra, Pagan, Khemer, Sri Vijaya, Sailendra and Majapahit; the familiar Indo-Sanskritic vocabulary in Thai language and Bahasa Indonesia; architectural monuments like Angkor Wat, Pagan, Borobudur and Lara Djonggrong; literary masterpieces like Ramkein, Amaramala, Arjuna Vivaha and Bharatha Yuddha; the *Wajang Kulit* based on Ramayana and Mahabharata themes; the living Indian traditions in the island of Bali — all these bear testimony to the courage and zeal of Indian princes, priests, poets, merchants and artisans and to the ingratiating and assimilable qualities of the peoples of Southeast Asian countries. The greatest of Indonesian nationalist leaders, President Sukarno wrote in a special article in *The Hindu* on January 4, 1946:

> In the veins of every one of my people flows the blood of Indian ancestors and the culture that we possess is steeped through and through with Indian influences. Two thousand years ago people from your country came to Jawadvipa and Suvarnadvipa in the spirit of brotherly love. They gave the initiatives to found powerful kingdoms such as those of Sri Vijaya, Mataram and Majapahit. We then learnt to worship the very Gods that you now worship still and we fashioned a culture that even today is largely identical with your own. Later we turned to Islam; but that religion, too, was brought by people coming from both sides of the Indus.

Norodom Sihanouk, the founder of modern Cambodia, echoed the same feelings. Inaugurating the Jawaharlal Nehru Boulevard in Phnom Penh in May 1955, Sihanouk declared:

> When we refer to two thousand years old ties which unite us with India, it is not at all a hyperbole. In fact, it was about two thousand years ago that the first navigators, Indian merchants and Brahmins brought to our ancestors their Gods, their techniques, their organization. Briefly India was for us what Greece was to Latin Orient.

Not much work has been done by Indian scholars on the impact of culture in Indian foreign policy. In fact, as far as Southeast Asia is concerned, the fascinating encounter among indigenous, Indian and Chinese influences deserves deeper study and sharper focus. I shall reflect on this theme at the concluding part of this essay. But I would like to highlight the abiding Indian influences in two countries, namely Indonesia and Thailand, by describing the impact of Ramayana in Indonesia and the festival of Navarathri in Thailand.

RAMAYANA IN INDONESIA

Ramayana is not only the epic of India, it is also the national epic of Indonesia. It had been a perennial source of inspiration in the past and continues to exercise its charm and influence even today. The simple story of Rama and Sita has been told and retold a million times in innumerable ways in different parts of the archipelago. No doubt, in the process of its diffusion and transplantation, the Ramakatha has undergone variations and adaptations. The immense vitality of the Ramayana tradition, in contemporary Indonesia, is a proof, if a proof is necessary, to the aptness of Brahma's assurance to Valmiki: "And O Great Sage, as long as the mountains stand and the rivers flow, so long will this story of Rama's heroic deeds be told and cherished on earth". K.M. Kannampilly, former Indian Ambassador to Indonesia, has aptly written: "For over fourteen centuries now, the Ramayana has continued to be a living force among the people of Southeast Asia, influencing their hearts and thoughts, inspiring their artistic creations and forming the mainspring of their cultural life. To them the hero and the heroine of the Ramayana have always been models of chivalry, nobility and faithfulness, characters of great spiritual beauty".

Even in the world scholarship, relating to Ramayana tradition, Indonesia has played a pioneering role. The Ministry of Information and Culture organized the First International Ramayana Festival in Jakarta in August-September 1971. Scholars and artists from India, Indonesia, Sri Lanka, Burma, Nepal, Malaysia, Singapore, Philippines, Vietnam, Laos and Cambodia participated in this unique seminar whose objective was to "promote deeper cultural understanding among nations". Four years later in 1975, New Delhi picked up the threads and on the occasion of the 400th anniversary of Tulsidas's Ramcharitamanas, the Sahitya Akademy organized an International Seminar on "Ramayana Tradition in Asia". The Sahitya Akademy again convened an International Seminar on "Asian Variations in Ramayana", in January 1981. These seminars and published proceedings are significant milestones in our understanding of the many splendoured Ramayana heritage.

The Ramayana, along with the Mahabharata, provides the base and has contributed to the efflorescence of the *Wajang Kulit* (the shadow or leather puppet theatre), known throughout Indonesia, especially Central and Eastern Java. The *Wajang* is not merely a popular form of entertainment, it is an inseparable part of Indonesian life and reflects the social order with all its complexities. Both physical and moral attributes are identified with different characters and, in the final analysis, the *Wajang* represents the triumph of good over evil. Even the orthodox Muslim Ulemas could not eradicate its appeal and came to terms with it by declaring that the *Wajang* was the invention of Sunan Kalijaga, an honoured Islamic saint. Though the main themes are derived from the Indian epics, the local genius has introduced many additions, deletions and interpolations in the stories. In the process, the influence of *Wajang* has not decreased, but continues to be growing. The stories can be divided into three groups — (1) *Caita Pokok* — *Pokok* means the trunk of a tree. The stories, therefore, revolve around the main characters of Ramayana like Rama, Sita, Hanuman etc. (2) *Caita Carang Dinapur* — *Carang* means branch which means the stories revolve around secondary characters like Vibhishana, Bali etc. (3) *Carita Carangan* — *Carangan* means a twig. In other words, the stories are far removed from the main theme and are figments of poet's imagination.

The *Wajang* season begins after the harvest and extends to the beginning of the rainy season. The manipulation of the puppet's movements, the control of the orchestra, the delivery of the dialogue — all are done by the *Dalang,* who is "at once a composer, improviser, producer, orator, singer, choir master, dance master and stage manager". A good *Dalang* identifies himself completely with the characters and is able to infuse the nobility of the story to the audience. While keeping within the bounds of the Ramayana, the *Dalang* also varies the presentation to suit the audience and mixes the narration with some earthly wit and humour. The *Wajang Kulit* performance is accompanied by a *gamelan* orchestra. The performance generally lasts throughout the night, although in urban areas nowadays it is generally reduced to three or four hours. Variations of *Wajang Kulit* include *Wajang Kokek* and *Wajang Wong.* A Malay scholar on Ramayana has testified to the fact that "a good *Dalang* can still draw a larger audience than a local open air cinema showing the latest Hollywood Coca Cola culture".

Ramayana has also retained its popularity because it has kept in tune with the dance-drama traditions of Indonesia. In the predominantly Hindu island of Bali, all the major dance drama traditions revolve around Ramayana. A large number of actors participate with men and women playing their respective roles. They dance and also deliver their dialogues. The chorus surrounding them play the role of the Vanaras or Rakshasas; sometimes they fight with each other and, at other times, they remain in the background. The Balinese dance opera is the most stylised of its kind in Indonesia.

Mention should also be made of the famous Ramayana scenes in the temple of Lara Jonggrong in Prambanan near Jogjakarta. These ninth century Saivite monuments contain in their balustrades and relief panels some of the most exquisite Ramayana scenes. The panels begin in a horizontal series at the main Siva temple and depict events starting from the Balakanta up to the arrival of Vanaras in Lanka. These are continued in the adjoining Brahma temple, but only detached fragments now remain. Visvamitra's visit to Dasaratha's court, the slaying of Tataka, Rama-Sita marriage, Rama's meeting with Parasurama, Rama's banishment to the forest, Rama chasing the golden deer, Sita's abduction, fight between Sugriva and Bali, Hanuman's visit to Ashoka Vana and the battle between Rama and Ravana — all these are depicted in detail and with remarkable finesse. These temples are held in great veneration by the local population. These imposing structures are the best examples of Indo-Javanese art and represent the apotheosis of Saivism in the archipelago. The Indonesian Government, during recent years, has been sponsoring dance-drama performances in the backdrop of these temples, during June-October. During the rule of the Majapahit dynasty, which represented the final phase of Hindu hegemony in Java, scenes from the Ramayana, especially from the Yuddhakanta, were sculptured in the temple of Panataran in East Java. Though the figures are stylized and sophisticated, they are not very natural and do not have the artistic excellence and visual appeal of those in Prambanan.

Ramayana and other epics spread to Indonesia along with the arrival of priests, Brahmins, merchants, kshatriyas, artisans and the poets. An Indonesian inscription in Sanskrit refers to Raghava (732 AD), while old Javanese inscriptions refer to Ravana (824 AD), Lanka (862 AD), Bharata (879 AD), Rama (880 AD), Ramayana (909 AD), Sita (910 AD), Vali (928 AD) and Lakshmana (928 AD). The earliest written version was the Ramayana *Kakawin* by Yogiswara of the 10th century. With the passage of time, numerous other versions appeared. According to one scholar, there are nearly 1200 versions of Ramayana in East Java alone. One of the Javanese versions, *Serat Kanda,* begins with Adam in Mecca and ends with the cremation of Rama and Sita.

How does one account for the dynamic vitality of Ramayana tradition in Indonesia? Does it not conflict with the tenets of Islam, the religion which 95 per cent of the Indonesians adhere to?

The explanation is to be found in Indonesian attitude towards life. The Indonesian mind believes in synthesis and is accustomed to the intermingling of diverse, apparently contradictory, elements. The average Indonesian finds no dichotomy in his obligations as a Muslim and his continued acceptance of earlier Hindu and animist practices. As a well known authority on Indonesia, Prof. J.D. Legge, rightly points out, "The propitiation of spirits, the observance of customary rituals surrounding the main stages of life, the resort to magical practices in curing illness may all be accepted by the same person, who is ready to observe the Moslem law in marriage, to accept the Moslem ritual of circumcision, or to follow the daily pattern of prayer, the weekly community worship and the annual month of fasting".

The first great religion to arrive in Indonesia was Hinduism and it was soon followed by the Mahayana form of Buddhism. Before the Hindus arrived, the people of the islands were animists. The new religions did not compete for people's support; they blended with the native animism and assumed new shapes. Siva merged with the Buddha and Siva-Buddha cult came into existence. In most parts of Indonesia, the banyan tree is still considered sacred and never cut down. Similarly, at the time of harvest, each stalk of paddy has to be cut in a different fashion and as quietly as possible to avoid disturbing *Devi Sri,* the guardian spirit of fertility. The belief in magic is quite common and the *kris,* the short ceremonial dagger, is endowed with magical powers and is worshipped every day.

Islam came to Indonesia in the 16th century and it spread throughout the archipelago in the course of the next three hundred years. It was brought by the merchants of Gujarat and had already undergone changes in the direction of mysticism that facilitated its adoption and adaptation in the Indonesian setting. As the distinguished Sociologist, Clifford Geertz, puts it, "Indonesian Islam, cut off from the centers of orthodoxy in Mecca and Cairo, vegetated, another meandering tropical growth on an already overcrowded religious landscape. Buddhist mystic practices got Arabic names, Hindu Rajas suffered a change of title to become Sultans, and the common people called some of their wood spirits *Jinns,* but little else changed".

However, it must be pointed out that the impact of Islam was felt in different ways in different strata of society. As the isolation of Islam broke down, with the establishment of contacts with centers of Islamic orthodoxy in West Asia, new groups began to emerge and occasional tensions took place between the "more faithful" and the "less faithful". Broadly these groups could be divided into three subvented categories: (1) The *Santri,* the devout Muslims, who consider themselves as the true followers of Islam, mainly belonging to the trading community; (2) The *Abangan,* the nominal Muslims, who in their daily lives, lay greater stress on the animistic aspects of the Indonesian syncretic religion, mainly belonging to the peasant masses and (3) The *Prijaj,* who stress on Hindu aspects and belong to the aristocracy in the towns. Numerically, it is the *Abangans,* who dominate the Indonesian scene and add colour and richness to the religious landscape. They patronize the *Wajang Kulit,* while the *Prijaji* are responsible for the enrichment of the more refined dance-drama traditions.

Thus over the centuries, Ramayana has inspired and influenced people in different parts of the world. Dr. V. Raghavan, the distinguished authority on Ramayana, has remarked:

> It is true that many stories and episodes have been added in different versions of Ramayana, especially in Southeast Asia, and in some of them some of the major deviations from the central Ramayana plot of Valmiki occur. But Rama is always the central figure around whom all other characters revolve and his life illustrates the message of the triumph of the good over evil.

NAVARATHRI IN THAILAND

Navrathri, the popular Indian festival, is celebrated in different ways in different parts of India. In Bengal, it is the *Durga Puja,* the worship of the Divine Mother, the primordial *Shakti.* Gujarat celebrates the nine-day period with song and dance, especially the famous *Garba.* In Tamil Nadu it is the occasion of social conviviality, the *Kolu* to which women invite one another and exchange *manjal-kumkumam.* In Karnataka, the festival is celebrated with great pomp and pageantry, culminating in a spectacular procession, led until very recently by the Maharaja of Mysore. In Delhi and Uttar Pradesh, it is celebrated as the *Rama Lila,* symbolizing the triumph of Rama over Ravana. On the final day, giant size effigies of Ravana, Kumbakarna and Meghanatha, stuffed with crackers, are exploded to the cheers and merriment of thousands of spectators.

The festival of Navarathri has crossed the Bay of Bengal and is celebrated on a grand scale in Bangkok, the capital of Thailand. It is celebrated with tremendous enthusiasm and, what is more, enjoys the full support and active participation of the local Thais and Chinese. The celebrations center round Sri Maha Mariamman Temple, located in Silom, the thriving business center of Bangkok. The Thais call the temple *Wat Kek* — foreigner's temple. Started on a modest scale by a Tamil business man, the temple over the years has developed into a grand structure. The priest, Nagamuthu, came from India some years ago and performs the pujas according to agamic rites. The temple is kept tidy and clean and has a serene atmosphere. In 1975, in deference to the wishes of the general public, the temple authorities installed the idol of Brahma. The idol of was specially made of *Pancha Loha* in Tamil Nadu, under the supervision of the famous sculptor Devasenapathy of Kumbakonam, and was consecrated with Hindu-Buddhist rites in October 1975. The most striking feature of the temple is the fact that it has happily blended with Thai religious landscape. In addition to the deities of the Hindu pantheon, the temple also has a beautiful image of Lord Buddha. Hundreds of devotees visit the temple every day, most of them of Thai and Chinese origin.

Navarathri, celebrated for nine days in the month of *Asvina* (October-November) is the most important festival of the temple. It commences with a Ganapathy Puja. After the Puja, Lord Ganesha is taken out in a procession around the temple. During the next nine days, pujas are performed in the morning and the devotees offer flowers, fruits, coconuts, ornaments and money. On the Vijayadashami day thousands of devotees throng the temple to join the grand procession. The procession consists of three decorated chariots, the first carrying the idols of Maha Uma Devi, Lord Ganesha and Lord Krishna; the second with the idol of Lord Subramania and the third with the idol of Karthavarahan (many consider the idol to be a Thai deity). Number of devotees are in a state of trance. Possessed with the spirit of Goddess Parvathi, they pierce their limbs with *soolam* and *alahus* and dance their way in front of the procession. Following them will be the devotees carrying *kavadis* and then the chariots. The majority of those who participate in the procession and go into trance and mortify their bodies are Thais and Chinese, who are non-Hindus. The spectacular procession, watched by thousands of people, winds its way slowly under the canopy of multi-coloured lights, through some of the busy streets of Bangkok and returns to the temple in the night. Arun Chetty, the live wire behind the celebrations and the Secretary of the Festival Committee, told me that no other procession in Bangkok, except those associated with Thai monarchy, attracts so much crowd as the Vijayadashami procession.

There is nothing surprising about the Thais celebrating the Navarathri with such devotion and fervour. The impact of India in the cultural life of Thailand is all pervasive. In addition to contacts with India, Thais received Indian cultural influences from the neighbouring Indianised kingdoms of the Mons and the Khemers. Even after embracing the Buddhist faith, the Thais still cling on tenaciously to many of the earlier Hindu traditions. An important contributory factor for the efflorescence of Indian culture in Thailand is the royal patronage. The royal courts became the centers of Indian culture. The royal title is Rama and the capital city was Ayuthia. Until very recently the Brahmins attached to the royal court cast the horoscopes, consulted omens and performed pujas for

Hindu and Buddhist deities. The complex coronation ceremony consisting of homa, ablutions, anointment and the actual coronation are based on Hindu rituals and are presided over by the chief priest called *Raja Guru.* The coronation itself is known by its Sanskrit name, *Rajabhisheka.*

There are eight families of court Brahmins in Thailand today. They claim that their ancestors originally came from Kasi. Since no women accompanied them, they married Thai girls. Today they speak only Thai language and have only a rudimentary knowledge of Sanskrit. But they try to adhere to Hindu rituals as much as possible, which they have inherited from their ancestors.

From the royal courts, Indian cultural forms percolated to popular level and blended with the life of the ordinary people. Thai language is full of Sanskrit words — *Ratha, Raja, Maha, Karuna, Shanti, Guru* — the list can be multiplied hundred fold. In Chiengmai, in northeastern Thailand, *Sankranti (Songhurant)* is still observed as the New Year's Day. Ramayana and Mahabharata form the basis of Thai literature and art. Ramayana known as *Ramkhein or Ramakritii* is regarded as a classic. Knowledge of Ramayana is an essential requirement for a refined Thai. The "Temple of the Emerald Buddha" in Bangkok has cloisters with murals depicting scenes from the Ramayana. Ramayana provides the basis for classical and popular theatre in addition to the shadow play. For a Tamil, it is an exhilarating experience to listen to the devotional songs of *Tirupavai and Thiruvampavai,* sung with great devotion, in the sacred month of *Markazhi,* corresponding to November-December.

CONCLUSION

As mentioned earlier, the fascinating encounter among indigenous, Chinese and Indian influences in Southeast Asia deserves greater attention from Indian and Southeast Asian scholars, alike. In this connection, I would like to submit these concluding thoughts for your consideration.

The spread of Chinese influence in Vietnam was an offshoot of political subjugation and consequent Sinicisation of the country. On the contrary, Indian influences spread to the region in a peaceful way. Except for the solitary incident of Chola invasion of Southeast Asia, in the eleventh century, no other Indian ruler embarked on military expeditions. Secondly, Indian contacts with Southeast Asia did not snap in the thirteenth century. Recent researches in maritime history clearly prove that the Keralites, Tamils and Gujaratis had extensive contacts with Southeast Asia during the medieval period. In fact, in the Islamisation of Southeast Asia, the Muslims from Gujarat and Malabar, Tamil Nadu and Bengal played decisive roles. Thirdly, Indian historians must re-evaluate the concept of "Greater India". The concept was a product of the Indian national movement and it gave

Indians a sense of pride in their glorious history. At the same time, its leading protagonists, more often than not, adopted a patronizing tone and denied Southeast Asian cultures autonomy of their own. To cite one illustration, Prof. R.C. Majumdar has written:

> "On the whole it is difficult to avoid the conclusion that Indian cultural influence deeply permeated the soul of diverse races in Asia over widely extended regions, and enabled them in many cases to emerge out of primitive barbarism."

Southeast Asian scholars are deeply sensitive and feel hurt because of this attitude of turning a "Nelson's eye" to the rich and virile indigenous cultural traits, which developed in different parts of Southeast Asia, even before contacts with Southeast Asia was established. Prof. Arun Das Gupta has convincingly pointed out that this concept of Greater India, in its older form, is not very useful. This does not mean we have to reject the unquestionable evidence of tremendous Indian influence in Southeast Asia. I suggest that instead of looking at Southeast Asian culture as an extension of Indian culture, we should treat the Southeast Asian region as a confluence area.

This balanced historical approach alone will provide the basis for benign cultural interaction between India and Southeast Asia.

I am left with mixed feelings, when I think of the enormous efforts that have gone into the study of the cultural evolution of Southeast Asian societies, I am, at the same time, conscious of the fact that much more remains to be done. Is the glass half empty or half full? The Indian scholars, committed to Southeast Asian Studies, should ponder over what Prof. Van Leur wrote few years ago about Dutch historiography: "The writing of real history has yet to begin".

Southeast Asian Studies was an important academic component of the Indian School of International Studies (ISIS), which was established in New Delhi in October 1955. The ISIS is a testimony to the academic vision and pioneering zeal of Pandit Hriday Nath Kunzru, Prof. Appadorai and Prof. M.S. Rajan. To quote Tagore's memorable phrase, like the Banyan Tree, the alumni of the ISIS spread to different universities and initiated teaching and research in International Relations and Area Studies. Facilities for academic training and research in Southeast Asian Studies are currently available in Jawaharlal Nehru University, Sri Venkateshwara University, Calcutta University and Madras University. Despite limited resources and inadequate support from the University Grants Commission, these Centres are doing fairly good work. But much more remains to be done.

It is a sad commentary that even after fifty seven years of independence, we do not have a research institution comparable to the Institute of Southeast Asian Studies in Singapore; Cornell University in the United States and the Monash University in Australia. It is imperative the Government of India and the University Grants Commission invest more resources in strengthening Southeast Asian Studies programmes, so that these Centres could develop into institutions of academic excellence and provide the much needed academic inputs for policy making.

"Given understanding and training, these Centres could also act as catalysts of academic interaction between Indian scholars and their counterparts in Southeast Asia. Mutual respect and appreciation can be fostered only by educational exchange and cultural co-operation. Senator Fulbright once remarked:

> "Civilization is what education exchange programs are all about. They are concerned in part with increasing man's knowledge about science and the arts. But they are primarily concerned with man's understanding of himself and of the national and world societies in which he lives."

The Senator added:

> "Educational exchange is not merely one of those nice but marginal activities in which we engage in international affairs, but rather, from the standpoint of future world eace and order, probably the most important and potentially rewarding of our foreign policy activities."

12

Central Asian and South Asian Cooperation

Potential to be Used and Utilized

F.G. TESHABAEV

In recent times the twin issues of international Cooperation and Security have become focus of attention and concern of everybody all over the world—from political leaders at the top, think tanks in between and common people, at the bottom. There are more, sometimes sidetrack sometimes core participants of this process-international organizations, global banks, leading corporations, permanent and occasional forums, which altogether are enhancing the scope of this historic and global analysis and search.

There are many reasons for that. First, the recent times are very turbulent and uncertain and insecure. Then local wars and international crises have threatened security and made cooperation almost impossibly difficult. Yet the countries and peoples moved on. The shocks of the collapse of old-world system and the terrorist attacks of global dimensions shattered the foundations of established relationships. But the focus on these issues has never diminished.

For every country and groups of countries, small and big regions it is in real terms the time of difficulties and hope. The above-mentioned two issues have become the categories of time and aspirations of the people.

The experience and logic of development had confirmed that it is imperative for countries and regions to deepen regional economic cooperation if they want development and prosperity because it will open unprecedented opportunities for social transformations and improvement of the lives of millions of people.

The path of Central Asian countries after their independence in early 90's could be a proof of this statement. The Central Asian states historically are bound with a strong set of economic relations. Now with these independent countries wishing to take part in the globalization process they have as never before the possibility of becoming full-fledged and equal participants in the process of globalization. From the very initial stages of their journey on the path towards development they had faced multiple challenges in national construction, regional cooperation and international integration. These were not separate tracks on which one could choose priorities and move in controlled manner. They all were intertwined.

The recent times have also brought the agreement between all countries that regional cooperation for the Central Asian republics is a vital imperative. Geographic characteristics of the region, comparatively small markets from the global point of view and urgency of mutually beneficial utilization of natural resources make all countries of the region interdependent. At the beginning of the process though interdependency was well recognized by countries of the region and their efforts alone could not bring the desired results.

At later stages the international community has started to pay more attention to the problems of regional cooperation in the Central Asian region. Regional cooperation is not only recognized as another intersect of this particular region but it is accepted as an element of wider process taking place in Europe and South East Asia. Thus the role of the deepening of the integration between Central Asian countries with wider international participation can not be separated from global developmental trends in the trade and economic cooperation in Asia as a whole. In these hugely complicated process joint efforts of the countries, the regions and the international organizations is quite necessary. After the efforts of countries of the region now Asian Development Bank, EBRD, Islamic Development Bank and World Bank have allocated $1 billion for different projects in Central Asian Region. Among projects selected there were first of all in the field of all the field of construction of transport corridors, regional utilization of energy and water resources and so on. All major events, be it the numerous international seminars, the Annual Board Meeting of EBRD, the visit of the President of the Islamic Development Bank and so on, focus is on the issues of regional cooperation. Just a few months ago — in November 2003 the Second Ministerial Conference on Economic Cooperation in Central Asia was held under the auspicious of Asian Development Bank. In May 2003, EBRD held its Annual Board Meeting in Tashkent. One of the features of this meeting was the agreement of multilateral institutions to work together to promote regional cooperation.

But one should admit it that there are number of complexities and risks on the path of regional cooperation. First of all, it is the fact which is called by foreign analysts as poverty problem, which local official language defines in different terms like weaker sections, socially protected groups and so on. The region is known to have some positive facts like rich natural resources, developed infrastructure as a pre-independence heritage, high level of literacy and vocational and professional skilled labour. At the same time it houses a large number of people who urgently need the support for a decent living. Second and more complex point is how to integrate quickly and at the same time to compete in different markets both national and international. No doubt it has many obvious advantages and hidden risks too. Successful integration implies the creation of globally comparative transport communication system, guaranteed high quality of manufactured goods and materials, and widespread network of social services. One of the basic and urgent requirements is the removal of trade and transport obstacles, which hinder regional cooperation. The role of trade for the region can never be underestimated in near and foreseeable future. Another difficulty is the question of common use of the water resources of the region, which is inseparably related to the problem of environmental protection.

One of the issues of recent experience is the indignation on the part of some countries of the region for solving the problems within their own national borders when the problems could have been tackled easily through regional cooperation.

There are many difficulties in the process. Certainly one of the main obstacles is the comparatively slow inflow of investments. Uzbekistan's strategy for regional cooperation has been based on some consistent points. It started to move towards cooperation for solving regional issues on every possible and practical way. As it may be remembered, Uzbekistan was among the first to raise the issue of regional and international cooperation to forge the solutions of urgent regional issues like Aral Sea problem. It was included in the first ever speech of the Head of the State to General Assembly of the UN. It always underlined the urgency of joint efforts of the countries of the region to solve regional problems. It tried to develop bilateral contacts as well as multilateral ones on different platforms of Central Asian cooperation on the whole range of issues. Along with this it supported the efforts of other side, both national and international. For example it wholeheartedly supported the Asian Development Bank programmes on developing transport communication line to the outside world for Central Asia.

There are different proposals on transport routes. But the route must have strict expertise in all respects. Those custom barriers, which do not comply with the lines of regional cooperation, should be re-examined and lifted if they are proved useless. But at the same time it is known that contraband and smuggling activities still continue to persist. The necessary barrier on their path is to be strong always. Certainly all these measures should be in conformity with the standards of WTO.

One of the important spheres for the regional cooperation is the implementation of practical principles in common usage of water and energy resources of the region. The countries should understand that the principle they prefer should be mutually complimentary to each other. The common concentrated efforts are required for the working out of the energy-saving technologies. Every country should be given chance to analyze thoroughly the implications of any particular step. For example, the high degree of commercialisation of usage of water resources at this juncture may require a cautious approach as the livelihood for millions of people depends on the availability of water for irrigation purposes during a particular given time of vegetation. One of the very crucial areas of cooperation should be the tackling of this problem through well thought out national policy in conjunction with the obligation emanating from international agreements. In other words bilateral cooperation is linked with multilateral cooperation and subsequently with regional cooperation. Recent issues of utilisation of water for irrigation and energy purposes show how the link is strong and should be taken care of.

When discussing regional cooperation of the transport system is vis-a-vis the regional cooperation. We could mention strategic priorities which are vital to provide efficiency to the system. One of the elements of efficiency must be its linkage of broader regional spaces. This requires the efforts of tackling Central and South Asian regional cooperation. In this field there is much potential like:

- development of transport corridors.
- working out of harmonized legal basis and norms.
- improvement of border control system.
- modernization of transport system in tune with the needs of regional cooperation.
- marketing and tariff regulations on the basis of competition.
- improvement of governance and finance system

The regional trade also has some vast potential like:

- simplification of custom procedures and documentation
- creation of conditions of civilised trade in conformity with standard of WTO
- implementation of efficient mechanisms to fight against smuggling in trade
- development of unified transit system, exchange of data and information in custom activity
- improvement of risk control and check after entry into the country.
- improvement of regional data collection system.

In the energy sector, the region has more common problems than in any other area. That is why there is a deep understanding among the countries of the region on widening cooperation on national and regional level. The satisfaction of expected demand for electric energy, the search for new sources of energy for the region as well as for export are today immediate issues of focus of Central Asian region. While Central Asian region is conducting long-term estimates of its resources for export it is necessary that South must be very closely involved in these processes.

Regional cooperation and security go together. Security situation in the whole world is full with uncertainties. Security is still under discussion. But South Asian countries especially India have developed very useful experience of tackling the problems of this kind. Certainly sharing the experiences are beneficial for all. That is why this line could be considered as another opportunity to start regional cooperation.

If one is to take a stock of regional cooperation, which is seemingly and obviously passing through its crucial stage of emergence, one should admit difficulties, but at the same time it is clear that despite difficulties the institutional structure of regional cooperation like transport, trade and energy is showing results. It is noticeable that international institutions are channelling considerable amount of resources to this end.

Take for example the issue of transport, which is admitted by everybody as crucially important. Uzbekistan is taking practical measures to enhance its input into this process. It started to operate Tashkent Kabul air-link and has expressed the intention to allocate concrete resources for the development of transport communications in Afghanistan. Within the framework of post-war rehabilitation programme it is implementing the huge work of construction of transport communications. Within a short time it has completed 9 bridges on Mazare-Sharif-Kabul axis. The largest regional custom services complex has been established in Termez with the collaboration of the UN and with financial help by Norway, Finland and USA.

This is mentioned here because it is obvious that the issue of transport is linked with both national construction and regional cooperation. Much has been said about it in Central Asia from the early days of independence. Almost all routes and corridors have been named and described by the experts. The existing ways of transport communications are still to develop to the extent when they will become the element of the system of regional transport network, not just like an exit and entry points. In other words it should provide all-basic requirements for free flow of goods and skills and people. The regulatory systems of transport communications must be harmonized between the countries of the region with more broad boundaries of concept and strategy.

As for the threats first among them being terrorism, the international community and leading powers have been taking mostly reactive action against it. The challenges of the 21st century are complex. The threats to security of human beings, national states, regions and globe as whole are emanating from terrorism, and terrorist actions of recent years have only brought death and destruction. The questions of tackling issues of humanity and life in our times await a proper answer and solution. That is why the mood of the century is beginning now to move towards practical actions for common existence and cooperation. The cooperation in the Central Asian region for the region's security concerns all. The individual countries and their governments are taking these issues as top priority. Once again latest efforts in the region like the setting up in Tashkent under the Shanghai Cooperation Organisation of the Centre for Fight against Terrorism is the indicator of structural and institutional progress in this direction. But struggle is going to be long lasting.

Central Asia and South Asia for a number of years have been in the process of becoming regions of major strategies importance. They involve and are engaged with the leading powers of the world. Their importance is set to grow. Perhaps more than any other regions of the world Central Asia and South Asia will be the avenues of much mentioned multipolarity in the world. While Central Asia is at the beginning of long a journey towards development and progress it is full of potential for fruitful cooperation on regional and global levels. The genuine desire of solving many probvlems of today like ethnic and religious radicalism, international narcotics trade and terrorism are the issues that are bringing the countries of the world more and more closer in the fight against them. Those who tend to be more pessimistic about the potential of regional cooperation should realize that there is no alternative to such cooperation, potentially and economically. Radical movements do not want to let them be materialized for the sake of social growth. Others have somewhat different agenda. Cooperation, among other things, means for every partner the freedom from outside influence despite how the pretext of such influence could be smartly formulated.

As a result of cooperation Central Asia could become the energy and transport hub for regional and world economy, which will be good for regional participants as well as for the international community.

It is clear that the Central Asia is becoming increasingly and deeply linked to the security issues of its southern and eastern neighbours. More and more countries of the east and west, north and south could play an important role in Central Asian Security. The region is also linked with other regions of the world. There is no doubt that in the process of formation of a clearly discernible and lasting geopolitical environment Central Asian and South Asian regional cooperation will be a factor of stability not only for the region itself but the whole world.

13

No Alternative to Collaboration and Cooperation Between Countries

Surat Mirkasymov

First of all I would like to convey to the hosts my heartfelt thanks for giving me a chance to be in this beautiful city of Kolkata and participate in this very important and timely organised international seminar.

The reasons of my happiness are: firstly, my diplomatic career started here in Calcutta, I worked as vice-consul of the Consulate-general of the Soviet Union from 1971 to 1975; secondly, my family loves this city of Rabindranath Tagore and Satyajeet Ray, city of knowledge with its famous university and libraries.

Now I would like to share my thoughts about the theme of the seminar. On 21 March 1 was talking to the students of Tashkent University of World Economy and Diplomacy about the life and creative works of Tagore.

While getting prepared for my lecture I read enough materials which gave me a good idea for my paper: I can draw needed ideas from the heritage of great personalities of India: Mahatma Gandhi, Jawaharlal Nehru and Rabindranath Tagore who did so much to bring together the people and states and consolidate different countries.

Mahatma Gandhi in his struggle for freedom of his country could bring together, under his banner of non-violence movement, people of India inspite of their differences in religions, languages, culture. He could prove that problems can be solved by peaceful means and compromise. Results are there to see independent and united India is very much there and she is now walking with vigorous strides to become a powerful state with highly developed economy, science-technology and culture.

Jawaharlal Nehru organised an Asian Conference before the independence of India. His idea was to consolidate and bring together all free Asian countries, but he could not implement his dream because of the "cold war" situation in the world. He was successful in organising the NAM with other leaders of the "Third World".

For lasts 7 years people of India have been singing:

> Jana-gana-mana-adhinayaka, jaya he
> Bharata-bhagya-vidhata.
> Punjab-Sindh-Gujarat-Maratha
> Dravida-Utkala-Banga,
> Vindhya-Himachala-Yamuna-Ganga,
> Uchchala-jaladhi-taranga.

In this sacred song Tagore invites all the states of India, Indian people with different religions to come close and be united. He knew that where there is unity, solidarity and order, there is growth and peace. Results are there for all to see. Today 28 states live together, struggle for their prosperity together and they are proud that they are united under the flag of India. Of course, there are all kind of problems in the country with more than one billion population and bouquets of different faiths: Hinduism, Buddism, Sikhism, Jainism, Parsis, Islam and Christianity. But in general, they always could find out the proper ways to live in harmony and jointly solve the problems of the country.

In contemporary time, when world has become very small because of the unbelievable growth of modern information technology and countries have become closer to each other and dependent on each other. In such situation time has proved that states can achieve their programmes to be implemented if they join their efforts. Now we have in different parts of the world many international and regional unions, associations, organisations of countries.

For example, European Union (EU), Association of South-Eastern Nations (ASEAN), British Commonwealth of Nations (BCN), Commonwealth of Independent countries (CIS), Shanghai Cooperation Organisation (SCO), South Asian Association of Regional Cooperation (SAARC) and etc. We cannot say that all the above international associations, unions are functioning successfully. But we can confirm that where there is real unity, of countries, strong trust between them, the organizations function well. For instance, European Union. All decisions of leading bodies of the Union followed by all member states with great care. As a result European Union has becam: politically, economically, militarily strong power. Very soon we shall be witnessing the ceremony where new constitution of the Union will be approved. This is the reason why other European countries also dream to be a member of the EU. This year in May membership of the European Union will grow from 16 to 25.

Unfortunately, we cannot say so about many other organizations. Conclusion: if countries want to find solution to their problems they should come closer to each other, stand shoulder to shoulder, join their efforts, try not only to understand the problems of the neighbour, but forget small ambitions and help as per as possible to solve them. From this point of view, we should welcome the changes in relations of two leading countries of this South Asian region India and Pakistan: if relations normalized between them, SAARC also will function properly, all decisions will work and bring real results. When leaders of two countries will sit together and sign the agreement of friendship and cooperation, that day will be great day. The victory day of wisdom. I would like to remind you that not so long ago, in 1963 leaders of two leading countries of Europe—France and Germany, President de Gaulle and Chancellor Adenauwer signed an agreement which closed forever doors to past enmity and opened the gates wide for future cooperation. This wise action of the two leaders destroyed the feelings of enmity and brought unity, changing step by step the psychology of the people.

Results of this historical action are there: united and prosperous Europe, rich and powerful France and Germany.

I hope that day is not far when the leaders of India and Pakistan will sign an agreement which will also close the doors to the past enmity of more than 50 years, and open the gates to the future of collaboration and cooperation in all fields of life. Than we would witness this region growing fast and becoming a very developed and prosperous region.

If we really want to build a new developed and secure Asia all the countries should join their efforts and fight against such common enemies as international and regional terrorism, extremism and narco business, which are blocking implementation of programmes directed towards eliminating economic and social backwardness. New states of Central Asia including Uzbekistan, because of civil wars and terrorism in neighboring countries, mainly in Afghanistan, had to suffer much: Firstly, to defend themselves from the real threat of Taliban regime and terrorist groups, like Islamic movement of Uzbekistan (IMU), located and trained in Afghanistan and the Government of Uzbekistan had to increase expenditure for defence equipment. Secondly, we could not bring investment into the growing economy, because of the threat from Afghanistan. The majority of foreign investors were afraid of loosing didn't want to take the risk.

The countries of West an East now understand clearly that the leadership of the former Soviet Union created the problem with its decision to send forces into Afghanistan. They couldn't solve Afghan problems and left others to find solution.

After 11 September 2001 many positive changes have taken place in the political situation in the region. Thanks to joint efforts of antiterrorist coalition of the countries under the flag of the United Nations and headed by the United States, Taliban regime and headquarters of Osama bin Laden of the Al-Qaeda international terrorist organisation were liquidated.

But "bomb blast in Madrid, in Tashkent and fighting of Pakistani army soldiers against terrorist Taliban groups located in mountain areas between Pakistan and southern Afghanistan make one sure that terrorist groups exist and will try to come together and implement their black deals.

It seems that life in neighbouring Afghanistan is slowly and step by step becoming normal. Adopting of the constitution and planned parliamentary election in September is good news. But Karzai government is still quite weak, even though it has the support from alliance states and the government of Afghanistan. According to some news they continue fighting with each other.

If Afghan problem is not solved soon, we will have to suffer. Mere statistics will not solve and soon, we all will have to suffer. Statistics inform that within 10 years customs system of Uzbekistan recovered tons of opium, which comes from Afghanistan on way to Europe. Afghan peasant earns 10 times more money from growing opium in one hectare of land than wheat. Afghan peasants should get alternate interest to grow more wheat. Efforts of the countries should be directed to help Afghan government to solve essential problems as soon as possible.

My country Uzbekistan is quite rich, with developed agriculture, industry plus rich natural resources and educated human resources. We have enough goods and commodities to export, to develop trade with other countries. Unfortunately it is land-locked. We need routes to seashores. Our government has tried its best in collaboration with neighboring countries to build new roads. For example we have signed an agreement with the governments of Afghanistan and Iran to build road from Uzbek city of Termez to Iranian border via Herat. We knew that the government of India also signed an agreement with Afghan and Irani governments to construct a road, which connects above-mentioned road with Iranian port of Chah-Bahar.

We hope that the normalization of relations between India and Pakistan, and improving situation in Afghanistan, we can use existing land routes which connect our Termez city with Delhi via Kabul, Peshwar, Lahore and Amritsar.

This type of cooperation and collaboration will definitely help to build New Asia, play great role in implementation programmes of economic and social development of these countries. I am sure that this seminar also will come out with useful good suggestions and recommendations to the governments of the East and West countries to collaborate with each other to build happy life on earth.

14

Indo-Central Asians Relations and a New Asia

SURENDRA GOPAL

European colonialism, beginning in the post-Vasco da Gama period in Asia and Africa consolidated itself in the era of Industrial Revolution and reached its peak in the 19th century. Though exploitation, political, economic and cultural, was its hall-mark, colonialism brought printing press and assisted ever expanding new education. The process was helped by steam engine which induced people's mobility. A new sense of identity and nationalism grew up in the colonies. Revolutions broke out against seemingly invincible ruler. The Asian determination to oust Europeans was steeled when Japan defeated Tsarist Russia in Russo-Japanese War of 1904-05. Four decades later, after the second World War, European colonialism was in full retreat from Asia and Africa.

The newly liberated countries, oppressed and exploited by metropolitan countries, embarked upon the path of development, social, economic and cultural. Basically the choice was between the ideologies of capitalism and communism, represented by USA and USSR, respectively. An intense cold war developed between the two super powers. The 'war' ended after almost half-a-century when in 1991 the Soviet Union disintegrated. Simultaneously the newly emerging forces of globalization pushed the ideological factor in the background. The USA was the unquestioned super power in the unipolar world.

International relations had to be recast. The question of security required new thinking in the new world perspective.

MAKING OF A POLICY

New sovereign states emerged on the ruins of the Soviet Union in the eastern Europe and in the heart of the Eurasian continent from Armenia to Kyrgysstan. They posed security problems to adjacent states including our country, India. Barring the Soviet regime, during the last two thousand and five hundred years, India had been repeatedly invaded.

The situation was grim. India today faces unprecedented problems, the foremost is the fear of the use of nuclear weapons.

The Soviet space station as well as nuclear installations were located in Kazakhstan, a newly independent state. Throughout its existence, the Soviet Union had ensured that the nuclear weapons were not to be used. Even though Russia, the major successor of the Soviet Union, had taken adequate precaution to prevent the use of nuclear weapons, one could not rule out the possibility of their misuse in new hands. There were solid reasons for visualizing such a situation.

Islamic fundamentalism was rapidly growing. Libya, Iraq, Iran and Pakistan and all Islamic states, were keen to acquire nuclear weaponry. They had made their intentions known to the whole world. These Central Asian States had dominant Muslim population. Their economy was pitiable. Oil-rich Middle Eastern States tried to lure them with big money. One could not predict their behaviour in the face of such allurements. At least their nuclear scientists could be 'hired' or 'invited' to assist the programme of nuclearisation.

With the demise of the Soviet Union, the communist ideology was given a burial. The danger was that the Islamic Fundamentalism could step in the ideological vacuum. In the neighbouring Afghanistan the Islamic fundamentalists, the Talibans, had obtained the upper hand. They could propagate their ideals or even forcibly try to impose them on their neighbours. They could invoke 'Islamic Brotherhood' to put across their message to the masses. India viewed this possibility with great alarm. India has around 160 million Muslims.

The emergence of a Turkish-speaking block extending from the Mediterranean to the Pamirs had to be taken into account. This could revive the moribund Pan-Turanism. A solid block of Turkish-speaking nations would alter the geo-political situation and India had to cope with this problem.

Finally, India visualized a far more serious problem. Pakistan, India's immediate neighbour and initiator of three wars during the last four decades was posing itself as the trustworthy friend of the newly independent Central Asian States, only on the basis of commonality of religion. Pakistan had been an active member of the USA-Sponsored Defence Pacts and Military Blocks. These military alliances, directed against the Soviets then had been denounced by the Soviet Union. The Central Asians, then a part of the Soviet Union, had more or less, shunned Pakistan. Pakistan thought that the death of the Soviet Union gave it a new opportunity to draw them within its own sphere of influence.

India had to prevent such a development because of the nature of its relationship with Pakistan which lost no occasion to show its hostility.

India's policy makers' immediate concern was to thwart neuclearisation of the area, ensure non-proliferation of nuclear weapons, and to keep the new sovereign states away from the ideologies of Pan Turanism and Pan Islamism. They had to ensure that Pakistan was not able to develop a cosy relation with them. India could hope to realize its aims as some favourable factors were operating.

First, though the Central Asian countries were sovereign nation states, they were still closely allied to Russia; both economically and politically because of compulsions of history and geography. Russia would not permit these states to have nuclear weapons. The presence of Russia was a guarantee that nuclear weapons would not fall into their hands. Super power USA and the 'big' neighbour China were also opposed to the nuclearisation of these Central Asian states.

The Central Asian states had been nurtured on a philosophy of atheism for seven decades and were not expected to be easily taken in by the fundamentalist Islamic propaganda. Tajikstan was an exception. Steeped in secular and scientific education, people were more receptive to the voice of nationalism than to the tenets of fundamental Islam.

Indian policy makers, after weighing the pros and cons of the situation, decided to work upon these positive points; they set about forging a relationship which could be mutually beneficial and strengthen liberal and democratic values and promote market economic forces in tune with the forces of globalisation.

India's formulation of the new policy was right. It was helped by non-interfering postures adopted by their immediate neighbours, Russia and China, the two largest countries in Euro-Asia.

India's initial policy moves were halting and hesitant as compared to Pakistan because India tried to ensure that they were in harmony with Russian sensibilities and did not fan Chinese fears

As time progressed, like all dynamic foreign policy initiatives, India incorporated new factors to suit India's interests better. India realized that the new states were rich in energy resources, petrol and gas. A mutually beneficial relation would help to solve India's chronic deficiency in these products. "Caspian basin held huge reserves which were waiting to be intensively exploited. According to an estimate[1] Turkestan has between 17 and three trillion cubic metres of untapped gas, estimated to be world's second largest reserve. Other Central Asian Republics together have oil and gas equivalent to that of Qatar, Oman and UAE, put together. They can produce seven million barrels of oil daily, but for the huge investments required."[2] India, as one of the largest consumer of hydrocarbons, was keen to benefit from the new source of supplies.

India could also hope to become a supplier of some consumer goods to the region, a market of over 55 million. This was a market with which Indians had become familiar during the eighties when plane-loads of Central Asians arrived in Delhi and carried back textiles and medicines.

For Indian authorities matters were made somewhat easier by the fact that the change of regimes had not meant a change of government, except in Tajikstan. In Turkmenistan, Uzbekistan, Kyrgyzstan and Kazakhstan, the old government wedded to secularism, with a pro-Russian tilt remained in power. Many in the Indian government were well acquainted with these leaders. The Indian policy makers took advantage of this and unfolded steps to convince these states of usefulness of continuing traditional friendship with India of the soviet era.

India convinced the Central Asian ruling elites of the harm that would accrue to them if they sided with the Talibans, who after ousting the Russians had imposed a fundamentalist regime in Afghanistan, where women were confined to the four-walls of their homes and the Mullahs dominated decision-making process in the government. The elite understood that a Taliban style government would be unacceptable to people used to equality of sexes, in homes, workplaces and educational institutions. Indian style governance, allowing freedom of beliefs and civil rights was suitable for them. It ensured a right mix of tradition and modernization.

UNFOLDING OF THE POLICY

India's relationship with Central Asia in Soviet times were only cultural and economic ; now they had to be reinforced with diplomacy as the security of India was involved. Pakistan, having tasted success in Afghanistan, in ousting the Soviets, opted for an aggressive foreign policy in the region; it projected itself as the true friend of Central Asian States and was not averse to play the Islamic card in the name of Pan Islamism. Though Pakistan had nothing to offer in economic terms, it sought to grant them access to the Arabian Sea through the port of Karachi or other ports on the Makran coast. It also played upon Central Asia's historic fear of Shia Iran and was offering the land-locked States an access to the sea bypassing Iran. Pakistan also sought to put forward itself as a long-standing friend of the People's Republic of China, their next-door neighbour. It claimed that it could keep China in good humour which would benefit the Central Asian States, as the Soviet shield had been withdrawn.

Pakistan's agenda in dominating Afghanistan and the newly independent Central Asian States was to ensure the so-called doctrine of 'strategic depth.'

Of course, the Central Asian States had their own problems. Tajikstan was confronted with a civil war, immediately after it became independent. Mujahdins from Afghanistan threatened it. The security of national frontiers against Afghan invaders was its first concern.

Uzbekistan at the heart of Central Asia, the largest populated state, had more cultivable land than the rest of the states except Kazakhstan.. Its mineral resources were enormous. Besides petroleum and gas, it was fifth in gold stock and seventh in its production, in the world. It was fifth in cotton production in the world. The tradition of monoculture, i.e. only cultivating cotton in the Soviet times had made it deficient in food grains.

The small Kyrgyzstan state was self-sufficient in food and dairy products.[3] Uzbekistan had more industries and traditionally it was more urbanized and had better facilities for higher education.[4] It was quickly given diplomatic recognition and today it is recognized by 170 countries.[5] On the other hand Kazakhstan had a large percentage of Russian population. In the Soviet times, Russia had created facilities for launching its space vehicles and storing nuclear weapons on its soil. Russia was afraid that these nuclear arms would fail into alien hands and jeopardize its security.Therefore, it carefully controlled the foreign policy of Kazakhstan.

Turkmenistan had discovered enormous quantities of oil and gas. It was also a corridor to Central and Southern Europe for the neighbouring Central Asian States. Its foreign policy aimed at ensuring its neutrality from the entanglements in which the other Central Asian States found themselves.

Hence, the Indian government, while formulating its policies, had to consider Central Asia as a unit and at the same time it could not forget the individual concerns of each country as well. It had also to compete with neighbours like Pakistan who invoked solidarity in the name of religion and/or language/or geography. For example, in 1999,Pakistani missionaries in Kyrgyzstan numbered forty and were the second largest group of foreign missionaries.

Forging of mutual trust and respect for each other's interest was a *sine qua non* for a durable and fruitful relationship and the Indian government set about the task with determination. India had no problem in formally establishing diplomatic relations with the newly established countries, though in certain cases there was a small time lag before the embassies could be established. India took six years to open an embassy in Dushanbe (Tajikstan).

Establishment of relationship with Uzbekistan was the easiest. India had a diplomatic presence in Tashkent during the Soviet days. The office was upgraded and Tashkent became the pivot round which India's diplomatic activities took place in other Central Asian republics.

The Uzbek President Karimov promptly responded. His first visit to India took place in August 1991. He followed it with visits in 1994 and 2000.[6]

The then Indian Prime Minister P.V. Narasimha Rao responded and visited Uzbekistan in 1993 and spelled out Indian concerns especially in relation to the growth of religious extremism. At the same time he pledged support to the legitimate interests of the newly independent country.

From then on exchange of visits at different levels between Central Asian States and India commenced. Attempts were initiated to establish mutually satisfying relationships; cultural, economic and political.

In Uzbeksitan India had a small economic presence towards the last days of the Soviet Union.The Tata and L&T group of Companies were constructing Hotels in 1990 in Tashkent and Samarkand, the capital of Timurid Uzbekistan. Indians were permitted to expand to expand their economic activities and allowed to set up new industries.

Indians started pharmaceutical companies in Uzbekistan.[7] In 2000, the turn over of trade amounted to $25.3 million.[8]

India's intense desire to obtain gas and petroleum, the two products available in plenty in the Central Asian States, was not lost upon these nations. They were conscious that new economic ties should be accompanied by close political relationship between the Central Asian States and India. Islam Karimov had mentioned that they had the largest reserves of gas and petroleum and 'the world cannot forget it.'

Geography had been a major hindrance to the development of closer economic relations between India and Central Asian States as they are separated by intervening states and do not have direct access to each other. These intervening states had their own agenda and were unwilling to see flourishing economic relations between these two regions. However, both sides showed keenness to overcome this geographical barrier. The idea of developing the North-South-Sea-Road corridor from Bander Abbas in Iran to Anzali and then to the Caspian port of Astrakhan was floated and was being vigorously pursued. The Central Asian States, under economic compulsions, are overcoming their traditional distrust of Shiite Iran because the unhindered access to the Persian Gulf opens up for them vast markets on the rim of the Indian Ocean where competition is less and the likelihood of economic gain is far greater than, either, in Europe or in China. Russia, so long their major purchaser and supplier, was restructuring its economy and was in no position to serve their immediate interests.

The above Indo-Central Asian interactions have to be seen in context the of Pakistani policies in the region.

Pakistan was trying hard to woo the Central Asian States since their inception.

While India was trying to forge mutually satisfying relationships with the Central Asian States, Pakistan tried to deflect Central Asian States from this course. In 1995 Ms. Bhutto, the then Pakistan Prime Minister went to Uzbekistan and almost immediately Saudi Arabia agreed to set up a joint venture worth $ 31 million. They wanted Uzbekistan to toe their policies. Uzbekistan, however, did not commit.[9] It's the then President Farooq Ahmad Khan Leghari visited Bishkek in October 1996 and promised to link Kazakhstan and Kyrgyzstan with the Karakoram highway so that their dependence on other Central Asian States for access to the outside would be reduced. He also asked them to use the port of Karachi rather than Bander Abbas in Iran to reach the sea as it would be shorter path.

To lure the Central Asian States to join the Islamic Bloc, economic allurements were put forward. A delegation of Islamic Development Bank based in Jidda visited Turkmenistan, Uzbekistan, Kazakistan, etc. in 1996 but not much came out of it. Kazakhstan would not be persuaded. It had applied for the membership of the North-South-Sea-Road corridor running through Iran.

Politically India and the Central Asian states started coming nearer after the latter realized the Chechen rebels, Talibans and Pakistanis were keen to stir up internal dissensions in the name of establishing Islamic polity.

The Central Asian Republics were convinced of Pakistan's close links with the religious extremism, terrorism and Talibans after the Islamic movement of Uzbekistan made a bid to stir trouble in Uzbekistan, Tajikistan and Kyrgyzstan in 1999. It is reported that 30 Kyrgyz soldiers lost their lives.[10] Uzbekistan had taken a little more time than other republics to reach this conclusion.

The Central Asian States were disenchanted by the pro-Taliban policies, pursued by Pakistan.

Pakistan attempted to join Shanghai Five Grouping formed by Russia, Kazakhstan, Kyrgyzstan, Tajikistan and China in 1996 in the face of mounting threat from Afghan fundamentalists. China was deeply concerned at the trouble it was facing at the hands of the religious fundamentalists and terrorists in its western-most province of Xinjiang, bordering both Afghanistan and Pakistan. It had promoted the Shanghai Five Group.[11]

The Chinese were friendly but noncommital. The Chinese foreign Ministry spokesman said, "but, I think, taking new members requires negotiated consensus of the five members of the Shanghai Five". The application was submitted to 'Group's current Chair, Tajikistan'.[12] But the Russian Foreign Ministry emphatically ruled out Pakistan's request. Its spokesman asserted, "it is a pure propaganda move".[13]

Uzbekistan was earlier lukewarm to the Group of Shanghai Five. Uzbekistan at first tried to adopt a neutral position on the question of growing Islamic fundamentalism along its border.

At a conference in 1996 convened in Tehran to chalk out a strategy to meet the threat being posed by the Talibanisation in Afghanistan, Uzbekistan abstained while Iran, Russia, India and four Central Asian States attended it.[14] Uzbekistan's reluctance to clearly spell out its stand against terrorism, prompted the three states Kyrgyzstan, Kazakhstan and Tajikistan to seek support elsewhere.

They found close allies in both Russia and China. The former was already suffering at the hands of Chechen rebels.

In early 1998 Uzbek Foreign Minister Abdulaziz Kamilov accused Islamabad of giving military training to Uzbek rebels. He said that some 400 Kyrgyz, Tajik and Uzbek rebels were undergoing training at illegal camps in Pakistan. He also accused the rebels trained in Pakistan were responsible for a series of attacks in Uzbekistan's Namagan region which led to the deaths of several government employees and law officers. The Pakistan government vehemently denied these charges.[15] But it was clear that Pakistan's bid to draw Uzbekistan in its orbit had failed.

The year 1999 proved to be a defining moment. Certain events forced the governments of Uzbekistan and Kyrgyzstan to shed their inhibitions and to commit their support to the ongoing struggle against religious fundamentalism and international terrorism. A major aim of the foreign policies of India and Central Asian States was the same. The Central Asian States corrected their pro-Pakistani tilt. In the international arena India and Central Asian States were coming together.

However, Uzbekistan had to change its stand when the Islamic fundamentalists tried to stir up trouble in Tashkent and caused a series of blasts in the capital. An attempt was made to assassinate President Islam Karimov on 16 February 1999. It was clear that the Islamic Movement of Uzbekistan (IMU), led by Namangani which had intruded into the Ferghana Valley, had well-established links with the Taliban. At a later date, in August 1999, armed bands entered Kyrgyzstan and the government forces had difficulty in putting them down. Some of the members of these armed bands also entered Uzbekistan and tried to create trouble. The Uzbek government was forced to bomb the guerilla's stronghold.

In July 1999 in Delhi the then Prime Minister Vajpayee had 'made a plea to the peoples of South Asia and Central Asia for taking the only possible route of "Peace, friendship and cooperation among the countries of the region". He described the people of the area as a "geocultural family of which we were, and continue to be members".[16] Nareshwar Dayal Secretary (East) Ministry of External Affairs on that occasion stressed the "Positive determinants of Indo-Central Asian Relations". There was the 'need to build roads and railway; pipelines would have to be laid to transport energy resources of South Asia; thus overcoming the access to the land-locked Central Asia".[17] Since then, Islam Karimov, the President of Uzbekistan has been actively pursuing the democratic agenda. Apparently the Pakistan's nuclear test of 1998 alerted him to the danger posed by a nuclearized Pakistan, supported by terrorists and fundamentalists. Such a position undoubtedly brought India and Uzbekistan and other Central Asian States together. In March 2000, Islam Karimov visited India and the Indo-Uzbekistan Joint economic Commission intensified its activities and to date has held four sittings.[18]

Meanwhile to ensure their security, as a follow up measure, in May 2001 a decision was taken to create a Rapid-Reaction Force consisting of a battalion 'from each of the four participants; Russia, Kyrgyzstan, Tajikistan, and Kazakhstan'. The force was to be subordinate to a 'joint headquarters based in Kyrgyzia'.[19] A statement added, "We will continue to jointly rebuff attempts to rebuff peace and tranquillity in Central Asia,..." Russia had also sought and secured the support of CIS nations in its fight against religious funamentalism and terrorism.

After Uzbekistan had hardened its stance against terrorism, at a meeting of the Shanghai Five in June 2001, it was admitted as a founder member of Shanghai Cooperation Organisation.[20] This showed that these countries were fully 'aware of the Taliban-led extremist links in their countries' and were determined that 'the problem of religions extremism, and terrorism be effectively controlled'.[21]

The turn of events in Afghanistan showed that the Talibans were keen to export their brand of Islamic fundamentalism and to establish Nizam-I-Millat, the Republic of Islamic fundamentalism, stretching from the borders of India to deep into the Volga country of Russia and Chechnya and Tatarstan. Hence, the small Central Asian States had no option but to turn to the democratic countries opposed to fundamentalism and this brought a better appreciation for India's bold stand against terrorism.

Uzbek scholars were forthright in assessing the role of India in fighting terrorism and religions extremism. Muhammad M. Yukbov, of the Institute of Strategic and Regional Studies of Uzbekistan stated, "India is quite experienced in handling fundamentalism and religious extremism, and since we are faced with almost identical problems, we will be glad to have the benefit of their knowledge.'[22] His colleagues Abdullah Zia Abdullaev and Isadjanov agreed with him and suggested that India, Uzbekistan and other countries of the region should cooperate and evolve a mechanism to fight fundamentalism and religious extremism.[23]

The Uzbek appreciation of India's position certainly influenced other Central Asian States policies towards India and this was reflected in visits of the Heads of States of Central States to India in 2001.

The leadership of Central Asian States was deeply affected by the events which took place in Uzbekistan and Kyrgyzstan, in July and August 1999, when armed bands (members of Islamic Movement of Uzbekistan) entered from Tajikistan into Uzbekistan and Kyrgyzstan and the government struggled hard to suppress the terrorists. The rebels were supported by Laden and they were planning to set up bases in the mountains to stir up further troubles.[24]

The experience impelled the two governments, of Uzbekistan and Kyrgyzstan, to take a definite stand against terrorism and religious extremism and this brought them nearer to the Indian position.

Earlier the rebels had imprisoned four Japanese geologists and German mountaineers and several others in Kyrgyzstan. They were released only after a hefty ransom was paid.

The foreign governments, especially the European Union countries, who were investing in the Central Asian States were worried about the growing instability in the region. The Central Asian States were nervous that this would affect foreign investments and would have a deleterious impact on their economy in the long run.

Pakistan made another desperate attempt to rope in Central Asian States to its side.

In November 2000, Pakistan's Chief Executive went on a two-day visit to Kazakhstan.[25] En route he met Turkmenistan's President Saparmurat Niazaov during a brief stop over to discuss Afghanistan. This was the third meeting of President Nursultan Nazarbayev with Gen. Musharraff, during the year. The aim was to remove Kazakhstan's perception that Pakistan 'is hand in glove with the Taliban regime in Afghanistan...' and this was to enhance political and economic relations with the Central Asian Republics. Central Asian States were in no doubt that India and not the Islamic Pakistan was their true friend.

To terrorise the Tajiks, the Talibans moved 1,000 gunmen to Tolukan border region, close to the Tajik international line but the Russians stationed there felt that they could repel any attempted intrusion on the part of the Talibans.[26] Even the Chinese in Western Xinjiang, bordering on Tajikistan, Kyrgyzstan, Kazakhstan and Afghanistan, were feeling the heat of Talibanism and Wahabism and were deeply concerned since Xinjiang was their gateway to capital Urumqi and Kazakhstan. The border trade with Kyrgyzstan, via the Turgurt pass, was too invaluable to be lost to fundamentalists. Hence, China extended its support to the Central Asian States for eliminating terrorism.[27]

Within less than a decade, Russia, the Central Asian States and China had all suffered from the ravages caused by the Talibans and the proponents of similar ideologies, both at home and abroad.

The experience impelled the two governments to take a definite stand against terrorism and extremism. This brought them nearer to the Indian position. The Tajik President Imam Ali Rakhmanov came to India in a four-day visit in May 2001.[28] Rakhmanov's worries were understandable. It is a frontline state and gateway for the Talibans to the Farghana Valley, i.e., both Uzbekistan and Kyrgyzstan. Russia, realizing the predicament of Tajikistan, stationed 30,000 troops to deter Taliban armed bands from crossing into Tajikistan.[29] During Tajik President's visit, India pledged support to Tajikistan and agreed to set up food processing industries. Certainly Tajikistan's conduct in restoring their reclining 42 ft. long and 9ft. high Buddha, found in 1960, brought to Indians their secular credentials, especially in the aftermath of the destruction of the Bahmian Buddhas by the Talibans. It was no surprise that the Indian government supported the Tajik government, which had endured civil war and political unrest through most of the 1990s.[30] A clear statement of their solidarity in fight against terrorism and religious extremism was made.

The Indo-Tajik declaration signed during the Tajik President Emomali Sharifovik Rakhmanov's visit in May 2001 covered the 'entire gamut of bilateral ties as well as regional and international issues of mutual concern'.[31] India offered a grant of five million US dollars to Tajikistan to tackle the acute drought situation and five agreements were concluded, such as one on economic cooperation and another for joint action against terrorism and drug trafficking.[32] The Tajik President offered to support India's candidacy for a permanent seat on the Security Council.

The clear formulation of a policy of resistance to the spread of religious extremism and terrorism by Shanghai Five and Uzbekistan encouraged the Northern Alliance which was battling the Talibans to send its Foreign Minister Abdulla to Moscow in July 2001 to 'build up international pressure to rein in the Taliban'.[33]

Thus when the events of 11 September 2001 took place in New York, the Central Asian States, Russia, China, India and Northern Alliance were bound to support each other against religious extremists and terrorists. When the USA decided to launch air strike against the Taliban positions in Afghanistan, Uzbekistan offered them the use of Tuzel Military Base, situated not far from Tashkent.[34]

Pakistan's attempts to wean away Central Asian States from adopting a line similar to that of India had proved futile.

The post-11/9 period witnessed a new direction to the foreign policies of India and the Central Asian States. Terrorism had bared its fangs and the whole world recognized its unsavoury character. The threat posed by it had to be met unitedly.

The Central Asian Republics and India decided to upgrade their economic relations by ensuring easier access to the markets of both the area. Since Afghanistan had been freed from the control of the Talibans by an international military action, the political scenario had changed. Pakistan had allowed international forces free access to its territory and its government had openly denounced terrorism and fundamentalism and agreed to support the new government in Afghanistan. Afghanistan and Pakistan agreed to serve as a new link between the Central Asian States and littoral countries of the Arabian Sea. India and Iran decided to open new routes to Central Asian States, via Afghanistan.

The port of Chabahar, on Iran's Makran coast close to Pakistani port of Gwadar in Baluchistan province, was selected as a new terminal port. A road is being built which would enter Afghanistan in the province of Herat and it would go on to Termez on the Oxus river in Uzbekistan.

Pakistan, aware of the changed mood of international politics, is reorienting its policy. It has withdrawn support to Talibans and al-Qaeda and pledged its support in suppressing terrorism. It has agreed to prevent nuclear proliferation by stopping supply or sale of nuclear parts to Libya Iran and North Korea. It has now reoriented its policy towards India. By establishing its credentials as an anti-terrorist state, as a believer in non-nuclear proliferation, and as a champion of regional cooperation, Pakistan is putting itself forward as a transit point for road-link between India and Uzbekistan. It is also keen that gas pipelines from Iran and Central Asia to India should run through it because it would bring immense economic benefits to it and also will be economically viable for India.

India is carefully assessing the moves of Pakistan; the Central Asian states also feel that the shorter route through Pakistan to India and other countries of South Asia would promote their economy as well.

Meanwhile, India has been continuously strengthening its relationship with the Central Asian states through diplomacy, intensified educational and cultural relations.

For example, Indian cultural centers were opened in Tashkent (Uzbekistan) and Almaty (Kazakhstan) with Vinod Bhatia and Naseem Bhatia as Directors, respectively. Both of them were familiar with the Soviet system and fluent in Russian as they had studied in Moscow for their Ph.D. degrees.

Besides, the Indian Government established, at the University of World Economics and Diplomacy in Tashkent and at the University of Osh in Kyrgyzstan, one Chair each to teach "Indian Civilization-study in Continuity and Change: Unity in Diversity". Indian scholars were appointed to these Universities. (Information supplied by Ms. Urmil Rawal, Sr. Programme Director, (ICC & C), ICCR, vide her letter No. ICC/ Mis./ 2002-03 dated 26 November, 2002)

Indian diplomacy became more active after the shock administered to it by the terrorist attack on Indian Parliament on 13 December 2001.

The event alerted the Central Asian states as well as USA to the scourge of terrorism with its philosophy to spare more of its opponents. Democratic nations had to close their ranks and fight it world-wide.

Central Asian nations shed their hesitancy and resolved firmly to confront the menace. China, too, openly came out in support of the anti-terrorist block. It agreed to collaborate actively with Russia, USA, India and Central Asian states against 'terrorism and fundamentalism'. The Central Asian States also forgot their traditional hostility to Iran. This is reflected in establishing the port Chahbahar on the Iranian coast. The policy of active opposition to terrorism once again brought the Central Asian States and India together. Henceforth, the focus of policies of India and Central Asian states was to ensure a terror-free region.

POLICY IN THE POST-9/11 PERIOD

In this period two considerations have been uppermost; fight against terrorism and promotion of economic development.

In 2002 the then Prime Minister Vajpayee travelled to Central Asia to gather support for India's stand.

When the Americans, along with their allies, took up the task of driving out the Taliban from Afghanistan, India supported the military action, though it did not commit its armed forces to participate in fighting. India already had a medical mission in Tajikstan to extend medical assistance to Tajiks fighting Talibans in Afghanistan. India also committed its resources for rebuilding Afghanistan, already devastated by decades of fighting and Taliban's oppression. This was to show Central Asian States India's goodwill towards its neighbours and also its technological capabilities.

Pakistan's new policy encouraged Iran and India to follow more actively the policy of opening up alternative routes to Central Asia and Afghanistan with the intention of overcoming 'Pakistan barrier'.[35]

The decision to develop Chabahar port aassumed importance after Iran's President Khatami was invited to India, during the Republic Day parade, on 26 January 2003, as the Chief Guest. Khatami was also clear in mind that Iran was the natural gateway between Eurasia and Indian Ocean littoral states.

Indian and Iranian perception about the energy resources of Central Asia coincided and therefore, they could act in tandem.

India's moves on deepening Indo-Iranian relation with a view to strengthen its position *vis-a-vis* Central Asia states became clear when the Iranian President publicly announced, "Iran welcomes the presence of India in scientific and commercial fields in Central Asia". (*Hindu,* 26 January 2003). President Khatami had in 2002 visited Central Asia and was keen have a share of Caspian oil wealth and was concerned at the growing military profile of USA in Central Asia.

While India and Central Asia were coming closer, India did not fail to take into account the new ground situation in the Central Asian States. It was concerned at the establishment of American military bases in Central Asia. It decided to take fresh initiative and started wooing Central Asian states, especially Tajikistan where there was no American soldier and where Indian government had sent doctors to render medical aid since northern Alliance had began its fight with the Talibans.

An Indian delegation had visited Kazakhstan in October 2002 after Vajpayee's trip in June 2002 and held talks about Kurmangazy oil fields in the Caspian.[36]

India had given a clear idea of its intentions to have a finger in its oil-pie when Punj-Lloyd of New Delhi won a stake in the Baten V. Ceyhan oil-pipeline running from Caspian to Ceyhan in Turkey.[37]

India's resolve to promote an Indo-Iran-Central Asian understanding also took in consideration China's growing involvement in the security and economy of Central Asian states. In December 2002, China signed with Kazckhstan "Good Neighbourly Treaty of Friendship and Cooperation".[38]

In 2002, India was concerned mainly to offset the growing influence of America, Russia and China in strategy and economic matters in Central Asia. In this task, India and Iran were acting together since both were concerned at the growing military might of great powers. India and Iran looked with grave concern at the growing militarisation of Central Asian unleashed by big powers, two of them Russia and China, their neighbours and the third USA, though situated far away had the potentiality to intervene because of the superiority of its military technology.

India's concern were manifested in steps Indian diplomacy started taking since the dawn of 2003.

First, India's the then Defence Minister George Fernandes decided to visit China.[39] This was to be the first visit by an Indian Defence Minister, in decades.

The Indian Foreign Minister, Yashwant Sinha went to Kyrgystand and Tajikstan and on return travelled through Almaty where he made the statement, "we are not in Central Asia to replace anyone. We see Central Asia as part of India's extended neighbourhood and our presence there is to promote a mutually inclusive relationship".[40]

This was also the first occasion when an India foreign Minister had visited Dushanbe, the capital of Tajikstan and he pledged India's help in building roads and developing hydropower.

Fear of terrorism and fundamentalism was so paramount that Shanghai group readied itself for 'regional security' by pooling their armed forces. This was the result of continuing failure of the Afghan government and the Allied forces to clear Afghanistan of Al-Qaeda elements who off and on continued to create trouble with the result that Mamid Karzai, the Afghan President was described as 'Mayar of Kabul'.

Furthermore, Pakistan's inability to control Al-Qaeda remanants caused more anxiety in the area. It was against this context, India continued enlarging its contacts with Central Asian states.

As a part of this strategy, Indian Prime Minister paid a visit to Beijing from 22 to 26 June 2003. The Chinese ambassador to India Hua Junduo wrote on the occasion that the countries were 'partners and rivals'. The need to stand up against terrorism had united the two sides.

A meeting of official of India and Kazakhstan took place in June 2003. From Kazakhstan, D. Sathojin and from India Lt. General Shantanu Choudhary took part in an exercise to share intelligence. They affirmed that the two sides were 'together on the issue of terrorism.[41]

In November 2003 Prime Minister Vajpayee travelled to Dushanbe, the first Indian Prime Minister to do so. The two sides agreed that both were keen to see stability in the region. They also felt that there was a vast potentiality of cooperation between the two sides especially in developing hydropower and mineral resources and many other fields. It must be noted that Tajikstan has silver mines.[42]

Military cooperation was also mooted. It was argued, "About 70 per cent of the equipment with Indian armed forces is of Soviet/Russian origin and nearly 100 per cent of that has commonality with what is used in the five Central Asian States." India decided to station some aircraft at the Farkhor military base in Tajikstan. Indian engineers were brought in to strengthen the runway, aircraft pens and other facilities.

The Farkhor base, also known as Ayni base, just 10 kms away from the Tajik capital, is the first Indian military base in foreign lands. (Gulshan Luthra, "India extends strategic reach with Tajikstan base".[43]

India has been going all out to develop friendly relations with all the Central Asian States. As a part of Indian effort to wean away Central Asian states from terrorist influences, India's the then External Affairs Minister, Yashwant Sinha paid a visit to Tashkent and reiterated India's close ties with Uzbekistan.

Diplomatic efforts are supplemented by other measures as well.

India has been giving scholarships to students of all the Central Asian States to study in Indian educational institutions and thus trying to add new dimensions.

It may however be pointed out that the task has now become extremely complicated because of the presence of USA armed forces in this area-and also its recent decision to give Pakistan the status of a 'Major Non-NATO Ally'. This would upgrade Pakistan's military strength and affect India's security.

India's effort to have a share in the Central Asian Energy resources is also beset with difficulties because of the problems of accessing them economically.

India now faces problem in establishing close relations. Given her democratic traditions, how much close India can get to the Central Asian States where the Heads of the State are unwilling to quit the seats of power, is problematic.

Rakhmanov, the Tajik President has secured popular mandate for two 7 year terms after the completion of his assignment in 2006.[44]

In 2002 the Uzbek electorate permitted Presiden Islam Karimov to run for two seven-year terms when his present term is over in 2005.[45]

In 1999, Suparmurad Niyazov, the Turkmenistan President, got a mandate to remain in office till his death.

In Azebaijan, after the death of the President, his son Aliyev won the Presidency.[46]

This is an important constraint before Indian policy makers in formulating a long-term viable and foreign policy towards the Central Asian States.

If India and Central Asia can coordinate their efforts and bypass Pakistan, 'an unreliable ally', probably the fate of Asia can be changed. The land from Caspian to the Pamirs can become economically prosperous and forward-looking territory.

REFERENCES

1. *International Petroleum Encyclopaedia* 1998, Oaklahoma, USA.
2. *The Times of India,* 23 September 2000.
3. *Central Asian Quarterly,* Vol. 3, No. 4, 1996, p. 23.
4. Aloke Raj, *Uzbekistan Gantantra, Kamyabi Ka Safarnama,* Patna, 2001, pp. 8-9.
5. Aloke Raj, p. 17.
6. *The Hindu,* 30 August 2001.
7. Alok Raj, p. 5.
8. *The Hindu,* 31 August 2001.
9. *The Hindu,* 23 November 1995.
10. *Asian Age,* 9 February 2001.
11. *The Hindu,* 29 April 2001.
12. *The Hindu,* 5 January 2001.
13. *The Hindu,* 6 January 2001.
14. *The Central Asian Quarterly* Vol. 3, No. 4, 1996, p. 5.
15. *The Times of India,* 19.2.1998.
16. Contemporary *Central Asia,* Vol. III, No. 1, 1999.
17. *Ibid.,* pp. 1-2.
18. Aloke Raj, p. 2.
19. *The Hindu,* 26 May 2001.
20. *The Hindu,*15 June 2001.
21. *The Hindu,*15 June 2001.
22. *The Hindu,* 17 July 200.
23. *Ibid.*
24. *The Hindu,* 12 August 2000.
25. *The Hindu,* November 2000.
26. *The Hindu,* 6 September 2001.
27. *The Hindu,* 11 September 2000.
28. *The Hindu,* 29 April 2001.
29. *The Hindu,* 29 April 2001.
30. *The Times of India,* 15 February 2001.
31. *The Hindu,* 11 May 2001.
32. *The Hindu,* 11 May 2001.
33. *The Hindu,* 11 July 2001.
34. *The Hindu,* 26 October 2001.
35. *The Hindu,* 3 February 2003.
36. *The Hindu,* 21 October 2002.

37. *The Hindu,* 7 November 2002.
38. *The Hindu,* 25 December 2002.
39. *The Hindu,* 27 January 2003.
40. *The Hindu,* 2 February 2002.
41. *The Times of India,* Patna, 25 June 2003.
42. Press Release, Dushanbe, 17 November 2003.
43. *Indo-Asian News Service,* 14 November 2003.
44. *The Hindu,* 23 June 2003.
45. *The Hindu,* 24 June 2003.
46. *The Hindu,* 17 October 2003.

15

South Asia and Pan-Asian Cooperation

D.R. Goyal

As India arrived on the threshold of independence, leaders of India's freedom struggle set about defining their role in international affairs. Jawaharlal Nehru declared India's resolve to keep away from bloc politics because the mentality behind it had plunged the world into two wars, within quarter of a century, and 'could again lead to disasters on a vast scale'. He warned the nations, freshly awakened into independence that once "foreign relations go out of your hands into the charge of somebody else, to that extent and in that measure you are not independent.... So our policy will continue to be not only to keep aloof from alignments, but try to make friendly cooperation possible. We approach the whole world on a friendly basis."[1]

That thinking was the result of his understanding of Gandhi. Nehru's view was that he was "for a vast majority of Indian people" wrote he, "he is the symbol of India determined to be free, of militant nationalism, of a refusal to submit to arrogant might, of anything involving national dishonour." Gandhi was also a symbol of the new nationalism; which was free from arrogance and avarice for subjugating others. He wanted India to be in the forefront of freedom struggles of other peoples and disliked the idea of his country being responsible for subjugating others.

The world today is face to face with the situation that Nehru had visualised in those days. End of Cold War, consequent on the collapse of Soviet misadventure in Afghanistan, had brought tremendous relief to humanity at large. It was hoped that international politics would move from confrontation to cooperation, turning the focus from pactomania to collective effort, towards banishing poverty, disease and cultural backwardness; the resources of the world would be deployed for human welfare rather than being wasted on developing weapons of mass destruction. But, alas, the fond dream soon turned to be a nightmare as had the dream of four decades earlier, the one dreamt at the end of World War II, in 1945. That is why Nehru's response inevitably to that situation comes to mind. Can we draw some lessons from, not only his words but actions to get out of this impasse? Let us therefore look at that.

POST-WORLD WAR II SCENE

At that time, the victors had proclaimed that the war against Hitler's Germany and Tojo's Japan was intended to end forever the threat of racist fascism and promote democracy and human rights in the world. The intentions were institutionalised in the form of United Nations Organisation, whose charter declared its objective was "to save future generations from the scourge of war" and to improve the quality of life all over the globe. Under its auspices, institutions were created to reduce the threat from nuclear weapons, to end racism, to promote human rights, to reduce mass poverty and hunger, to protect cultural heritage etc., etc.

Despite these high-sounding intentions and lofty goals, the multiple imperialism of pre-war period was replaced by two major powers which began to divide the world in order to build their spheres of influence. USA, the self-proclaimed land of freedom, that had once revolted against the British overlordship, adopted the role of earlier European imperialists and began to enlist the newly independent nations of Asia, Africa and Latin America to serve its strategic interests to dominate the globe. On the other side emerged the Soviet Union which began to compete with this American bloc by forging its own bloc. Thus, the world began to be divided between two conflicting power blocs and the logic of confrontation took its toll of human values.

In that situation the altruistic ideals of creating a brave new world of peace and freedom was forgotten. The strategies to surpass the rival blocs, in terms of assured destruction, led to prioritising war materials to welfare measures; leaders on both sides seemed to have adopted the Nazi slogan that had eulogised bullets over bread and butter. The independence of nations began to be circumscribed in the name of ideologies, in an effort to win more and more adherents. Forgotten were the ideals of saving the world from racist hatred and establishing an international regime, based on equality and freedom of nations, as also to save the world from the 'scourge of war'.

The United Nations Organisation, the international institution created for the purpose, was sought to be converted into the instrument of the US and its allies, with the veto right to the rival power as a mere concession. As a result, it either succumbed to the US pressure or was left paralysed. The phenomenon was seen manifest in the thwarting of struggle against Apartheid in South Africa, in promoting Zionist racism against the just demand for a state of Palestine and rights of Arabs within the territory of Israel. Communist China's entry into the world body was wilfully delayed and theworld economy made subservient to dollar. Anglo-American conspiracy plunged the Indo-Pak subcontinent into an unending and totally wasteful conflict over the so-called Kashmir dispute, ignoring the democratic secular aspirations of the Kashmiris who had, hand in hand with the freedom fighters of India, struggled against feudal autocracy, just to serve the designs of the Anglo-American combine in the Great Game they had been playing in Central Asia.

The war between the power blocs got averted because of the fear of mutual destruction, but small wars were triggered in different parts of the world, in which the newly independent countries were embroiled. The wars compelled the countries concerned to build their respective arsenals which boosted the military-industrial complex of the big powers and seriously damaged the process of socio-economic reconstruction that the newly independent countries aspired to undertake. The result was that the people who had broken the imperialist stranglehold again became dependent on the old imperialism. The supposed era of independence became a huge illusion.

It is relevant to recall the sad story, partly because the complications caused in that process are still lingering and more because the new situation has assumed a more sinister aspect in the absence of a countervailing force to check the arrogant shenanigans of the new superpower. The dream, induced by the end of Cold war, was shattered as the world witnessed the rise of a new hegemon, the United States. It emerged as the unchallenged superpower, drunk with its military and economic power which it thought could bend the nations of the world to its will. Just as several new nations fell to the illusions and allurements, put on offer by the bloc chiefs, at that time today most of the world succumbing to the defeatist idea that there is no alternative than to surrendering its superior might and accept its agenda.

WASHINGTON'S DUBIOUS ROLE

When the Cold War ended, Washington establishment declared its political aim as promotion of democracy and replacing centrally controlled economic system by free market. No questions were raised as to why it was patronising feudal autocracies and militarist regimes in different parts of the world? Or, why it was supporting tyranny of terrorist Israel that had been trampling under foot the legitimate national rights of Palestinians and brazenly defying scores of UN resolutions? Nor was the 'free market' prescription sought to be rationally explained, not at least till it brought disaster on those who took to it with alacrity.

After 9/11, the call from Washington has gone out to all to fall in line with its strategy against terrorism. Again it remained unquestioned as to why the modern scourge had not registered on its mind before that, though several other countries, India and Israel in particular, were facing it for decades prior to that heinous crime?

Rulers in Washington were also not asked to explain whether they regretted the use of the same forces, which they describe as terrorism during Cold War period and why they continued to hug the same elements till they displayed the temerity to subject the US embassies in Africa to bombing. Why don't they realise that Israeli actions are breeding more terrorists in the Arab world? They are ignoring the rogue state's misdeeds even though it is creating problems for its own friends in Middle East. They helped Saddam Hussain's war against Iran just because it had put an end to Reza Shah's monarchy that had usurped the country from Mosaddeq's democracy. And, it is punishing Iraqis for crimes of Saddam because he showed the guts to support Palestinian resistance more than any other Arab regime.

The entire record hardly shows concern for democracy or earnestness about the war against terrorism. Otherwise action against Taliban and Al-Qaeda and consolidating a democratic alternative should not have been left in the hands of Pakistan. Ignoring the fact as to how Gen. Musharraf has been playing ducks and drakes with democracy how its role in harbouring terrorists that have been a menace to its neighbourhood and the world at large, its role in proliferation of nuclear weapons, Musharraf's Pakistan has been proclaimed to be the 'closest non-Nato ally'. Is it because it opted to do America's job against Afghan extremists? Or, is it because Gen. Musharraf can turn round and remind Washington that whatever it has been doing has always been at the bidding of Washington?

The approach to economic development is similar to the one reflected in the case of promoting democracy and curbing terrorism, that is, the operation fits into overall US ambition to dominate the nations of the world. So, the theories are floated about limitations of nationalism in a situation where time and distance have been overcome by technological development, especially in the field of information technolology.

Whereas the market strategy in economy is being found wanting for egalitarian development, nationally as well as internationally, the recent US military operations in Afghanistan and Iraq have rung alarm bells all over the world and regional combinations are emerging in different parts of the globe to defend national sovereignties as also to arrest the unilateralism, increasingly evident in US actions.

The motivation behind these actions has been discovered in the report submitted by a Commission for 'Strategic Energy Policy Challenges for 21st Century' appointed when Bush senior occupied the White House. The report advised following line of action:

(a) The nation's oil policy, foreign policy and defence policy are converging.
(b) Iraq remains a destabilising influence.......... to the flow of oil to international markets from the Middle East. Saddam has also demonstrated the willingness to use the oil weapon and to use his export programme to manipulate oil markets.
(c) The US should conduct an immediate policy review towards Iraq including military, energy, economic and political/diplomatic assessments.... The US should then develop an integrated strategy with key allies in Europe and Asia, and with key countries in the Middle East to restate goals with respect to Iraqi policy and to restore a cohesive coalition of key allies.

History is witness to the policy towards Iraq adopted since those years marked by the end of Cold War. It was a prelude to what has now happened to Saddam and Iraq. On the eve of invasion of Iraq, Colin Powell, the head of State Department under Bush junior, had testified before the Senate Foreign Relations Committee that overthrow of Saddam regime could "fundamentally reshape the map of the Middle East in ways that could enhance US interests." This has been achieved and is now being followed up with pressure against Syria, Iran and Libya with the perspective of Greater Middle East initiative which is significantly silent about a just peace between Israel and Palestinian authority. Those who are supposed to be affected by the proposal, sought to be endorsed by G-8 in coming June, have created a storm of protest throughout the Arab world.

ROLE OF ASIA

What role can Asia play and what would building Asia mean as a remedy for this impasse, this high-handedness of a superpower in unipolar world that has presumed that it has the responsibility and power to reshape the world order closest to its own heart's desire?

The answer can be found in the various initiatives taken by the Asian nations then facing the problem of defending and consolidating their newly acquired sovereignties. Today that problem is facing almost the entire globe; as is evident from US action in Iraq after bypassing the United Nations.

Newly independent India then, despite the unfortunate setback to its aspirations, was full of idealistic energy and ideas about rebuilding human relations on the basis of cooperation rather than conflict and confrontation. Gandhi's message was still ringing in the minds of men of goodwill. According to Einstein, Gandhi was humanity's answer to the nuclear bomb. His successful struggle against the brutal might of British imperialism with mass mobilisation on the basis of non-violence, had opened new vistas for rearranging human affairs. Under his leadership, Jawaharlal had declared that India's struggle was a part of world-wide struggle for freedom. It was an echo of the assertion of Maulana Azad that loss of communal unity would not be the loss of India alone but of entire humanity.

Full of such lofty ideas, India took the initiative to convene an Asian Relations Conference in New Delhi, in March 1947. It was attended by delegates from China. Egypt and Western Asian Arab countries, Iran, Indonesia, Indo-China, Turkey, Korea, Mongolia, Siam, Malaya, Phillippines, the Soviet Republics of Asia, Afghanistan, Tibet, Bhutan, Nepal and Ceylon (Sri Lanka). There were also observers from as far as New Zealand. The idea, in the words of Jawahar Lal, was to confer with fellow Asians "about the present and the future, and lay the foundation of our mutual progress, well being and friendship".

That initiative was misinterpreted in Europe and America as 'some kind of a Pan-Asian movement' directed against non-Asians. It was a repetition of the British accusation against those Muslims who were struggling to free their countries from their stranglehold. Nehru's response to it was: "For too long have we of Asia been petitioners in western courts and chancelleries. That story must now belong to the past. We propose to stand on our own legs and to cooperate with all others who are prepared to cooperate with us. We do not intend to be the plaything of others."

The Indian leader had spelt out the spirit behind the conference in the following words:

> "In this crisis in world history Asia will necessarily play a vital role. The countries of Asia can no longer be used as pawns by others; they are bound to have their own policies in the world affairs. Europe and America have contributed greatly to human progress and for that we must yield them praise and honour, and learn from them the many lessons they have to teach. But the West has also driven us to wars and conflicts without numbers, and even now, the day after a terrible war, there is talk of further wars in the atomic age that is upon us. In this atomic age Asia will have to function effectively in the maintenance of

peace. Indeed, there is today conflict in many countries, and all of us in Asia are full of our own troubles."[1]

Reiterating his stand during India's freedom struggle, he asserted:

> "We seek no narrow nationalism. Nationalism has a place in each country and should be fostered, but it must not be allowed to become aggressive and come in the way of international development.... The freedom that we envisage is not to be confined to this nation or that or to a particular people, but must spread out over the whole human race. That universal human freedom also cannot be based on the supremacy of any particular class. It must be the freedom of common man everywhere and full opportunities for him to develop."

CHANGE IN CONCEPTUAL FRAMEWORK

Author quoted Nehru at some length knowing well that the dominant forces in the world have made Nehru-baiting a favourite pastime. Nehru does not need defence, because his ideas remain crucially relevant for defence of national sovereignties and progress of all the newly independent countries. The votaries of the 'end of ideology' thesis dismiss him as motivated by Marxist ideology, as it was practised in Soviet Union that tends to make the role of state supreme in human affairs. Careful reading of his above statement, as also the planned economy he ushered, contradicts this view because he talks of 'freedom of common man' and 'full opportunities for him to develop'. It is, of course closer to the ideal of Marx but is certainly different from the practice in Soviet state, though it was claimed to be Marxist; Nehru has clearly spoken of his aversion to 'supremacy of any particular class' whereas the Soviet Union believed in the supremacy of the 'working class'.

Nehru's Marxist proclivity was tampered by Gandhi's insistence on primacy of man which meant providing opportunity of growth to all, irrespective of class, with the proviso that the opportunity should not be used to circumscribe the realisation of others' potential; indeed his test of a strategy of development was how it helped the last man, the poorest to come up. The idea was to make the process of development painless.

With these ideals before him he interacted with leaders of Asia and Africa, individually and collectively, first at Bandung and then at Belgrade. The effort culminated in the founding of Non-Aligned Movement (NAM) which was pooh-poohed as trade union of underdeveloped countries. It is noteworthy that the movement, at the outset, steered itself clear of ideological differences becoming a hurdle to cooperation on issues of vital interest to humanity. The critics did not realise that, though economically yet to be developed, the Asians possessed a wealth of philosophical treasures that gave them confidence and the grit to stand on their own legs and, in fact, significantly influence developments in the international sphere.

The controllers of contemporary international discourse may not agree but it is a fact that NAM became a major force for peace and disarmament. It inhibited the power blocs from confronting nations with threats of war, much less of nuclear war. Whatever steps they took , were taken in the name of peace. As such, probably for the first time in world history, war-making was not treated as a matter of pride or credit. Its slogan of disarmament may not have compelled the possessors of weapons of mass destruction to give up their endeavours to build more and more lethal arsenals but it did create a moral climate that pulled the confrontationists back from the precipice. The end of Apartheid in South Africa goes entirely to the credit of NAM.

Despite very limited success in achieving the goals, it set before itself, there is no gainsaying that it has left behind a cultural legacy which prevents even successful war-mongers from taking pride in their achievements. The most outstanding example of this is the documentary on American foreign policy, *The Fog of War,* which focusses on the career of Robert McNamara. The film by Errol Morris has recently won the 'Best documentary' Oscar. Its great merit is presentation of McNamara through interviews in which he appears regretting his role in the World War II, in Cuban crisis of 1962 and in America's Vietnam war.

About his role in World War he says that, had the Allies lost, he would have been prosecuted as a war criminal, because his fire-bombing strategy killed nearly a million Japanese civilians, including 1,00,000 in Tokyo in a single night. At the time of Cuban crisis of 1962, he was Secretary of Defence in the Kennedy Administration. A minor official in State Department had persuaded Kennedy to adopt a conciliatory approach in dealing with Khrushchev. In this context, McNamara says in the film "From October 16 to 28, 1962 we literally looked down a gun barrel into nuclear war. We lucked out; luck prevented nuclear war."

On Vietnam, McNamara does not appear a hawk. He had, in fact counselled Kennedy to pull out American military advisers out which he was about to do when he was assassinated. Kennedy's successor Johnson wanted to build his politics on punishing the Vietnamese for defiance of the American might. In the film McNamara makes a sensational revelation that the Tonkin Gulf incident, which was the excuse given for carpet bombing, never actually happened. In the film, McNamara concludes his interview saying, "The human race needs to think about conflict. Is this what we want in the 21st century?"

It is a fair question to which Nehru's words indicate the answer. His role at that time does not have to be repeated because the environment has changed from bipolarity to unipolarity. The threat today is not clash of power blocs but of one power holding humanity to ransom with its attitude 'if you are not with us you are the enemy'. India's role in late forties and early fifties calls upon it to mobilise the protesting forces for a fair and just, world order.

Hope had been seen by perceptive observers in the then Prime Minister Vajpayee's efforts to act on Nehru's adage that one can chose friends but not neighbours. His efforts to put back bitter confrontation with Pakistan and China and usher an era of cooperation seemed to be bearing fruit. Apprehensions are however expressed that the current India-Pakistan bonhomie is the result of US pressure, because both the neighbours are tending to vie with one another to curry favour with Washington. It is necessary to undertake such initiatives independently because, as Nehru had pointed out, 'too close an embrace of a power like the US can be suffocating'. This danger has to be understood by both and can be averted if they place their relationship in the perspective of mutual needs and advantages and in the larger perspective of Asia.

Nehru had the disadvantage of a hostile Pakistan backed to the hilt by the Western bloc. Vajpayee was free from that disadvantage and had the additional advantage of the cordiality between the two neighbours being welcomed and encouraged all over. India has already taken steps to coordinate policies with the countries of South East Asia, Africa and Latin America. With Russia it has revived traditional relations of cooperation. This can be expanded to other countries of Europe because they also share the apprehensions about US designs.

The climate is propitious because there are no signs of efforts to build an anti-US bloc but to persuade the policy makers in Washington to get out of the 'American interests first' syndrome and think of its national interest in terms of wider human interest so that others can share its perspectives without fear of losing their identity.

REFERENCE

1. Inaugural Speech, March 27, 1947.

16

Eurasia Calling

Significance of Cooperation in a Changing World

P.L. Dash

The peace time birth of several independent and sovereign states, on the debris of the communist system, implied that their future role in the shape of things to come, in the region is likely to remain significant for a long time to come. The larger countries continued to focus on smaller countries, and contours of reality slowly unfolding in each of them, watched avidly how these newly independent countries progressed in their path to democracy and nation building; and finally what role they could possibly play in the post-Cold War structure of international relations. In the past decade, such jockeying of bigger and smaller states, is nowhere better evident than in Eurasia. Aside from the attention paid by states, truly stunning is the treatment given by the scholarly world to the study of post-communist society in the countries of Eurasia. By now, fourteen years after the Soviet break-up, the research output on problems facing Eurasia on different problems constitutes a sizeable literature in the realm of knowledge. Similarly the problems of facing an unexpected transition unprepared and grappling with a prolonged political, economic and social instability without any structured agenda are as stunning as they are uniquely bewildering. The epicenter of attention has, therefore, truly shifted from Cold War rivalry between the two big powers to post Cold War competition and cooperation among big and small states of Eurasia.

While events of cataclysmic importance such as the Soviet disunion and 9/11 conditioned Eurasia in a fashion never seen before. What singled out the region, as a territorial entity, was the emergence of China and India in a big way to play tangible regional and global role as independent actors. This was happening, when Russia was recuperating from the shocks of collapse, and parallel to the dwindling role of Russia, there were evidences of growing importance of the USA, particularly after 9/11. The primary US attention was focused on China, secondarily on Russia and tertiary attention was paid to India. In order to circumvent a resource rich area such as Central Asia, the concerned countries of the region, as well as the US, quickly realized the importance of the area lying between east of the Black Sea and west of the Tienshan mountains. Within the Eurasian landmass, all three Asias — West Asia, Central Asia and South Asia-suddenly became important in the US scheme of things for a variety of reasons. While contiguous countries of the region did not lose their sight of a looming US importance, the inevitability of their increasing role and growing importance placed them either in rival position vis-à-vis the US or conditioned them to play a subsuming role to largely safeguard the American interest. Within the ambit of a this study, a modest attempt has been made to throw light on the growing importance of Central Asian states and the role of China, Russia and India in the changing context of conflict and cooperation as well as to assess the US role in the region in the aftermath of 9/11.

CENTRALITY OF CENTRAL ASIA

As a single geo-cultural space, Central Asia has remained a compact region over centuries, that has assimilated into itself multicultural ethos of world civilizations. As a geo-political entity, history had witnessed Central Asia providing meeting points and battle grounds to many conquerors from east and the west alike. In the post-Cold War scenario, Central Asia has become an arena of competition among many interested powers for its geo-economics. The abundance of natural and mineral resources and the colossal deposits of natural gas and oil in Caspian basin have been central not only to Central Asia, but to many a country attracted to the region to gain a foothold. However, each country pursues its interests in its own way: Turkey for a common cultural space, Russia for not allowing the region to slip in to the sphere of influence of other countries, China for materializing her economic and strategic objectives, the USA for balancing out Sino-Russian influence in the region and projecting its own objectives of democracy building and Pakistan for buffeting a wave of Islamic renaissance. The relationship of each of these countries with Central Asia was voluminous and deserved special scholarly treatment. However, what remained of utmost importance to us, for a variety of reasons, was how Central Asia has remained central to India; and this requires a brief analysis.

Firstly, Central Asia was central to India for strategic reasons. The Soviet break-up had as much altered the security scenario in the region as it did in India's north. Need arose to gauge the strategic depth of Central Asia, in the changing context, and it is in this backdrop that India began assessing her pursuits. For India, the appearance of five independent countries in her northern neighborhood dramatically altered the existing equations. The political and ethnic volatility prevailing in Central Asia through the 1990s enhanced India's security concerns in the north, and evidently these concerns included the tenuous ties, still emerging with the new states. Amidst worries, India, somehow, felt that her security horizon was broadened from the north of Kashmir to the north of Kazakhstan. Secondly, the geographic location of Central Asia is central to India. It is from this area that conquests were undertaken by invaders in the past. An unstable neighborhood is unwelcome and the area in constant ferment may threaten national interests of all countries in the region. Thirdly, political developments in the surrounding neighborhood were central to India. Developments in Afghanistan and Pakistan were of sinister import. An Indian aeroplane was hijacked to Kabul, that led to the release of a hard-core terrorist from Indian prison, and the released terrorist drove down from Kabul to Pakistan in full view of the world on television. The whole event was politically unpalatable and diplomatically unprecedented. It cast a morose shadow on the morale of Indian security forces and such incidents threatened to spill over to Central Asia too.

Fourthly, the resource potential of the Central Asian countries was central to India. Rich in oil and gas, gold and other minerals, the Central Asian countries were an alluring area of emerging commerce. They kindled shining hopes for future, and India being one of the major countries in the neighborhood, was naturally interested in expanding commercial ties with Central Asia. Fifthly, Central Asia's sixty million people are central to Indian business community. They provide a sizeable market for Indian export. As traditional Indian gift items were popular from the Soviet era, India was expected to harvest yield from commercial transactions. Everyone celebrates birthday and should occasion arise for sixty million people to buy one item each as gift on birthdays, and that too an Indian item, the magnitude of sale would be expectedly high. Sixthly, the secular ethos of these new states was central to India. The neighboring countries were aflame with radical Islam and apprehensions abound that fundamentalist Islam may spread to Central Asia. Over the years when Central Asia demarcated between Islamic revivalism in the social and religious contexts and radical Islam in the political context, the secular ethos evinced a sort of contemporaneous approach to Islam, that India and Central Asian states espoused.

Seventhly, Central Asia's response to globalization is central to India. It was a closed economy in the Soviet era and has not eschewed state control completely.

In a complementary sense, the marketizing economy and democratizing polity in Central Asian countries may like to learn from the Indian experience in reforming their economy. Eighthly, viable regimes that could ensure political stability in Central Asia, is central to India. Although the degree and level of democratic reforms have varied from one country to another in the region, by and large, the same regimes have been continuing in power in Central Asia for the past 13 years. Their attitude to India has remained warm, positive and friendly, providing a fecund ground for bilateral ties to prosper.

Ninthly, in the aftermath of 9/11, the demonstrative interest of the USA in Central Asian military bases is central to India. The Manas airbase in Kirgyzstan is leased to the USA, where, varying reports say that some 800 to 3,000 troops are stationed.[1] Similarly at the Khanabad airbase in Uzbekistan, some 1,700 US troops are located. Given that Russia has leased out the Kant base from Kirgyzstan some 180 kilometers away from Bishkek and Russian troops are there in Tajikistan, the regional juxtaposition of these troops seems relevant in the changing context. Further added to this picture is the sizeable US military involvement in Afghanistan, Pakistan and Iraq that enhances the worry, making Central Asia central to all in the neighborhood, including India.

Further central to India is the role Central Asian countries are likely to play, as a bridge between Russia and India in bilateral and trilateral trade, commerce and security relations. The paradigm shift that the region has followed in the past decade in embracing those countries traditionally inimical to Russia tells us a tale of probable military rivalry in future. The form of rivalry may be different, but the content would remain the same and that would not only affect India exclusively, but also other countries too. It would remain central to India's diplomatic interest as to how smaller countries of Central Asia evolve a foreign and security policy pattern to accommodate interests of bigger countries, such as Russia, China, India, the USA and others, in the years to come.

The eleventh factor central to India is the nascent Central Asian national armies. Inevitable for their defence in each country, the genesis and growth of these armies have been slow, lopsidedly dependent on Russia and varied in their degree of preparedness in each country. India has been training officer cadres for some of these countries at the National Defence Academy in Khadakvasla and may pursue a proactive policy of helping Central Asia build national defence systems. The twelfth factor of centrality of the region to India remains inherent in the two magnificent corridors of communication linkages being talked about. The North-South corridor and the Eurasian Continental Bridge would be the lifeline of communication linkages in the future. However, keeping aside, what the future would entail, the existing cross-country road network along the Old Silk Route could easily be harnessed, should there be only political commitment to peaceable communication between Pakistan and India. The related moorings of all these twelve dimensions of centrality of Central Asia's location put the region on a high pedestal of cross-country competition, big and small, all afield in one game. Competing powers evince their interest in Central Asia and this itself puts the region into limelight and centrality.

EMERGING CHINA

As Asian countries begin to play their weighty role in Eurasian affairs, China singles out itself as a major player in all scheme of things as much in Eurasia as in the Asia Pacific. The incredible economic growth of China, in the past one and half decades, has stunned all other countries. What makes China an attractive destination for foreign investment is the fact that it has successfully sustained an economic growth of 7-9 per cent since 1987, occasionally even higher, and has successfully blended communist control with emerging capitalism. Over the passage of time into future, as demands for skilled manpower would steadily grow, the two Asian demographic giants-India and China-would be the precious centers of supplying human resources. Asia already accounts for 70 per cent of the world's population or more than 3.5 billion people, likely to grow to 5.7 billion by 2050.[2] Of these 3.5 billion, nearly 2.5 billion live in China and India. While European and North American demographic figures will not substantially change from the current data of just 1 billion population, there will be a remarkable shift in manpower management. Home to 1.3 billion people, one fifth of the world's population, China has successfully demonstrated as how to overcome the lingering shadows of poverty and how to combat pessimism, with determination to grow and branch out.

The most populous nation on earth has also the largest army, the PLA, and the fastest growing economy. Although a major revision in military policy was brought about in the last decade, it has left its imprint on the armed forces, implying that they need to be more professional than they were earlier under Deng Tsiao Ping. Taking into account the "experience of 1979 border war with Vietnam and observation of the Gulf conflict in 1991, the PLA has been numerically slimmed from 4.2 million men in 1985 to 2.9 million in 1996"[3] It is also a nuclear power, one of the permanent members of the UN Security Council, with a veto power, and has an area of 3,705,820 square miles, just falling short by 11,976 square miles of the USA. China has several attributes to attract tourists, business and laymen alike, like a magnet. And it indeed does attract. A brief, comparative analysis of assets and performances of the two neighbours—China and India, provides glaring gap between the two and also why China is preferred over India. China's GDP of $1.2 trillion and per capita income of $1100 are more than double of India's. Its foreign exchange reserves of $285 billion is thrice more than India's, it exports annually goods worth of $280 billion, which is five times more than India's, Its Foreign Direct Investment of $45 billion are ten times higher than what India has been able to attract.[4] A combination of all these factors makes Chinese market huge in respect of all products, at least 3-4 times the size of the Indian market. Regulated flow of FDI, flexible investment environment supervised by the state and inexpensive labour market taken together have made China as one of the major investment destinations in Eurasia, at the turn of the century.

Armed with all its inherent qualities and cozy with easy money flowing from foreign lands and Chinese diaspora, China has posed a virtual challenge to its big neighbours, both Russia and India in every parameter of growth. China's increasing influence in Eurasia is also a challenging factor for many, including the USA. These challenges are visible in three clear dimensions: infrastructure development in surface communication and technology, persuasive diplomacy in a changing environment and economic and commercial contacts with countries from far and near alike. In the realm of expanding surface communication network, a shinning example that becomes visible in modern China is her ever growing railway network in near inaccessible regions of her far west. In recent years it has built a 1,400 kilometer long rail line between Xingxiang capital Urumqi and Kashgar.[5] This is a major linkage of mainland China with Xingxiang, and a viable route of commerce between China and adjacent Central Asia. In fact, China has been laying "between 600 to 1,000 kilometers of new track every year, a construction rate faster than America's at the height of its rail boom".[6]

While China's vision of communication encompasses "wheels of steel" from Singapore to London by 2010, a major obstacle facing mainland China is the lack of connectivity via Central Asia to the Soviet era rail network. China is well connected with the Trans-Siberian railway line in three directions: from Shengyang via Changchun to Harbin and Vladivostok in the far eastern sector, from Beijing via Ulanbator in Mongolia to Irkutsk in the middle sector and from Zhengzhan via Urumqui to Perm in the expansive western sector. However, it requires a rail link between Kashgar and Jalal-Abad and in the middle of this sector comes 3,752 meter Turugart Pass of the Tien Shan. Preliminary engineering studies done by the Kirgyz railway ministry has estimated that such a rail line would have 28 tunnels and 42 bridges and would cost of $2.9 billion.[7] This line would be China's exclusive gateway to Central Asia and enable China to completely bypass Russia and could largely sidestep Kazakhstan. For the energy security of China in future, this line will be of paramount importance because it could carry oil from Tehran and gas from Turkmenistan to remote areas of western China.

Secondly, the proactive and persuasive diplomacy is the currency China has been using to buy friendship in the past decade. It has actively involved itself in three major fora: the APEC, the Shanghai Five and the project called Eurasian Continental Bridge — all multilateral platforms of cooperation, all viable forms of interaction in recent memories and all within the framework of a globalizing, integrating world, where boundaries seem disappearing. China's adroit diplomacy also includes having good relations with the neighbours, ensuring peace in the fissiparous ethnic pocket of Xingxiang and Tibet and expanding national interests beyond boundaries. In order to achieve her objectives, China has been ardently pursuing bilateral, trilateral and multilateral course of diplomacy.

In the APEC, a 21-member body of nations from east and west alike with a combined GDP of $16 trillion dollars in 1998 and 42 per cent of global trade, leaders have been discussing issues of mutual benefits since 1989, the year of establishment of the organization.[8] Soon after APEC charted its economic objectives in the Blake Island summit hosted by former US President Bill Clinton, in November, 1993, it is over a decade now that its leaders have been regularly meeting to discuss nitty-gritty of free trade issues in the Asia Pacific and how it would benefit the economic growth of the region. Similarly, in the Shanghai Five, a regional forum with China, Russia, Kazakhstan, Kirgyzstan and Tajikistan as members that originated in Shanghai in April,1996, China has been playing a proactive role to moderate her objectives, mainly to iron out border issues.[9] Since all member countries share a border of 7,000 kilometers, a forum such as the Shanghai Five, has allayed mutual fear of armed hostility and added to the confidence building among themselves. Within the framework of the forum and acting on a bilateral platform, China has persuaded its neighbours, particularly in Central Asia, about the futility of separatism in Xingxiang province and has obtained diplomatic assurances from them that they would not protect, harbour or encourage separatists, espousing the cause of united Uyghurstan.

Thirdly, the Eurasian Continental Bridge is an off-shoot of China's prudent economic diplomacy of the past decade. Aimed at connecting Qinhuangdao harbour in far eastern China with Rotterdam in the Netherlands, this 10,800 kilometer land-sea-land transportation bridge would be a life supporting transportation system for thirty countries of Eurasia. This would be a shorter line than the existing trans-Siberian rail and is likely to cut cost by 20 per cent, time by half and distance by 2,000 kilometers. This will provide the Chinese market easy accessibility to Eurasia, to market their goods and other countries and vice versa. China has therefore been looking to put a viable transportation system in place for the benefit of her future. The growing economic potential and increasing diplomatic and political influence that China has been acquiring in recent years precipitate her aggressive penetration not only westward to

Central Asia but also eastward to the other areas. In the South China sea, China has virtually regained control over the Paracel Islands from Vietnam in 1974 and has subsequently built an airfield there. It has acquired the Mischief Reef too, from the Philippines in 1996. It also contests sovereignty over Spratly Islands with Vietnam, the Philippines, Malaysia and Brunei and has disputes with Japan over Senkaku, a string of island in the East China Sea which the Chinese call Diaoyu.[10]

This growing economic, political and diplomatic influence, however, comes to China at a price. And the price of growth is ecological disaster and environmental degradation across China. Bad air quality has caused nearly two million deaths in the past decade. China has been witnessing unseen pollution –heavy metals and noxious chemicals from factories, fouling the water in China's major rivers. Two thirds of China's major cities are seriously short of clean water. Acrid plumes from factories bellow into the azure sky, making it perennially hazy. As Chinese are becoming wealthier, they consume more meat, leaving the animal waste and livestock remnants into rivers and lakes, turning them from blue to green and resulting in eutrophication and suffocation of fish that in turn, harms human health. A revealing depiction of "China's Growing Pain" of ecological disaster has been recently published in the National Geographic.[11] In any case China remains a post of attraction in Eurasia never to be ignored in foreseeable future.

RUSSIA'S FAR EAST

Although the pangs of transition continue to haunt Russia all through these years, Russia under Putin has been trying to assert her role in the changing geo-political and geo-economic environment in her Far Eastern periphery. A country that was expanding for centuries since the time of Peter the Great found itself suddenly nonplussed when it faced the stark realities of shrinkage, stemming from the Soviet disintegration. The aftermath was interesting. In her foreign and security policy realms, Russia was on the horns of a dilemma, toeing the line of three pressure groups: radicals, occidentals and Orientals. Those, who looked radical, wished Russian foreign relations to be framed on the lines of empire building. Headed by Vladimir Zhirinovsky, they wanted Russian soldiers to "wash their boots in the warm waters of the Indian Ocean",[12] an impractical proposition at a time of sagging image and nagging difficulties. The other group was represented by Andrei Kozyrev, Yeltsin's foreign minister, who looked at the occident for resolving Russia's problems, forgetting that Russia was unique in evolving its seminal ethos to future; albeit through dismay and difficulties. This was once again a policy doomed to death and within just five years into that policy, Russia felt dejected with her experiment of Euro-Atlantic approach. Opposed to these two was a third one, more pragmatic and more balanced. Headed by the foreign minister turned Premier, Evgenyi Primakov, this group looked at the orient to reaffirm Russia as a Eurasian power and revive her shrunken image. Beginning January, 1996 and since, Eurasian policy postures have even handedly balanced out Russian approach, to the east and the west alike.[13] While not entirely overlooking the occident, it has never ignored the orient, too. This policy postulate implies that in the Eurasian context, Russia's relations with China, Japan and India are particularly important, while it admits to the porosity of her 'near abroad' as a soft underbelly. It is worthwhile in this backdrop, to deal with Russia as a Far Eastern power of far reaching importance.

Russia's resource potentials in the Far Eastern sector presupposes a tangible role for the country to harness them in the national interest. A vast swathe of 6.2 million square kilometers of landmass, rich in gold, diamond, oil, coal, gas, timber and several other useful industrial raw materials, the Russian Far East is more than one third of the area of the Russian Federation. The region's natural and mineral endowment strikingly contrasts with its sparse population: only 7 per cent of Russia's population live there. Emigration statistics of the past decade reveal that most of the population settled in the region, through material inducement of the state, had left lock, stock and barrel to European Russia for permanent settlement. and that has reduced the Far East population by 10 per cent of what it was in 1989. Low birth rate and high mortality rate are two other factors that provide a bleak picture to the extant reality of depopulation.

In the Far East, demography is not Russia's asset, the real assets are its wealthy disposition in oil, gas, gold and diamond. Demography hurls as much of problems as insalubrious weather conditions, a disturbingly destabilizing tendency for future depletion of population that may cause alarm. Imagine the contrast: on 6.2 million square kilometers of land inhibit only 8 million Russian citizens with wealth that lay unexplored. And across the southern border, on 2 million square kilometers of Chinese territory, live 130 million Chinese citizens, 30 times more densely than those live in the Russian Far East. There is likely to be regular interaction across the border, however, full-proof you make it. As a result, reasonable estimates say that there is already a sizeable Chinese population numbering between 20,000 to 1,00,000, living in the Russian Far East[14] Boris Yeltsin had admitted in April,1996 that there were 1,80,000 illegal migrants, mostly Chinese, living in the Khabarovsk territory alone. In the southern districts of Far East, the Chinese migrants are estimated to be around 2 million.[15] This clearly implies that the two areas of distinct demographic contrast will be subjected to greater mobility of labour. Russia would require workforce that Chinese would supply. And Chinese would need jobs that Russia would supply.

And this demand and supply game would concretely boil down to ensuring the energy security of the region. China has a growing demand for oil and gas that would increase with the passage of the years and Russia could supply it through new pipelines. Similarly, Russian demand for consumer goods could be met entirely by China in that area. Even if both countries do not change to market capitalism, their barter could prevail over mutual deals that can be called "oil for food and goods". Thus pipeline connectivity is likely to be the future bond of Sino-Russian relations in the Far East, inasmuch as it would cater to huge market of China, Japan and the Korean peninsula and be the principal source of energy supply for them.

Currently, China imports about half of her oil requirements from the Middle East. Its native infrastructure of coal based energy is not only outdated and expensive, but also environmentally hazardous. It would certainly prefer a market closer to home. Similarly, Japan imports 99.5 per cent of her energy requirements, and it would prefer a market nearer home. Russia's Far Eastern reserves, mostly untapped, is a blessing in disguise for both of them. However, what impedes the transaction is the absence of pipelines to supply gas and oil to these up-market economies. After a decade long negotiations and considerable study of feasibility, the Chinese National Petroleum Company and Russia's YUKOS had signed an agreement, in May 2003, to build a $2.5 billion worth pipeline along a stretch of 2,400 kilometers from Angrsk near Irkutsk to Daqing in China with a view to transport to China 5 billion barrels of Russian oil between 2005 and 2030. This would effectively increase daily Russian export to China from 40,000 barrels per day now to 6,00,000 barrels then.[16]

The Russo-Japanese pipeline deals are still rosier, which Putin considered worth pursuing. This would be a pipeline of $4.5 billion built entirely on the Russian territory from Irkustsk to Nakhodka that could provide an outlet to Russian oil supply to the entire Asia pacific. Japan is so hospitable to the idea that it has kept the obvious future in sight, and after Angarsk-Daqing deal was inked, it offered Russia a $ 7 billion low interest credit to develop its Siberian oil fields. While plenty of feasibility studies have focused attention on the Caspian oil reserves in recent years, there has been comparatively little spadework on feasibility of exploiting Siberian oil. The Chinese and Japanese initiatives are really forward looking in their nature. Apart from the inherent interest that China, Russia and Japan display as beneficiaries to lay Russian oil and gas pipelines of the future, others too have commerce in their far-sightedness. British Petroleum, Shell, Sidanko and Rosneftegazstroi have undertaken various projects, some viable and others unviable, to market Russian oil and gas in Chinese and Japanese markets. In November, 1997 British Petroleum took a 10 per cent share in Sidanko and also a 40 per cent holding in Sidanko's 60 per cent interest in Russia to develop Kovyktinskoe gas condensate field. Estimated by BP to have a reserve of 700 billion cm of gas, Koviktinskoe will require $10 billion to be in production line in ten years time in order to supply gas to China, Japan and Korea.[17]

As gradually becoming clear, Russian engagement in oil and gas exploration in the Far East in collaboration with interested partners is likely to increase, in the years to come. West Siberian basin remains core of Russia's oil industry, providing the country 70 per cent of its national output. Russia has developed offshore fields of Sakhalin for export, too.[18] However, east of lake Baikal right up to Sakhalin provides a vast panorama of unexplored oil and gas fields awaiting exploration. Inclement weather combined with hostile nature often makes the area inaccessible. In any case, Russia cannot ignore the energy requirements of China, Japan and Korea as much as these countries cannot ignore the source of energy available at their doorstep. The more the demands for energy, the greater will be the prerequisite for mutual collaboration.

Among the various maps, charts and plans that circulate in the realm of energy politics in the post Soviet space, Russia's Far East assumes significance because of two reasons: the potential of the reserve and proximity to potential markets. The Far East pipeline politics has attracted relatively less attention of analysts and researchers than the Caspian. However, there have been concerted efforts to join Russian and Caspian pipeline network, so that it benefits the energy consumers in China and Japan. Firstly, US oil company Exxon, Japan's Mitsubishi and China's National Petroleum Company had conducted a feasibility study on the 8,000 kilometer long gas pipeline that starts from Turkmenbashi, runs through Uzbekistan, Kazakhstan and China and thus connecting Japan with Turkmenistan.[19] This mega project of the future will not only benefit the producers and consumers of oil, but also bring transit tariff to countries that allowed oil and gas to be piped on their territory. Secondly, important for the Asia-Pacific energy sector are the tangible efforts made to pipe Kazakh oil from its Tengiz and Aktyubinsk fields to Xingxiang in western China and from there via mainland China to the Koreas. Besides, China too has a huge a market for oil and gas. There are four proposed pipelines that connect Russia with China and Japan: (i) from Irkutsk to Beijing via Ulan Bator; (ii) From the west of Beijing, a branch line travels toward the Koreas; (iii) Angarsk is connected to Daqing in Manchuria and (iv) The existing pipeline from Komsomolsk travels via Sakhalin peninsula to Hokkaido, in northern Japan.[20]

Thus, looking closely at Central Asia and Caspian, as a pocket of energy rich and cash poor strip of land, plus the Russian Far East in abject poverty as an additional pocket plus the vast landmass of reformed China as a third pocket, it seems probable that the process of globalization will bring demand and supply of energy to the fore and countries of the region will have enough commonalities to interact. With Japan being the only developed economy in the area, this mutual interests and dependence on one another will compel each of these countries to ensure greater responsiveness to each other's requirements. Political and economic activities will shift theater to where energy reserves could be exploited and this is certainly likely to be Eurasia with engagement of such influential countries as China, Russia, the USA, Japan and India. It is for the first time, after the Soviet disunion and for the first time in this century, that so many countries are vying with one another to take advantage of the regional frailties vis-a-vis fabulous resource endowment.

THE INDIAN ENIGMA

The economic liberalization process initiated by the Narasimha Rao government in the early 1990s was almost coincidental with the Soviet collapse. The ills of socialist management methods were coming to the fore. India's reform measures to move away from the License Raj, toward a more open economy, soon began paying dividends. By the mid 1990s, it was clear that major countries of Eurasian region were marketising their economies; while the world in general was globalizing; and India did not wish to lag behind in this inevitable process of transformation. Transformation of India's economy was further essential because her geographic location, demographic size and strategic importance were a mismatch with her economic ability, denying her the rightful economic role to play in the region. It is the largest country in South Asia with a billion plus population. Yet her regional economic role remained largely confined to the SAARC. As the century was approaching its close and the world was changing fast, the future of each country was becoming uncertain and their economic and political role remained undefined. In such a situation, India undertook her cautious recourse to economic reforms that blended her traditions with modernity. Soon it became an investment target because it was a huge market. As sector after sector opened up to competition, subsidies were slashed and inducements were given to industry and entrepreneurs to compete with free market forces.

However, India is a country of contrasts. Its urban rural divide is amazing. It uses the archaic mode of transport like bullock carts as well as modern jets. Its industries produce low cost goods for millions of poor and high cost quality products for the affluent. In the ladder of prosperity, it has at the apex states such as Goa, Punjab and Maharashtra and at the nadir Bihar and Orissa. It has high-tech hospitals in mega cities and dilapidated primary health centers across the countryside. It has prestigious technological and management institutes such as the IITs and IIMs and thousands of rural engineering and management colleges.

However, what makes India a strategic investment target is the size of her market, the untapped sectors of her economy, the high potential of human resource availability, resource-rich states, and to back it all, cadres savvy with English language that provide them a gateway to the world. In the rapidly changing post-Cold War scenario, while combination of all these attributes remained a rarity, what made India conspicuous in South Asia is her growing influence in the subcontinent, her traditional wisdom prevailing in foreign and security policies and her increasing regional stature. The possibility of an expanding market, in hitherto less accessed areas, is what allures the foreign investors. For instance, take the banking sector: despite a phenomenal growth in banking activities, 65 per cent of the Indian householders are yet to open a bank account and that itself is an indicator of future expansion of the banking sector. Take the automobile sector: despite traffic clogged roads in metropolitan cities, only 6 per cent urban families have a car as against 13 per cent in Delhi, the highest in the country. And this implies that the market potentials are high in auto industry too. Similarly, only 23 per cent urban families have telephones as against 4 per cent in rural India, and that itself suggests a huge market opportunity in telecom sector.[21] Similarly, the housing sector, service sector, agriculture and many other areas are optimistically looking upward for progress. Future possibilities, combined with crimson hopes for palmy days ahead, is what makes India a strategic destination of great economic activities.

All these gave India the aura to assert her diplomatic and political clout in South Asia, talk about venturing into Central Asia, make a strategic triangle with other two regional giants in Eurasia-Russia and China and play a possible conduit in resolving the Afghan imbroglio. On her part, India also could not remain a mute spectator to what has all been happening in her neighborhood. Cross-border terrorism continued to wreck havoc in Jammu and Kashmir. The forces of destabilization attacked the legislature of that state and the Parliament of the country to vent their rage on democratic institutions. Kargil happened and subsequent negotiations with Pakistan failed in Agra, All this while, infiltration continued its tresspass on Indian territory. Hopes were dwindling about a probable cease-fire. In such a situation, 9/11 completely altered the regional security scenario, when the US decided in favour of deeper engagement in Indo-Pak relations, sometimes even overtly supporting India, and often aligning with Pakistan. The situation entailed a saga of different tastes unknown in the fifty plus years of Indo-US relations. Thus, the emerging new India, an India at the beginning of the 21st century, ought to be viewed in the changing regional context rather than in isolation.

As India emerges as an important power, it encounters a set of interrelated hurdles, primarily stemming from her western neighborhood. The relations with

Pakistan through all these years have weltered in the tides of time and have largely remained strained, cross-border terrorism has continued and the issues remain unresolved, instability in Afghanistan has enhanced drug trafficking and money laundering, growing influence of Islamic forces in Pakistan and that of regional war lords in different Afghan pockets have kept the region volatile. The active US involvement in Afghanistan, Pakistan, Iraq and her leasing out of military bases in Central Asia have enhanced apprehensions about future US role in the region. Countries such as India and the US, India and Russia, China and Russia have entered into partnership of uncertain duration, pronouncing joint objectives and a desire to work together, but finally nothing tangible has come about, apparently implying that partnership does not bear early first. However, post 9/11 issues bind India and the US as never before: terrorism and nuclear proliferation, both originating from Pakistan and their regional implications for South Asia.

While Pakistan continues to remain in limelight as a pronounced non-NATO ally of the US, India and the US have both combined their efforts to combat these twin evils of modern times. Both countries have emphasized on improved Indo-US ties. Views of both countries are synonymous about building a democratic civil society in Pakistan, the Indo-US approach to global terrorism rhymes together with desire of many other states, particularly those, who have been victims of terrorist outrage in recent years. It seems as if common platforms, common paradigms and common approaches drive Indo-US motives in the post 9/11, save that of Iraq. Will these two democracies of the world be able to downsize the menace of terror? The efforts need to be concentrated not entirely on geographic Eurasia, not necessarily on Indo-Pakistani ties, not exactly on Afghanistan or Iraq or Pakistan; but on a different plain in the entire Islamic world on eliminating the yawning gap between the haves and the have-nots, between the rulers and their subjects and between the Mullahs and the modern world. Better education and a civil society will be an anathema to the ills plaguing the Islamic world.

CONCLUSIONS

The developments of recent years remain incredible in many a sense. When Europe was following integration of the European Union and the US was pursing globalization, the former Soviet land witnessed disunion and disintegration. Meanwhile, the former communist countries passed through unprecedented transformations, but continuously reaffirming their faith in "unity in diversity" and "unity is strength" as a result of which many regional organizations emerged, transformed and transmuted themselves to demonstrate their proactive role.[22] All these regional organizations have been concerned with security, terrorism, mutual economic cooperation, political and diplomatic collaboration and economic integration. Economy has now assumed a larger role than earlier. The growth of China and India and the revival of Russia indicate that their Eurasian significance is vital and they hold the lever to future prosperity. While oil and hydro carbon wealth of the Caspian region gives them hope about an alternative arrangement in place, the US presence in the region gives them apprehensions and sleeplessness as much as rising Islamism. Except Russia, China and India, shaky regimes rule all round and their political volatility is an explosive factor for the economic health of the region. The situation is very much likely to continue, and bilateral and trilateral cooperation would continue to overwhelm the region in importance, amidst raging disputes and conflicts.

REFERENCES

1. Charles William Maynes, America Discovers Central Asia, *Foreign Affairs*, Vol. 82, p. 122. Also see *Mid Day*, 3 May, 2003, p. 8.
2. Fareed Zakaria, As Asia Rises, 'ASIA' Falls, *News Week International*, July-September, 2001, Special Edition Issues *Asia*, p. 6.
3. The growing Importance of China as a Regional and World Power, Background Brief, Foreign and Commonwealth Office, London, September, 1997, p. 5.
4. Rohit Saran, Can India Challenge China? *India Today*, 30 June, 2003, p. 50.
5. *The Economist*, 12 February, 2000, p. 30.
6. George Wehrfritz, The Orient Express, *News Week Special Edition*, July-September, 2001, p. 35.
7. *Ibid*, p. 35, Also refer to the map at pp. 30-31.
8. P.L. Dash, Russia in the Asia Pacific: Evolving Pattern of Relations, *Indian Journal of Strategic Studies*, Vol. XXIV, 2003, Allahabad, p. 4.
9. News from China, 1 May, 1996, p. 6.
10. The Growing Importance of China, *op. cit.*, p. 5.
11. Jasper Becker, China's Growing Pains, *National Geographic*, March, 2004, pp. 68-91.
12. Vladimir Zhirinovsky, Posledneyi Brosok Na Yug, LDP Publication, Moscow, 1993, p. 113. (In Russian)
13. For an exhaustive discussion, please refer to N.I.Atolskoy, Russkii Uzel' *Euroaziiastva: Bostok v Russkoi Mysli*, Belovogie Publishers, Moscow, 1997. (In Russian)
14. Rajan Menon, The Sick Man of Russia, *The National Interests*, Fall, 2003, p. 102.
15. Background Brief; Population Movements on the Countries of the Commonwealth of Independent States, Foreign and Commonwealth Office, London, July, 1996, p. 2.
16. Rajan Menon, *op. cit.*, p. 100.
17. Fred Thackeray, The Only way Out, Petroleum, *Economist*, August, 1998, p. 33.

18. *The Economist*, 15 November, 1997, p. 69.
19. *Summary of World Broadcast*, SWB-I SUW/0563, WE-2,20 November, 1988.
20. Russia Energy Survey — 2002, International Energy Agency in Cooperation with Energy Charter, Paris, 2002, p. 14. (please refer to the maps).
21. For the first time, Census of India conducted a household amenities and assets survey that revealed some amazing findings. For a lucid presentation with commentaries, Please see, Rohit Saran, India Today, 28 July, 2003, pp. 34-42.

    Apart from the Commonwealth of Independent States (CIS), there are other regional organizations such as Eurasian Economic Community (EEC) which was earlier Custosm Union with Russia and Belarus, Central Asian Cooperation Organization (CACO) earlier known as Central Asian Economic Community, the 56-member Organization of Islamic Conference (OIC), Central Asia Regional Economic Cooperation (CAREC) that includes countries such as Mongolia, Azerbaijan, China's Xingxiang (Turkmenistan is likely to join) Shanghai Cooperation Council (SCO), A group of poor countries in the CIS called (CIS-7) that includes Armenia, Azerbaijan, Georgia, Kirgyzstan, Moldova, Tajikistan and Uzbekistan, (GUUAM) Georgia, Uzbekistan, Ukraine, Azerbaijan and Moldova and Asia-Pacific Economic Community (APEC).

17

India-Russia Strategic Partnership

Implications for Common Security of Asia

R.S. Yadav*

The end of Cold War has led to the transformations and restructuring of International system in substantial form. Two developments in the form of emerging unilateralism in global politics and globalization in economic sphere have emerged as outstanding features of the post-1990s world order. These changes are not only related to the relations among the major actors, but have also affected the foreign relations of numerous states. Being no exception, India -Russia relations are also affected in a significant way by these developments. Both are coping with the emerging strategic and economic situations owing to the fallouts of these catastrophic events. Both have started on a hesitant note due to their new engagements and reorientations of their foreign relations, in general, and building new bridges with the only superpower, in particular. At bilateral levels, relations between them in a substantial way must have economic bearings as both are passing through the process of structural reforms in their domestic affairs. However, the legacy of past relations between the two, alongwith multiple developments of global and regional levels, circumscribed them to engage with each other in mutual cooperation and ultimately led to strategic partnership. This strategic partnership is not confined to their bilateral interests only but has regional and global ramifications, too. Countries of Asia will be affected both in terms of their security and development by this new situation. Since these twin forces are working simultaneously and are of interdependent nature, these are bound to have significant implications for this continent. The present study is a modest endeavour to find out the impact of these bilateral ties in the context of Asian developments.

Before analyzing the development and implications of strategic partnership between India and Russia, it is necessary at the outset to spell out concept of 'strategic partnership' and 'Common Security'.

Strategic Partnership

Indo-Russian relations in the post-cold war era have started in the form of 'strategic cooperation' and are moving in the direction of 'strategic partnership'. If these two terms are to be understood it becomes clear that 'strategic partnership' concept is more wider and comprehensive than strategic cooperation. In case of the latter, it would "imply a more proximate exchange and cooperation of views by both countries to the common challenges posed in the economic, political and security spheres."[1] Strategic partnership, on the other hand, would "imply a relationship which would not only incorporate strategic cooperation but also an added emphasis on converting the strategic convergences between the two nations into more meaningful defence and security cooperation.... In other words an evolving alliance relationship, but short of it"[2]. Thus, the countries involved in a strategic partnership have to be "mutually interested in long-term economic, military, technological cooperation with similar, if not identical, security threats and perceptions of the coming world order."[3] India-Russia emerging ties to a great extent are not only interested in developing their bilateral economic, political and military relationships, but are also based on their common perceptions about the future of Asia and the world. To a great extent Moscow-New Delhi relationships meet the requirements of the above definition due to following reasons:

(i) India-Russia economic and political relations are on an upward swing.
(ii) Defence cooperation between the two is gaining strength day by day.
(iii) There is a broad identity of views between the two countries on the basic regional and global issues.
(iv) The gap between the views of India and Russia on the issue of nuclear non-proliferation is not so wide and can be bridged or at least appreciably narrowed down.
(v) There are obvious parallels in the security challenges faced by the two countries.
(vi) Emerging convergence on security matters between the two is more akin to the idea of common security in Asia.

(vii) In the context of globalization, liberalization and privatization both are not only facing the similar problems but are sharing common perceptions to get rid of the adversial impacts of these phenomena.

Thus, the emerging strategic partnership between India and Russia is not limited to defence cooperation between the two, but is rather involved in a more comprehensive outlook of cooperation among these states. Besides, it is based on the convergence of their perceptions about the future of Asia and emerging world order. Finally, this partnership is not against any third state, rather it is devised as a means to regulate the regional and global international affairs so as to preserve peace and stability in their region and the world.

Common Security

The concept of 'common security' could be visualized in the context of emerging threats of unilateralism, in the post-cold war era. The theoretical underpinnings of this concept have been derived from "Independent Commission on Disarmament and Security Issue" (ICDSI) or popularly known as Palme Commission of 1982,[4] underlining the need of the "commitment of mutual survival". It is stressed that "nations must come to understand that the maintenance of world peace must be given a higher priority than the assertion of their own ideological and political positions."[5] The call for common security, thus was clearly a political counter move to the prevalence of unilateralism. It was a plea to restore the legitimacy of negotiated solutions, bilateral and multilateral.

To operationalize the idea of common security the practice of collective solutions must be followed. According to Vayrynen, these solutions have three basic ingredients which together form a kind of alternative — C^3, i.e., Communication, confidence, cooperation.[6] Primary requirement for the development of common security is the establishment of smooth communication among both the countries and understanding of interpretation of similar communication by both of them. This communication is pre-requisite for the growth of confidence among states. CBMs are associated with the predictability of activities by potential adversaries and with the reassurance of their non-aggressive intentions. Such reassurances can either be verbal commitments to peaceful behaviour or concrete action of restraining and reducing military capabilities and interventionist policies. Finally, cooperation refers to functional exchanges to increase the interdependence between the states. These steps obviously lead to the strengthening of bilateral ties and at the same time help in the growth of common perceptions between the two about the outside world.

Consequently, Indo-Russian building of communications, CBMs and finally cooperation among them will not only strengthen/re-vigorate their earlier ties, but it would lead to convergence of their mutual perceptions in regard to regional and global concerns. In this context, the region of Asia is bound to emerge as an area of concern for both the states. Hence, common security for Asia and development for this region are likely to be affected significantly by the enhanced Indo-Russia ties.

In the post-cold war era, Indo-Russian relations started on a low profile, as Russia was busy in developing a balanced approach in South Asia. Besides, due to continued pragmatism of Gorbachev era, Indian sub-continent still occupies one of the last place in the list of Russian foreign policy priorities. This was very much evident from the "Concept of Russian Federation's Foreign Policy" released in the end of 1992. Though visits of Bourbolous (Secretary of State) and Yevgany Primakov (Head of Russian Intelligence Service) have brought out some sort of reconsiderations on the part of Russia. However, a "new beginning" of the process of change started only after the visit of President Yeltsin to India in January 1993. Signing of 10 agreements, including the Treaty of Friendship and Cooperation, and resolving the long pending issue of debt repayment between the two normalized their ties and tilted Russia's balance in South Asia in favour of India.

The period between 1993-96 could be considered as a turning point for emerging strategic cooperation between the two as it laid down the trajectory for Indo-Russian strategic partnership. This change has been caused by the exchange of visits by the important dignitaries of both the countries during this period — President Boris Yeltsin (1993), Prime Minister Viktor Chernomyrdin (1994), Foreign Minister Yevgeny Primakov (1996 March and December) from the Russian side; and Prime Minister P.V. Narsimha Rao (1994), External Affairs Minister Pranab Mukherjee (1995 May and August) from the Indian side. Besides this, numerous parliamentary delegations paid mutual visits during this period. Moreover, the period of 1993-1995 can be regarded as turning point in Russia's national development. Russia was disenchanted with its pro-Western approach in its foreign policy. "The hasty and thoughtless westernization of the country led to the political crisis of Spring-Autumn 1993, resulting in an attempt of stage a Coup d' et at the beginning of October. The elections to the Duma showed that nationalist feelings and disenchantment with the West was gathering momentum among the political elite."[7] Finally, the Yeltsin-Kozyrev tilt towards West was over visualizing America's policies towards the eastward expansion of NATO.[8] The changes in Russian foreign policy towards India became more significant with the coming of Yevgeny Parimakov as Foreign Minister in January 1996.

The above changed context, along with the treaty of Friendship and Cooperation of 28 January 1993; Declaration of Further Development and Enhancement of Cooperation of 30 June 1994; and the Moscow Declaration on the Protection of Interests of Pluralistic States of 30 June 1994 worked as important factors in building strategic relationship between the two countries.[9] However, Russian Prime Minister Yevgeny Primakov's visit to India, after the Pokhran II, from 20-22 December 1998, strengthened their cooperation further. Because during this visit, besides signing of 7-agreements between them, both agreed on long term strategic cooperation, recognizing India's position on Kashmir and endorsement of its claim for the permanent seat of the UN Security Council.[10]

The formal 'Strategic partnership' agreement between India and Russia was signed during the visit of Russian President Putin to India, in 2000.[11] This has taken India-Russian ties to new heights. It has significantly contributed to the further deepening of the strategic dimensions of relations between the two countries by conclusion of ten agreements, including defence deals worth 3 billion dollars. The declaration proclaims the "establishment of relations of strategic partnership between them based on mutual understanding and long term confidence in each other" and envisages the "elevation of their multifaceted ties to an even higher and a qualitatively new level" by imparting them a "specially close and dynamic character both in the bilateral field and in the international arena"[12]. The preamble of the declaration refers to the "conviction that it is necessary to build a multi-polar global structure based on sovereign equality of all states and peoples" and "desire to jointly contribute to the strengthening of international peace and security as well as to the promotion of the establishment of a new, just and stable world order....[13] This development of partnership has not only enhanced the multi-faceted cooperation between them, but has also influenced the prospects for common security in Asia. The improvement or strengthening of their bilateral ties is manifested through their changing relations in following areas.

Defence Cooperation

Despite the disintegration of erstwhile USSR, India and Russia are still major partners in defence deals. Three levels of defence cooperation continue to prevail between the two countries — (a) supply of arms by Russia; (b) helping India in the production of nuclear energy; and, (c) institutionalization of defence deals. In 1991, India was dependent in a big way on Soviet arms — 65 per cent for its army; 80 per cent for its airforce; and 85 per cent for its navy. This is still continuing, either in the form of supply of spares for the old Soviet arms or purchase of new technologically advanced weapons.[14] For the supply of weapons India and Russia signed numerous MOUs during the visits of Primakov (1998), Putin (2000), Vajpayee (2001), George Fernandes (2003) etc. for building long term strategic partnership up to 2010. Russia is the main supplier of MIG-AT Jet Traver; SU-30, MIG-27, MIG-29 Fighter air craft. Kamov-31 and Kamov-28 helicopters; 300-T Tanks; 4TU-22M3 Backfire Strategic bombers; Akula class nuclear submarines; and, finally Gorshkov aircraft career to India.

India-Russia defence relations strengthened with their cooperation in the nuclear field. Earlier Soviet Union had supplied nuclear fuel for Tarapur nuclear plant, despite the protests from the United States. Later Rajiv Gandhi-Gorbachev agreed to set up two nuclear power plants of 1,000 megawatt capacity each at Kudankulam, in 1988. But it was actually implemented only with the Soviet assistance after the signing of agreement with Russia in 1998 during the Primakov's visit to New Delhi. It has been viewed by experts that the Indian nuclear power engineering market is estimated to be $30 billion, of which Russia is competing with the French and American companies to acquire a major share. Besides, India is planning to raise its level of production of nuclear power from 2,000 to 6,000 megawatt by 2010 and subsequently to 20,000 megawatt by 2020.[15] In this scenario, possibility of large share of Russia can not be ruled out at present.

For long term defence cooperation, mere supply of arms will not be sufficient, rather an institutional framework between the two is needed. Both countries are aware of this fact. Consequently, Russia is not only selling arms to India but is also providing technology for its reproduction, either independently or through joint ventures. Both the countries are also engaged in the setting up of such joint ventures in Third countries, as well. The protocol signed in Moscow by Defence Minister George Fernandes on 17 January 2003 is a significant land mark in the Indo-Russian Military-Technical Cooperation. Now India is involved in the Russian programme for development of a fifth generation combat aircraft and plans to set up joint ventures in defence industry patterned after Indo-Russian Brahmos Company for production and marketing of supersonic cruise missiles. These joint venture will yield benefit for both the defence and civilian sectors in both India and Russia.[16] Thus Russia has not only cooperated towards the requisition of India's need for arms and supply of spares, but both have also well adapted themselves with the changing needs of globalization and privatization. Besides, both have not looked at their cooperation from the narrow perspective of mutual security, but are very much orienting themselves to the changed context of regional and global milieu.

Political Understanding

The above partnership is the product of emerging political understanding among them on numerous bilateral, regional and global issues. This is evident from the fact that in recent past important leaders of both countries visited each other, e.g. President Vladmir Putin (2000 and 2002), Defence Minister Igor Ivanov (2002), and Prime Minister Vajpayee (2001 and 2003) and Defence Minister George Fernandes (2003) etc. These visits signify the emerging commonalities between India and Russia on issues of vital interests. In this changed context both are sharing their perceptions on the problems of strengthening the United Nations, new world order, democratization of the international organization, improvement in global financial institutions, security and stability in Central Asian Republics, nuclear non-proliferations etc. Besides, India and Russia are making a common effort to do away with the problem of international terrorism. This has become all the more important in the wake of crisis in Afghanistan and 9/11 September event in the United States. However, the terrorist activities in Kashmir and Chechnya provided a sound bond for common approach toward this menace. Indian and Russian initiatives in 2000, in the United Nation's Security Council, is a proof for such thinking. Even this fact has been reiterated in the strategic partnership document where both agreed on their concerted efforts to "fight against international terrorism, separatism, organized crime and illegal trafficking in narcotics."[17]

India and Russia are building their partnership through improvement of their relations with China. And both acknowledge that a 'strategic triangle' among India-Russia-China is required to promote peace and stability in Asia. Prime Minister Primakov's remarks on this issue during his visit to New Delhi in 1998 could be visualized in this context. Though India did not accepted this idea in an explicit manner. But both are individually making efforts to improve their bilateral ties with China. The simultaneous visits of President Putin to China and India in December 2002 has been considered a step forward in the direction of consolidation of ties between the three. To some extent this could also be inferred from the similarities found between the declarations of Beijing and New Delhi, issued after the visit of President Putin. All the three hold similar views on various international issues including terrorism, Iraq, West Asia, Afghanistan, developments in Central Asian Republics, role of United Nations and the regional security.[18]

India and Russia also share common perception regarding the peace, stability and development of Central Asian Republics (CARs). If Russia is worried about this region because of its close neighbourhood, then India is also very much concerned, due to likely spill over impact it is going to have in this country. On the issue of terrorism, Islamic fundamentalism and political instability, in this region, both India and Russia are equally worried. Both are keenly watching the competitive -influence-building attempts by the outside powers in this geo-strategically volatile region. The availability of oil around Caspian Sea, terrorist activities in Afghanistan with its linkages in Tajikistan, Islamic fundamentalist resurgence and its support from the neighbouring states etc. have brought both India and Russia closer to each others' foreign policy initiatives in this region. Though, a regional cooperation organization—Shanghai Cooperation Organisation (SCO) with the support of Russia and China has been formed, but Putin is continuously making efforts to engage India into this organization. Thus, strategic partnership has enhanced and strengthened sound political understanding between the two countries.

Economic Cooperation

Though economic factor has acquired primacy in the post-cold war global politics, yet the Indo-Russian partnership could not grow to the level of their cooperation in defence and political areas. This is evident from Indo-Russian trade and joint ventures run by both the countries. A look at the Indo-Russian trade statistics given below reveals this factor in a more explicit manner.

Table 1: Indo-Russian Trade, 1993-94 to 2001-02[19]

(Indian million US$)

Year	*Indian Exports*	*% of Indian Exports*	*Indian Imports*	*% of Indian Trade Total*	*Total Trade*	*% of Indian Trade*
1993-94	648.60	2.92	256.89	1.10	945.49	1.98
1994-95	807.38	3.07	504.54	1.76	1311.92	2.39
1995-96	1046.55	3.29	857.53	2.33	1904.09	2.78
1996-97	811.84	2.42	628.96	1.16	1440.80	1.98
1997-98	954.12	2.72	679.02	1.63	1633.14	2.13
1998-99	706.26	2.14	545.42	1.29	1254.68	1.66
1999-2K	948.99	2.58	623.94	1.25	1572.93	1.82
2000-01	869.93	1.97	517.19	1.03	1387.12	1.47
2001-02	796.83	1.82	538.36	1.05	1332.19	1.41

If a close look of the above table is made then it could be discerned that volume of India-Russia trade is not significant. Approximately their bilateral trade is 1.5 per cent of the total trade with Russia. India's share of import and export is nearly 1 per cent and 2 per cent, respectively. This has become all the more difficult due to non-existence of proper banking, financial institutions, convertible currency etc. between them. Moreover, the demand for hard currency for their mutual export-import, is another serious problem between the two. Additionally, India has to pay 1 billion US $ annually to Russia as a part of its payment for debt up to 2005, followed by a smaller amount till next 33 years. The economic situation became more critical due to a weekly auction of rupee debt fund by the Vnesheconombank (Bank of Foreign Economic Affairs).

However, things are on an upward swing now as the governmental level Indo-Russian Inter-Governmental Commission on Trade, Economic, Scientific, Technological and Cultural Cooperation has been working towards promoting bilateral cooperation. It covers cooperation through 11-working groups, which ultimately are bound to influence their bilateral trade. Moreover, the recent agreement on Indo-Russian transport corridor may also help in enhancing bilateral trade by reducing transport costs. Present route, which passes through Suez Canal and enters into the Russian port of St. Petersburg via Kotka (Finland) and Rotterdam (Netherlands), is long and time consuming. The new route will be Mumbai-Bandar Abbas (Iran) — Astrakhan (Russia). Work is underway for construction of a 250 kilometer long railway line linking Bakdash on the Korobogozgol Bay on the Caspian Sea in Turkmenistan to Yeralievo in Kazakhstan. From Yeralievo to Russia the railway line is already functional, ships will carry the railway train across the Arabian Sea from the Persian Gulf port of Bandar Abbas.[20] However, by which time and to which extent this will boost their bilateral trade is difficult to infer at the moment.

Despite some problems in trade number of Indian public sector companies are actively working with the Russian companies. State Bank of India, Canara Bank, India Trade Promotion Organisation (ITPO), Tea Board of India and ONGC (Videsh) are actively collaborating with Russian Companies and government enterprises. ONGC (Videsh) is not only collaborating with the Russian oil company, but is also competing with the Japanese and American companies in Sakhalin oil exploration project. India has already invested approximately US $1.7 billion in this project and is likely to get oil to the tune of 2 to 4 million metric ton and 5 to 8 million cubic metre of gas annually. The only apprehension lies in the fact that this project is in the hands of the public sector companies, in both the states, which are progressively moving towards privatization. In that situation the fate of this project is very difficult to predict. Despite availability of different trade avenues, attempt towards diversification of trade, and successful working of some joint ventures in different areas, the certainty about strengthening of economic cooperation between the two is moving at a much much lower pace than expected and a situation of uncertainty still looms large.

The strategic partnership between India and Russia has not only enhanced multi-faceted cooperation between them, but has also significant implications for emerging new world order, in general and building up of a new Asia, in particular. It will have deep bearings for the adjoining regions, as well as, development of pan-Asian security in following ways:

(i) The end of cold war has led to the emergence of unipolarity in the world order through the assertive foreign policy followed by the United States. It has not only destabilized the regions adjoining India and Russia, but has also violated the very dictates of International organization. Happenings in Afghanistan and Iraq have questioned and marked the very functioning, and even existence of the United Nations. Thus, a concern for multipolarity in international system has been one of the considerations in building relations between India and Russia. The recent decision of Washington to designate Pakistan as a "major non-NATO ally" (MNNA) further justifies the need for reviving their earlier ties.

    While signing the strategic partnership agreement in 2000 both proceeded with the "conviction that it is necessary to build a multi-polar global structure based on sovereign equality of all states and peoples, democratic values and justice confirming their adherence to the common ideals of peace, democracy, rule of law, human rights and fundamental freedoms, non-violence and secularism....[21] and wish to "contribute to the strengthening of international peace and security, the democratization of international relations, as well as to the promotion of the establishment of a new, just and stable world order...."[22] This was reaffirmed by Prime Minister Atal Bihari Vajpayee's address to the Russian Science Academy (12 November 2003) when he observed that the Indo-Russian relations have helped us to "evolve a comprehensive vision" in "promoting peace, security and stability both in Asia and the world."[23] Consequently, both advocated for the establishment of a multi-polar world as it is an unavoidable trend for the benefit of world peace and opposed to any country seeking any kind of unilateralism and hegemonism in the post-cold war era.

    Hence, it is noteworthy that while highlighting 'Global Challenges and Threats to World Security and Stability' (13 November 2003) both stressed that: "United Nations Organisation has a vital role in tackling major international issues. The United Nations can and should be reformed to reflect the current realities, with a view to preserve and enhance its efficacy and efficiency."[24] Its reform, however, must presuppose respect for and observance of the UN Charter, instead of discarding or bypassing it. Though the above assertionism is similar to the earlier idea of 'common security' opposing unilateralism, yet this assertiveness is not in explicit opposition of the United States America.

Rather this time opposition was there through 'engagement and containment' of the USA, as well as, considering the USA as their cooperative partner in the world by both the states. In their relationship with the United States, though both proceed from their respective divergent national interests and different ways, yet hold the similar constructive stand point of avoiding confrontation.

(ii) Another, similar but related interest to be achieved through this partnership is the evolution of 'triangle for peace and prosperity' by involving China as their third partner.[25] Though it was not explicit, but some experts are of the view that indirectly that thinking was prevailing during Prime Minister Deva Gowda's visit to Moscow, in March 1997.[26] During that visit, despite NATO's meeting at Helsinki, Yeltsin had shown much warmth than expected and Russia devoted due attention to that visit. Besides, the simultaneous presence of Chinese Foreign Minister Quan Quichen in Moscow gave birth to the speculation about the emerging triangular cooperation between India, China and Russia. During Primakov's visit to New Delhi in 1998 this idea was formally put forward by Russia. This idea of "strategic triangle" was based on the commonlity of approach followed by three sides on a number of issues, such as:

(i) India-China relations in the changed context not only acknowledged but also reaffirming their firm conviction for the continuation of Panchsheel (five principles of peaceful coexistence). The broad similarity of it is found in Indo-Russian strategic partnership document as well; where it has been stated that this partnership is "based upon the principles of sovereignty, equality and territorial integrity of states, non-interference in their internal affairs, mutual respect and mutual benefit."[27]

(ii) The three are making bilateral or concerted efforts towards the establishment of multi-polar world order.

(iii) They are opposed to any kind of hegemonism and unilateralism and are not in favour of any kind of interference in domestic affairs in the name of human rights, democracy or any other such pretext.

(iv) Despite the difference of approach on the issue of nuclear non-proliferations in the context of NPT and CTBT, all are in favour of nuclear disarmament, as the ultimate goal for the world.

(v) They are in favour of strengthening of the United Nations as a mechanism for resolving international conflicts.

(vi) They are also in favour of the growth of new international economic order to cope with the advertial impact of globalisation on the developing countries.

These shared interests and identical approaches, viewed Kaushik, are likely to serve the three countries in achieving a successful break through in the direction of triangular cooperation. During the last few year some attempts in this direction have also been made by them. Modest beginning by India-Russia-China, in the form of informal meetings of foreign ministers of three countries during the UN session in 2002, is a clear manifestation of this initiative. Moreover, establishment of military bases in Central Asian Republics and Pakistan, during Afghanistan crisis, were looked with serious concern by all the three states. Besides, the apprehensions regarding destablization in the adjoining region is bringing out a common response from these states. Finally, the recent economic situations prevailing at global level is also a favourable development for the growth of strategic triangle between them.

(iii) Establishment of peace and stability in the Central Asian region has been an important factor in the foreign policies of India and Russia, due to their convergence of geo-political interests.[28] In the post-cold war period, the growing Islamic factor increasingly seeking to assume aggressive fundamentalist overtones in some of the Central Asian Republics and fueling secessionist movement in the Chechen Autonomous Republic of Russia, also impinges on the situation in India where a secessionist movement in Kashmir is being sustained through transborder terrorism. Talibanization of Afghanistan, Tajikistan and Pakistan has given birth to warlord culture or "Kalashnikov culture" which has emerged as a serious danger for the fragile ethnic mosaic of this region. Hence, the above onslaughts could create problem of stability and disorder in this proximate region of India and Russia.

Due to emerging globalization and liberalization, this region has also attracted attention of India and Russia. Availability of vast resources of oil and natural gas reserves have attracted the influence-building activities of advanced nations. Three states of Central Asian Republics (Kazakhistan, Turkmenistan and Uzbekistan) possess the world's largest oil fields and natural gas. Caspian Sea region is perceived as the Third largest area of oil after Persian Gulf and Siberia. Kazakhstan is also described as being on the way to becoming another Kuwait. Besides, different republics posses a significant quantity of resources of uranium, gold, silver, aluminium, cotton etc., which have implications beyond this region. Moreover, various MNCs are engaged in competition for the exploration of oil from the area. Important companies involved in this competion are Chevron (USA), British Gas (UK), Agip (Itlay), Elf-

Flaine (France), Lukoil (Russia), Gazprim (Russia), ONGC (Videsh) (India) etc.[29]

Existing multi-religious, multi-cultural, multi-lingual and multi-racial set up in India and pluralistic composition of Russian society brought about a convergence of interest between the two with the Central Asian Republics. Both the states favoured the continuation of plurality and multi-cultural system of governance in these republics. This conviction for plurality is well explicit from the 1994 "Moscow declaration on the Protection of the Interests of Plural States" signed by Boris Yeltsin and P.V. Narasimha Rao during the latter's visit to Russia. It criticized and condemned the "forces of aggressive nationalism, religious and political extremism, terrorism and separatism, which strike at the unity of pluralistic states" and urged the world community to respect and strengthen their territorial integrity.[30]

Thus, Central Asian Republics, due to its geo-strategic, geo-political and geo-economic linkages, provide convergence of interests between India and Russia. The latter is interested in the development of cooperation between India and the Central Asian states, as a means of counter balancing the influence of Central Asia of neighbouring Islamic countries, as well as the USA and other Western countries. India, for its part, is concerned to counter the influence of its arch-rival, Pakistan, in Central Asia, believing that Islamabad's close links with Central Asia would enable Pakistan to acquire strategic depth in any future war against India.[31]

(iv) Finally, threat of international terrorism in Asia has been another factor bringing the two countries closer and simultaneously affecting this region by way of their emerging partnership. India and Russia affirmed their belief for the "cooperation in the fight against international terrorism." It is because the development in Chechnya and Kashmir, along with the happenings in Afghanistan created a convergence of interest between the two. Both India and Russia also submitted their proposals to the UN on how to deal with this problem. Visualizing the gravity of the situations in their "Joint Declaration between India and Russia on Global Challenges and Threats to World Security and Stability" (13 November 2003) both have evolved "essential steps in effectively and comprehensively dealing with the threat of international terrorism"[32] as under:

- creation of environment for total rejection of terrorism and absolute unacceptability of any of its forms;
- consistent and uncompromising approach to terrorism and giving up "double standards";

- preventing the flow of funds for terrorist activities;
- effective implementation of the UNSC Resolution 1373 aimed against those who support, fund or abet terrorists or provide them shelter or asylum to engage in cross-border terrorism;
- promotion of confidence between members of the anti-terrorist coalition by, inter alia, due consideration of interests of each one of them and ensuring that the fight against terrorism is strictly based on rules of international law and principles of the UN Charter;
- reinforcing national and international legal instruments for countering terrorism, making the existing anti-terrorist conventions genuinely universal, and earliest completion of negotiations on the draft conventions in the UN, including the comprehensive convention against international terrorism submitted by India and the international convention on suppressions of the acts of nuclear terrorism submitted by the Russian Federation;
- steadfast cooperation to prevent terrorists from acquiring weapons of mass destruction, their means of delivery and materials and technology related to their manufacture;
- improvement of mechanism of legal assistance and extradition in order to ensure the inevitability of punishment for terrorist crimes;
- efforts to promote coexistence of different religions, cultures and civilizations by stressing greater mutual understanding and respect amongst them, especially the idea that terrorism can not be identified with any particular religion or ethnic group.[33]

The above concerted efforts made by both the countries are not only within their bi-lateral considerations, rather it encompasses a thinking about Asia and the world. Because happenings in the proximate regions of Russia and India are bound to have repercussions and destabilizing effects throughout Asia.

However, the emergence of common security of Asia is not easy to establish. There are number of theoretical and practical problems in the buildings of a secure and stable Asia. Theoretically, establishment of multipolar global order can not be visualized with the concurrence of the hyper power i.e. USA. Whereas through this partnership both India and Russia are engaging the USA in an accommodative role, yet it will be largely dependent upon the American response to this thinking. Similarly, some scholars are skeptical about the establishment of strategic triangle between India, Russia and China.[34] But some experts rule out such apprehensions.[35] However, it is certain that at this moment a consensus has been missing among the three countries on building of such partnership. Until and unless differences on major issues between them are resolved such development is rule out, for the present. Thus, Asian security will be dependent upon the development of common perception between India, China and Russia; and simultaneous accommodation of their interests by the USA.

Practically, there are certain problems which are of global nature, hence cannot be resolved by either the concerted efforts of India and Russia, or by the developing commonalities with other states of Asia. For instance, terrorism is a world wide phenomenon, having global roots and repercussions. Hence, India-Russia partnership alone can not resolve such issues without the support of world community. Similarly, peace and stability in the region of Central Asia can not be strengthened without the support of all the concerned powers. Besides, until and unless India and Russia are successful in their economic reforms and are able to strengthened their economies, building of a new Asia will continue to be adversely effected. Moreover, despite development of sound understanding between the two on some critical issues (i.e. nuclear non-proliferation), complete convergence between all the powers and major Asian states is required.

The convergence of interests and growing bilateral Indo-Russian relations — despite some bilateral and regional constraints — signify a strategic partnership between them encompassing multi-dimensional interests. Their relations in turn are bound to have positive implications for the development and security for Asia. Both India and Russia are opposed to unilateralism and hegemonism. They agree on the necessity of building a multi-polar global structure and are accordingly reorienting their relations in the context of the changed world order, by agreeing on common strategies to combat global and regional problems. They are adopting policies of accommodation in the region and are making efforts to reinforce the importance of national and international institutions. Their mutual relations encompass the interests and security of Asia and vice versa. This also portents a triangle for peace and security.

But it has to be accepted that common security for Asia can not be built without a multi-polar world order based on accommodation and acceptability to other major powers, especially the hyper power. Present efforts by India and Russia is a modest beginning to enhance their bilateral cooperation with another important Asian power, i.e. China. This effort, however, has neither been build in the form of an alliance or bloc, nor it is directed against any third state. Rather, it is being developed with a sense of accommodation with other important powers. Thus, a good beginning has been made by India and Russia in terms of strategic partnership, but efforts are required to strengthen the same to attain the goal of 'Common Security' with the help of other like minded states. However, success towards their duration will be dependent upon how far both can strengthen their economic and political systems to cope up with new realities; and how far their concerns are addressed by the other states in the region and by the only super power. If their experiment succeeds, despite minor differences, it will inevitably strengthen the forces working for the establishment of global peace. Hence, in present times a due consideration to this new thinking is not only essential but is also inevitable.

REFERENCE

1. Subash Kapila, "China's Quest for Strategic Cooperation with India: Perspectives", *South Asia Analysis Group*, Noida, Paper No. 936, 2004.
2. *Ibid.*
3. Artem Rudnitsky, "Russia and India: In Search of a New Strategy", *World Affairs*, Vol. 3, No. 2, April-June 1999, p. 82.
4. For basic tenets of the doctrine of Common Security see, ICDSI, *Common Security: A Blueprint for Survival,* New York, 1982; and Raimo Vayrynen, ed., *Policies for Common Security,* London, 1985.
5. On the debate of this approach see, Reinhard Mutz, *Common Security: Elements of an alternative to Deterrence Peace,* Hamburg University, 1986; Robert Axelrod, *The Evolution of Cooperation,* New York, 1984; Johan Galtung, *There are Alternatives: Four Roads to Peace and Security,* Nothingham, 1984; and *World Politics* (Special Issue), Vol. 38, No. 1, 1985.
6. Raimo Vayrynen, "Common Security: A Metaphor and an Incipient Doctrine", *World Futures,* Vol. 24, 1987, p. 179.
7. Rudnitsky, n. 3, p. 84.
8. For details regarding early foreign policy orientations of Russia see, Devendra Kaushik, "Commonwealth of Independent States and India," *International Studies,* Vol. 30, No. 2, April-June 1993.
9. For details see, Devendra Kaushik, "India and Russia in the Post-Cold War Period: Imperatives for Building a Strategic Relationship "in Lalit Manshingh, et al., *Indian Foreign Policy: Agenda for the 21st Century,* New Delhi, 1998, Vol. 2, pp. 291-98.
10. John Cherian, "Primakov's Visit", *Frontline,* 15 January 1999; and Baidya Bikash Basu, "Primakov's Visit", *Strategic Analysis,* Vol. 22, No. 11, February 1999. Also see, Jyotsana Bakshi, "Russia's Post-Pokhran Dilemma", *Strategic Analysis,* Vol. 22, No. 5, August 1998, pp. 721-36.
11. For the text of documents and critical appraisal see, "Indo-Russian Strategic Partnership for Enhanced Cooperation", *Strategic Digest,* Vol. 30, No. 11, November 2000, pp. 1154-56; "Visits of Mr Vladimir Putin, President of Russia, to India: Statements and Speeches", *Strategic Digest,* Vol. 30, No. 10, October 2000, pp. 1453-59; Devendra Kaushik, "India-Russia Relations New Prospects", *World Focus,* Vol. 24, No. 1 January 2003; Jyotsna Bakshi, "India-Russia: Strategic Partnership: President Putin's Visit", *Strategic Analysis,* Vol. 24. No. 8, November 2000, pp. 1539-44; and Baidya Bikash Basu, "Putin's Visit and Future of India-Russia Defence Cooperation", *Strategic Analysis,* Vol. 24, No. 9, September 200, pp. 1763-69.
12. *The Hindu,* 4 October 2000.

13. "Indo-Russian Strategic Partnership for Enhanced Cooperation", *Strategic Digest,* Vol. 30, No. 11, November 2000, p. 1554.
14. Rudnitsky, n.3, p.86. Also see, Basu, n.10; and John Cherian, "Clinging the T-90 deal", *Frontline,* 16 March 2001.
15. Kaushik, n. 11, p. 54.
16. *Ibid.,* p. 5.
17. "Indo-Russian Strategic Partnership for Enhanced Cooperation", n. 13, p.1556.
18. Kaushik, n. 11, p. 5.
19. R.S. Yadav, *Bharat ki Videsh Niti: Ek Vishleshan,* Kitab Mahal, Allahabad, 2004, p. 181.
20. Kaushik, n. 11, p. 6.
21. "Indo-Russian Strategic Partnership for Enhanced Cooperation", n. 13, p. 1554.
22. *Ibid.*
23. http://meaindia. nic.in/speech/2003/11/12ss01.htm.
24. http://meaindia.nic.in/declare statement/2003/11/13 jd01.htm.
25. For details see, Devendra Kaushik, "The Triangle for Peace and Prosperity", *World Focus,* Vol. 24, Nos. (10-11-12), Oct-Nov-Dec. 2003.
26. M.L. Madhu, "For Multi-polar World: Role of Russia, China and India", *The Tribune,* 22 May 1997; V.P. Dutt, "India's Options: Russia's Slow Emergence", *The Tribune,* 19 April 1997; Alexai Almanov and Sergai Strokov, "Moscow Looks Eastward", *Outlook,* 9 April 1997; and *Times of India,* 26 March 1997.
27. "Indo-Russian Strategic Partnership for Enhanced Cooperation", n.13, p. 1554.
28. For Indian interests in this region see, R.S. Yadav, "India and the Central Asian Republics", *World Focus,* Vol. 20, Nos.10-11-12, Oct-Nov-Dec. 1999.
29. *Ibid.* p. 63.
30. For text of the declaration see, Jyotsna Bakshi, *Russia and India: From Ideology to Geopolitics,* New Delhi, 1999, Appendix I, pp. 291-93. Also see, "A New Entente: Narsimha Rao's Moscow visit", *Frontline,* 29 July 1994.
31. Anita Inder Singh, "India's Relations with Russia and Central Asia", *International Affairs,* Vol. 71, No.1, January 1995, p. 80.
32. http://meaindia.nic.in/declare statement/2003/11/13 jd01.htm.
33. *Ibid.*
34. Rudnitsky, n. 3, p. 96. For comments by Alexander Salitsky and Sham Lal see Kaushik, n. 25, p. 46.
35. Kaushik, n. 25, pp. 44-48. Also see, Chintamani Mahapatra, "India, China and Russia: Strategic Triangle is Possible", *Strategic Analysis,* Vol. XXII, No. 11, February 1999, pp. 1793-96.

18

Asian Powers and Central Asian Security

Ajay Patnaik

Since the collapse of the former Soviet Union, five small states came into existence in the Central Asian region. The region suddenly acquired immense geopolitical significance and also experienced a power vacuum. For some, historical, cultural and religious affinities could give them advantage for spreading their influence. This region became key to the security of many neighbouring countries, big and small. The fear of some adversary, filling the vacuum, prompted the other to seek influence in the region. Regional rivalries were key to competition for influence in Central Asia. Turkey, Saudi Arabia, Iran, Pakistan were eager to gain maximum influence at the cost of their regional rivals. These were the big two neighbours—Russia and China—which share border with some of the Central Asian countries and have co-ethnics in those states. Existing border disputes and ethno-demographic composition added to the security worries of Central Asia vis-à-vis their powerful neighbours. Militarily and economically weak, Central Asian states, in the initial phase following independence, followed an open-door policy with their Islamic neighbours with the hope that an extended cultural neighbourhood would stabilise their independence and insulate them from pressure of their more powerful neighbours.

However, driven by their narrow geopolitical objectives, southern neighbours sought to expand their influence in the region at each other's expense, which prompted scholars to speak of the "New Great Game" in Central Asia. Conflicts within and among them were extended to Central Asia. It became the location where the future of conflicts and strategic gains or losses of its southern neighbours were sought to be determined. This resulted in making the region so volatile that the big powers could not but engage themselves more comprehensively. Regional rivalries were getting mixed up with the religious radicalism and terrorism. With the coming to power of the Taliban in Afghanistan, Central Asia's threat perception heightened and the relationship with most of its Islamic neighbours cooled down. The role of powers, such as Russia, the United States and China increased in the region to ensure regional stability.

Central Asia's security dimension has evolved through three phases. The first phase was till the mid-1990s, before the coming of Taliban to power. The second phase includes the Taliban years in Afghanistan. The third stage set in since September 11 terrorist attacks in the United States.

THE FIRST PHASE: STRUGGLE FOR CULTURAL SUPREMACY

At the time of independence there was a perception that this region would be volatile and conflict prone, given the nature of inter-ethnic relations and disputed borders between the Central Asian Republics. The series of riots that shook the region in 1989-90 were reasons to believe that wars, civil wars and ethnic cleansing would be the order of the days ahead. It is to the credit of these nascent Asian states that in the last more than a decade they have neither traversed the Yugoslav way or of the Caucasus. The states are committed to respect the Soviet drawn borders and the emigration from the region has been mostly of the Slavic minorities, for a variety of reasons. The indigenous minorities have stayed and in some cases their numbers have grown. In certain cases like in Tajikistan, the role of the minority group has been instrumental in ensuring victory for the ruling group (Uzbeks in Tajikistan during the civil war). Tajikistan, which witnessed a bloody civil war, has come out stronger with greater consolidation of Tajik nationhood, so much so that they were able to sustain the struggle of their co-ethnics in neighbouring Afghnistan during the Taliban days in power.

For consolidating their independence and nationhood, the new states of Central Asia looked to relatively more powerful and rich neighbours for support. During the early days of independence, the euphoria of nationalism and religious revivalism propelled these new states towards their Islamic neighbours. Funds started pouring in from Saudi Arabia, Iran, Pakistan and Turkey to augment religious and cultural institutions. Groups, propounding political Islam, were finding ideological and material support from these states. A struggle for cultural influence in the region was launched by some of the neighbouring countries, especially between Iran and Turkey. Some argued that due to historical, cultural and religious ties and because of their own weakness, Central Asian states would come under the influence of a regional bloc dominated by one of the above two regional powers.[1]

Central Asian states became members of ECO, OIC and other such regional groupings; to strengthen their ties with the Islamic countries. However, soon they found out that these powers were interested in spreading their own brand of ideology to obtain hegemony that hardly helped in ensuring security or development in Central Asia. Competing perspectives and limited objectives of Central Asia's southern neighbours (in West Asia as well as in South Asia) were bound to impinge on their capacity to have a strong influence in the region. Apart from not being economically rich themselves, their involvement also carried the danger of arousing Russia's suspicion, which it ultimately did.[2] The involvement of Iran in Tajikistan brought Russia right back to Central Asia, after initial hesitation. The CIS Collective Security Treaty of 1992, stationing of Russian troops etc. again made Russia deeply engaged in the region.

THE SECOND PHASE: INVOLVEMENT OF NEIGHBOURING MAJOR POWERS

The rise of the Taliban and its coming to power in Kabul dramatically changed the security scenario in Central Asia. The region was in the danger of being sucked into a world of radical Islam, the foundations of which had been laid in Afghanistan. However, the victory of the Taliban also ended the illusion that secular and moderate Central Asia can integrate with their religious neighbours in a larger cultural space for mutual advantage. Some states like Iran changed course feeling the heat from the Taliban and others like Saudi Arabia and Pakistan sided with the Taliban and lost the goodwill of the Central Asian states. Russia became the major security guarantor of Central Asia and China looked beyond economic opportunities in the region to issues of regional stability and religious extremism. India, worried and harried by the escalation of cross-border terrorism, emanating from Pakistan and Afghanistan, looked at Central Asia as a region with which its security interests converged and in a limited way became politically and militarily engaged in the region. Symptomatic of these changes were the settlement of the Sino-Central Asian border problems and the creation of the Shanghai Five. Iran's role in conflict resolution in Tajikisan and India and Iran's role in co-ordinating their efforts with Russia, to help the Northern Alliance in Afghanistan, were symbolic of the positive role that Asian powers could play in preserving the stability of Central Asia.

Another worry facing the emerging Asian powers like China, India and Iran in the Central Asian region was their being denied access to energy resources of Central Asia, which came to light mainly during this period. Given the fact that energy requirements of China and India are growing at a faster pace, they would not like to be deprived of the energy pie by big superpowers like the US or

Russia. Iran has the added advantage of being the shortest and cheapest route to transit Central Asian oil to warm waters.

THE THIRD PHASE: US PRESENCE IN CENTRAL ASIA

The terrorist bombing in the United States on 11 September radically metamorphosed the geopolitics of the Central Asian region, which became vital to the US security interests. Both energy and international terrorism drew US physical presence to the region. Though earlier it operated though NATO's peace programmes, it now became the main security alternative for the Central Asian states. The US presence in the region has alarmed Russia and its engagement with the region has equally grown. There is a danger that, in the short-term, US-Russia co-operation could marginalise the Asian powers in the region and jeopardise their interests. However, there are ways in which countries like China, India and Iran have made themselves relevant in stabilising the region and to meet some of their security needs.

This study looks at the positive role that some of the Asian countries—China, Iran and India-have played and are playing to resolve conflicts, help in regional stability and in some sense become security alternatives in areas that may not be adequately taken care of by the two superpowers. India and Iran's links with the present government in Afghanistan and Tajikistan, China's steps to meet the threat perceptions of Kazakhstan and Kyrgyzstan are important indicators that as interested parties Asian powers can neither ignore the Central Asian region nor be marginalised there.

CHINA: THE POTENTIAL MAJOR PLAYER IN CENTRAL ASIA

China's contiguity, significant size, burgeoning economy and powerful military make it a potential major player in Central Asia. At the time of Soviet disintegration its major apprehensions ranged from ideological and political problems to security challenges along China's northern frontier provinces. Issue of ethnicity and religious revivalism, in addition to the lingering problem of border disputes, were key problems that defined the security parameters of China's relations with Central Asia. Added to this has been the problem of drug trafficking. According to Gerald Segal, Chinese policy, in the region at that time, was cautious and gradual, a posture reflective of complex and potentially explosive issues that link China's own inner Asia, primarily Xinjiang and the new Central Asian states.[3]

China was also concerned about the nuclear threat emanating from CA. Though Nazarbaev declared, in early 1992, that Kazakhstan has a right to remain nuclear, under US persuation, it signed the NPT as non-nuclear weapon country in May 1992 and on 23 May 1992, it signed the Lisbon Protocol of START treaty maintaining its non-nuclear status. By mid-1995 all nuclear warheads in Kazakhstan were either transferred to Russia or destroyed. Before that in February 1995 the Chinese government issued its security assurance to Kazakhstan and urged all nuclear-weapon states to undertake the same commitment.

Central Asia's concerns included territorial disputes and presence of that Chinese forces on the border, in huge strength. There were also apprehensions over China's nuclear testing and Chinese economic projects on Central Asia's border, that might cause environmental problems. China's rising military and economic power is both a matter of advantage and concern. China looks towards Central Asia's rich deposits of oil and gas and other minerals and metals, access to which is vital for China's rapid industrial development.

There is a mutual concern regarding religious extremism and cross-border terrorism. While China fears that such movements could emerge from Central Asia to threaten China's northwest region, Kazakhstan and Kyrgyzstan are concerned that separatist movements by Uighurs in Xinjiang could create problems in their own states.[4]

The initial strategic concern for China, over this region, was to stabilize the north-western frontier and create a favourable external environment vis-à-vis the Central Asian neighbours. China shares nearly 3,500 km. border with Kazakhstan, Kyrgyzstan and Tajikistan. Border problem has mainly been sorted out on the basis of (1) respect for agreements already entered into in the Sino-Soviet border talks, (2) recognition of existing treaties as basis for future negotiations, (3) willingness to settle all disputes in accordance with the established rules of international law, (4) mutual consultation on equal footing or mutual accomodation.

The Sino-Kyrgyz and the Sino-Tajik Joint Communiques in 1992 and 1993 confirmed the principles of respecting previous agreements with the former Soviet Union, recognition of existing treaties, settlement of disputes through established principles of international law and mutual consultation and accomodation. Sino-Kazakhstan border agreement signed on 27 April 1994 finalized in principle the delineation of the 1,700 km. long Sino-Kazakh border. Understanding was also reached on the Sino-Kyrgyz and Sino-Tajik border also.[5] Talks to resolve the long-standing border issue culminated in a Summit of the five in Shanghai, in April 1996, the focus of which was to settle the border issue and secure tension-free relationship among them. The April 1996 Shanghai Five agreement on mutual military confidence building measures was the first collective agreement between Russia, China and three Central Asian republics.

Besides, an accord on mutual troop reduction on the borders to a level that would make offensive action impossible, the parties agreed not to use force or threaten to use force in case of disputes nor would seek unilateral military superiority. In the next Summit at Moscow in 1997 Russia proposed a zone of peace along the borders. The Moscow Agreement on Mutual Reduction of Military Forces in the Border Region signed in April 1997 committed the five countries to reduce military forces in the border and maintain only defencive troops; not to use weapons or threaten to use them to seek to maintain military superiority; to reduce number of ground forces, air forces, air defence forces and border defence forces, and the number of major weapons deployed for the length of 100 km. on either side of the border; to define the size of the forces remaining after the reduction and the manner and timetable of this reduction; to exchange relevant information on their forces deployed, in the border region; and to conduct regular verification of the implementation of the agreement. The agreement is valid till 2020, but can be extended. The information exchanged on the military forces in the border area will be kept secret from third parties.[6]

On 4 July 1998 China and Kazakhstan signed an agreement that brought an end to their long-standing border disputes. The joint declaration signed by the Shanghai Five leaders in Dushanbe on 5 July 2000, emphasized and gave highest priority to state sovereignty. Thus border disputes are unlikely to pose any security crisis in the near future.

In 1996, at the time of its formation, the Shanghai Five formed a regional border security forum and agreed to cut their armed forces along their common border and refrain from using force against each other. Apart from exchange of military delegations on a regular basis since 1995, China provided an aid of 11 million Yuan to Kazakhstan's armed forces, during the visit of the Kazakh defence minister in April 2000. It is seeking closer military ties with other Central Asian states as well. The Turkmen defence minister, who visited China in September 1999, expressed interest in cooperation in the field of military training and use of equipment. A Chinese military delegation visited Tajikistan on 13 July 2000. Of late China has also enhanced its military ties with Uzbekistan, which is under great pressure from Islamic militancy and extremism. According to Oliker, before September 11, apart from Russia, China was the only other power to supply lethal weapons to Central Asia. China provided Uzbekistan with sniper rifles as well as flak jackets. China has provided Kyrgyzstan assistance worth $6,00,000, to include tents and army gears, and in June 2001 the Kyrgyz and the Chines defence ministers agreed to the training of Kyrgyz soldiers at a training centre in Guangzhou in China.[7]

China's other major concern is to efficiently handle separatist and religious extremist infiltration and their negative influence in the Xinjiang region. Chinese initiative in this regard resulted in an agreement at the fourth summit of the Shanghai Five in Bishkek in August 1999 to make joint effort to fight ethnic "separatism, religious extremism and international, terrorism". At the Almaty Summit in 1998, China secured a vital pledge from its partners to reject "all manifestations of national separatism and religious extremism" and to ban on their territories activities harmful to state sovereignty, security and public order of any of the five states. It was declared at the Summit that any form of national splitism, ethnic exclusion and religious extremism was unacceptable.

China, underlines Schoeberlein, has reasserted itself into Central Asia in the years since the appearance of the IMU. Beijing is supplying weapons and military equipment to Kyrgyzstan to help in its fight against the IMU, and is also concerned about the activities of separatist Muslim Uighurs in its western Xinjiang province, which borders Tajikistan and Kyrgyzstan.[8]

The threat of Islamic extremism in Central Asia, fuelled by Taliban regime in Afghanistan, appears to have triggered effective rapproachment and co-ordination between the five states. Terrorist camps in Chechnya, Xinjiang and in the Ferghana valley region and the southern belt bordering on Afghanistan have been a major source of worry.[9] That is why, in January 2002, the SCO decided that its focus would be Chechnya, Xinjiang, and the IMU.

The presidents of all the member states signed a charter at the above summit transforming the SCO security bloc into a fully-fledged international organization with a permanent secretariat based in Beijing. They also agreed to set up a regional antiterrorist structure to be based in the Kyrgyz capital, Bishkek, and signed a political declaration underlining the SCO's joint goals. According to Putin: "The charter makes provision for the creation of a regional antiterrorist structure as a permanent organization within the SCO....The signing of the agreement will be a significant contribution by all SCO members to the creation of a global system fighting against terrorism."

The political declaration says that the aim of the Shanghai group is to fight terrorism, prevent conflicts, and ensure security in Central Asia. It says that the organization "is based on principles of mutual respect of the sovereignty, independence, territorial integrity and inviolability of the borders, non-intervention into domestic affairs, non-use of force or threat of force, and equality of all members."

Expanding multilateral trade was high on the agenda. The political declaration states clearly about the participants' intention to step up negotiations on creating favourable conditions for trade and investments, and to develop a long-term programme of multilateral economic co-operation. According to the document, projects for improving transportation, power generation, water use, and energy will be given priority. Nazarbaev said the SCO could help to "solve military problems" in Asia.

In January 2004, the Shanghai Group formally operationalised two permanent bodies-a secretariat and an anti-terrorist set-up. The Secretariat will handle organisational and paperwork for the SCO's apex bodies, which include four councils: of heads of states heads of government, foreign ministers and national co-ordinators. On the same day, a regional anti-terrorist structure was unveiled in Tashkent. "With the two working bodies in place, SCO begins operating as a full-fledged international organisation complete with its working mechanism and budget", Russian foreign ministry source said.[10]

A major strategic concern for China is related to the economic aspects of China's relations with Central Asia. The former has emphasised a gradual regional economic co-operation between the latter and Xinjiang. Immediately after the emergence of new states, China established rail and road links with bordering Central Asian republics. Cheap Chinese consumer goods flooded the region. China has also extended access to sea for the land-locked states through its ports on the Pacific, which helps the latter in their search for alternative routes and reduces their dependence on Moscow. In view of the Western projects to take Caspian oil and gas westward thorough a new network of pipelines, China is keen to ensure that the Caspian oil and gas are not delivered only to the west. The fact that China may be importing 3 million barrels of crude oil per day by 2010, makes it necessary for cross-border co-operation in this sector.[11]

In the field of energy, the economies of CAR and China are mutually complimentary. Turkmenistan and Kazakhstan are the main partners of China. China is particularly interested in gaining access to Turkmen gas and thus ensure future energy security. A joint statement issued during President Jiang Zemin's visit to Ashgabat on 6 July 2000, attaches special importance to strengthening mutually beneficial co-operation in the energy field. Central Asian republics also realised that increased co-operation with China will link their economies with the Asia-Pacific economic boom.

China is perhaps the more successful non-CIS power in finding a foothold and ensuring its access to the Central Asian republics. From the Chinese perspective, according to Guangchang Xing, the strategic importance of Central Asia will increase and this region will have considerable influence in the world. The future role of these states, however, will depend not only on their own strength but also on how they co-operate with their neighbours and what issues they pursue.

China considers that Central Asia, in the context of Eurasia and these states, have a linking role not just in the geographical sense but also in a political and cultural sense; a bridge between East and West. Though during his visit to Kazakhstan, former Premier Li Peng declared that his country will not seek either a political or economic sphere of influence, China believes that if there were to be turbulence around the 'bridge', the future political and economic co-operation in the whole Eurasia would be seriously affected. That is why Chinese political and economic co-operation is viewed as vital to the stability and prosperity in the region. Apart from these, China and Central Asian states have shared since 1991 several security concerns in the region, says Xing.

Geopolitical factors indicate a high priority for economic and trade contacts between Central Asia and China. Their economic structures are complimentary. The opening of the 'second Eurasian land-bridge' and the improvement of transport connections have provided a solid material basis for improving relations. This land-bridge is an important route for China to be the link of the Central Asian states with the Pacific. Increased co-operation with China and the Pacific states would enable the Central Asian states to join the 'dynamic Asian heartland', i.e., the emerging 'Pacific economic ring'. China provides not only a large market but the projected oil and gas pipelines to China would further boost the economies of Central Asia, Xing goes on to argue.[12]

IRAN'S ROLE IN CONFLICT RESOLUTION AND REGIONAL STABILITY

The creation of five independent states in Central Asia brought new challenges and opportunities for Iran. Iran had historical and cultural ties with the region since ancient times. Its geographical location close to the region has its advantage. It shares Caspian Sea with Kazakhstan and has a long border with Turkmenistan. It can offer Central Asia an outlet to the open seas through the Persian Gulf.

Ethnic and linguistic factors were likely to facilitate Iranian influence in the region. According to Herzig, in the early years of Central Asia's independence (late 1991 to early 1993) both the Iranian government and quasi-state Islamic Foundation took initiatives to lead, encourage and shape religious revival in Central Asia, which included sponsored missionary activities, distribution of religious books, broadcasting of Iranian television and radio in Central Asia, training of mullahs in Iranian madrassas and opening of religious schools and mosques. Iran was reportedly supporting the Islamic Revival Party of Tajikistan. The initial fervour however calmed down, as Saudis and Pakistanis entered in a big way in this fray and lately Iran has been less aggressive in religious proselytising and has concentrated more on good diplomatic and economic relations. Soon Iran began to appreciate the need for the regional peace and stability in Central Asia, which, if threatened, could affect Iran's national security.[13]

A more pragmatic policy towards the region was initiated during the visit of President Rafsanjani in 1993, when religion occupied a very small part of the discussion and greater emphasis was laid on peace, stability and co-operation, especially in the economic field.[14]

Though Iran has not developed any military-security ties with the Central Asian republics, it has taken an active role in conflict resolution and mediation. In the case of Tajikistan, its position shifted to that of a peace-maker.[15] Iran became a key supporter of the UN-backed mediation efforts and was instrumental in securing the acceptance of the Islamist-led United Tajik Opposition (UTO) to a cease-fire in 1994. Eventually President Rakhmonov visited Tehran in 1995 and the final peace accord was signed in 1997, for which Iran received a lot of international goodwill.

The success of the Taliban drew Iran closer to countries that were threatened by the Taliban brand of radicalism. Following the killing of 10 Iranian diplomats in Taliban's Mazar-e-Sharif in August 1998, Iran started troop mobilisation and military manoeuvres involving nearly 70,000 revolutionary guards and 2,00,000 regular troops close to Afghan border. Like Tajikistan, Iran too was host to huge number of refugees (estimated to be about 1.5-2 million) pouring in from Afghanistan. Apart from being a country that was directly affected by the civil war in Afghanistan, Iran also had to take into cognisance the persecution of Shia minority under the Taliban rule. Together with Russia Iran became a major sponsor of the Northern Alliance and, after the ouster of the Taliban from power, Iran also played a constructive role at the Bonn Conference that discussed the future set up in Afghanistan.[16]

Iran's image as a radical Islamic country and US hostility to the Islamic republic has handicapped Iran's advantage, as an immediate neighbour (bordering Turkmenistan) located between the Persian Gulf and the Caspian Sea. The advantage of a potential transit country for Central Asian energy and US effort to by pass Iran further underlined Iran's need to go beyond Islamic ideology and look for allies. US military presence in Afghanistan and Central Asia has added to Iran's security worries. Its role in conflict resolution in Tajikistan and support to anti-Taliban coalition-the Northern Alliance-has endeared it to countries such as Tajikistan and Uzbekistan. The visit of President Khatami to the region in 2002, resulted in a number of agreements, which included improvement of transport infrastructure in Uzbekistan to facilitate transit of goods to China from the Persian Gulf, opening of a trade centre in Bishkek in future and focussing on Iran as an export route for Kazakh energy. A limited amount of Kazakh oil is exported through a swap arrangement with Iran and a pipeline carries Turkmen gas to northern Iran.

Iran has improved its bilateral relations with China. Both countries link their own security to that of the Central Asian states and Afghanistan. This perspective was underlined during President Khatami's China visit when the two countries expressed their desire to co-operate in developing regional transport (including pipeline) infrastructure to link West and East Asia. China, in Tehran's perception, could become an additional counterweight to the United States in Central Asia. According to Herzig such strategic considerations could have been behind Tehran's decision to award the contract, for the construction of the Neka-Tehran pipeline, to a Chinese consortium.[17]

Similarly Iran has improved co-operation with India to develop trade access to Central Asia, bypassing Pakistan and Afghanistan through a rail link to Turkmenistan. A tripartite agreement among the above two and Turkmenistan was signed on 22 February 1997 at Teheran, on international transit of goods. This enabled goods from India to reach Turkmenistan through Iranian port of Bander Abbas and from there by road and rail. India and Russia are developing a new transit route through Iran to Novorossisk which is being developed for transport of goods between India and Russia.

The prospect for Indo-Iranian co-operation in Turkmenistan already exists. India has already held talks with Iran and Afghanistan for developing the Iranian port of Chah Bahar, as the nodal point of a new trade corridor in Afghanistan. Since Afghanistan and Tajikistan are neighbours, the extension of this route to Central Asia from the former can expand Indo-Central Asian trade ties. Given the never-ending nature of tension in Indo-Pakistan relations, it is unlikely that India would be interested in depending on energy through pipelines across Pakistan.

Some experts are of the view that Iran is going to play a positive role in Central Asia and focus on developing political and economic ties with the region. Not just develop long-term relations with Tajikistan, but with Uzbekistan, too, Iran is trying to mend its fences and develop better relationship. Hoping to play an important role in future in Caspian development, Iran's interest in maintaining stability in the Central Asian region is going to outweigh any political role based on Islamic ideology or ethnic ties.[18]

WAR AGAINST TERRORISM AND INDO-CENTRAL ASIAN CO-OPERATION

With the coming of Taliban to power in Afghanistan in 1996 the threat to security of the Central Asian states as well as India grew manifold. Mounting cross-border terrorism supported by the Afghan government, backed by international terrorist groups and sustained by drug money, became the biggest challenge to their external security and internal stability.

The victory of Taliban in almost the whole of Afghanistan opened the doors of new possibilities for the fundamentalists. Both, India and Central Asia came under increasing pressure. The common threat of terrorism resulted in a growing convergence on the need to devise ways to combat and in a unity of approach to meet this menace. India, realising that Central Asia held the key to the two of its major worries — Pakistan's expanding influence over Afghanistan and beyond; and the threat of a growing belt of fundamentalism sponsoring cross-border terrorism — chose to cooperate closely with the secular governments in Central Asia. It provided financial assistance to the Northern Alliance that enabled it to acquire weapons and ammunitions. The diplomatic support was not confined to just maintaining the Embassy of Afghanistan in New Delhi, representing the Rabbani leadership. In all diplomatic fora, India condemned the Taliban and it also played a crucial role in the campaign against international recognition to the Taliban, which was recognised by only three states till about the end. India played host to the families of the leadership of the Alliance hounded by the Taliban.

The defeat and ouster of Taliban has put on hold Pakistan's hopes of achieving some strategic edge over India. The positive development has been the weakening of the destabilising forces that were unleashed, since the Taliban take over, threatening countries such as India, China, Russia and the Central Asian states. The informal alliance of India and Central Asian countries, that had developed in the course of sustaining the United Front (Northern Alliance), contributed substantially to the campaign against terrorism.

While the US-led war against the Taliban might have hastened the fall of Taliban from power, the existence of the Northern Alliance made the change to an alternative government, far easier. However, given the still unstable situation in Afghanistan the need for continued co-operation between India and Central Asia is very critical.

Even after the ouster of the Taliban from Afghanistan, India neither feels totally secure or comfortable about the reports of renewed attempts to destabilise Afghanistan, despite US presence, in both Pakistan and Afghanistan.[19] Indian policy makers believe that Pakistan still continues with its policy of what India's foreign secretary describes as "sustainable terrorism" and the international community has been unable to address to India's concerns.[20] To counter its own marginalisation, India would have to focus on greater involvement with this region.

India has reportedly renegotiated the use of Farkhor in Tajikistan, as a base for assistance to Afghanistan. Earlier it had built a military hospital and an airstrip there to help the Northern Alliance. The hospital shifted to Kabul after the fall of Taliban. India signed a bilateral agreement during Indian defence minister's visit to Dushanbe, in April 2002. According to the agreement, "India will train

Tajik defence personnel, service and retrofit Soviet and Russian military equipment and teach English to army and air force personnel", reported *Jane's Intelligence Review*.[21]

Stephen Blank thinks that India's present policies are oriented to play a larger role throughout Asia in both defence and economics by establishing strategic partnership with key players.[22] He also suggests elsewhere that beyond purely economic and military links, India has upgraded its military profile in Central Asia, to the extent of acquiring an air base at Ayni in Tajikistan. This, he underlines, "testifies to India's new interest in capability for power projection missions as well as its ability to threaten Pakistan from the rear and deny it a strategic hinterland".[23]

Such views seem to exaggerate India's capabilities and ambitions. India has not so far done anything to suggest expansionist or hegemonic designs in the region. During his visit to Central Asia in February 2003, India's External Affairs Minister Yashwant Sinha made India's involvement with the region clear by stating "We are not in Central Asia to replace anyone. We see Central Asia as part India's extended neighbourhood and our presence there is to promote a mutually inclusive relationship".[24]

FUTURE OF INDO-CENTRAL ASIAN COOPERATION

The present government in Afghanistan is yet to be stable and, given Pakistan's displeasure over the composition of the present Afghan leadership, India feels the urgency of providing economic and other developmental as well as humanitarian assistance to Afghanistan. For India, access to Afghanistan is not possible through Pakistan. As a result, it has chosen the Central Asian route and that too through Tajikistan, the most reliable and close ally during the Taliban days in power. The facility provided by Tajikistan has enabled India to remain involved in the developmental process in Afghanistan and help it meet many of its socio-economic challenges.

The joint declaration signed by Prime Minister Vajpayee and Tajik President Rakhmonov during the former's visit to Tajikistan in November 2003 made a pointed reference to "steady progress in defence exchanges and the intent to intensify relations in this area". Indian air force engineers are repairing and upgrading the runway at Ayni. Tajik president Rakhmonov said that the Indian military transport aircraft had participated in military exercises in Tajikistan and declared "I would like to state for the record that we will continue military co-operation between the two countries in all areas".[25]

Another promising prospect could be India-Kazakhstan co-operation. Kazakhstan has shown a great deal of inclination for intensifying ties with India and has allowed

India to invest in its oil sector. It has given special attention to defence co-operation between the two countries. India and Kazakhstan have established a forum not only to co-operate on fight against terrorism but also for an 'early action' in finalising agreements in military and technical co-operation. President Nazarbaev has been persuading India to join the Shanghai Co-operation Organisation (SCO). During the February 2002 visit of Nazarbaev to India, the Joint Declaration stated that India's membership in SCO "would add to the strength of that organization".[26] Similar sentiments were expressed during Prime Minister Vajpayee's visit to Kazakhstan in June 2002, during which a protocol on military-technical cooperation and an agreement on setting up an India-Kazakhstan Working Group for joint fight against terrorism and other crimes was signed.

Though the pressure to focus on Pakistan's movements in Afghanistan and the Central Asian region would continue, India should simultaneously concentrate on enlarging its economic profile in the region, which remains marginal compared to other major actors. It needs to increase its investments in Central Asia to create a viable infrastructure to access the resources in the region. This would help in giving stability to India's long-term strategic ties, apart from benefiting from trade and economic opportunities in Central Asia.

TOWARDS AN ASIAN SECURITY AND CO-OPERATION MECHANISM

Nazarbaev has been the moving spirit behind an Asian mechanism, like the OSCE, to co-ordinate multilateral efforts for peace and stability in Asia and create an effective and universal structure ensuring security on the Asian continent. Mooted first at the 47th UN General Assembly in October 1992, the idea and his efforts finally resulted in the formation of CICA and its first Summit in Almaty in June 2002. The Almaty Act, approved at the meeting spoke of, among other things, guaranteeing regional security to promote the peaceful settlement of existing conflicts and to prevent new ones. The other document, "The Declaration on Eliminating Terrorism and Dialogue Among Civilizations" calls upon the UN to play a "central role" in developing a framework to fight terrorism.

CICA as a security forum can potentially become an international security structure that would allow its member states to broaden the sphere of joint interest despite different foreign policy priorities as well as resolve issues important for the whole continent. Its 16 member states occupy about 89 per cent of the Asian landmass and 72 per cent of that of Eurasia, with 3 billion people (about 45 per cent of world's population) living in this vast space. The members also include some of the largest developing economies of the world like Russia, China and India and attract considerable share of global volume of investment. Spanning over the Caspian region and the Persian Gulf, the hydrocarbon reserves and production of CICA members represent a significant proportion of the world's resources base and production.

However, this initiative is yet to take off in any substantial manner and may not meet the threats faced by the Central Asian states even if it materialises. Central Asia's security needs would be taken care of by both superpowers mainly and by regional frameworks like CIS Collective Security Treaty and Shanghai Co-operation Organisation. Nevertheless, positive role played by some Asian powers like China, India and Iran would make them attractive partners of Central Asian states in meeting some of the security challenges in the region. Their role may not be in terms of overt and overwhelming military support but would remain important all the same. Through confidence building measures, assisting in conflict resolution, technical-technological help, providing access to sea and cheaper markets and consumer goods, the above three Asian powers can improve the security scenario in Central Asia.

REFERENCES

1. Mathew Edwards, "The New Great Game and the new great gamers: disciples of Kipling and Mackinder", *Central Asian Survey*, Vol. 22, No. 1, March 2003.
2. According to Shireen Hunter, Iranian Islamic model or West's promotion of the Turkish secular-democratic model did not have any chance to succeed simply because they did not have the resources to permeate the region. "Iran's pragmatic regional policy", *Journal of International Affairs*, Vol. 56, No. 2, 2003, p. 134.
3. Gerald Segal, "China and the disintegration of Soviet Union", *Asian Survey*, Vol. 32, No. 9, 1992.
4. Olga Oliker, "Conflict in Central Asia and South Caucasus: Implications of foreign interests and involvement", in Olga Oliker and Thomas S. Szayna (eds.) Faultlines of Conflict in Central Asia and the South Caucasus, Rand, Santa Monica, 2003, p. 215.
5. However, with Tajikistan dispute remains over an area of about 20,000 sq.km. in the mountainous region of Pamir. Guangcheng Xing, "China and Central Asia", in Roy Allison and Lena Johnson (eds.), *Central Asian Security*, Brooking Institution Press, Washington DC, 2001.
6. *Ibid.*, p. 160.
7. *Ibid.*, p. 216.
8. RFE/RL, Prague, 10 September 2001.
9. Ma Jiali, "Central Asia: Geostrategic situation and big powers' policies", *Contemporary Central Asia*, Vol. III, No. 1, 1999, p. 45.
10. Vladimir Radyuhin, "Shanghai group comes of age", *The Hindu*, 11 January 2003.
11. James P. Dorian, Brett Wigdortz and Dru Gladney, "Central Asian and Xinjiang China: Emerging energy, economic and ethnic relations", *Central Asian Survey*, Vol.16, No. 9, 1997, pp. 461-86.

12. Guangcheng Xing, *op. cit.*, pp. 158-59.
13. Edmund Herzig, "Iran and Central Asia", in Roy Allison and Lena Johnson (eds.), *Central Asian Security: The New International Context*, Brooking Institution Press, Washington DC, 2001, p. 176.
14. *Ibid.*, pp. 177-78.
15. Among many agreements Iran signed with the Central Asian states, only two relate to security; one for military and border co-operation with Turkmenistan signed in 1994 and the other a letter of understanding on defence co-operation signed with Tajikistan in 1997. Beyond these there have been some limited initiatives with Turkmenistan on co-operation and sharing of intelligence to tackle the drugs trade and transnational crime. *Ibid.*, p. 187.
16. *Ibid.*, pp. 186-87.
17. *Ibid.*, pp. 1992.
18. Olga Oliker points to the silence on the part of Iran to Uzbekistan's persecution of Islamic groups and Persian-Speakers as an indication of Iran's shifting focus from ideology to economic opportunities and regional stability. "Conflict in Central Asia and South Caucasus: Implications of foreign interests and involvement", in Olga Oliker and Thomas S. Szayna (eds.) *Faultlines of Conflict in Central Asia and the South Caucasus*, Rand, Santa Monica, 2003, pp. 209-12. Shireen Hunter suggests that Iran should come to terms with reality and must reach a *modus vivendi* with the US to achive its goals in Central Asia, despite the growing volume of trade between Iran and the region-from $74 million in 1994 to $430 in 2000 with Turkmenistan, from $220 million in 2000 to $500 million in 2002 with Kazakhstan. Shireen Hunter, *op. cit.*, pp.146-47.
19. According to Firdous Syed, President, Kashmir Foundation for Peace and Development Studies, Kashmir, more than half the Taliban core survived the US assault and continues to be active in parts of Afghanistan and in the Federally Administered Tribal Areas (FATA) in Pakistan. *The Hindu*, 5 October 2002.
20. Indian Foreign Secretary Kanwal Sibal's press conference on 4 October 2002, *The Hindu*, 5 October, 2002.
21. *Ibid.*
22. Stephen Blank, "India and Central Asia: the return of strategy", *Central Asia-Caucasus Analyst*, 11 September 2002.
23. Stephen Balnk, "India's Continuing Drive into Central Asia", *Central Asia-Caucasus Analyst*, 14 January 2004.
24. *Tribune News Service*, 1 February 2003, Chandigarh.
25. *India Discussion Forum*, www.indolink.com, 14 November 2003.
26. Rahul Bedi, "India and Central Asia", *Frontline*, *op. cit.*

19

Regional Cooperation in Central Asia

VASUNDHARA MOHAN

The break-up of the Soviet Union in 1991 resulted in the emergence of independent Central Asian states. Independence brought about fundamental changes in the political and economic systems and society of the Central Asian states. The end to Soviet rule provided not only political freedom to the Central Asian republics but also an opportunity for developing democratic societies. However, in the new found freedom, the region came face to face not only with the complexities of building institutions for establishing a democratic society and a market-based economy but also the problems of security.

In the sphere of economy and society, the collapse of Central planning, to which the Central Asian republics were accustomed to, and separation from Russia had a profound impact. The practices followed by the Soviet regime and its treatment of Central Asia as a unified economic zone had ensured intra-regional cooperation. Major industrial complexes were under the control of the Centre, which determined the production plans, leaving minor activities either under dual (Moscow and the republics) or solely under republican control. Moscow and its bureaucracy did not seem to believe that the republics had their own aspirations and needs. By and large, the Central Asian production profile, quantum of trade and its direction were managed by Moscow for the benefit of the Union, as a whole. Moscow, however, included non-Russian nationalities in the decision making process and extended huge subsidies for strategic industries.

Vast natural resources without the technology and means to exploit them made the independent Central Asian states easy targets for the outsiders. Similarly, the Central Asian region, with its vast Muslim population inquisitive, if not thirsting, for religion which was denied to them under the Soviet rule, was a fertile ground for militant Islam. Finally, poverty in the region was an opportunity for international trade in human trafficking. The region, therefore, needed not only inter-regional cooperation but also security against outside aggression. This paper tries to examines as to what extent the erstwhile Soviet Republics, which depended on each other during the Soviet regime, have been able to achieve and maintain cooperation among them in the last more than a decade that they have been independent and if they have not been able to see eye to eye, then what are the reasons.

SOVIET LEGACY

With a view to exercising political control, the Soviet government created Central Asian republics with irregular and sometimes economically and ethnically irrational borders, denying ethnic homogeneity and cutting natural economic areas. Although the territory of Central Asia was ostensibly divided on the basis of nationality, the ethnic composition was actually mixed in a number of localities. The fertile Ferghana Valley, for instance, was divided among Kyrgyzstan, Uzbekistan, and Tajikistan. Similarly, the Leninabad region of Tajikistan and the Osh region of Kyrgyzstan are separated from their capitals by snow-covered mountains. Both the areas have a high admixture of ethnic Uzbeks, a situation that has led to violent confrontations over land and water rights.

The general economic structure of the former Soviet Union had followed centralised economy. All economic decisions were made by Moscow and these decisions had to be followed very strictly. The centre covered the entire Soviet Union in its planning and the hierarchical system and did not allow local managers to make any changes or corrections in the centralised decisions. Very detailed price controls created a non-economic pricing system. Therefore, there were no liquid funds or a conception of money in the real sense. The Soviet industrialisation policy was to transform Central Asia into a specialist supplier of raw materials. Uzbekistan was a big net importer of machine tools; Kazakhstan also relied on other Commonwealth of Independent State (CIS) countries for machine tools. Tajikistan imported its tractors, cars and trucks; Kyrgyzstan imported all its needs of fertilisers and gasoline: Turkmenistan had no coal and had also to import many essential food products.

The pattern of economic integration of the Central Asia into the Soviet system, for over seven decades, did not create infrastructure sufficient to facilitate their trade with each other once independence was achieved. Railroads and pipelines had been built primarily to carry raw materials from Central Asia to the processing plants in Russia and Ukraine. Consequently, Kyrgyzstan had no direct rail link from Bishkek even to Osh, its second largest city, or to Almaty. Kazakhstan's metallurgical and energy base was linked primarily to Russia. Similar was the case with the alignment and capacity of the gas pipelines. Even the visitors from the west were handled from Moscow, resulting in the Central Asian officials in the industry having little or no direct contact with foreign decision makers.

POST-INDEPENDENCE SCENARIO

Independence and the accompanying collapse of Central planning resulted in a severe economic depression in Central Asia, a region consisting of over 55 million population. The inability of the independent Central Asian governments to continue supporting social infrastructure like childcare facilities, transportation, domestic heating, free school meals with subsidies etc., greatly affected the morale of the population. The economic slide and lack of social assistance pushed increasing number of families, especially those with large number of children, and individuals with special needs, into poverty. Deterioration of the healthcare system is visible in the prevalence of diseases and rising infant and child mortality. These problems are more acutely felt among the poor, especially in remote areas.

The economic problems are by no means on account of the absence of resources but because of the Soviet policies that made the Central Asian states dependent on each other and all of them on Russia. Independent Russia has not shown any inclination to continue to carry the burden of supporting Central Asian states, with which the latter could have established closer ties, supporting each other. However, the political culture in which the leaders of independent Central Asian states were bred made them turn authoritative, in order to strengthen their hold on the new states. Secondly, these leaders chose the path of 'export globalism' i.e., "dealing on world markets for the sale of raw materials and the purchase of capital and some consumer goods".[1] Instead of giving preference to other states of the region in trade, the Central Asian States sought most-favoured-nation treatment from the western countries and membership in the World Trade Organization, along with loans, technical aid, and investments from national and multilateral sources. In fact, some of them took protectionist measures against the others of the region, affecting the development of inter-state trade.

At the beginning of the 1990s these former Soviet republics faced the crucial problem of choosing a new path of development. The crisis of post-Soviet society on one hand and global challenges of new geopolitics on the other, made these young independent states launch structural reforms and establish ties with the outside world. However, the results of the reforms have not been positive, and the independent Central Asian states are still undergoing immense social problems, and economic collapse to some degree or the other. Repressive politics of non-democratic regimes in some of the states have added to the miseries. One of the obstacles for successful reforms and effective integration of these countries into the world economic system is their social legacy. The social development in the Central Asian states is a mix of traditional society and Soviet power structures. Although under the Soviet regime the traditional societies of Central Asia adjusted to the communist state-party hierarchies, traditional social features like clan-patronage principle, the system of kinship rights and responsibilities did not entirely disappear. Such features were only dormant during the Soviet rule to surface once the states achieved independence.

EFFORTS AT REGIONAL COOPERATION

Regional cooperation has been the oft-repeated official proclamation of the Central Asian leaders. As the USSR was disintegrating, the 'leaders of the newly independent states of Central Asia, considered the option of creating a regional Central Asian Union in the form of a confederated Turkestan.[2] Islam Karimov, President of Uzbekistan was the chief proponent of the idea. Although the idea was ultimately rejected, the four states, with the exception of Tajikistan, have recognised their common ethnicity. Except Tajik, the languages of the remaining four states are closely related; and the religious practices are similar. The Central Asian states had all the requisites for a high degree of, if not total, integration.

One of the first regional initiatives of the post-Soviet period was the establishment of the Commonwealth of Independent States (CIS), by Russia, Ukraine and Belarus, whose Presidents signed a resolution at Minsk on 8 December 1991 declaring the demise of the Union and establishment of the CIS. Though the Central Asian leaders were initially agitated at the formation of such a 'Slavic Union', they finally decided to remain in a political community that corresponded to the political space of the former Soviet Union. Along with Yeltsin, the leaders of the former Soviet republics (excluding Latvia, Lithuania, and Estonia) met in Alma Ata on 21 December 1991 signed a declaration creating the CIS and bringing the USSR to an end.

The CIS being neither a political union nor a federation or confederation, has shown little vitality in the military, political, or economic areas. Early efforts to preserve economic unity were destined to fail. Divisive reactions surfaced during 1991-93 with the collapse of the Russian economy and currency. Various protective measures were taken everywhere at that time to prevent the flow of necessary food, energy, materials, and consumer goods to higher price areas. By

1993 the common rouble zone collapsed as Moscow could no longer prevent the former republics from expanding their rouble credits and contributing to the zone's hyperinflation. The CIS leaders (who included the Central Asians also) were trying to create an Economic Union, to foster a free trade area, create a customs union with reduced internal tariffs and common external tariff.

However, the Central Asian leaders had their own parallel agenda. Earlier in 1990, Kazakhstan, Kyrgyzstan, Tajikistan, and Uzbekistan joined forces in order to restructure their national economies and formed a sub-regional structure, the Central Asian Cooperation Organization (CAC). After independence, the idea of regional integration was given a new boost by their desire to facilitate reform of their national economies and to become part of the global economy. On 30 April, 1994, Kazakhstan, Kyrgyzstan, and Uzbekistan signed the treaty on the formation of an Integrated Economic Space (IES), aimed at implementing joint programmes to step up the economic integration and envisaging the free movement of goods, services, capital, and manpower, as well as coordinating credit, budget, tax, price, customs, and currency policy. This treaty was later signed by Tajikistan on 26 March 1998. On 17 July 1998 it was officially named the Central Asian Economic Community (CAEC).

The formation of CAEC was dictated by the need to find ways to make rational use of the region's common resources due to the drastic cutback in economic trade ties with the former union republics and the extremely limited opportunities for gaining access to markets beyond the CIS. The fact that Russia had no coherent and efficient policy in Central Asia also played its role in this process. The CAEC states stressed that their rapprochement did not mean regional isolation and was not aimed against the CIS, and declared the open nature of CAEC. In 1996, Russia was granted the status of observer in the CAEC, and in 1999, Georgia, Ukraine, and Turkey obtained this status, also.

Although the Presidents of the Central Asian countries had declared "regional economic integration" as the policy that they would pursue and created the structures mentioned above, the decisions were not implemented by their governments.[3] For want of political will, all integration initiatives remained mostly as statements of intentions. Economic integration calls for the renunciation of economic sovereignty to some extent and its transfer to the supranational level, which the Central Asian states were not prepared to do.[4] Instead of integration, the Central Asian states started following their own separate development agenda and policies of transformation.

Kazakhstan has adopted a radical transformation of the Soviet economic system into a market economy. Kazakhstan's currency is fully convertible and its oil sector has integrated into the world market. Uzbekistan has pursued a phased program. The Uzbek government controls prices and has strict control of foreign currency, banking and trade, thus creating 'severe policy incompatibilities in the Central Asian region.'[5] In both cases, the process of transformation has been plagued with delays, inching forward only under the pressure of the IMF.[6] In July 2000, Uzbekistan took the unusual step of adopting an additional level of visa controls, stepping out of the unified Soviet visa regime, by requiring that Kyrgyzstan residents apply for a visa to cross into Uzbekistan. Kyrgyzstan has adopted a pro-reform strategy. As a member of WTO, Kyrgyzstan has to open its markets for China, another WTO member. If Kyrgyzstan were a part of Central Asian common market, the import of Chinese goods would not be limited in Kyrgyzstan.[7] Tajikistan is committed to the reform path, but its commitment far exceeds its capacity to carry out reforms.[8] Tajikistan's ethnic problems, geographical location, poorly developed infrastructure make its desire at economic integration a difficult proposition. President Niyazov of Turkmenistan, who exercises monopoly on political power, has embraced commercial relations without market reforms. Domestic political institutions have no influence on the economic and foreign policy formulations of *Turkmanbashi*, as Niyazov is called. Turkmenistan places 'less emphasis on Central Asia regional cooperation and more emphasis on relations with the Caucasus, the Middle East, Iran and Caspian engress routes.'[9]

Thus, with such differing ideologies and economic and foreign policies among the constituents, the Central Asian Economic Community remained a mere name. It was only a programme, expression of a hope to overcome together the crisis that was caused by the disintegration of the Soviet model economic system. During the ten years of the CAEC's existence, none of the set aims viz., a common market, regulation of customs tariffs and taxes, common export policy, and common currency, were achieved.

At a Presidential-level meeting of Uzbekistan, Tajikistan, Kazakhstan, and Kyrgyzstan held in Tashkent in January 2002, it was declared that "economic integration is not a common aim any more" and the Central Asian Economic Community was renamed "Central Asian Cooperation" (CAC). The CAC was meant to promote security and political cooperation, and economic integration, and address problems associated with sharing water resources. Uzbek President Islam Karimov said that the Central Asian states and Russia were making joint efforts to prevent a possible incursion by Islamic militants into Uzbekistan and Kyrgyzstan. He stressed that "ensuring security is now the most important regional issue and all countries of the region should pursue a policy of "integrity of security." Other aspects of regional cooperation were, thus, pushed aside, although for the record, the Presidents of the Central Asian states discussed regional cooperation, maintaining peace in the region, terrorism, religious extremism, and joint fight against drug trafficking. The constituents of the organisation continued to officially discuss questions of active cooperation within the framework of the CAC and strengthening the 'current low level of cooperation.'

FACTORS AFFECTING REGIONAL COOPERATION

One of the areas in which the Central Asian states have failed is in agreeing to a preferential tariff structure in intra-regional trade. In fact, the existing tariffs are not only low, but the governments are unable to collect taxes even at the existing rates. Tariffs are relatively insignificant as compared to other barriers affecting trade among the Central Asian countries. These include prevalence of bribes and other unofficial payments, poor roads, hijacking of trucks carrying goods, and unofficial police stops. The governments have also been finding it difficult to collect taxes from shuttle traders, mostly middle-aged women, who transact business in cash, especially in US dollars. In spite of the problems, informal trade among the Central Asian countries appears to be working reasonably well. However, organised intra-regional trade is not flourishing as much as trade with the non-CIS countries, at least according to official estimates.

For the businessmen, both indigenous and foreign, a free trade in Central Asia means a larger market. But, unlike the businessmen who understand the necessity of normal commercial relations, the statesmen who control major resources have other motives, which often rank above commercial interests. Leaders of Uzbekistan and Turkmenistan have been giving priority to order and stability in their countries, over economic growth. They are afraid that active trading across borders is a threat to national security. For example, by Uighurs living in Sinkiang province of China and Kazakhstan might threaten the political status quo in China's northwest border area and hence the national security of Kazakhstan. Through suppression of opposition and strict control of the media, the autocratic governments of the area seemingly appear to enjoy broad support for their policies. According to many observers, Uzbek president Karimov believes that Uzbekistan should be the hegemonic power in the area, owing to its greater size, central location, and cultural advantages. Naturally, his brother presidents do not agree, and such disagreements often break up their frequent meetings before real progress can be made.

Another aspect affecting the establishment of strong economic ties is the inability of some of the Central Asian states to give up the soviet legacy of state trading, which has not helped in creating a strong private sector. A bulk of the trade in the energy sector is state-to-state. Consequently, when the customer-state fails to pay, the supplying state has been resorting to shutting off supplies, provoking either a diplomatic crisis or sometimes retaliation. This has happened even with water. The Syr Darya, Amur Darya, and several smaller rivers flow from Kyrgyzstan and Tajikistan to irrigate much of the arable lands of Uzbekistan and Turkmenistan, before joining Aral Sea. When the downstream states refuse to help Kyrgyzstan maintain the dams on the Naryn headwaters, the Kyrgyzstan has the option of releasing water at its own convenience, not when it is needed.[10]

Central Asian regional cooperation is also affected to a certain degree by ethnocentrism prevailing in these countries, except, perhaps in Turkmenistan. In the years before and after independence, bloody conflicts occurred in the Ferghna valley, including clashes between Uzbeks and Meskhetian Turks in Uzbekistan and between Kyrgyz and Uzbek in Kyrgyzstan. Although these clashes did not escalate into major regional conflicts, they demonstrated that ethnic tensions in the region have the potential to develop into explosive situations. In a 1993 survey of 2,067 people, only about 10 per cent of the respondents felt that their countries should rely on other Central Asian countries. Almost 50 per cent preferred to "go it alone." A cognisable number of respondents preferred seeking help from Western Europe, Japan, the USA, or even Russia in preference to fellow Muslim or Central Asian countries. More people said they would prefer not to work with another Central Asian "than with a Russian." Very few (about 10%) of the respondents said nationality would make no difference in working with a colleague.

Language has also become a point threatening regional integration of the Central Asian region. In spite of the existence of different languages, Russian continues to be the medium of inter-ethnic communication. Independent Central Asian states found it difficult to decide on the official language, due ethnic diversity of their populations. Attempts to give primacy to indigenous languages over Russian has naturally enraged Russian speaking population of the region, who consider it an infringement on their fundamental right. Under Kazakhstan's law, 50 per cent or more of all broadcasts should be in Kazakh and all ethnic Russian officials should gain proficiency in the native language. Under Turkey's influence, Uzbekistan has introduced Latin alphabet in schools from 1996 and Turkmenistan has printed textbooks in Latin. However, Tajikistan has expressed its intention to adopt Arabic. Uzbekistan's switch over to Latin alphabet has created problems for Uzbeks living in Tajikistan and Kyrgyzstan. Teachers in Uzbek schools in these countries demanded introduction of Latin alphabet. If the children do not learn Uzbek language the way it is taught in Uzbekistan, they would become strangers in their own motherland. But, if they switch over to Latin, they would be aliens in Tajikistan and Kyrgyzstan, where Cyrillic is used in the schools. The problem is explained by a researcher as under:

> "Thus, language will be an important factor in the separation of Central Asia into three or four new regions: Uzbekistan will use mainly the native language

> with Latin script; Tajikistan, as the one of the least Russified Muslim nations, will be subject to cultural influence from Iran; Turkmenistan continues its isolation; and Kazakhstan and Kyrgyzstan will retain the use of the Cyrillic alphabet within the Russian - dominated zone of communication. At the same time, English is beginning to seriously undermine the role of Russian, through out the Soviet successor states."[11]

THE CASE FOR REGIONAL COOPERATION

Regional integration facilitates easy transfer of capital, helps equalization of incomes and living conditions. A free trade area in Central Asia would constitute a much larger market than any of the isolated countries. An economic union allowing free movement of factors of production as well as goods would attract foreign investors. A large economic area, united politically for foreign policy purposes, can negotiate better prices on certain imports and preferential loan rates. To gain access to the regional market, foreign equipment suppliers would be forced to lower prices and improve terms. All these advantages would seem to apply to Central Asia, were it to move towards economic union in the future.

On the other hand, continued state trading in staples and energy, together with export globalism and very slow privatisation of enterprises, results in the slow growth of not only the indigenous business class, who would have a natural interest in trade with neighbouring countries, but also the liberalization of currency and banking practices. State monopoly might result in accrual of most of its revenue from the centralized sale of raw materials like cotton, gold, or petrochemicals or through leases for exploration, but does not permit the birth of indigenous manufacturing, which is essential for employment generation. Encouraging foreign-financed businesses has only created monopolies, which, in turn, has been discouraging the growth of domestic competition. Hence native entrepreneurs have remained small and mobile, holding their assets in cash, precious metals and jewellery, or real estate.

Openness across regional borders would not only increase competition, but also facilitate reduced government interference in the market. However, to counter such interference and the corruption it breeds, one needs a strong parliamentary opposition and independent judiciary. These countries should also understand that their economies are inter-dependent. Kyrgyzstan supplies electricity, hides and wool, and non-ferrous ores to its neighbours. Kazakhstan is a supplier of coal, chemicals and fertilizers, as well as non-ferrous minerals. Uzbekistan supplies natural gas and cotton. All these rely on specific factor endowments. Furthermore, the complementarity that exists could be enhanced by regional cooperation in manufacturing investment.

However, the Central Asian states have been trying to use the strong points of their economy to dictate terms to the others. Tajikistan for instance, relies heavily on Uzbek for fuel supplies, while Uzbekistan's cotton industry, the mainstay of its economy, depends on water flowing from Tajikistan's mountains. The economy of these two countries are closely integrated. But independence has seen each trying to go its own way, often with difficulty and mutual mistrust. In December 2003, the two countries negotiated water and energy-sharing deals, on a year-to-year basis. A high-level Tajik delegation's visit to Tashkent, led by the Tajik Prime Minister, focused on bilateral economic ties and signed two cooperation agreements on deliveries of gas and lubricants, rational use of water and energy resources. Tajikistan's trade with Uzbekistan accounts for about 25 per cent of Tajikistan's annual trade turnover. The level of trade has grown steadily in recent years. It stood at $120 million in 2002, but amounted to $110 million over just the first eight months of 2003. Apart from trade, the two countries have common problems like drug trafficking, international terrorism, and religious extremism.[12]

The gas-for-water agreement between Uzbekistan and Tajikistan was not an end in itself, and both the countries are yet to sort out their border problems. With a view to preventing the entry of the extremists of the Islamic Movement of Uzbekistan into its territory, Uzbekistan unilaterally planted mines along the Tajik-Uzbek border. Since 2000, about 60 Tajik civilians are reported to have been killed by these mines. Tajik nationals crossing the border complain about the frequent and illegal detention by the Uzbek police officers demanding bribes. Tajik transport firms have also complained that Uzbek customs officials often refuse to open a border-crossing point used mostly in winter due to the closure from piling up of snow on a road linking northern and southern Tajikistan. On the economic front, Uzbekistan has often cut gas supplies to Tajikistan, as the latter owes more than $100 million.

Yet another evidence of lack of cordial relations among the Central Asian states is found in Uzbekistan's refusal to permit the transit of electricity from Kazakhstan, through its territory. Every year in winter Tajikistan is compelled to buy 1 billion kilowatt hours of electricity from Kazakhstan. But due to Uzbek opposition to the transit of the electricity to Tajikistan, the latter has been able to receive less than 30 per cent of its needs from Kazakhstan through Uzbekistan. The Tajik government has tried for six months, during 2003, to solve the problem of electricity transfer through Uzbekistan, with little result. As late as in November 2003, the Managing Director of IMF commented:

> "All countries in the region need to ensure that *arbitrary restrictions* and corruption do not interfere with the flow of goods and services. And reinforcing

> cooperation in the areas of water and energy will be crucial for the development of the region and also for addressing serious environmental issues, for example regarding the Aral Sea. The CIS-7 initiative has boosted regional economic cooperation in the areas of regional tax issues, social sector reform, public expenditure policy, and financial sector issues. It will be important to build on this important stepping-stone."[13]

Even from the security angle, the Central Asian republics are in no position to set up their own national armies, and therefore are vulnerable to foreign aggression. In the former Soviet Union, 35 per cent of the young men, who were recruited into the Soviet Army, were non-Slavs. Of these, two-thirds of the soldiers were of Turkic origin. However, in the officer corps, the non-Russians were only 10 per cent. Consequently, even though the Central Asian republics would like to create their own national armies, there is a lack of trained indigenous officers. Further, Central Asians who served in the Soviet army were utilized for non-combat duties and, therefore, did not have combat experience.[14]

The fact of the matter is that the persons ruling these states do not wish to let go their power nor want their countries follow another's example. It may be recalled that under the CPSU's personnel policy, ethnic representatives of each titular nationality were appointed as the first secretaries, while the second secretaries mostly were Slavic. Although the CPSU appointments policy created a cadre of Central Asian officials, only a few of them were offered all-Union careers. Consequently, very few of the republican officials had any foreign education nor had any exposure to international experience, which would have changed their mind-set. Thus, the Central Asian republics now have a shortage of statesmen with diplomatic experience to deal with their neighbours, leave alone with the outside world.

In January 1996, Russia, Belarus and Kazakhstan signed an Agreement on the Customs Union among the three states. Kyrgyzstan and Tajikistan entered the Union in 1996 and 1998 respectively. However, this Union remained ineffective. In 31, May, 2002, the Eurasian Economic Community (EurAsEC) was formed in Minsk, replacing the Customs Union. President of Kazakhstan N.A. Nazarbayev, who promoted the idea, was elected as the chairman. But within two months, in July 2002, Russia introduced limitations on the import of Kazakhstani metal production. At the First Economic Forum of the Eurasian Economic Community, held in Moscow in February 2003, to activate the process of economic integration, the President of Kazakhstan emphasized the need for the introduction of a common currency, possibly before 2011.

Prior to the above meeting, the Presidents of Russia, Belarus, and Kazakhstan and Ukraine signed an agreement on the formation of the Common

Economic Space. The agreement envisaged the creation of a regional integration organization, harmonization of an appropriate legislation and economic policy, and the formation of a united regulating interstate independent Commission on trade and tariffs. Formation of this supranational economic regulating body distinguishes this initiative from the previous efforts. But, these efforts are seen as Russia's attempt to dominate the region, on account of which, the Central Asian states are discouraged from joining these 'Unions', as a condition for entering the World Trade Organization. It may be recalled that as early as in 1997, a pro-western alliance, GUAM (Georgia, Ukraine, Azerbaijan and Moldova) was formed to counter Russian domination. GUAM was later transformed into GUUAM, with the joining of Uzbekistan. Russia did not like either GUAM or GUUAM, considering them as efforts at destroying the CIS.

Kyrgyzstan, Kazakhstan, and Uzbekistan were enthusiastic proponents of yet another institution, the Central Asian Free Trade Area (CAFTA) and signed agreements in 1993 and 1996 which would have allowed completely tariff-free trade, among the three countries. However, Uzbekistan, which had acceded formally, held out restrictions in important categories. Since 1996 the non-convertibility of the Uzbek *som* prevented any substantial expansion of mid-level trade between Uzbekistan and its neighbours. Time and again the three presidents have postponed hard decisions on creating any single economic zone. Meanwhile, petty disputes among the Central Asian neighbours, over non-payment of bills for fuel, transit fees, and water continue to prevail.

Central Asian economists recognize that regional cooperation would be favourable for the regeneration of Central Asian industry and ultimate growth renewal. Even by early 2000, no Central Asian country had recovered the level of GDP it had achieved in 1989, though Uzbekistan is close. Besides exploiting natural resources for export, renewed growth in Central Asia will depend to a great extent on local manufacturing facilities. But efficient production requires a minimum assured output to achieve reasonably low costs, which, in turn, depends on the demand. For example, production of automobiles or farm machinery is subject to economies of a scale that cannot be fully exploited within Kyrgyzstan, or even Uzbekistan. Similarly if earlier Russia supplied electronics and other consumer appliances to a large market in Central Asia, Kyrgyzstan produced certain consumer goods for a larger Soviet market. Such trade having now ceased altogether, revival of civilian machine building in Central Asia is possible only if there is an easy access to nearby markets. In view of accumulated technical skills in all these countries, the potential for development is considerable if trade outlets can be assured.

CONCLUSION

Regional cooperation in Central Asia could go a long way in mitigating the effect of small domestic markets and extreme distances to industrialized countries that determine the economic landscapes in each Central Asian republic. Improved transport systems and policy environments, supportive of trade, would help arrest the widespread economic decline in the region. Regional cooperation and a common economic space would immediately benefit a large number of small traders, many of whom are women who have moved from restructuring state enterprises and government agencies into the private sector. Improved road transport is especially needed to encourage the development of small businesses. Improved rail transport will similarly lower the costs of operations and prove an incentive to new investment in large enterprises. Strengthening the potential for expansion of agriculture and industry would limit the ongoing labour redundancies and unemployment. Regional cooperation also offers scope for addressing some of the very difficult poverty issues such as the lack of adequate infrastructure in border areas.

Recent developments demonstrate that the Central Asian states have failed to cooperate with each other in achieving many common regional economic and political objectives, except, perhaps, in saving the Aral Sea. Such cooperation is not impossible in view of not only the common cultural and historical experiences but also the diversity and inter-dependency of their resource base. It is all the more necessary if they wish to avoid Russian domination, of which they are apprehensive about. Economic logic points to the advantages of regional cooperation. As long as the Central Asian states retain state hold and influence over trade and production, their actions so far do not, for the most part, conform with their many verbal commitments to regional cooperation. Financing for truly cooperative projects is small, and petty interferences at the borders do occur. The two most promising regional institutions, the Intergovernmental Commission and the Central Asian Bank, are still struggling to find their place and influence. Economic policies in these countries discourage mid-sized businesses that would most benefit from a free regional market. Political frictions among the states of the region and their preference for dealing with outsiders, outside the CIS, perceived to be more capable and less dangerous, are responsible for the failure to put rhetoric into practice. If regional cooperation is to increase, with all its benefits, it will require leadership from the inside or determined and patient assistance from the outside.

In spite of the fact that the Central Asian countries are facing the threat of international terrorism, they have failed to act in unison in countering the danger. They agree that Afghanistan poses the worst danger for the southern parts of the

CIS, and the creation of an extreme radical Islamic state in Central Asia is a major goal of international religious extremists and terrorists groups. But, except setting up international terrorism centre in Central Asia and similar cosmetic measures, nothing tangible has been done. The Central Asian states also face problems arising out of international drug mafia, acute poverty, deteriorating health standards etc., all of which need a joint effort. If their inability to come together is one problem, the unilateral actions taken by some of the countries is yet another. For instance, the CIS Secretariat complains: "Uzbekistan does not contribute to resolving the problem by creating an iron curtain and planting land mines that are banned by international conventions that kill civilians living in border areas."

As President Nazarbayev said in an interview: "The future of the CIS depends on the successful resolution of three key issues. The first of these is political. It is a matter of turning the CIS into an efficient instrument of multilateral cooperation and the settlement of political problems and conflicts. But, so far politics has overshadowed economics in the CIS and we all understand how fragile and short-lived such a bond is. Thus, preservation of the Commonwealth of Independent States requires that we immediately make up for lost time in economic integration. This can be done by the CIS republics that have a similar social, economic and political foundation. To be more precise, these are the states that have achieved results comparable to Russia in the liberalization of economics and public life."

There has been no shortage, either of declarations of intent, or of specific programmes of measures, or even of separate alignments within the CIS (the Collective Security Pact, the CIS Customs Union) intended to promote such cooperation. But the overwhelming majority of the hundreds of measures agreed on have never been implemented. In early 1998, the then-CIS Executive Secretary, Ivan Korotchenya, calculated that of the 887 documents drafted since the CIS was created, only 130 had been signed by all member states. Speaking in an interview in September 2003, Islam Karimov said: 'most of the 400 various documents signed within CIS were not working today. During the first years of the CIS, certain countries sought to focus more attention on political and military issues. In other words they yearned for the former Soviet Union and sought to restore it.'[15]

According to Islam Karimov, even today, some CIS states were striving to create new superstructures within the CIS that would enable them to supervise organizations. He gave the examples of the "quartet" [single economic space between Russia, Ukraine, Kazakhstan and Belarus], the "quintet" [the Customs Union of Russia, Ukraine, Kazakhstan, Belarus and Kyrgyzstan], Eurasia and so on.

Independence, the collapse of the Soviet-trade system, and the need to resolve regional issues, have led the Central Asian states to experiment with various institutional forms of economic cooperation. In addition, there have also been negotiations concerning trade in oil, electricity, and gas; water rights; and for cooperation concerning reconstruction of the environmental problems in the Aral Sea area. These activities reveal an underlying commitment to economic cooperation, an understanding and appreciation by the respective Governments that common solutions must be found to regional problems.

Ever since the inception of the CIS, the issue at stake that has plagued the member states is whether it is desirable to reach consensus on shared common objectives and on measures to ensure the optimum degree of cooperation in achieving those objectives. But, the question presupposes that CIS member states will, if necessary, subordinate their own interests to that of the CIS as a whole, and that they will refrain from adopting policies that could undermine the CIS. One of the things that the events of 2003 illustrated was that countries making up Central Asia are travelling along increasingly divergent paths. None of the five Presidents who delivered their new year eve messages to their countrymen and the world, spoke about the status of cooperation among the Central Asian states or of their plans to improve upon the existing level of cooperation. Those that touched foreign policy referred to their improved relations with Russia. Even this has to be taken for its face value.

REFERENCES

1. C.S. Martin Pechler, 'Regional Cooperation in Central Asia: Promises and More Promises' *The Fletcher Journal of Development Studies,* Vol. XVI, 2000.
2. Gleason, Gregory, Inter-state Cooperation in Central Asia from CIS to the Shanghai Forum', in *Europe-Asia Studies,* Vol. 53, No. 7, 2001, p. 1077.
3. W. Schneider-Deters, *Regional Cooperation in Central Asia: Vision and Reality,* http://www.kisi.kz/English/Geopolitics/11-04-03Schneider-Deters.pdf.
4. *Ibid.*
5. n. 2, p. 1084.
6. n. 3.
7. *Ibid.*
8. n. 2, p. 1083.
9. n. 2, p. 1084.
10. n. 1.
11. Tabyshalieva, Anara. 'The Challenge of Regional Cooperation in Central Asia: Preventing Ethnic Conflict in Ferghana Valley', *Peaceworks* No. 28, United States Institute of Peace, Washington DC, 2000.

12. Antoine, Blua. 'Central Asia: Tajikistan, Uzbekistan Try To Improve Strained Relations'. *RFE/RL*, 30 December 2003.
13. 'Opportunities and Challenges for Central Asia' Horst Köhler, Managing Director of the International Monetary Fund, At the Conference for the Tenth Anniversary of the Introduction of the *Tenge,* Almaty, Kazakhstan, 14 November, 2003, IMF.
14. Devlet, Nadir. 'Ethnicity and Power: Relations Between the Central Asian States' in *Journal of International Affairs*, Vol. II, No.1, March-May 1997.
15. Justine Burke, 'Most signed CIS agreements "not working today" — Uzbek leader' Uzbek President Karimov in an interview in Tashkent, *Uzbekistan Daily Digest,* 19 September 2003.

20

The Main Factors that Influence the Security of the Middle East After the Iraqi War

Zhang Jianwei

The strategic status of the Middle East is of great importance. The resources of oil and gas are abundant, various contradictions combine with each other, the conflicts and wars keep cropping up, and that the peace and development in this region are badly influenced. Although the possibility of another large-scale war is decreasing, after the Iraqi war, the factors that influence the security and stability of the region still exist. Especially the serious "aftereffects" left by the Iraqi War which has put the region in a volatile and unstable situation.

The factors that influence the security and stability of the Middle East are the United States, the nationalities and the religion.

FACTOR ONE: THE UNITED STATES

Because the United States can not change its position on the problem of the Middle East, the regional terrorism can not be eradicated.

The settlement of the problem of the Middle East can not be achieved without the United States. However, the United States has always adopted double standards on the problem, hence the conflicts between the Palestine and Israel have not been solved now for over a long period of time. The situation of the Palestine people worsens increasingly and the Islamic world, especially the Arabic countries, have shown strong dissatisfaction. By grabbing this opportunity, some Islamic extremists expand their power and take terrorist actions, which leaves grave impact on the regional security and stability and triggers off the terrorist activities around the world.

Before Iraqi War, the United States carried out the policy of "containing Iraq and overturning Saddam administration". The United States did not effectively stop the continuous bloody conflicts between Palestine and Israel. After the War, in order to relax the relations with Arabic countries, the United States pushed forward the plan of Road Map to Peace in the Middle East. However, the United States didn't really exert pressure on the implementation of the plan nor force the two sides to compromise with each other, so that the plan was held up at the beginning stage.

Guaranteeing the absolute security of Israel in the Middle East is the consistent position and strategic policy decision of the United States. In a short period of time, Palestine and Israel can not walk out from the vicious circle of retaliation. In a long period of time, even if the United States intensify its strength of mediation, it is impossible for the United States to change its consistent position and the Palestine-Israel problem can not be solved fairly. As long as the terrorist activities were not curbed from the root, the countries in the region would continue to face the threat of terrorism.

Some countries in the region will continue to face the pressures of the United States and will lack guarantee of the security and stability.

By taking an excuse of anti-terrorism and destroying WMD, the United States launched Iraqi War and overturned the Saddam administration, which has paved the way for comprehensively controlling the Middle East and its oil. However, the United States won the war, yet it did not bring real peace to the region. The post-war Iraq is in chaos. The political arrangements develop slowly, the economic reconstruction works with difficulties, the religious contradictions unceasingly intensifies, the terrorist bombs are thrown here and there, the security situation continues to worsen and the anti-America emotions increase day by day. Meanwhile, the war further stimulated the anti-America and hate-America feelings of the Islamic world and Muslims of all countries. The terrorist bombs were hurled in succession after the war in Turkey and Saudi Arabia have shown that the United States and its alliances would face even more serious terrorist threats.

After the Saddam administration was toppled, countries which were regarded as radical ones, like Iran and Syria were confronted with unprecedented pressure. In order to avoid being the next target of the United States, the countries adjusted their policies one after another and tried to ease their relations with the United States. Because there is lack of mutual trust between the United States and Iran and Syria, the contradictions between them are deeply rooted and the social systems and ideology are completely different, countries, including Iran and

Syria would not like to follow the orders of the United States while the United States will continue to exert pressure or even sanctions on the two countries and ask them to abandon the ideas of developing WMD and stop their support of terrorism. The relations between the two sides will possibly be intense at any time. At the same time, the big powers will continue to compete with the United States for the right to speak on regional affairs. There are still profound crises hidden in the Middle East.

The proposal of Great Middle East made by the United States will perhaps bring new changes to the situation of regional security.

In order to completely transform the Middle East, the United States is brewing a proposal of Great Middle East, which includes 22 Arabic countries and some Islamic countries, including Turkey, Iran, Pakistan and Afghanistan. The United States strives to push forward the comprehensive reform of all countries by starting with the politics, economy, democracy, human rights and education and finally realize the democratization of politics, liberalization of economy, secularization of religion and pluralism of society of all countries. The action, that was called the most ambitious effort on democracy, was attacked and resisted by the leaders of Arabic countries when it was still in the process of study. The reason for such a result is that the plan did not only neglect the Palestine-Israel issue that was of concern by the countries in the Middle East, but also neglected the specific politics, history, religion, nationality, culture and social traditions of the Islamic countries. It is probably the one-sided plan of the United States.

There exists a big gap which is hard to bridge between the ideal of the United States and the reality of the Islamic world. The situation in Iraq after the war has shown that the democracy of western style is unsuitable to Islamic countries and will even lead to contradictions and conflicts. President Bush had hoped to make Iraq a country of experiment that pushes forward the democracy of western style. However, the post-war Iraq has become the main arena of the international terrorism and a land mine positions that is hard for the United States and Britain to get the release from. Once the United States implements its Great Middle East Proposal, the contradictions between the two sides will surely be intensified and their relations will be worsened. Even more, it is possible to lead to the increase of terrorist actions targeted at the United States. On the other hand, the traditional alliances of the United States like Saudi Arabia and Jordan will face the dual pressure of the American democratic transformation and the anti-America feelings of the masses. If not properly handled, it will give rise to the instability of the political situation and the upheaval of the society and finally lead to the change of the regional political structure.

FACTOR TWO: NATIONALITY

The contradictions between the Arabic countries and Israel will still be the main problem that influences the regional security and stability.

The contradictions and conflicts between the Arabic nations and the Jewish nations have been existing now for several centuries. The contradictions and conflicts between the Arabic countries and Israel are the central embodiment of the contradictions between the Arabic nations and the Jewish nations and the contradictions between the Judaism and Islam. Although the two sides long for peace, one side stresses the concept of "land for peace", while the other side stresses "security for peace". The peace talk between Syria and Israel has been stagnated for a long time. On the issue of sovereignty and security of Golan highland, both sides will not make concessions easily. As long as Israel does not return the Sabaa Farm to Lebanon, the Hizbullah will not stop the attacks on Israel. The conflicts between the Palestine and Israel have never stopped, the terrorist bombs and bloody retaliations are mixed together. Salon administration forcefully built the Wall of Isolation and wanted to abandon the peace talk with Palestine. The prospect of the peace talk tends to be dark and the peace and security is nowhere in sight.

The Kurdish question will probably become a new hot issue of the region.

Kurd is one of the oldest nations in West Asia with a population of 22 million. Most of them live in Turkey, Syria, Iran and Iraq. Kurdish question is one of the most conspicuous questions of nationality in the Middle East for over a century. Over a long period of time, Kurdish nationality has never abandoned its effort for seeking national autonomy and building an independent Kurdish country. But it has not succeeded yet. The governments of Syria and Iran control the Kurds by making a combined use of favour and disfavour to keep peace and stability. The Kurds in Turkey have suffered several times on account of cleaning up by the Turkey government and their power has decreased greatly. However, the Kurds in Iraq set up Kurdish autonomous region in North Iraq, in 1991, with the support of the United States and their strength and influence has been further enhanced after they helped the United States topple the Saddam administration. According to the temporary constitution, promulgated by Iraq, the federal system will be in existense in Iraq, which means that the Kurdish will gain high-level autonomy. In a short time, the Kurds will not seek independence, but they will not give it up easily, either. Although the effect of a "country within a country" has not set off a chain reaction for the time being, it will undoubtedly stimulate the Kurds in other countries to strive for national self-determination and increase the difficulties for the countries concerned to guard against them. Some countries, including Turkey are worried about that and the rights entrusted to the Kurds by the Iraqi constitution have led to strong dissatisfaction.

FACTOR THREE: RELIGION

The contradictions between the Shiite Muslims and the Sunni Muslims will create troubles to the new Iraqi government.

During the period of Saddam administration, the Sunni Muslims were in power, yet the Shiite Muslims that accounts for most of the population were oppressed. The resentment between the two sides has led to armed confrontations many times. After the war, the Sunni Muslims have become the focus that the US-British armed forces have to guard against. The influence of the Shiite Muslims has increased and the political status of the two sides has reversed. After that, the Shiite Muslims successively suffered the terrorist attacks and have been seriously injured. Although the Sunni Muslims did not necessarily create those terrorist bombs, the terrorists wanted to take this as an opportunity to express their discontent and provoke the conflicts between the Shiite Muslims and the Sunni Muslims so as to disturb the US plan of the reconstruction of Iraq. In order to prevent large-scale conflicts and internal disorder, the two sides now adopt the manner of relative self-restraint. If the gap of the political status of the two sides was widened in the future, the contradictions between the two sides will probably be intensified, which will seriously threaten the security and stability of Iraq and bring new unstable factors to the region.

The continuous growth of the Islamic radical forces has brought about great security dangers.

In recent years, due to the slow development of the political reform, the stagnancy of economic development, the widening of the gap between the rich and the poor and the prominent social problems, the Islamic radical forces have gained ground to some extent and have gradually expanded. These people discriminate against the modern civilization, hate the West and western culture, criticize the regime in power as the puppets of the West and advocate to establish a strict country with the combination of politics and religion. In order to achieve that, they instigate the religious feelings of the people to express their discontent of the government by making use of every religious occasion and wait for an opportunity to engage in terrorist attacks. They also create turmoil and panic in society. Meanwhile, after the Taliban regime was overturned, some members of Al-Qaeda move stealthily back to the countries in the region. They keep in touch with the local radical and extremist forces, save up energy and wait for chance, which has become a cancer that will influence the security and stability of all countries in the region.

21

The Al Qaeda Threat to Southeast Asian Security

Problems and Prospects

S.P. Singh

While functioning both operationally and ideologically at local, regional and global levels, the Al Qaeda has enormously threatened the Southeast Asian security in the recent years. The various international intelligence agencies, led predominantly by the CIA and the FBI, are engaged in confronting the biggest ever challenges to this far-flung region, which have been thrown up by the first multinational and the most feared terrorist outfit of the 21st century. Having a global reach, across the entire continent, this group has catapulted terrorism as an integral part of the most coherently organized international instrument with avowed commitment to the substitution of corrupt western influence in the Muslim–populated Southeast Asian region. After the world's most devastating terrorist outrage on 9/11, it has been acknowledged as the pioneering vanguard of the worst variety of global Islamist threat. The Al Qaeda, the shadowy body of the Islamists, and its other associate terrorist groups have been alleged by the CIA to have infiltrated one-fifth of all the Islamic NGOs sprinkled all over the world in general and the Southeast region in particular. The Al Qaeda has managed the strategic depth even among the European, North American and Australian Muslims.

The Al Qaeda aims at the replacement of the existing Muslim regimes with Islamic polity in accordance with the tenets of the *Shariat.* Its associate groups in West, Central and Southeast Asia have been acting in concert with British, German, French, Spanish, Belgium, Canadian, Italian, Albanian,

Bosnian and US cells. The Al Qaeda has developed indelible connections with Abu Sayyaf Group (in Malaysia and the Philippines), Palestinian Islamic Jihad, Islamic Jihad (in Egypt), Jemaah Islamiah (in Indonesia), Islamic Army of Aden, National Islamic Front (in Sudan), Islamic Movement of Uzbekistan, Salafist Group and Armed Islamic Group (in Algeria), Lashkar-e-Toiba and Jaish-e- Mohammed (in Kashmir), and various terrorist outfits in West and Central Asian countries.

The multi-national, multi-ethnic and multi-lingual Al Qaeda groups predominantly share Sunni Muslim fundamentalist groups, but after the Afghanistan debacle, they have stepped up co-operation with Hezbollah, the minority Shiite militia from Lebanon, with the backing of Iran. Over the years, it has cut across sectarian classes and has drawn followers from all strata of society.

In recent years, the Al Qaeda has concentrated its operations in various parts of Southeast Asia. After 11th September, which was like a wake-up call to the USA and its traditional allies, experts have been continuously unearthing unimpeachable evidences testifying to the existence of numerous locally trained separatists and terrorist groups in the Southeast Asian region, having long running connections, both locally and globally. The various Islamic terrorist organizations in this area are aiming at creating Islamic Super State consisting of Indonesia, Singapore, the Sultanate of Brunei and parts of the southern most areas of the Philippines, Thailand and even Cambodia.

The Al Qaeda made first inroad into Southeast Asia with the despatch of Muhammad Jamal Khalifa to this region as far back as in 1988. Osama bin Laden deputed Ramzi Ahmad Yousef to the Philippines after he bombed the World Trade Center in February 1993. Khalifa backed him in training the Abu Sayyaf Group (ASG) in terrorist techniques.

PHILIPPINES

It was in the course of the trial of Yousef in the USA, after he was detained in the aforesaid bombing case, that the details of Al Qaeda network in the Philippines, during 1988-93, came to be known to the world [1].

In 1994, the Al Qaeda plotted to kill Pope John Paul II during his visit to Manila and a year later, it made an abortive attempt to assassinate President Bill Clinton during his state visit to the Philippines. As part of the Al Qaeda-sponsored *Oplan Bojinka* in 1994, which was plotted by Yousef, Philippines president Fidel Ramos, his two aids, numerous foreign envoys along with several top defence and police personnel were to be killed.

Yousef's plot was aimed at bombing chief business offices, departmental stores, churches, main government buildings and the US Embassy in Manila. The Al Qaeda had also gone to the limits of plotting to bomb 11 US Airplanes over the pacific. Due to Yousef's timely detention, however, series of the well-planned mishaps, including the one to crash an explosive–laden aircraft on to the Pentagon and CIA headquarters, were averted.

It is worth mentioning here that Jamal Khalifa, one of Laden's top associates and his brother-in-law, subsequently led the ASG in the southern part of the Philippines.[2]

Initially, the ASG was led by Abdurajak Janjalani, a native Muslim, who fought in Afghanistan, as a mujahiddin. Osama is said to have forged links with Janjalani and introduced him to Yousef in Peshawar. It is believed, says Gunaratna, that the ASG's organization, ideology, target selection and tactics are deeply influenced by the Al Qaeda.[3] The ASG has taken leading role in bombing the churches, murdering the missionaries and the foreign priests as well as abducting the American tourists in the Philippines [4.]

In addition to the ASG, members of the Moro Islamic Liberation Front (MILF) are also believed to have been trained in the Al Qaeda camps in Afghanistan. The MILF has been reported to have arranged for the huge collection of weapons as well as explosives, which were used in attacking on US, Australia, Israeli and British targets in Singapore.

The Al Qaeda, which had earlier formed a special Moro sub-brigade in Afghanistan for fighting against the Soviets, later picked up a few hundred Moros from the Mindanao region in southern Philippines. Those Moros were organized and trained for fighting a Jihad in order to set up an independent Islamic state.

In order to ward off the close connections of the Al Qaeda, with both the ASG and the MILF, the Bush Administration has shared armed forces intelligence with the Philippines Government and provided it with training assistance as well as two hundred military advisers also in February 2002.

Recently the Philippines government arrested Rahman al Ghazi, an Indonesian explosive expert for forging linkage between Islamiah of Indonesia and the MILF, which has threatened to attack any joint Philippines-US forces. While committing all out support to the US led global campaign against terrorism, the President of the Philippines has offered logistical support, the country's air space, intelligence reports and the two former American navel bases Clark Air Force Base and the Pubic way.

In addition to clearing the anti-money laundering legislation to forestall the flow of terrorist and drug-money, Manila has called for a tri-nation anti-terrorist coalition with Malaysia and Indonesia. Recently, they have agreed to draft an agreement, which would facilitate the various measures required to combat terrorism and border crimes. The Philippines government has further agreed to receive advice and logistical support from the US troops in its fight against ASG.

The Philippines is the only country besides Afghanistan to receive US troops in the global fight against terrorism. In addition to the 500 support and technical personnel the US contingent consists of 160 special operation forces including Navy SEALS, the armies green berates, marines armed special forces. The US forces, while providing only technical support, advice and training, will not participate in combat. Since 31 January, 2004, however, joint training exercises have been conducted for the "Balikitan' (shoulder-to-houlder) operations against the Al Qaeda and allied terrorist groups in the Philippines.

INDONESIA

There have become available several evidences of clandestine Al Qaeda operations in Indonesia, which has been continuously marred by violence, terrorism and separatism perpetrated primarily by numerous radical Islamic groups. The Jemaah Islamia (JI) is alleged to be involved in several bombings in Indonesia, in the Philippines, including explosions in Jakarta as well as Manila in December 2000, which took 35 lives [5]. The JI is said to have expanded the Al Qaeda network in the entire Southeast Asian region in association with the Kumpulan Mujahidin Malaysia (KMM). It is alleged to have executed the terrorist attack on nightclubs in Bali in 2003 which was reportedly plotted by Khalid Saikh Mohammad.[6] Abu Bakr Bassy is said to have led the JI. Bakr was detained on complaints from Singapore and Malaysia but was released for want of concrete evidences of involvement in the terrorist activities. It is alleged that the Indonesian government is soft on him for fear of Muslim backlash in the country. Critics maintain that in July 2003 five Al Qaeda terrorists sneaked into this country with a view to blowing up the US Embassy in Jakarta. The US officials, however, hold that they were allowed safe passage by the Indonesian authorities to slip away from the country in order to escape from the resultant terrorist crackdown in the event of their detention.

Initial denials, notwithstanding, the Indonesian government acknowledged, in December 2003, the presence of Al Qaeda training camps on its soil.

Engaged in the killing of several Christians, this group is led by Jaffar Umar Thalib, believed to have interacted closely with Laden in the 1980, though he has denied any such ties including receiving monetary assistance from the Al Qaeda.

The country's Foreign Minister has denied any ties of local Muslim outfit with any international terrorist network.

Another militant Muslim group named Lashker-e-Jihad has been setup in Indonesia with the sole agenda of founding an Islamic state on its soil.

There are reports that Indonesian Islamic Liberation Front (IILF) has received direct training from the Al Qaeda in Afghanistan as well as from the trainers in some pockets in the Philippines.

Just a few months ago, the Bush administration despatched a secret Delta force to the Indonesian capital to bolster its feeble security arrangement.

The US Congress has passed a bill in December 2003, which has permitted the Indonesian security personnel to take part in counter-terrorism-training programmes. In addition to the sanction of non-military assistance to Indonesia, the Bush administration has granted a sum of $10 million to this country for the training of its police, customs and bank officials. It has proposed intelligence sharing.

Indonesian response to anti-terrorist activities amounts to loud rhetoric but no substantial action. Critical of Indonesia's feeble response, the neighboring countries have mounted their pressures on it.

It is true that this enormously poor, largest Muslim, and hugely scattered country has long been embroiled in bloody secessionist movements and recurrent sectarian violence between the Muslim majority as well as Christian minority. President Megawati Sukarnoputri has, no doubt, chosen to support George Bush in his global attack on terrorism. She was one of the first heads of state to meet Bush, offer condolence and pledge support to the USA in the post 9/11 period. Back home, however, she was dissuaded by some of the largest protests denouncing US military campaign in Afghanistan. The violent reaction of the country's 176 million Muslim did not allow her to respond positively.

MALAYSIA

Some recent evidences have revealed that numerous Al Qaeda related terrorists have been filtering in and out of Malaysia, which has been used as a staging ground for a couple of abduction cases by the Abu Sayyaf terrorist group of the Philippines. With the recent report of the FBI, that Malaysia has been a primary operational launch pad for 9/11 attacks this tiny country has caught the attention of strategic thinkers. Although critical of the FBI reports, Prime Minister Mahathir Mohammad has acknowledged the identification of 50 natives with Al Qaeda ties.

Yazid Sufaat, an important suspect, has been recently detained under the controversial Internal Security Act. This, Malaysian chemist has been associated with the Jemaah Islamiaah of Indonesia and Hambuli, the notorious terrorist, who has been the leader of the Kumpulen Mujahidin Malaysia (KMM). This terrorist organization seeks to establish an Islamic state composed of Malaysia, Indonesia and the Muslim dominated Philippines.

In December 2003, the government of Mahathir has taken strong measures against Al Maunah, an Islamist sect of Malaysia, and has ordered the hanging of three of this group and life imprisonment for its 16 members on the charges of treason. He, however, has been critical of creating "more terror" through the US –led coalition. Mahathir tried to impress upon the world leaders, at the World Economic Forum in February 2004, that they should try to understand Muslim grievances and "listen to the views of others". Sufaat is alleged, by the US officials, to have known at least two of the hijackers on board the ill-fated planes on 9/11. He helped Bin Laden, both financially and organizationally, in the expansion of Al Qaeda's network throughout Southeast Asia.

SINGAPORE

Of late, the activities of the Al Qaeda in the affluent city-state of Singapore have triggered off alarm bells in the entire Southeast region. While blaming Abu Bakr of the Jemaah Islamiaah for plotting to bomb the American Embassy including other Western installations in Singapore, the intelligence community of this country has unearthed numerous evidences testifying to direct linkages between this group and the Al Qaeda. Along with the Philippines, Singapore has also fully supported the anti-terrorist coalition with the US. Since 9/11, it has set up a national security secretariat within its defence ministry in order to oversee counter terrorism measures. By way of tightening its border security, it has made it necessary for the citizens of Iran, Saudi Arabia, Sudan, Pakistan and Egypt to obtain visas before entering Singapore.

CONCLUSIONS

From the foregoing account of the activities of the Al Qaeda and its associate Islamist groups, sprinkled over the Southeast Asian countries, it becomes obvious that these elements are deeply entrenched in this volatile region. The intricacy of the workings of the various terrorists conflicts, their elaborate networking, elusive nature of the native partners, clandestine activities of the perpetration of terrorism and the complicities of their involvement in the drug- trafficking as well as money laundering businesses have contributed enormously to the consolidation of Al Qaeda in this remote region. It augurs well for all the countries in this area that all the governments have acknowledged the need of cooperation for further enhancement of legal, military and political arrangements. Although the words of the heads of state are not matching with their deeds, it is worth noting that

Indonesia, Malaysia and the Philippines have agreed to finalize an accord with a vow to combating terrorism. This may lead further to the creation of a Rapid Response Force. The long existing Forum of the Association of Southeast Asian Nations is already available for coordination among them in the field of security arrangements. This organization, at the Brunei Summit in November 2003, has already adopted the ASEAN Declaration on joint action to counter terrorism. Procedures for collaborative efforts are being finalized. The ASEAN initiative has earned high credibility in the anti-terrorism global coalition. Its success will further pave the way for stronger and broad anti-terrorism framework through the collaboration efforts of ASEAN –Plus-Three (Japan, South Korea and the USA, ASEAN- China summits, ASEAN Regional Forum as well as US-ASEAN Dialogue. All this augurs well for the progression of the global fight against terrorism.

REFERENCES

1. Simon Reeve, *The New Jackals: Ramzi Yousef, Osama bin Laden and the Future of Terrorism,* London, 1999, p. 157. See also *Ramzi Ahmad Yousef,* Intelligence Report, Kuwait, 1996.
2. See Muhammad *Jamal Khalifa,* Biographical Profile, Directorate for Intelligence, Philippines National Police, Manila, n.d.
3. Gunaratna, Rohan, *Inside Al Qaeda: Global Network of Terrorism,* New Delhi, 2002, p.174.
4. *Ibid.*
5. "Muslims Groups Hunt for the Americans", *The Jakarta Post,* 24 September 2001.
6. "Anti-US Plots", *Los Angeles Times,* 7 Febraury 2002.

22

Changing Dynamics of Regionalism in Southeast Asia

SHANKARI SUNDARARAMAN

The theme of this conference specifically refers to pan-Asianism. Taking into consideration the shifts that have occurred in the global scenario since the dawn of the new millennium this theme is not only relevant but also needs to be discussed at this juncture. The most defining moment in this period has been the 9/11 terrorist attacks upon the United States and the subsequent assertion of unilateralism. The inability of the United Nations to curb the US action in Iraq and the manner in which the US has carried out its actions, leave little doubt about the unrivaled military superiority of the US. These two factors give rise to the urgency for a debate which focuses upon redefining the patterns of regional cooperation in Asia. There are within this scenario, two critical components that have a serious impact upon the Asia-Pacific region, in general. First the US action precludes the fact that the era of unilateral power will remain uncontested by any single power, at least for some time to come. Second, for the smaller Asian countries this is rather significant since the US action has undermined multilateral approach which was envisioned by the leaders of the post colonial period and was articulated by the events such as the Bandung conference of 1955. While several scholars have opined that the 21st century will be the Asian century, in my opinion, it was the 20th century and the idealism of leaders such as Nehru, Nasser and Sukarno that remains the hallmark of Asian identity. Taking into consideration the current global scenario there is an imperative to draw upon the lessons left behind by that generation of leaders and make attempts to progress towards 'building a new Asia', as suggested in the theme of this conference.

In addressing the problems and prospects of regional cooperation in Asia, it is significant to bear in mind that various regions of Asia do not fit in any specific pattern of generalization. While determining the nature of the political and security landscape in Asia, cognizance must be taken of the fact that the diversity of the Asian canvas itself acts as a limitation. Even within the distinct regions of Asia this diversity is very much at play, thereby making it difficult to weave together a common agenda for development and security in the region. In the current paper I focus specifically on regionalism in Southeast Asia — which today is undergoing a critical phase of transition in terms of what the region sees as it's political, economic and security calculations. Southeast Asia regionalism today is challenged by the dictates of diverse interests among the regional members both in terms of the development and security.

PROBLEMS OF ASEAN REGIONALISM: COPING WITH THE CHALLENGES OF CHANGE?

One of the most successful regional groupings in Asia has been the ASEAN. From its inception till date — though there have been periods when critics of ASEAN have been in a rush to place its obituary, it has shown resilience and the willingness to restructure itself according to the changing global environment. The success of ASEAN, as a grouping, has been well described by Michael Leifer in an authoritative work on the way in which ASEAN had originated. Based on the twin streams of legal-rational and social-cultural approach, the ASEAN followed a 'common adherence to conventional international norms'.[1] Moreover the underlying principle of state behaviour toward each other was to be founded upon the 'respect for justice and the rule of law in the relationship among the countries of the region', with an emphasis on adherence to the United Nations Charter.[2] However there is a view that the success of ASEAN rested upon its ability to utilise both the approaches in combination. In addition to this the uniqueness of ASEAN has been underscored by the use of the principle of consensus — both *musyawarah* or consultation and *mufakat* or consensus, were used as the principle rules of the decision making process.[3] This principle of consensus was justified as a 'regional cultural style' of functioning and became the modus operandi for the ASEAN.[4]

Another distinction of the ASEAN was that the very concept of security in Southeast Asia differed from the Western view, which was essentially state related and relied on the logic of military capacity to protect the nation from external threat. In the case of Southeast Asia, the original five members of ASEAN, from its inception in August 1967, have recognized an approach that has always been more inclusive and holistic.[5] In fact from its inception the ASEAN had aimed at the formation of some kind of a 'collective political defence'.[6] The most ardent voices that supported this notion, within Southeast Asia were from Indonesia and Malaysia. Indonesian leaders at that time stressed the need to include domestic challenges to security, which arose from issues relating to communist insurgency, ethnic tensions as well as economic and social disparities. Similarly the Malaysian leaders, too, emphasized that comprehensive security would include the non-military challenges. Moreover, the weakness of the socio-political cohesion of the new states, the problems relating to regime stability, intra-state disputes, inter-state ideological divides and the presence of external powers in the region all contributed to the endorsement of such a holistic approach to security in the region.[7] Such a view, in the early years of ASEAN's emergence, was significant because member states had to contend with problems relating to the insurgencies, ethnic tensions — the particularly with relation to socio-economic inequities. The notion of ASEAN's comprehensive security was further enhanced by factoring in the view that 'inclusive regionalism and multilateralism' were complementary approaches to managing security; which had hitherto been defined more narrowly by bilateralism and nuclear deterrence, thereby leading to an espousal of cooperative security.[8]

Another factor that went toward measuring the success of ASEAN was the economic gains, which the region achieved by the mid-eighties. From the late sixties till the early nineties there was no doubt that economic development has been one of the pillars of regionalism in Southeast Asia. Espousing a model of export driven economies, with closed domestic markets and no room for import substitution, these economies achieved a high degree of growth, which was a crucial factor for the cohesiveness of the ASEAN.

However, for almost a decade ASEAN has been faced with several challenges. For this presentation I will look at two temporal junctures within which I see the changes occurring in Southeast Asian regionalism. These are the 1997 financial crisis and the 2001 terrorist attacks in the United States. The reasons for choosing these two time frames is significant as they represent the two critical periods under the influence of which Southeast Asian regionalism has evolved and restructured itself. In this section I will briefly touch upon a few events that have posed a challenge to the ASEAN.

The 1997 Financial Crisis

First, the 1997 financial crisis has had an impact that is asserting itself even today. While the countries of the region did not face the same problems it has left some countries more affected than the others. As a result of this, members had become more inward looking in the process of trying to deal with both their economic recovery as well as maintaining political stability.[9] Moreover, there was also the emergence of bilateral tensions and the weakening of intra-ASEAN ties — a clear example of this is that of Singapore, which had been the least affected, was seen by other members as not having been supportive to the needs of the member states and was called a 'fair-weather friend' by some member countries. Moreover in the aftermath of the crisis, there has been criticism that the ASEAN had been unable to provide 'a united front in dealing with the challenges of globalisation'.[10] A view emerged within the region that the East Asia model based on its vision of rapid economic development did not cover social and political inequalities. Three factors contributed to this view. First, globalisation was basically seen as a response to global factors.[11] Second, the process of globalization itself had been articulated and led by the regime in power with the hope that economic prosperity would lead to regime consolidation.[12] Third, the region had not opened up in a collective manner but had introduced globalisation at various stages and that led to the implementation of the first order adjustments and not to the second order adjustments.[13] Moreover, there was recognition that the traditional notion of the state as the key player in the security dialectic gets transformed under the impact of globalisation as it can contribute to a heightened awareness of divisibility and can shift the focus from the sovereign state to the internal social elements, that are at play. As a result of globalisation there is increasing 'porosity or irrelevance of state boundaries' because of which there is growing exposure to and interaction between internal social groupings and external forces.[14] The financial crisis of 1997 underscored this view and the political legitimacy of that state came to be challenged, particularly in the case of Indonesia.

The focus of the debate on globalisation also saw the emergence of differences within the ASEAN — among the groups who advocated greater globalisation as part of the efforts to build deeper economic ties with the west, such as Singapore and Philippines and those who felt that some countries were left far more affected than the rest — Indonesia was of this opinion. The specific case of Indonesia is critical to this analysis — there is a view that the difference in the centre-periphery arrangement had become more sharpened as a result of the centralised economic polices of the New Order regime and had unleashed issues relating to identity, in a quest for greater control over economic assets.[15] Even among the new members such as Vietnam and Laos this fear is there — their entry into the WTO places demands on the reduction of tariff and the removal of non-tariff import barriers for TNC's.[16] These divergent views among the members has led to the strains within the regional organisations such as the ASEAN, APEC and the furtherance of the AFTA. The issue was also raised at the APEC Ministerial meeting, that took place in October 2003 at Bangkok, which set up the Economic and Technical Cooperation (ECOTECH), which could address issues relating to the social dimensions of globalisation.[17]

The significance of this relates to the fact that the region has begun to address this issue and also find space for maneuvering within the given set of circumstances to look into economic development and also set in place measures to address the problems relating to it. One such measure was the furthering of the ASEAN plus three processes — which began as an initiative to address macro-economic risk management, with an emphasis on strengthening the banking and financial sectors, and reform of international finance structures.[18] Added to this it was also to look at issues relating to the social and human index, as well as those relating to culture and information.[19]

The Enlargement of ASEAN

The second challenge to ASEAN, as I see it, is the enlargement of ASEAN and its expansion to include four new members — Vietnam, Myanmar, Laos and Cambodia. As a result of this ASEAN has diversified, both politically and economically. In fact it is believed that the political diversification of ASEAN has led to the dilution of the ASEAN way. At one end of the spectrum are countries that are completely authoritarian in structure such as Myanmar, where the political fissures are very deep. On the other side of the spectrum are those that are on the democratic path, such as Thailand and Philippines. In between these are those that are semi-authoritarian such as Singapore, Malaysia, Brunei and Cambodia. Vietnam and Laos follow the communist model and Indonesia has just begun the democratisation process.[20] Both as a result of the crisis and the expansion of ASEAN, there has been an increase in intra-ASEAN tensions and bilateral tensions among the members. Even within ASEAN the challenge of democratic transition has led to a shift in the way in which the member states have altered their behaviour towards each other. Moreover there has been an erosion of the two principle elements of the ASEAN approach which are its policy of non-intervention and consensus. This has led to the intra-ASEAN schisms over many issues. For example — there was criticism from the Philippines over the treatment meted out to Anwar Ibrahim, which would, in other circumstances have been considered a part of the domestic issue and would not have merited any discussion at all. Moreover, at the time of Cambodia's entry into the ASEAN, in 1999, the grouping almost came to vote on the matter. This went completely against the 'ASEAN way' which was to be based primarily upon consensus and consultations.

Moreover the inclusion of newer members into ASEAN has diversified security interests of the members, too. It is important to remember that the core security values of the original five members were not shared by the new members of ASEAN. This disparity itself was difficult to resolve. In fact, initially when the issue of inclusion of newer members arose there were differences within ASEAN to find compatible approaches. For example at the time of Vietnam's inclusion Singapore had concerns relating to the economic compatibility of Vietnam with the rest of the members while Thailand rejected the idea.[21] In fact the Thai suggestion had been for the formation of a loosely knit grouping of Southeast Asia-10, which would have a ten year moratorium for the inclusion of the newer members into the actual ASEAN itself.[22]

However, with Singapore dropping its reservations to Vietnam's inclusion, the Thai objections too found little favour and Vietnam was finally admitted.[23] Similar differences were also evident at the time of Myanmar's entry, where the issue of the junta's human rights record cropped up. However, the view that the ASEAN should take a decision that was not contingent upon the Western approach to Myanmar was clearly articulated by both Indonesia and Malaysia, which were key players in the ASEAN. There was a view that the consensus policy within ASEAN and the sovereignty of the region could not be compromised, over issues relating to the Western interpretations of human rights.[24]

Simultaneously, with the enlargement of the ASEAN, one sees the weakening of the Indonesian state structure, which has again added another dimension of vulnerability to the ASEAN and has contributed to a weakening of the ASEAN structure.[25] There is no doubt that Indonesia was one of the most vital links in the ASEAN chain — and was considered the '*primus inter peras*' within the ASEAN. One of the key factors for ASEAN's success was the capacity to maintain political stability among the countries. This was seen as a key ingredient of economic development which would in turn contribute to greater regime consolidation.

With the political collapse of Indonesia, following the financial crisis, a major source of ASEAN's strength was undermined. Added to this another vital member, Malaysia, saw challenges within the political structure in the manner in which the Anwar Ibrahim affair was handled. This followed by the uncertainties relating to the succession issue ensured that two of the most vital elements of the ASEAN chain were hampered by developments within the state and so the focus on the challenges from the inclusion of new members did not receive the necessary attention.

Regional Responses to Terrorism

In the aftermath of the WTC bombings, two statements made by the US President George Bush had direct implications for Southeast Asia. The first statement that those who were not with the US, were against them and the second that the 'theatre of war would not stop at Afghanistan', is crucial for the Southeast Asian region, which itself is trying to cope with the growing problem of religious revivalism and with fringe groups seeking refuge in radical Islamic ideology. These fringe elements have the capacity to create instability, thereby affecting both economic development and the further consolidation of the democratic processes, that have come in after the financial crisis. The impacts of the WTC attacks had two significant reactions from within the region. In the initial stages, regional ties among the ASEAN countries were under some strain. Statements from ASEAN leaders on possible linkages, that the groups within the region had with the Al-Qaida, caused some level of bilateral tensions. For example a statement by Senior Minister Lee Kuan Yew that Indonesia was proving to be a hotbed for terrorism had been regarded as a controversial remark, which furthered bilateral tensions.[26] In response to this statement, the Indonesian Foreign Affairs Minister, Hasan Wirayuda, on an official visit to Kuala Lumpur, expressed Indonesia's concerns over the strains in bilateral relations. Moreover, the fact that Lee Kuan Yew had made a statement to the press, rather than through the usual proper channels that had been established in the region for discussion of such issues, remains a valid point. However, the regional members did come together to address the issue and, in the course of time, this became a rallying point for the ASEAN. It is worth noting that as a result of the Asian financial crisis the intra-ASEAN linkages had been undermined leading to tensions and fissures within the regional grouping. The 'war on terrorism' has reconfigured these dynamics and there is once again a revival with relation to the intra-ASEAN equations. One of the indicators in this regard was the fact, that in the aftermath of the Bali bombings, that the regional players orchestrated their support for the actions taken by the government in Indonesia and gave their consent for Bali as the next venue of the ASEAN summit, that took place in October 2003. This was a clear articulation of confidence in Indonesia's capacity, to both respond to the attacks and to provide a safe environment for the next summit.

This culminated in a series of regional response that took shape over the past two years. These responses have been briefly highlighted below:

(a) In November 2001, at the Brunei meeting of the ASEAN Heads of States Governments, the ten members of the ASEAN signed the 2001 ASEAN Declaration on Joint Action to Counter Terrorism. This declaration unequivocally condemned the September 11 attacks and extended its sympathy to the victims. It also stated that it viewed all acts of terrorism as, "a profound threat to international peace and security, which would require concerted action to protect and defend all peoples and the peace and security of the world".[27] The declaration also endorsed that it did not associate terrorism with any particular religion or race, and stated that the ministers concerned would be tasked to ensure that follow-up action on this would be of prime concern to the ASEAN, particularly in terms of strengthening the national and regional mechanisms to combat terrorism.[28]

(b) In May 2002, Malaysia, Indonesia and the Philippines signed a trilateral security pact at Kuala Lumpur called the 'Agreement on Information Exchange and Establishment of Communications Procedures'.[29] Under this agreement the signatories would cooperate to counter cross-border terrorism and to break the militant network in the region. This came as a crucial step in addressing the serious misgivings among countries of the region. The agreement provided a framework for the countries to facilitate cooperation among them and also adopted procedural steps which could address issues relating to security of the borders. One of the most important clauses of the pact was the move to establish a Joint Committee, highlighting the SOP's-sharing of airline passenger lists, strengthening border patrol, joint exercises and training to combat terrorism.[30] The Agreement is currently among the three members but is open to the rest of ASEAN, at a later date, if need be.

(c) The third initiative at the regional level was the issuing of a Joint Communiqué by the Special ASEAN Ministerial Meeting on Terrorism that took place between May 20-21, 2002, at Kuala Lumpur. The significance of this has been the agreement to execute a work programme on terrorism. The salient features of this agreement include exchange of information; compilation and regulation of relevant laws and regulations of the ASEAN members; compilation and dissemination of bilateral and multilateral agreements and information on relevant international treaties where feasible; development of legal mechanisms at the bilateral as well as the multilateral levels to facilitate counter terror strategies; enhancement of cooperation in law enforcement and intelligence sharing and the development of regional training programmes in counter terror tactics.[31]

While these three form the basic response, in terms of the regional initiative, the ASEAN has also enlarged the scope of the terrorism issue by not confining its linkages within the region alone. Both with the United States and India it has issued a Joint Declaration for Cooperation to Combat International Terrorism.[32]

PROSPECTS FOR MOVING BEYOND ASEAN TO PAN-ASIANISM: AGENDAS FOR SECURITY AND DEVELOPMENT

Having touched upon the key issues that have emerged as challenges to Southeast Asian regionalism, in this section of the paper some basic approaches and initiatives that further the process of regionalism to go beyond the limits of ASEAN and allow for a larger matrix of development and security related linkages to be formed are being examined. In this assessment two critical player emerge — India and China. In terms of both its security and economic dimensions ASEAN has identified both India and China as key players. The waning focus that had been given by India to ASEAN and vice versa changed with the end of the cold war and the beginning of India's Look East policy.[33] Three factors drew India closer to the ASEAN — first, ASEAN's increasing political and strategic importance in the Asia-Pacific region; second, the emerging potential that the region had as a trading partner and third, the fact that the two regions could mutually benefit as sources of FDI towards one another.[34] Both in terms of security and economic ties, linkages have improved since the onset of the Look East policy. For the present discussion focus will be on two events that have strengthened these ties.

Development of Security Linkages: The 1998 Tests and After

India became a member of the ASEAN Regional Forum (ARF), which is a multilateral security platform of the Asia-Pacific region.[35] While its membership to this grouping had enhanced the security ties with the region the Indian nuclear tests of May 1998 saw some initial reactions, especially from individual countries. However, the region did not let this hinder the enhancement of ties with India. There were reactions within the media, of both Malaysia and Thailand, to the Indian tests which criticised India going nuclear.[36] This remained at the level of individual countries and was not reflected in the manner in which ASEAN-India relations progressed. In fact, Vietnam even welcomed India's nuclear posture, and was supportive of India's decision while recognising the fact that it could act as a deterrent to other countries, even though none were actually named in this regard.

Two factors that have contributed towards reinforcing the security linkages are India's accession to the Treaty of Amity and Cooperation (TAC) and its willingness to endorse the Southeast Asia Nuclear Weapons Free Zone

(SEANWFZ). The TAC agreement provides a basic framework for the regional security cooperation by laying down the ground rules for interstate relations between the countries of the region and India. According to the former Indian Foreign Secretary, Mr. Kanwal Sibal, "our accession to the treaty is an additional step forward in the implementation of our 'Look East' policy. It is reflective of our desire for fostering closer cooperation with ASEAN as well as our determination to cooperate in the maintenance of peace and stability in Southeast Asia."[37] The willingness of India to accede to the TAC goes a long way in ensuring the region of the peaceful intent of India's policy towards it. Moreover, the very facts that the TAC is designed and based on the provisions of the United Nations charter as well as the fact that it endorses within its structure the principles of the Panchasheel, makes it more acceptable to India. Initially the TAC emcompassed only the original ASEAN members and it took some years before the states of Indochina acceded to this treaty. However, the expansion of the TAC to include countries like India also indicates the willingness of the regional countries to allow for the enlargement of the institutional framework for security which the region has followed. The inclusion of countries like India and China brings about a diversification of security interests and allows this to be discussed within a common framework, thereby increasing the multilateral approach to security.

Added to this, India's willingness to endorse the Southeast Asia Nuclear Weapons Free Zone (SEANWFZ) is another vital step in furthering India's security interest in the region. India's willingness to endorse the treaty goes a long way in assuring the region of India's intent and also to ensure that the regional perspectives on the nuclear issue are both respected and recognised. By endorsing the SEANWFZ agreement, India has ensured that, the ASEAN would look at India's security needs as a factor emanating from the compulsions of the geopolitical position that India holds, rather than being a derivative of any hegemonic designs on India's part.[38]

The latest initiative in terms of closer security linkages was arrived at during the Second India-ASEAN Summit held at Bali in October 2003, where a Joint Declaration on Cooperation for Combating International Terrorism was signed. While reiterating the view that the need to fight the menace of terrorism must lie within the framework of the United Nations, it laid down two basic objectives. First, it stated that, there was a need to 'reaffirm the importance of having a framework for cooperation to prevent, disrupt and combat international terrorism through the exchange and flow of information, intelligence and capacity-building'[39] . Second, it stated that, 'the purpose of this cooperation is to enhance the efficacy of those efforts to combat terrorism'.[40] In terms of the scope of the agreement and the levels of cooperation that it envisages, it basically promotes 'exchange of information, cooperation in legal matters, free cooperation in enforcement matters, institutional capacity building and training'.[41] One of the provisions also looks at the transportation, border and immigration controls related to the flow of people, money and material. This would address other outstanding issues related to terrorism such as money laundering and drug trafficking.

Enhancing Economic Ties with ASEAN

The November 2001 agreement to host annual India-ASEAN summits led to the institutionalisation of the 'ASEAN plus one' as a formal structure of the ASEAN's annual processes. The First India–ASEAN summit laid the roadmap for the structuring of the Framework Agreement, which was concluded during the Second India-ASEAN Summit of October 2003. The ASEAN-India Framework Agreement is a watershed in the economic ties that bind the two regions and also enhances the existing bilateral and multilateral arrangements within the region. At the bilateral level, India is already evolving Free Trade Agreements (FTA's) with both Singapore and Thailand. The most significant aspect of the India ASEAN Framework Agreement is that it enhances the potential for deeper economic integration with the region. The Framework Agreement will act as a roadmap for the implementation of the Free Trade Area with the ASEAN. This Framework Agreement would cover goods and services, investment, and trade facilitation measures.[42] The current volume of trade between India and the ASEAN stands at about US $10 billion. There is a scope for a further increase, as India's economic performance improves and the ASEAN completes its recovery from the 1997 crisis. The Framework Agreement also enhances the early harvesting of these initiatives thus bringing closer the move to create a Free Trade Area between India and the ASEAN.[43] Moreover at the multilateral level the BIMSTEC already acts as a bridge between South and Southeast Asia. Added to this the Mekong-Ganga Cooperation also acts as a vital link with the region.

One of the most vital components of the India-ASEAN Free Trade Area is the development of infrastructural links between the regions. In this context there has already been some progress with the opening of the Moreh-Tamu-Kalewa road link. This link with Myanmar provides the India's northeast with a direct access to the Southeast Asian region and not through Calcutta. The Framework Agreement also envisages the development of a railway link that connects New Delhi with Vietnam.[44] This would be a significant step and once implemented it would prove to be a critical network in facilitating movement of both goods and people. As part of the infrastructural development the open skies agreement is also crucial — private airlines will be allowed to operate flights to and from the region specifically targeting the enhancement of the tourism sector. India's role within the BIMSTEC, as well as the implementation of the proposals of the FTA under the Framework Agreement, are both significant as they enhance the deeper economic ties with the region and they must be viewed as the blueprint for India's incorporation into the APEC.

There has also been an increasing view that the ASEAN policy of 'looking west' at India has been dictated to some extent by the emergence of China as a power to contend with. Within ASEAN the reaction to China has always been along two parallels; those who advocated a closer alliance with China and those who preferred a distance with China.[45] As India's economic and military position is now stronger, the ASEAN will certainly use it as a counterweight in its relations with China. One prevalent view is that Southeast Asia is India's `natural area for its future focus',[46] especially given the proximity to the region and the long established ties that India and the region have had. What will remain a challenge for India is that its broader strategic perspective for the Southeast Asian region should not be contingent upon the China factor, but should be based on a more intensive approach that includes economic and security linkages that are all-weather relationships.

ASEAN's Engagement with China

The view that China is considered a rising power has been well emphasised by its economic success which has led to an expansion of its share of global trade. This expansion has ensured that China is poised to move from the seventh position in terms of its GDP to take a second place, only behind the United States.[47] This growing economic might of China is also buttressed by the fact that it has been emphatic in terms of asserting its view in terms of what it regards as its vital security interests — particularly with reference to issues relating to Taiwan and its claims over the Spratly Is, notwithstanding the fact that it repeatedly advocates multilateralism as the major plank of its foreign policy. For ASEAN the post cold war period has seen a deeper interaction with China. The view that closer economic interaction with China would minimize the threat from China, in terms of its strategic consolidation, has primarily driven the ASEAN-China relations. However issues relating to the Spratly's dispute remain unresolved and the fact that China has begun its military modernisation and expansion is a factor that is of critical concern to the ASEAN region.[48]

One of the significant efforts, in this drive to establish deeper economic ties with China, has led to the proposal of the China-ASEAN Free Trade Area. The implementation of the CAFTA is seen as a win-win strategy for both China and the ASEAN. China stands to gain because it would lead to the development of its inland provinces of Yunnan and Guangxi, which would narrow the developmental gap between the inland and the coastal regions of the country. In the case of ASEAN there was fear that the rise of China as an economic power would detract from its own economic success in the region. The CAFTA will enhance this and lessen the gap between China and the ASEAN itself. Moreover, it would also offer the newer members of the ASEAN the growth of formal and informal trade with China, which would reduce their dependence upon the other members of ASEAN. In terms of infrastructure development, too, it would enhance the facility of the inland waterways and provide for better transportation and communication facilities.[49]

CONCLUSION

In terms of both its economic dimensions and the security aspects, Southeast Asian regionalism has been able to transform and readjust itself taking into consideration the changing global environment. In the effort to address the issue of furthering pan-Asianism, the agreements with both India and China as well as the sub-regional initiatives are crucial steps in the right direction. The emergence of both the India-ASEAN FTA and the CAFTA is vital as it provides the largest and most encompassing economic agreement for most countries of the region. This is also enhanced by individual countries signing FTA among the bilateral partners thereby providing a web like intricate pattern of economic ties emerging within the Asian region — these linkages will be based upon the economic growth within the region and while it increases the economic dependence among the countries it will provide measures for addressing security issues which impinge upon the region as a whole. The consolidation of these ties will no doubt act as an anchor in a region that is witnessing rapid and fundamental change.

REFERENCES

1. Michael Leifer, *ASEAN and the Security of Southeast Asia,* London, Routledge, 1989, p. 24.
2. *Ibid.,*
3. Tobias Nischalke, "Does ASEAN Measure Up? Post-Cold War Diplomacy and the Idea of Regional Community", *The Pacific Review*, Vol. 15, No. 1, 2002, p. 93.
4. Michael Leifer, n.1, p. 27.
5. For a detailed analysis of ASEAN's security perceptions at the time of its formation and the challenges thereafter please see, Amitav Acharya, *Constructing a Security Community in Southeast Asia*, London: Routledge, 2001.
6. Tim Hixley, "ASEAN's Prospective Security Role: Moving Beyond the Indochina Fixation", *Contemporary Southeast Asia*, Vol. 9, No. 3, December 1987, Singapore, ISEAS, p. 196.

7. Amitav Acharya, n. 5, p. 4.
8. For a detailed analysis see David B. Dewitt, "Common, Comprehensive and Cooperative Security in Asia Pacific", *The Pacific Review*, Vol. 7, No. 1, 1994.
9. Kusuma Snitwongse, "A New World Order in East Asia?", *Asia-Pacific Review*, Vol. 10, No. 2 November, 2003, p. 44.
10. Amitav Acharya, n. 5, p. 6.
11. Hadi Soesastro, "Globalisation, Development and Security in Southeast Asia: An Overview", in David b. Dewitt and Carolina G. Hernandez, eds. *Development and Security in Southeast Asia*, Volume III: Globalisation, Ashgate: Burlington, USA, 2003, p. 21.
12. *Ibid.*
13. *Ibid.*
14. Christopher Hughes, *'Globalization and Security in the Asia-Pacific: An Initial Investigation'* (presented at the 8th Meeting of the CSCAP Working Group on Comprehensive and Cooperative Security, 19-21 October 2000, Kuala Lumpur, Malaysia), at the website http://www.warwick.ac.uk/fac/soc/CSGR/wpapers/wp6100.pdf
15. For details see, Vivienne Wee, *Political Faultlines in Southeast Asia: Movements for Ethnic Autonomy As Nations of Intent*, Working Paper Series No. 16, Southeast Asia Research Centre, City University of Hong Kong. See also, Vivienne Wee and Kanishka Jayasuriya, "New Geographies and Temporalities of Power: Exploring the New Fault-lines of Southeast Asia", *The Pacific Review*, vol. 15, No. 4, 2002, pp. 475-95.
16. For detailed analysis see, Nguyen Phuong Binh, *Globalisation and Its Implications for Southeast Asian Security: A Vietnamese Perspective*, Working Paper No. 12, Institute for Defence and Strategic Studies, NTU: Singapore, May 2001, pp. 8-12.
17. For details see, Fifteenth APEC Ministerial Meeting Joint Statement Summary of Key Issues at the website http://www.apecsec.org.sg/apec/ministerial_statements/annual_ministerial 2003_15th_apec_ ministerial.html#15AMM_Statement.
18. Carlyle A. Thayer, "ASEAN Ten Plus Three: An Evolving East Asian Community?", Pacific Forum — Comparative Connections, 4th Quarter, January 2001 at the website http://www.csis.org/pacfor/cc/004Qchina_ asean.html.
19. *Ibid.*
20. Paul Dibb, "Strategic Trends in the Asia-Pacific Region", in Paul D. Taylor, eds., *Asia and the Pacific: US Strategic Traditions and Regional Realities*, Naval War College Press: Newport Rhode Island, 2001, p. 11.
21. Far Eastern Economic Review, 4 August, 1994 (Hong Kong), p. 15.
22. Cited in Tobias Nischalke, n.3, p. 102.
23. Far Eastern Economic Review, 4 August, 1994, p. 15.
24. For details and comments by leaders from within the region see *Asian Defence Journal*, Vol. 6 and 8, June and August 1997.
25. Kusuma Snitwongse, n. 9, p. 44.
26. The Jakarta Post (Jakarta), 20 February, 2002. Internet Edition.

27. 2001 ASEAN Declaration on Joint Action to Counter Terrorism at the website http://www.aseansec.org/2001_asean_declaration.htm
28. *Ibid.*
29. Joint Communiqué Special ASEAN Ministerial Meeting on Terrorism 20-21 May, 2002, Kuala Lumpur, at the website http://www.aseansec.org/sammter.htm
30. The Jakarta Post (Jakarta), 9, May, 2002. Internet Edition.
31. 2001 ASEAN Declaration on Joint Action to Counter Terrorism at the website http://www.aseansec.org/2001_asean_declaration.htm n. 8, p. 2.
32. In view of the scope of this paper only reference to the initiative with India is made while that with the US is not being discussed, as it falls outside the purview of pan-Asianism. The ASEAN-United States Joint Declaration for Cooperation to Combat International Terrorism, was signed during the visit of the US Secretary of State Colin Powell to Southeast Asia, in July 2002. The agreement reaffirms ASEAN's commitment to the UN Security Council Resolutions 1373, 1267 and 1390. Its objective was the endorsement of a framework for cooperation among the signatories, that would effectively combat the threat of terrorism. With an emphasis on the 'flow of information, intelligence sharing and capacity building', the basic scope of the declaration aims at promoting US-ASEAN ties through a mutually accommodative framework for combating terror. For details see, ASEAN-United States of America Joint Declaration for Cooperation to Combat International Terrorism at the website http://www.aseansec.org/print.asp?file=/newdata/6.htm
33. The settlement of the Cambodian conflict brought about a changed environment internationally that allowed for closer ties to develop between India and the ASEAN. The fact that India had backed the Heng Samrin government in Cambodia was an issue of discord between the two. The polarisation of the factions at the domestic level was also indicative of a similar trend at the international level by virtue of which India and ASEAN found themselves taking diametrically opposed positions.
34. India and ASEAN Dialogue Partnership at the website http://www.meadev.nic.in/foreign/asean.htm
35. For details see, Shankari Sundararaman, "The ASEAN Regional Forum: Reassessing Multilateral Security in the Asia-Pacific", Strategic Analysis, Vol. 22, No. 4, July 1998, pp. 655-65.
36. An editorial in the Bangkok Post titled 'The Nuclear Club Offers No Honour' was critical of India's decision to go nuclear and stated that the long held policy of disarmament was being undermined. The Bangkok Post (Bangkok), 18, May, 1998. The Malaysian paper, New Straits Times, also carried an article titled 'KL Deplores Indian Nuclear Test', this is cited in Kripa Sridharan, "Regional Perceptions of India", in Frederic Grare and Amitabh Mattoo, eds., n. 15, p. 77.
37. *Indian Express,* New Delhi, October 9, 2003.
38. Shankari Sundararaman, India and ASEAN, *The Hindu,* Madras, November 19, 2002.
39. ASEAN-India Joint Declaration For Cooperation to Combat International Terrorism at the website of the ASEAN at http://www.aseansec.org/15277.htm
40. *Ibid.*

41. "India, ASEAN Declare Terror War, Sign Trade Pact", *Indian Express*, October 9, 2003.
42. Framework Agreement on Comprehensive Economic Cooperation Between the Republic of India and The Association of Southeast Asian Nations at the website http://commerce.nic.in/agree_asean.htm
43. *Ibid.*
44. *Ibid.*
45. For details see the following, Chung-Si ahn, "ASEAN-Vietnam-PRC Triangle and Its Implications for Peace and Stability in Asia", *Korean Journal of International Studies*, Vol. 19, No. 1, Winter 1987/88, pp. 65-86. Also see Chang Pao-Min, "The Sino-Vietnamese Conflict and its Implications for ASEAN", *Pacific Affairs*, Vol. 60, No. 4, Winter, 1987/88, p. 634.
46. Paul Dibb, "Strategic Trends in the Asia-Pacific Region", in Paul D. Taylor, eds., *Asia and the Pacific: US Strategic Traditions and Regional Realities*, Naval War College Press: Newport Rhode Island, 2001, p. 15.
47. Kusuma Snitwongse, n. 9, p. 38.
48. For a detailed analysis see, Derek Da Cunha, "Southeast Asian Perceptions of China's Future Security Role in its "Backyard", in Jonathan D. Pollack and Richard H. Yang, eds., *In China's Shadow: Regional Perspectives on Chinese Foreign Policy and Military Development*, Rand: 1998, pp. 115-26.
49. For details see, Sheng Lijun, "China-ASEAN Free Trade Area: Origins, Developments and Strategic Motives", ISEAS Working Paper International Politics and Security Issues Series No. 1 (2003), ISEAS, Singapore at the website http://www.iseas.edu.sg/ipsi12003.pdf.

23

Russia and the Asian Giants

The Problems and the Prospects of Cooperation (Energy Sphere)

SERGEI LOUNEV

Unresolved legacies of the Cold War and other historical epochs still exist in the Asia-Pacific region, but there is no open challenge to the security-military, political, economic, cultural-of RF from East and South Asian states (and vice versa) as one can see mutual interests in addressing possible conflicts and different problems in the region. The whole system of international relations in the region has been traditionally based on bilateral links. May be now is the time to consider the possibilities of the emergence of "concert of great powers", in the region.

Close analysis of all these different problems shows one major one that covers practically all issues and that is the base for all concrete difficulties: Mutual distrust.

It is possible to solve problems if there is the growth of mutual trust. Of course, one can see new problems in the bilateral relations but the level of its gravity is much lower. For instance, any deterioration of the situation in China will have huge destabilizing impact on the security environment of Russia taking into account many thousand kilometers border. China still causes certain distrust in Russia, especially characteristic among the representatives of the nationalistic forces. The part of the regional elites of neighboring China regions have negative perception of China. Now 7 million people live in the Russian territory to the east of Lake Baikal, and the population of only one neighboring Northeast province of China is more that 100 million people. Many fear that China can

Table 1: The Problems in the Bilateral Relations of Asian Giants

Japan-China	*Japan-Russia*	*Japan-India*	*China-India*	*Russia-India*
• The history issues (different attitudes towards the events during the Japanese war with China in 1937-1945); • Territorial disputes (Chinese claims on Senkaku islands); • The future of Taiwan; • Human rights issues; • Chinese criminals and illegal immigrants in Japan; • The lack of Chinese readiness for a compromise on different political subjects; • China as a potential regional superpower that can use military measures to establish regional hegemony • Enlargement of the economic and political role of China in South-East Asia; the appearance in China of the idea of «Greater East Asia» without Japan and South Korea; • The negative attitude of China to the U.S.-Japan alliance • Japanese apprehensions about the possibility of full-scale domestic crisis in China.	• Historical issues and historical memory; • Territorial problem; • The lack of real long-term partnership and long-term plans.	• Nuclear programme of India.	• The evaluation of China by India as its strategic opponent and the Chinese attitude towards India as to a major Asian strategic opponent; • Border problems; • Chinese-Pakistani relations (especially military cooperation); • The perfection of nuclear weapon in China; • Chinese military build-up; • Nuclear programme of India; • Tibet immigrants in India.	• The deterioration of economic subsystem

Table 2: The Russian-Chinese Relations

	Soviet-Chinese differences in the mid 1980s	*The present situation*
1.	Military opposition	Agreements on the non-use of force (1994); the adoption of measures for the establishment of confidence in the near-boundary territories (1996), the creation of demilitarized zone within the limits of 100 km from the boundary (1997); multi-billion Russian arms supplies to China
2.	Political confrontation	Big number of summits (practically every year); declaration of strategic partnership, Treaty on friendship and cooperation (2001)
3.	Border problem	The end of demarcation of the border (1997)
4.	The practical lack of economic cooperation	Very rapid development
5.	Different positions on international and domestic problems	The mutual support on practically all vexed questions (Tibet, Chechnya, Taiwan, Afghanistan, Iraq, Afghanistan, etc.)

contribute to the disintegration of the Asian part of Russia. That means that the level of mutual trust is not enough.

Economic cooperation is the best way to achieve this trust. In my opinion, the comprehensive development of economic ties may overweigh all political, military and cultural differences and help any Asian giant to build mutual confidence with its neighbors. Economic interdependence in the region will compel all sides toward positive interaction and cooperation.

For quite some time, the Asia-Pacific region has been viewed as a major area for growth of international cooperation in the coming century. Thousands of works have been published all over the world on the growing prosperity among the "Pacific Community" and the region has become a symbol of openness, innovation, progress and has acquired a somewhat mysterious image of the place where economic "miracles" occur with regularity. High dynamics in every sphere of human activities, until recently, seemed deeply rooted in the nature of the region, per se. It looks that last dozen years are bringing some changes to such understanding. Erection of a new formation in the West limits approximating «flying geese» pattern and «catch-up development», that demand to reconsider new forms of economic cooperation to regain competitive advantages of the Asia-Pacific region.

Economy is the most fruitful possible area of regional cooperation. Russia's new commitment to multilateral consultation and dialogue, wherever possible, can be viewed as constructive for the development in this direction. And the sphere of energy is the most important one.

Russia's Asian part possesses vast resources. The paradoxes of the situation are: they are primarily transported to Europe while Asia is a much better choice; Western investors are often more active than Asian ones; the infrastructure of the region is very backward in spite of tremendous wealth potential.

Specialists from Harvard predict that for the next 25 years annual increase of GDP per capita in China and India will comprise of 5- 6 per cent. Many researchers consider that in 10 years China's GDP, calculated on purchasing power capacity, will overtake or even exceed the US GDP, and that India will be practically be equal with Japan. According to the recent forecast of CIA, in 2020, GDP of China will amount to $ 20 trillion that will be more than the joint GDP of the USA and Japan (13.5 and 5.1 trillion dollars respectively). It means that energy consumption in the Asian countries, mainly in China and India, will be increase year after year.

Table 3: Total Energy Consumption (Quadrillion British Thermal Units)

	2001	*2025*	*Average annual per cent growth*
Japan	21.9	23.3	0.3
China	39.7	60.3	1.8
India	12.7	23.5	2.6

According to Paris-based International Energy Outlook, 2003, total energy consumption in Japan amounted to 21.9 quadrillion British thermal units (Btu) and it is projected to increase by 0.3 per cent annually and by 2025 it will reach the figure 23.3 quadrillion Btu. Total energy consumption in China is projected to increase by 1.8 per cent annually over the 24-year projection period, from 39.7 quadrillion Btu in 2001 to 60.3 quadrillion Btu in 2025. Total energy consumption in India is projected to increase by 2.6 per cent annually, from 12.7 quadrillion Btu in 2001 to 23.5 quadrillion Btu in 2025.

Oil and gas are the world's foremost source of primary energy consumption and Russia may play a very important role in supplying Asian giants with hydrocarbons. Oil's share of world energy consumption amounted to 39 per cent in 2001 and gas's share to 23 per cent. In the near future the natural gas' share will increase, without doubt. Oil's share may drop, but not dramatically.

Table 4: Consumption of Oil (Million Barrels per day)

	2001	*2025*	*Average annual per cent growth*
Japan	5.4	6.5	0.8
China	5.0	10.9	3.3
India	2.1	5.5	4

Table 5: Consumption of Gas (Trillion cubic feet)

	2001	*2025*	*Average annual per cent growth*
Japan	2.8	3.6	1
China	1.0	6.1	7.9
India	0.8	3.4	6.1

Oil is the second largest source of primary energy consumption in China. In 2001, natural gas accounted for 2.7 per cent of China's primary commercial energy consumption, but its consumption has been growing fast. China has become a net overall oil importer since 1993. In 2002, the net imports reached 1.6 million barrels per day. International Energy Agency expects oil production in China to decline slightly to 3.4 million barrels per day, by 2025. China's oil consumption is projected to increase over the 24-year projection period by 3.3 per cent annually i.e. from 5.0 million barrels per day in 2001 to 10.9 (9% of world oil consumption) million barrels per day, in 2025. If the forecast is correct it means that in 25 years China will import 7.5 million barrels per day.

China's gas consumption is projected to increase by 7.9 per cent annually from 1.0 trillion cubic feet in 2001 to 6.1 (3.5% of world gas consumption) trillion cubic feet in 2025. In 2002, British Petroleum listed 48 trillion cubic feet as China's proven natural gas reserves; that means that on this level of consumption Chinese own reserves will be exhausted in less than 10 years.

India accounted for 12.5 per cent of total primary energy consumption in the Asia-Pacific region. Oil and gas currently meet about 42 per cent of energy consumption of the country. It is estimated to reach half of energy consumption by the end of the first quarter of the 21st century.

The current level of domestic production of crude oil amounts to about 33 million metric tonnes per year and that of natural gas around 65 million standard cubic meters per day. India's oil consumption is projected to increase by 4 per cent annually from 2.1 million barrels per day in 2001 to 5.5 million barrels per day in 2025. India's gas consumption is projected to increase by 6.1 per cent annually from 0.8 trillion cubic feet in 2001 to 3.4 trillion cubic feet in 2025.

So, India will still be heavily dependent on import of oil. Net imports of crude oil and petroleum products have already more than doubled in the past ten years and comprise 20 per cent of the total value of Indian imports. Estimates of Indian government indicate that in five years oil imports will meet 75 per cent of total oil consumption. At present, India does not import any natural gas but demand is supply constrained and imports will begin evidently in near future.

Oil is the primary energy in Japan and Japan has to import hundred per cent of its need. Japan's oil demand decreased for the third consecutive year but Japan's oil consumption is projected to increase over the 24-year projection period by 0.8 per cent annually from 5.4 million barrels per day (7 per cent of world oil consumption) in 2001 to 6.5 (less than 6 per cent) million barrels per day in 2025. Gas currently meets about 13 per cent of energy consumption of the country and practically the whole amount is imported. Japan, gas consumption is projected to increase by 1 per cent annually from 2.8 trillion cubic feet in 2001 (3 per cent of world gas consumption) to 3.6 trillion cubic feet in 2025.

All these energy import dependence implies vulnerability to external price shocks and supply fluctuations, which threaten the energy security of the all three countries. China has a certain capacity to maximize oil and gas production. India has much less such opportunities. Japan has practically no chance. But even China's dependence on import will grow.

One can point out that China and India's primary energy consumption is dominated by coal. But the growth of coal production has its limits. And adverse environmental impacts are the major factor. For example, fly ash is generated during the combustion of coal in power generation. China and India occupy the first places in the world among these indices.

More than 120 million tonnes of fly ash are produced every year in China and 80–100 million tonnes-in India. Acid rains are generated in China due to coal-fired energy, and they cause severe health hazards, spreading in neighboring countries, including Japan.

Another thing is the dependence of Asian giants on one region of the world — Middle East. In 2003, Middle East imports represented 76 per cent of Asia-Pacific region's total oil imports. The share of Gulf amounted to 88 per cent of Japanese import of oil. If we take the import of gas, Japan's dependence on the Middle East is much less (about 22 per cent), with Indonesia and Malaysia accounting for 51 per cent of the import. Middle East supplies three-fifths of China's oil imports and practically all Indian oil imports.

This situation dictates the necessity to diversify the sources of oil and gas imports, increasing the share of oil and gas imports from other regions, especially taking into account the growth of instability in that region. The Middle East was always a turbulent zone, with ceaseless internal and external conflicts. Moreover, in the final decades of the 20th century the revival of native civilization values in the region, transformed itself into alienation from the principles of European civilization. The current advance of Western technology, of science, education and mass (Americanized) culture, has provoked certain rejection in the Middle East. The growth of Islamic terrorism is only one of the exogenous manifestations of this alienation.

By the 1990s, the Arab oil-exporting states of the Persian Gulf redistributed their oil revenues and raised per capita income to the levels found in the developed countries. But during the last decade the situation has worsened in many countries. In Saudi Arabia, for instance, per capita income dropped by 4 times and now amount to $ 6,000 only. The big share of young in the population combined with a sharp decline in the living conditions of the youth and an undulating rise of unemployment contributes to the growth of tension. The process of Islamization enhanced the role of social groups who are critical of the local elite.

After the the Iraqi war the situation is continuously deteriorating. There is a high possibility that new terrorist attacks of Islamic extremists may jeopardize the safety of oil and gas transportation routes.

The events taking place after 9/11 demonstrate the rigid stances in the development of world system. First, clear unipolar system is being formed, its leader has subordinated the overwhelming majority of the countries, even those, which had occupied with respect to it neutral or oppositional position. Furthermore, USA completely rejects the joint solution of world problems under the control of the UN, and dictates the methods of relations with the nearest allies. Second, violence does become the most important tool of maintaining of order in the world system and the subordination of all countries to USA. The USA accepted unprecedented military budget, and, furthermore, significant sums are passed in the fight with the terrorism. Thirdly, the conflict, which appears in the world system, is developed entirely according to S. Huntington-collision of civilizations. Impression is created, that the actions against world terrorism, intentionally are seen as against Islam (Afghanistan, Iraq, Somalia, Yemen, Moslems in the Philippines, etc.). At the same time even old allies of the USA reject their unconditional support.

The reasons declared by the USA about the necessity to occupy Iraq (weapon of mass destruction, the dictatorship of Saddam Hussein, genocide of ethnic and religious minorities) can deceive no one. Weapons of mass destruction have still not been found. In the world there are much worse dictatorships and grave violations of human rights. The international war in Zaire began in 1998, took away the lives of almost 3 million people, but the American media did not even report about this. In reality, the Iraqi oil (11% of world's reserves) was the main target. Not incidentally, 41 of 100 top American officials are directly connected with the petroleum companies. Moreover, the USA tries to obtain complete control over the Middle East. Russian scientists are sure that in 5-7 years American reserves of oil will be over. That's why the control over oil production is absolutely vital for the USA. Evidently Washington will not continue its "revolutionary" foreign policy course for some time, but nobody knows for how long and who will be the next target. Some experts name Saudi Arabia; currently trusted and cherished friend of the USA. Thus the American control of the Middle East may make all countries dependent on the supplies from this region extremely vulnerable.

Russia worries a lot about the future of Sino-American relations. With the end of Cold war Washington lost a valid element of its foreign policy: the basic strategic enemy, whose presence determined during the half century not only the configuration of world system, but also targets and tasks of American foreign policy course and a strict block system of the West, in which no one challenged American leadership. Therefore for maintaining their political influence and possibility to preserve the role of the world arbitrator, the USA attempted to find such a common enemy that could consolidate the Western countries. From the 1990s, many American politicians began to promote China for the role of the main enemy of a free world, more and more frequently. And China can be considered as the only candidate — though hypothetical one-for the status of a second superpower and the USA denies this possibility for any other. And the independent foreign policy course was always the main target of China and India, and subordination to someone in no way finds place in their plans[1].

There is a possibility of third scenario concerning the future of the Middle East: the maintenance of status quo. Then it'll be a long period of uncertainty and sporadic new conflicts are likely to take place. After some time the situation will begin to develop according the first or second scenario.

All these scenarios demand the searches of alternatives for Japan, China and India. Many experts began speaking about Central Asia as a possible supplier of oil and gas to Asian countries.

The estimations of the reserves of oil and gas, especially in Caspian Sea, are extremely contradictory. American experts evaluate their cost as $4 trln., Russian specialists, as a rule, give considerably smaller numbers, and Central-Asian and Transcaucasian — larger numbers. The tendency of the Central-Asian and Transcaucasian ruling circles toward overstating of its resource potential is completely understandable: this is possibly to create illusion among people about the possible transformation of their countries into a new Kuwait and to distract attention from the real situation in the social and economic sphere. It gives the opportunity to preserve authority and to draw foreign investments. For the USA the region is an important potential reserve for the future, especially if some complications in the relations with the countries of the Persian Gulf occur (American own petroleum reserves will be exhausted in this decade). The clearly exaggerated reserves of hydrocarbons in Caspian Sea also permit to pressurise oil-extracting countries. There is also a task to protect the leading positions of American companies.

Obviously, the reserves of oil and gas in Caspian Sea are highly exaggerated. For instance, it was declared that Azeri-Chirag-Gyuneshli chain contains 500 million tonnes of oil. However, independent experts estimate the number at 75 millions tonnes. Evidently the small reserves of Caspian shelf in the Azerbaijan zone do not exceed the annual output of oil in Russia; moreover more than 70 per cent of them are located very deep, which sharply raises the price.

In all likelihood, attention should be focussed exclusively on the proven reserves. By 1991 it was discovered in the shelf of Caspian Sea-in the Azerbaijan sector that there are reserves of 150 million tonnes of oil in the Turkmen, 79 million tonnes, in the Kazakhstan-673 million tonnes. Only Turkmen and Russian coast was relatively unexplored. The world level of Soviet geological survey gives grounds to assume that the most profitable layers were known, and reserves of oil found are located very deep. Ecological considerations were the base for the absence of works on the output of Kazakhstan oil. The reserves of this oil are quite big but oil is of quality that demands the construction of special oil refining installations. Moreover, the high percentage of active hydrogen sulfide in the oil makes it necessary to use anticorrosive pipes during the laying of pipelines. Azeri oil is of high quality but the reserves are not much.

Proven reserves of oil and gas in the Caspian Basin (including Russian and Iranian sectors) are evaluated respectively as 30 billion barrels and 7 trillion cubic meters. These reserves comprise approximately 3 per cent of the world reserves. For the comparison let us note that the reserves of oil and gas in the Persian Gulf are 8 and 6 times more. So, over the long period transformation of Caspian Sea into a new Persian Gulf will not occur. It cannot be compared even with the potential of Russia that possesses one third of the world's reserves of gas. Proven reserves comprise 48 trillion cubic meters, and potential as 235 trillion.

In spite of all attempts of the countries of the region, the USA, Great Britain and Turkey and in order to decrease the dependence of the southern former Soviet republics on RF did not succeed in proposing to alternative to Russian hydrocarbons or to the transport of raw material from the region through the Russian territory.

Even the closest Asian markets are problematic for potential Central Asian oil and gas export routes. For oil, the main export route is via Turkey only. In 1997, China signed an agreement with Kazakhstan and promised to build a 3,000 km pipeline, connecting western Kazakhstan with China's northwestern Xinjiang Autonomous Region. The project turned out to be uneconomical and has been shelved. There are even fewer options for gas exports. For instance, Turkmenistan had four projects to construct gas pipelines to east (up to Japan), south and west (to Iran and Turkey). All four projects did not materialize and in

2003, Turkmenistan signed a contract with Russia, regarding the largest part of gas exports.

It doesn't mean that it is necessary to ignore Central Asia. But evidently the investments and participation in oil and gas production are the only economic and reliable course. It is possible to find some new forms. For instance, Turkmenistan and Uzbekistan can provide Russia with gas that'll go to Europe but Russia will reorient supplies from its Asian part to Asia. International statistics prove oil export from the USSR to India. But in reality India was supplied with Iraqi oil, Iraq bought Soviet arms, and India exported some goods to the USSR. This cooperation was very profitable and fruitful.

On the whole, Asian countries shouldn't have any hopes about the import of hydrocarbons from the Caspian region.

At the same time Russian energy sector, with prospects for regional interdependence, can contribute to energy security and serve as a barometer of regional integration. Though not the only economic factor, Russia's energy sector is important for regional economic calculations. In 2003, Russia produced 620 billion cubic meters of gas. According to Paris-based International Energy Agency, Russia possesses 30.5 per cent of the world's gas reserves (1680 trillion cubic feet) — in comparison to Turkmenistan's 1.3 per cent and Uzbekistan's 1.2 per cent. In 2003, Russia produced more oil than Saudi Arabia (421 million tonnes) and has 12 per cent of the world's oil reserves. According to Russian Energy Strategy adopted by Russian government in 22, May, 2003, Russia will produce 490 million tonnes of oil and 665 billion cubic meters of gas, in 2010.

The existing potential of Russia's cooperation with Asia is very high. The problem is easy when it concerns maritime provinces: the paradigm of Asia Pacific is absolutely suitable. The development of infrastructure in remote regions — due to the presence of the essence of continental conditions, another type of resource endowment, and difficult access to foreign markets, specific political and cultural situation — is a complicated task. Historically it was performed by national states. But for the present international cooperation in continent of Asia is possible. The modernization in Asia's heartland poses the necessity to broaden the existing potential for continental cooperation and, perhaps, to implement the system of preferential treatment of trade and investment between the countries in some geographical areas and industrial sectors. "Strategic" interests may primarily include such spheres as human development, fuel supplies, and search of new energy sources, transportation and ecological projects.

Russian factor in energy supply to Asian countries was ignored for a long period of time. For instance, in 1972, the USSR suggested construction of a oil pipeline from Western Siberian oil fields to the Pacific port Nakhodka but Japan declined the offer due to China's pressure. In 2001, Japan imported from Russia slightly over 0.1 per cent of the total amount of its oil purchases. But there are colossal opportunities. Japan invests now in different Sakhalin projects. There is an interesting project of construction of oil pipeline Angarsk-Nakhodka though it competes with Angarsk-Daquian (China) pipeline. Russian officials support mainly the first one while Russian private companies defend (though not very successfully) the pipeline to China.

Russian gas exports can play greater role. Natural gas has all the capabilities to be converted very soon into the basic energy source. If gas was inferior to oil in 1973 as two parts of the source of electricity, then in 1993 it already exceeded oil by this parameter almost to third. In last quarter of century only nuclear power engineering had the higher rates of increase, but increase in its production began sharply reducing since 1985. The development of gas industry can assume locomotive status for the revival of Russian economy.

Natural gas resources in the Russian Far East and Eastern Siberia have sufficient potential to meet Asian needs, with a supply potential from Pacific Russia of as much as 12 trillion cubic meters. Only three years ago proven gas resources of RFE and ES were estimated at 6 trillion cubic meters. And potential gas resources of the region amount 55 trillion cubic meters. Given the distances involved, natural gas pipelines from these regions are likely to be more economical than supply from greater distances in Western Siberia or Central Asia. And it is an attractive alternative to liquefied natural gas (now Japan is a consumer of half of world's export of gas in the form of LNG). In May 2003, "Sakhalin Energy" (operator of the project "Sakhalin-2") and Tokyo Gas signed the agreement about the deliveries of the Sakhalin liquefied natural gas into Japan with a volume of 1.2 million tons per annum during the period of 24 years. But there is still a possibility of constructing pipelines. Russia has obtained successes in fulfilling "The Blue Stream" project that includes a sea section (around 400 km). The gas pipeline was being laid on the bed of the Black Sea.

The realization of different projects-Sakhalin's, Irkutsk's and Yakutsk's-could offer a wide range of benefits from increased economic activity: enhanced regional energy security, new opportunities for resource development, facilitating foreign capital flows into eastern Russia, improved of environmental quality, and regional development and co-operation. Natural gas projects, however, require large, long-term financial commitments, with considerable exposure to risk and cost overruns. Therefore, substantial efforts are needed to stabilize tax systems, foreign investment protection, security of transfer of earnings, clarification of arbitration procedures, and transparent energy policies (all of which pose challenges in the Russian context).

There are also great opportunities of Russian supplies of cooking coal to Japan and Russian deliveries of electricity to China.

The prospect of a strategic and inexpensive energy supply from Pacific Russia to China, Japan and India provides a major opportunity for increased regional integration, involving energy companies, investors and governments. It is a key part of the vision for a more integrated Asia, and may provide an impetus for institutionalized cooperation on a regional basis that has previously been lacking. Each country in the region has chosen to address energy and natural resource issues independently or, as in the case of China and Russia, bilaterally, without resorting to regional cooperation, but there are likely to be significant benefits in developing an appropriate mechanism for cooperation.

For instance, evidently it is possible for Japan and China to stop being competitors in the realization of Angarsk project. India invests $ 2 billion in Sakhalin 1 project that gives an opportunity to unite the efforts of Asian giants to augment their energy security.

Many experts speak about the necessity to organize Pacific Energy community and to establish a regional energy security system. But there is also a possibility to create Energy organization of Asian giants (Russia, Japan, China and India).

Adjustment of the geographic orientation of Russia's international economic links would bear fruit immediately.

REFERENCE

1. The possibility of establishing a unipolar world is unacceptable for Asian giants. The normalization of bilateral relations on the boundary of the 80-90s is connected with this factor. Already in December 1991, during the first visit to India of a Chinese premier after 1960, in the course of the talks both sides expressed the readiness to sharply activate contacts in the case of the hegemony of one country in the global system of international relations.

24

Interaction and Confidence-Building Measures in Asia

An Asian Forum

MEENA SINGH ROY

For the countries of Asia and its neighbouring regions, the need for peace, stability and greater cooperation has never been so important as it is now. Asia is possibly the only continent still beset with the perennial regional conflicts, many of which have their roots in history and the colonial past. Uncontrolled process of militarisation is going on, and high level of economic and political instability is still being maintained. Peace and stability in Afghanistan seems to be an area of major concern, despite the end of Taliban rule, violent turbulence in Iraq continues to affect the entire region, conflict in Sri Lanka continues to affect the people of that country, tension in the Korean Peninsula and South China sea remain worrisome, ethnic violence in Indonesia has still not ended, and the presence of jehadi elements in Pakistan-Afghanistan make the situation still very critical in these countries. Ethinic conflicts, political tensions, border problems continue to remain the potential source of destabilization in the former Soviet States. There are greater issues to be resolved within Asia, between Asian entities than between Asia and the rest of the world.

Therefore, the need for stronger linkages, more effective regional mechanisms of cooperation and greater cooperative networks, among the people and societies of Asia, has become an absolute necessity. Almost everywhere except in Asia, exist forum for discussion of essential problems. In Europe, the Organization on Security and Cooperation and several other structures, in America, the Organisation of American States, in Africa, the Organisation of African Unity. In this context, the Conference on Interaction and Confidence Building Measures in Asia (CICA) is surely an important Central Asian initiative, which aims at creating a regional mechanism of preventive measures in Asia and development of a new system of relations between the states of the vast Asian region The present study is an attempt to understand, examine and critically analyse the strengths and weakness of CICA. Following important issues have been addressed:

- What is CICA. its structure and functioning?
- How important is this forum?
- Should CICA be considered a unique Asian forum promoting dialogue among civilizations?
- What are the challenges/limitations?
- What lies ahead?

STRUCTURE AND FUNCTIONING

The CICA is a structure, uniting the countries of Asian continent, which aims at strengthening mutual relations and cooperation between Asian states with a view of stabilizing and safeguarding the region. The President of the Republic of Kazakhstan initiated the idea of CICA, in October 1992, in United Nations General Assembly and in February 1993 in a meeting of NATO. The forum was created in 1994.

The main bodies working within the framework of CICA are a special working group (SVVG) and a Contact group (CG). Primary aim of SWG is the preparation of CICA documents. Representatives of ministry of foreign affairs (MFA) of 16 CICA states, including observer states and international organisations, take part in sessions of SWG.[1] Since its creation in 1994, 12 sessions of SWG have been held. The first session was held in March 1995 and the last, in June 2001.[2]

Since October 1992, when the idea of creating CICA was put forward by the President of the Republic of Kazakhstan, in the 47th General Assembly of UN, the development process of the organisation had passed through several stages. During the first stage several meetings of experts of the Ministries of Foreign Affairs of member states were held. The first meeting was held in April 1993 where 12 members participated, the second meeting was held in August-September 1993 with 28 members attending the meeting and third meeting took place in October 1994 where in 29 members participated. The main achievement at this stage was an agreement where all the participants felt that the existing disagreements among the member nations should not become an obstacle to the common approaches, to solve the problems of safety and cooperation. The skeleton of the conference, consisting of 15 countries of Asia, 9 observers, and 4 international, organisations was also agreed.[3]

During the second stage, a meeting of the Ministers of Foreign Affairs of CICA member-states states was held on September 14, 1999 in Almaty. The main achievement of this meeting was the signing of the first official document of the Conference-the Declaration of the Principles, regulating the relations between CICA member- states. The legal bases of system of the Asian safety with a plan of actions, measures and mechanisms of maintenance of stability in region were also incorporated. The participants adopted the Resolution of the ministerial meeting, where they confirmed their support to the development of the CICA process as regional forum. They also decided to work out a document within the CICA framework to be signed by the Head of States and the Governments. During this period the other basic CICA documents such as "The Rule of Procedures" and "The CICA structure and Institutes" were also adopted.[4]

In addition, on voluntary basis a permanent Contact Group, comprising of representatives of the Embassies of member-states was accredited in Almaty in December 1997. The aim of this Contact Group is to hold consultations and exchange opinions concerning the documents of the Conference. The expertise of the academicians of Asian countries and international organisations, during the inter-session period, was also welcomed. Another important moment in the course of CICA process was the international colloquium "Asian security in the context of convocation of CICA", held in Almaty, on 21-22 October 1998.[5]

During the third stage, the regular session of SWG, within the CICA framework took place on 12-14 of April 2000. Here it was decided that measures should be taken to implement the provisions of Declaration of Principles. This Declaration was considered to be the guarantor of success of future activities of CICA. During this session the participants also adopted the structure of the document to be signed by the Heads of States and Governments. In the period between 26-31 of March 2001 the regular session of SWG was held in Almaty to continue the work on elaboration of summit documents. The following working groups, on preparation for summit, were created:

- The working group dealing with the organisational issues of summit,
- The working group dealing with the Security issues of the summit,
- The working groups dealing with issues of providing informational support to the summit.

Executive Secretariat of the CICA summit was created, and is currently situated in the MFA building, in Almaty. On June 4-9, 2001 the last SWG meeting was held to prepare the draft of CICA Summit Document. According to the results of last SWG meeting it was recommended to organise the Senior Official Meeting during the period from 4-6 of September 2001 to finalise the text of the Summit Document. There after the Senior Official Meeting took place on 4-6 September 2002 in Almaty. It was in this meeting that Summit Document was completed and named as Almaty Act.

Finally the first sixteen-nation summit of Conference on Interaction and Confidence-Building Measures in Asia (CICA) was held in Almaty on 3-5 June 2002. This summit was called to formalize the creation of a new Asian Security Organisation. The conference was attended by delegates of all member states, International organisations and observer countries. During this meeting the Almaty Act was signed and declaration on eliminating terrorism and promoting dialogue among civilizations was adopted.

Declaration on terrorism is a two page document and it condemns all forms and manifestations of terrorism committed; no matter when, where or by whom. Declaration also emphasizes that no consideration, whatsoever, can be invoked to justify terrorism. The declaration very clearly identifies "separatism as one of the main threats and challenges to security and stability" in the region. It also says "Member states will not support any separatist movement on the territory, of another member states". The central role of the United Nations, its General Assembly and Security Council was emphasized, in developing the framework for this forum. The Declaration said, 'We are fully committed to fighting terrorism and strengthening bilateral, regional and international cooperation, in accordance with the UN Charter, required to meet this challenge". The declaration addresses issues of illicit arms and drug trafficking as well. Member states also pledged to support the efforts for the global elimination of all weapons of mass destruction and prevent proliferation of nuclear, chemical and biological weapons.[6]

Almaty Act consists of four sections and 35 provisions. There is also a short preamble. The first section deals with the security and cooperation and lays down certain principles and norms of behaviour. The second section deals with the challenges to security like terrorism, drug trafficking, illicit trafficking of small arms and light weapons, and racism. Third section pertains to Confidence Building measures. The last section is about the structure and institutions of CICA.

According to Almaty Act, it was decided by the member states that for the effective functioning of the organisation, the structure of CICA would consist of following:

- There would be meeting of the Heads of State or Government, every four years, in order to conduct consultations, review the progress of, and set priorities for CICA activities. Special meetings could be convened, as necessary, by consensus. Meetings of the Ministers of Foreign Affairs would precede Summit meetings.
- The Minister of Foreign Affairs will meet every two years. These meetings would be the central forum for consultations and examination of all issues related to CICA activities. Special meetings can be called by consensus.
- To follow-up the previous CICA decisions, the Committee of Senior Officials would meet at least once a year. Their work would be to carry out consultations on the current CICA issues, oversee the work of Special Working Groups and coordinate the work of other meetings. One of their works would also be to make necessary preparations for the organisation of the Summit and ministerial meetings, including elaboration of draft documents.
- Special working group would be established to study specific issues relevant to CICA's areas of interest and to carry out the tasks mandated to them. They will have to submit the results of their work to the Committee of Senior Officials.
- To discuss issues of a specific and technical nature the member states could convene meetings of other ministers or the competent national agencies and institutions.
- Academic and professional inputs would also be provided.
- The establishment of the Secretariat of CICA has been supported by member states in Almaty Act. This is mainly to provide follow-up and administrative support for regular meetings and political consultations and other activities mentioned in Almaty Act. The Minister of Foreign Affairs has been entrusted with job of finalising the elaboration of all aspects related to the establishment of the Secretariat.[7]

As per the decisions of first CICA summit and Almaty Act, the session of Committee of senior officials of CICA member states, observers and international organizations was held in Almaty on 16-17 January 2003. During this session decision on creation or two special working groups, one on measures of trust of CICA and Statute of Secretariat of the CICA and catalogue on Confidence Building Measures, was accepted. Further in 11 February, 2004, the next session of Committee of senior officials of CICA states was held in Almaty to study and discuss the above mentioned draft documents. It is planned that the draft of the Catalogue was to be adopted at the session of Ministers for Foreign Affairs in

October 2004. The Measures of trust of the CICA and Statute of Secretariat of the CICA would be adopted during the second summit of CICA Head of the States in 2006. Same year the opening of Secretariat of CICA is also supposed to be held.[8]

HOW IMPORTANT IS CICA? : THE CRITICAL ASSESSMENT

The importance of CICA should be viewed in the context of challenges that Asia is facing today, the need of establishing a forum for dialogue, and the requirement of some kind of collective mechanism to settle the old disputes and prevent the new ones, in this region. In this context can CICA be considered a unique Asian forum promoting dialogue among civilizations and cultures?

Given the centrality of Asia in the world politics and the region still beset with perennial conflicts, CICA surely is an initiative, which aims at the creation of an effective mechanism of preventive measures in Asia and the development of a new system of relations between the states of the vast Asian region. The main aim of the CICA, as declared by the heads of states, has been to boost cooperation by working out multilateral approaches to ensure peace, security and stability in Asia. It is also an important organisation from the point of view that the total area of the territory of its participants amounts to 38.8 million sq. km, or approximately 89 per cent of all the territory of the Asian region and 72 per cent of the territories of the Eurasian continent. There live more than 2.8 billion people that make 45 per cent of the total population of the globe.[9] In terms of economic potential the gross domestic product of the countries of Asia amounts to 13 trillion dollars. In addition, the CICA member states occupy leading positions in the world oil reserves (40%) as well. Therefore, should the CICA members successfully achieve some kind of economic cooperation, including cooperation in energy sector, which is crucial for both supplier as well as consumer nations it could become an important forum providing the necessary guarantees ensuring the sustainable economic growth for its member nations, in future. The increasing process of globalisation does create a precondition for unified approach by the CICA member states towards greater economic cooperation. But how things would unfold in coming years is yet to be seen.

At present it is difficult to say how affective the CICA mechanism is or would be in future, as it is just a nine-year-old forum and, still is in process of learning and testing. However based on the current regional and international trends certain hypothetical conclusions can be drawn.

In political arena the first CICA summit, though considered as historic by most of the leaders, produced mixed results. President Vladimir Putin described

CICA, 'Timely and fruitful to the utmost," and called this summit a unique event and also felt that this was the first time the leaders of 16 countries came together to discuss the questions of strengthening security and stability in the region, and mechanism which will make it possible to settle the old conflicts and to help prevent new ones.[10] According to Russian Foreign Minister Igor Ivanov CICA may contribute to fighting terrorist threats, while its ultimate goal is to form a secure Zone throughout the Asian continent.[11]

The main achievement of the first CICA summit has been the signing of the Almaty Act and the Declaration on eliminating terrorism and promoting dialogue among civilisations. Both these documents have been designed to strengthen security and increase mutual trust among the member nations. In this context the CICA summit documents present future oriented instrument in field of security and cooperation in Asia. The summit was also seen as a complete achievement for the foreign policy and diplomacy for Kazakhstan. This success was measured less in terms of its conceptual evolution as an effective security forum but more in the context of timely initiative to diffuse tension in South Asia.[12]

According to this scholar who was in Almaty, the public response to CICA within Kazakhstan was somewhat mute and subtle. To the general people this concept remains unfamiliar. There has neither been a serious nor informal national debate on CICA. Media was generally critical and questioned the Kazakh official's attempt for resolving the perplexed international issues when it has a host of domestic and regional problems to be addressed first. Some described this attempt as a public relations exercise by President Nazarbayev to boost his international image, while others felt the initiative as a non-starter.[13]

The importance of CICA, in terms of tackling the problem of nuclear proliferation, should not be overlooked. Perhaps, CICA could take a lead in spearheading the campaign for Asian NFU as the first step towards progressive delegitimisation of nuclear weapons. This view point was also expressed by the then Prime Minister Shri Atal Bihari Vajayee at CICA summit. He said, "...CICA, therefore, has to evolve certain reliable ground rules that would promote peace and security in Asia, by reconciling the diverse concerns and interests of the countries of the continent. One of the most important ground rules is that of nuclear weapon states should not indulge in nuclear blackmail. India has already adopted the doctrine of no first- use. We believe that adoption of this by all nuclear weapon-states would be an important confidence-building measure for Asia and the world.[14]

CRITICAL UNCERTAINTIES

There are critical uncertainties pertaining to the functioning and effectiveness of the CICA. Despite CICA being an extraordinary Central Asian initiative, most observers feel that the CICA is too amorphous an idea representing too many conflicting interests to evolve as a functional forum for Asia. It is felt that the Forum is seeking an agenda larger than that of the United Nations. So far it does not have structured mechanisms for practical cooperation between its members, including in the military sphere. It intends to function primarily as a forum for dialogue. During its first summit, the India Pakistan crisis dominated the scene and in terms of defusing the tensions between India and Pakistan it was not a success. But it certainly is important in terms of initiating a forum for dialogue for Asian countries. While highlighting the difficulties in reaching a consensus, in a forum on a particular issue, it was stressed by President Nursultan Nazarbaev that CICA could benefit from the experience of the CIS Collective Security Organisation and of the Shanghai Cooperation (SCO).

The CICA has so for been able to function and survive, mainly because there is a convergence of interests among the other organizations (CSTO, S.CO), which are effectively functional in the region. Secondly; Kazakhstan due to its political stability, economic prosperity and geostrategic location has been able to sustain this forum.

At the international level CICA members appear to be motivated more by the need to safeguard their narrow national interests than the conceptual framework. The Chinese seem to be skeptical about CICA maturing into a conflict resolution mechanism. Within China, the dominant discourse is that of SCO rather than, of CICA.

Therefore, the success or failure of this organisation, to a great extent, would depend on the effective functioning, seriousness with which the member nations cooperate with each other, giving priority to the commonalties rather than their differences and also the changing patterns of alliance systems in the region where the great powers are involved in creating their own sphere of influence. This situation is even more critical in the region like Central Asia because these states are more vulnerable to such influences due to their weak political and economic positions.

The factors complicating the process of CICA are the following:

- Territorial disagreements between some of the CICA member countries: This problem poses a threat for all the Asian countries, without exception, in view of the fact that practically each country has various religious, ethnic and cultural groups and if there are possibilities of negative developments of a situation that would introduce additional intensity in interstate relations. Examples of tensions between Israel-India-Pakistan and some of the Central Asian Republic can be pointed out.

- Problems related to disarmament and arms control: In this respect many Asian countries have not joined the basic international agreements in sphere of disarmament and arms control. There is already an existing pattern of arms acquisition by Asian nations. In some regions of Asia, arms race is taking place, which pushes the states to armed confrontations. As a result, the exclusive circle appears, which is pernicious both for the countries involved in conflict and for the whole region, as such.
- Currently there are number of existing conflicts in Asia, which generate lack of trust and suspicion among the nations. Thus, lack of mutual trust and understanding among the member nations further complicates the functioning of the CICA.
- The wide spectrum of understanding and upholding of national interests among the member states of CICA and their own vision of solving the regional and global issues is also a limitation. These diverse viewpoints are likely to create differences of opinion among the member states. Which in turn is likely to affect the smooth functioning of CICA. The problem in establishing any effective regional structure in Asia is often compounded by the fact that.the national priorities do not always coincide with the regional priorities.
- The regional dynamics, within the Central Asian region, could also be a critical factor. The Uzbek-Kazak rivalry is one such example. Therefore, lack of confidence and trust among the Central Asian states will impede its prospect to become a viable security forum for Asia.

It is important to take note of the views expressed during a recently held international conference in Taskkent. It was argued by some scholars and experts that despite frequently signed agreements and existence of various important regional organizations, in the region, the effectiveness of these organizations, in addressing regional problems, remain relatively low. Whereas few others rejected such an opinion and felt that this kind of criticism was misplaced and argued that central Asian states are newly created are still in very young and are the first decade of their independence are still involved in the process of learning and defining their national interests and looking for the appropriate partners. If one looks at the experience of other countries one finds that the process of learning and testing has been very long. In this respect it can be said that these organisations are not doing badly.[15] Therefore, it can be argued that though there are problem areas in CICA yet it is a useful instrument for strengthening bilateral relations and also an important forum for countries to exhibit their position with respect to the problems faced by them.

INDIA AND CICA

India has fully supported the idea of CICA since its inception. It has been participating in all its meetings and working groups. The visit of the then Prime Minister Atal Bihari Vajpayee to Almaty, in June 2002, exhibits the kind of importance India has given to CICA process. For India, this visit can be evaluated at two levels; bilateral and multilateral. At bilateral level this visit could be seen as a step towards strengthening the existing ties with Kazakhstan. India and Kazakhstan signed three agreements, a memorandum on military and technical cooperation, an agreement on cooperation in tourism and an agreement on setting up joint working group for combating international terrorism. India's readiness to invest in Kazakhstan's oil and gas industry was conveyed by Atal Bihari Vajpayee. The Prime minister and the Kazakh leader identified four major sectors, comprising oil and gas, information technology, pharmaceuticals and small-scale industries, or cooperation between the two countries, media also agreed to promote joint ventures in information technology by extending full support to the establishment of a software technology park about 30 km from Almaty. Preconditions appeared for cooperation in space research, remote probing, and biotechnologies, as well. In a special gesture to India, Kazakhstan renamed the Pinfilova Street in Almaty after Mahatma Gandhi. President Nazearbaev expressed Kazakhstan's interest in joining the north-south transport corridor so that economic cooperation could be expanded, which otherwise was being hampered due to the absence of optimal transportation routes between the two nations.

At multilateral level it has been an achievement as far as the problem of terrorism is concerned. The Almaty summit did give an opportunity to India to put forth its problem of cross-border terrorism; sponsored by Pakistan into the territory of Jammu and Kashmir. In this sense the signing of declaration on "Eliminating Terrorism and Promoting Dialogue among Civilizations' and 'Almaty Act' was a major gain for India.

India's approach to CICA should be that of moving towards greater economic cooperation and linking Central Asian region with South Asian region, in terms of increasing trade and cooperation in energy sector which is a crucial factor for all member states. While dealing with CICA India also needs to carefully view its policy towards other central Asian countries, China and Pakistan. India must continue to actively participate in the CICA's structural and institutional mechanisms.

While Asia may appear to be in turmoil, the hope and optimism of building a peaceful Asia remains strong. For a long time the challenge for Asia has been to create collective, peaceful and cooperative mechanism, ensuring a mutually beneficial environment in which human development could be pursued without disruption, at a pace acceptable to all. It is important to note here that Asia is the only continent from where innovative approaches for containing and managing conflicts, even resolving them, are coming about. Although the diversity of Asia does not apparently permit a clear model for security cooperation yet it is a hope that CICA would stand out to be an Asian framework for peace through cooperation in the future, where sharing commonalties would be the priority, rather than the areas of disagreement.[16]

REFERENCES

1. These member states are Afghanistan, Azerbaijan, Egypt, China, Israel, Kazakhstan, Kyrgyzstan, Mongolia, State of Palestine, Pakistan, Russia, Tajikistan, Turkey, Uzbekistan, India, and Iran. The USA, Japan, Australia, Indonesia, Thailand, Ukraine, Korea and Vietnam, have an observer status in CICA. The United Nations, Organisation of Security and Cooperation in Europe and League of Arabian States also participate in the CICA.
2. A.G. Kozhikhov, *Conference on interaction and Confidence Building Measures in Asia (CICA) Question and Answers, Reference Guide,* Center for Foreign Policy and Analysis, Almaty, 2001 p. 11.
3. CICA: Prospects of Process, Information Provided by the Embassy of Kazakhstan in India.
4. *Ibid.*
5. *Ibid.*
6. Text of Declaration on eliminating terrorism and promoting dialogue among Civilizations.
7. Text of Almaty Act, *Almaty,* 4 June, 2002.
8. Draft Document on Statute of CICA Secretariat, CICA Rules of Procedure and CICA Catalogue. Also see briefing organized on CICA on 23 March 2004.
9. A.G. Kozhikhov, *op. cit.*, p. l0.
10. News from Russia, Vol. V, No. 23, 7 June, 2002, p. 3.
11. *Sergei Blagov,* "Post-Soviet diplomacy faces check of Asian realities", http://www.atimes.com/c-asia/DE04Ag05html
12. P. Stobdan, "Central Asia and India's security" Paper presented at IDSA weekly 'Fellows Seminar' on 30August 2003.
13. *Ibid.*
14. Statement by the then Prime Minister Atal Bihari Vajpayee at the CICA Summit, *Almaty,* 4 June, 2002, <http://meadev.nic.in/speeches/pm-cicasummit-4june2002.htm>
15. Views expressed in the International Conference on, "Central Asia in the XXI Century: Cooperation, partnership and Dialogue" held in Tashkent on 13-15 May 2003 and in India "Central Asia regional Conference" held in Tashkent on 3-5

November 2003. The regional organizations like The Economic Cooperation Organisation (ECO), the Central Asian Economic Community (CACE), the Eurasian Economic Community (EEC), the Shanghai Cooperation Organisation (SCO), the Collective Security Treaty Organisation under the CIS (CSTO), and the Central Asian Cooperation Organisation (CAC).

16. Meena Singh Roy, "CICA: Unique Asian Forum" The Kashmir Times (Jammu), June 25, 2002.

25

Japan and Asia

Sanjana Joshi

It is widely accepted that since the Meiji Restoration "a wealthy nation and a strong military" have been the twin objectives of Japanese security policy and that since the defeat in the Second World War military security has been embedded in a broader definition of national security. In keeping with the dictum that "economic progress is in the end more decisive" post-World War II Japanese Foreign Policy was guided by the Yoshida Doctrine[1] — concentration on economic and social reconstruction while relying on the United States for Japan's basic security and non-involvement in local conflicts. Japanese perceptions and correspondingly the policies with regard to the regional security environment were articulated in terms of *seikei bunri* i.e. separation of politics and economics. And, Japan's approach to regional relations in Asia came to be characterized as "economic multilateralism combined with security bilateralism"[2] wherein Japan's foreign relations were largely a function of Japan-US relations.

Since the 1990s, it has been variously suggested that with the end of the Cold War there has occurred the "re-Asianization of Japan"[3] as Japanese leaders began to support multilateral approaches to the region's security problems. One of the first examples of this change in position was the diplomatic initiative known as the Nakayama Initiative. Under the leadership of Foreign Minister Nakayama, in 1991 Japan proposed the creation of a new regional multilateral security dialogue that would build on the existing Post-Ministerial Conference (PMC) of the Association of Southeast Asian Nations (ASEAN).[4] Prior to the Nakayama Initiative Japanese leaders had been firmly opposed to the development of multilateral security institutions in Asia, fearing that these would undermine Japan's alliance with the United States.

No doubt, since 1945, Japan has carefully avoided putting its relations with the United States and with Asia in 'either-or' contexts claiming that both are essential to its national interests.[5] Yet when it had to choose, it often chose the United States over Asia.[6] The Fukuda Doctrine of 1977 succeeded to some extent in moving Japan from its "separation of politics and economics approach" and Japan expanded cooperation with the ASEAN countries by providing economic leadership and diplomatic support for efforts in dealing with Vietnam and Cambodian crisis.[7] However, one of the main tenets of the Fukuda Doctrine was that Japan would not play a military role in the region and until the mid 1980s Japan shied away from proposals for regional dialogue.[8]

Even today Japan's relationship with the United States remains the keystone of its foreign policy. Inoguchi Takashi describes this state of affairs as "*Karoke Diplomacy*" arguing that Japan's foreign and security policy is circumscribed in a "set menu" of alternatives provided by the United States.[9] "Depending on circumstances, Japan may have some limited leeway in deciding who, when, where, what or how it will engage internationally. But the essential choices are often predetermined by Washington with little scope for initiative, or innovation, from Tokyo."[10]

In 1951 the two countries signed the United States-Japan Security Treaty which stated that "Japan desires, as a provisional arrangement for its defence, that the United States of America should maintain armed forces of its own in and about Japan so as to deter armed attack upon Japan" and that "Japan will itself increasingly assume responsibility for its own defence against direct and indirect aggression, always avoiding any armament which could be an offensive threat".[11] The Treaty of Mutual Cooperation and Security between the United States and Japan further reinforced the bilateral security alliance in 1960, which stated, "Each Party recognizes that an armed attack against either Party in the territories under the administration of Japan would be dangerous. to its own peace and safety and declares that it would act to meet the common danger in accordance with its constitutional provisions and processes."[12]

This division of roles has undergone "redefinition" over the years, with Japan assuming greater responsibility but there has been little support for a complete "reassessment" of the ties with the United States. It is therefore imperative that we assess Japan's role in Asia within this framework, specifically the issue of "burden sharing".

The collapse of the Soviet Union and the end of the Cold War brought the issue of Japan's "burden sharing" into sharper focus. The United States appeared to be turning inward. In 1990, the US announced that it would make a ten per cent reduction of its forces in the region. The US troop presence in Asia steadily declined from 1,41,000 in 1988 to 98,000 in 1992. America's intentions regarding its long-term military commitment to the Asian region were not publicly clarified until 1995 when the so-called Nye Report, "US Security Strategy for the East Asia- Pacific Region,"[13] was published.

Meanwhile in the wake of the first Gulf War, Japan's failure to contribute personnel to the multinational coalition assembled in the Gulf and Tokyo's so-called 'checkbook diplomacy' fell short of international expectations and engendered negative responses, especially from the United States.[14] Japan's initial response to Iraq's invasion of Kuwait was in line with its traditionally passive stance in international affairs. It took Japan three weeks to formulate a positive commitment to help the United States and the Western Allies restore the status-quo, and simply amounted to a monetary contribution of 1 billion dollars. A financial contribution had also been the Japanese response to the earlier threat to Gulf oil access during the 1987-88 Kuwaiti oil tanker flagging crisis. At that time Japan had provided economic assistance to construct shipping navigation aids in the Persian Gulf.

In August 1990, however, the situation was qualitatively different. Iraq's invasion of Kuwait raised the issue of how regional conflicts could be controlled after bi-polar super power competition had ended. The crisis was perceived as the first test to see how the United States and its allies could address regional conflicts jointly when their collective interests were at stake. The response of the Japanese government was interpreted as signaling that it continued to expect the United States to protect Japan's interests without Japanese participation. This international criticism sparked off vigorous domestic debate over Japan's international security role. The debate was further sharpened by Prime Minister Kaifu's proposal to authorize the dispatch of 1,000 unarmed troops and civillians to the Gulf to give non-combat support to the multinational force present there. Thwarted in its efforts, the Kaifu government then initiated an attempt to dispatch air-force transport planes to evacuate refugees. The Flight Squadron 401 of the First Air Transport Squadron at Komaki base in Aichi Prefecture was prepared for this mission, but this could not be realized as the Gulf War came to a quick end.

These measures earned Japan little credit, as they risked no Japanese lives. Nor were Japan's actions perceived to be spontaneous and voluntary. However, important lessons were learnt from this episode. The Japanese leadership and public realized that Japan needed to participate more directly in international security issues and for the first time, Japan's 1991 Diplomatic Blue Book called for going beyond "cheque-book diplomacy." In June 1992, the governing Liberal Democratic Party (LDP) pushed through the Upper House of the Diet the law enabling the Japanese Self Defence Forces to participate in UN Peacekeeping Operations.

From the perspective of Tokyo, then, multilateralism was a useful tool to keep the United States engaged in the region and to respond to American demands for increased burden sharing. For example, the paper presented at the ASEAN-sponsored meeting in Manila on 5-7 June 199137 by Yukio Satoh, then Director-General of the Information Analysis, Research and Planning Bureau of the Foreign Ministry, who played the primary role in advocating multilateral security cooperation within the Japanese government, stressed that the US participation in such a dialogue was "critically important for the sake of mutual reassurance" as the future direction of American and Japanese policy was the two major concerns in the region.[15]

Nakayama's 1991 diplomacy reflected Tokyo's policy of a 'multiplex mechanism' "composed of bilateral and multilateral arrangements and frameworks of cooperation designed for a variety of purposes"[16]. It has four pillars:

1. economic cooperation;
2. diplomatic efforts to settle sub-regional conflicts and disputes;
3. a broad range of (bilateral) security arrangements and cooperative relations;
4. a regional political dialogue.

The first pillar, economic cooperation, refers to bilateral cooperation as well as such existing multilateral cooperation as ASEAN, ASEAN PMC, PECC and ESCAP (Economic and Social Commission for Asia and the Pacific). The second pillar of diplomatic efforts to settle sub-regional conflicts and disputes places emphasis on Cambodia and the Korean Peninsula. The third pillar includes a set of bilateral alliances with the United States. The fourth pillar, a regional political dialogue aims to raise a sense of mutual reassurance between Japan and the countries in the Asia-Pacific region.

Japan's policy on security multilateralism at this point had two dimensions—Multilateral efforts toward the settlement of conflicts and disputes would work at the sub-regional level whereas multilateral dialogue to reduce tension and promote confidence would operate at the regional level. This two-dimensional approach was enunciated by then Prime Minister Kiichi Miyazawa at the National Press Club in Washington D.C. on 2nd July 1992 where he asserted the significance of regional political dialogue. In his words, "For the security of the Asia-Pacific region, it is most effective to take the two track approach, which aims, on the one hand, for the promotion of sub-regional cooperation to settle conflicts and disputes and, on the other hand, for the promotion of regional political dialogue to increase a sense of mutual reassurance. These two efforts should advance in tandem."[17]

Subsequently Prime Minister Miyazawa's speech in January 1993 in Bangkok placed the promotion of regional political and security dialogue as the first among the four pillars of Japan's ASEAN policy and clearly pointed to Japan's willingness to assume a leadership role in regional security multilateralism. "In this period of transition for the international community, the countries of the Asia-Pacific region need to develop a long-term vision regarding the future order of peace and security for their region. For this, various ideas should be thrashed out through political and security dialogue among the countries in the region. I hope that some picture of the future of this region's security will be gradually distilled through such a process, based on shared perceptions and concerns. Japan will actively take part in such discussions."[18]

Japan thus started to assume a larger political profile in Asia during the early 1990's, although it did so quietly, generally working behind the scenes. Japan played a key role in the creation and evolution of the Asia Pacific Economic Cooperation forum (APEC). The ASEAN Regional Forum (ARF), a multilateral mechanism for addressing regional security concerns, was also arguably an initiative of Japanese origin. And, Japan's decision to allow Self-Defence Force participation in the 1992 UN peacekeeping effort in Cambodia marked a major departure from past constitutional interpretation-and represented an important symbolic step in Japan's quest for regional leadership. In similar vein the 2001 *Diplomatic Bluebook* of the Ministry of Foreign Affairs (MOFA) of Japan articulates that "the most realistic and appropriate approaches for the enhancement of the region's security environment should be viewed as developing and strengthening both bilateral and multilateral frameworks for dialogue and cooperation in a multi-tiered manner."[19]

According to Lisa J. Sansoucy[20] this policy to maintain the United States engagement with Asia is a response to two major obstacles Japan faces in formulating independent policy towards Asia particularly East Asia. The first is the "Japan Problem," or the ways in which the history of Japan's wartime aggression in the region continues to constrain its current security policy options. The key, as Ralph Cossa points out, has been "defining adequate support to the satisfaction of both nations, and in a manner not threatening to Japan's neighbours."[21] Because the "Japan Problem," ie. Japan's history of aggression and colonialism in the region makes neighboring states extremely wary of any increases in Japan's military activities in the region and continues to constrain Japanese security policy. These constraints operate across both Northeast and Southeast Asia. And a key response to this dilemma of "adequate support" vis-à-vis regional concerns" has been Japan's initiative for multilateral regional security dialogue.

The second is the "China Problem," or the lack of consensus among Japanese security policy makers over the nature of Chinese power and intentions. The priority that policy toward China has commanded in Japanese foreign affairs has varied over time. During the period of United States-backed "containment" of China, there was a sharp divergence between official policy and popular attitudes in Japan. As a loyal ally of the United States, the Japanese government was committed to non-recognition, whereas popular sentiments favoured diplomatic relations and expanded trade. When the Tiananmen Square incident occurred in 1989, Japan was initially reluctant to apply sanctions but soon fell in line with the Western countries. The entire episode demonstrated that the US factor still weighed heavily in Japan's Asia policy even as the Cold War was coming to an end.

The end of the Cold War had complex implications for Japan. The Soviet Union, a longtime major threat, collapsed and declined, and left Japan with much more peaceful borders. At the same time, China has emerged as a great economic and military power in East Asia. Under these circumstances Japanese policymakers struggled to form a consensus from which to engage China. Most experts however made it clear that Japan would not deal with China by itself but through the support of US moves to check China if it became aggressive on security issues. "Because only the deterrence capabilities of the United States can respond effectively to Chinese tendencies, maintaining America's presence in East Asia is critical to regional peace and stability (Morimoto 1997)". Others argued that both Japan and the United States should engage China in reaching constructive views on regional security. "The United States and Japan should encourage China to participate in creating a common security order in the Asia Pacific region (Takahashi 1997).

Indeed, one of the first questions raised in formulating the Nakayama Initiative was whether China should be included as a member in a regional multilateral security institution.[22] Prior to 1993, Japanese support for multilateralism, exemplified by the Nakayama Initiative, was aimed at keeping the United States engaged in the but after 1993 the primary focus in Japan's strategy shifted to using security multilateralism as a tool to engage China. Thus, Japan's regional security policy of multilateralism was constructed with two audiences in mind. On the one hand, Japanese foreign policy makers were mindful of pressures from the United States to take on a greater role in the maintenance of regional security and, on the other hand, they wanted to engage China.[23]

However a series of events served to remind Tokyo that the end of the Cold War did not eliminate all the possible sources of instability in East Asia and brought renewed attention to the importance of the US-Japan alliance. These included Beijing's 1992 law reaffirming Chinese claim to the Senkaku Islands, the 1994 crisis over North Korea's nuclear weapons programme, Chinese nuclear tests in 1995 and 1996, Chinese military exercises in the

Taiwan Strait in March 1996 and popular protests over the disputed Senkaku islands that broke out in Hong Kong and Taiwan in 1996. These created momentum for the revision of the Guidelines for Japan-US Cooperation from 1997 onwards, and then the passage in May 1999 of legislation to enable the SDF to provide logistical support to US forces in order to deal with "situations in areas surrounding Japan that will have an important influence on Japan's peace and security." Japan's response to the September 11 and subsequent participation in the US actions in Afghanistan and Iraq have further enhanced the scope of Japan's bilateral security measures. And, once again relations with the United States have become the focus of Japanese policy.

At the same time given the unwillingness to radically alter the military component of its security policy it therefore appears that Japan has creatively interpreted burden sharing in terms of a growing role in Asian security. There are clear advantages to doing so:

(a) It resonates with the spirit of the October 2000 Armitage/Nye report that called on burden sharing by Japan to evolve into power sharing.
(b) There is greater domestic acceptance for such a role than sending troops abroad.
(c) It allows Japan to delicately distinguish itself from the larger American military strategy in Asia.
(d) It mitigates regional antagonism that tends to regard any change in Japan's security profile as a revival of militarism.

This is not to suggest that efforts at Asian security cooperation regard the US-Japan alliance in adversarial terms but certainly we need to view Japan's activism in Asian security issues in a more realistic and pragmatic manner. It is unlikely that Japan would be a reliable partner in forging Asian cooperation that aims to check US unilateralism.

REFERENCES

1. For a detailed analysis see Kenneth B. Pyle, *The Japanese Question: Power and Purpose in a New Era,* Washington DC, AEI Press, 1992.
2. See the collection of essays in Peter J. Katzenstein and Takashi Shiraishi, eds., *Network Power: Japan and Asia,* Ithaca, NY, Cornell University Press, 1997.
3. See Yoichi Funabashi, *Asia Pacific Fusion: Japan's Role in APEC,* Washington DC, Institute for International Economics, 1995.
4. Paul Midford, "Japan's Leadership Role in East Asian Security: The Nakayama Proposal and the Logic of Reassurance," *Pacific Review* 13, No. 3, 2000, 382.

5. For a detailed analysis see Akira Iriye, "The United States and Japan in Asia: A Historical Perspective" in Gerald L. Curtis, ed. *The United States, Japan and Asia: Challenges for US Policy,* New York: Norton, 1993, pp. 29-52.
6. Akitoshi Miyashita, "Introduction: A Framework for Analysis" in Akitoshi Miyashita and Yoichiro Sato ed. *Japan's Foreign Policy in Asia and the Pacific,* New York, Palgrave, 2001, pp. 1.
7. Christopher W. Hughes, "Japan's Subregional Security and Defence Linkages with ASEAN's, South Korea and China in the 1990s" *The Pacific Reviw* Vol. 9, No.2, 1996. pp. 230-31.
8. *Ibid.*
9. Inoguchi Takashi and Purnendra Jain "Introduction: Beyond Karaoke Diplomacy" in Inoguchi Takashi and Purnendra Jain ed. *Japanese Foreign Policy Today,* New York, Palgrave, 2000, pp. xv.
10. *Ibid.*
11. Text of treaty available at http://www.yale.edu/lawweb/avalon/diplomacy/japan/japan001.htm
12. Text of treaty available at Japan Ministry of Foreign Affairs website http://www.mofa.go.jp/region/n-america/US/q&a/ref/1.html
13. United States Department of Defence, Office of International Security Affairs, *US Security Strategy for the East Asia-Pacific Region* (Washington, DC: February 1995).
14. See Courtney Purrington, "Tokyo's Policy Responses During the Gulf War and the Impact of the 'Iraqi Shock' on Japan," *Pacific Affairs* 65 (Summer 1992), pp. 161-81. For an analysis of the effect of the Gulf War on US-Japan relations, see Walter LaFeber, *The Clash: US-Japan Relations Throughout History* (New York: W.W. Norton, 1997), pp. 385-89.
15. Yukio Satoh, "Asian-Pacific Process for Stability and Security," in MOFA, ed., *Japan's Post Gulf International Initiatives,* Tokyo: MOFA, August 1991, pp. 43.
16. *Ibid.*, p. 42.
17. Quoted in Fukuda Tamotsu "Japan's Evolving Interests in Multilateral Security Cooperation in the Asia-Pacific: A Two-Dimensional Approach" http://eprints.anu.edu.au/archive/00002521/01/Japan_evolving_interest.pdf
18. For an English translation of Miyazawa's speech in Bangkok in January 1993, "Japan will act together with ASEAN," *Jakarta Post,* 23 January 1993, p. 4.
19. The Ministry of Foreign Affairs (MOFA), Japan, *Diplomatic Bluebook 2001,* Tokyo: Okurasho Insatsu Kyoku, 2002. Also see The Defence Agency, Japan (JDA), *Boei Hakusho: Heisei 13-nen-ban,* Defence White Paper 2001, pp. 74, 212.
20. See Lisa J. Sansoucy "Japan's Regional Security Policy in Post-Cold War Asia" http://www.ciaonet.org/wps/evm01/sal01.pdf.
21. Ralph A. Cossa, "US-Japan Security Relations: Separating Fact from Fiction" in Ralph A.Cossa (ed.) *Restructuring the US-Japan Alliance: Toward a More Equal Partnership",* Washington DC, CSIS, 1998, p. 46.
22. Lisa J. Sansoucy "Japan's Regional Security Policy in Post-Cold War Asia". http://www.ciaonet.org/wps/evm01/sal01.pdf
23. *Ibid.*

26

Problems of National Security of Kyrgyzstan in Modern Situation

AINUR ELEBAEVA

The multipolar world and the mushrooming transitional and transferred threats created a fundamentally new security system in Central Asia. The old relationships, based on military components have been replaced with a more flexible and dynamic world with many centres of power. This has forced the new independent Central Asian states to identify their foreign policy priorities and the most suitable partners in an effort to ensure regional stability.

Recently, Central Asia has found itself once more in the centre of events of world importance, it has become an arena of struggle for influence that reflects the old regional problems and new global realities. Ambitions of the new players and rivalries of the old regional powers, Russia and China in the first place, are intertwined here.

What is more inadequate is that the political and economical possibilities of all Central Asian countries force them to co-operate with strong partners to consolidate the regional positions in the world. Russia and China are two permanent members of the UN Security Council — this creates a certainty that these two influential members will defend the interests of the Central Asian states, which partly coincide with their own, in the Security Council.

Our country's stronger and developing multilateral relations with Russia is one of its key and long tern foreign policy priorities. Such relationships are of special importance for Kyrgyzstan for historical and cultural reasons, because of traditional friendship between the two nations and shared interests in political,, economic, scientific and technical, humanitarian, cultural and others spheres. Relationships between Kyrgyzstan and Russia received a new foundation when the Soviet Union ceased to exist. Today they are developing in full conformity with the Declaration of Eternal Friendship, Alliance and Partnership signed by Presidents Akaev and Putin on 27 July, 2000.

It is very important that we co-operate closely in the foreign policy sphere and co-ordination of practical measures at the global and regional level, in collective security, defence and guarding our borders, peacekeeping actions in the CIS conflicts zones, migrations policies, illicit trade in arms and drugs.

We have achieved the best results in our concerted antiterrorist efforts, we have already created Collective Forces of Rapid Deployment with the headquarters in Bishkek, along with a branch of the CIS of the Antiterrorist Centre in the Kyrgyz capital. There are plans to set up an Antiterrorist SCO centre based in our capital.

A working meeting between Presidents Akaev and Putin that took place in May 2002 within a framework of the jubilee events marking another anniversary of the CIS Collective Security Treaty was of signal importance. The Russian side treated with understanding the position of Kyrgyzstan that wanted more active bilateral trade and economic contacts, military-technical co-operation and resolution of certain financial problems. President Putin supported the initiative of our republic to give the new lease of life to the relationships among the defence Ministries, he also instructed the RF Defence Ministry to organize steady supplies of military hardware and other equipment to Kyrgyzstan on easy terms and to charge domestic rates for repairing helicopters used by the Armed Forces of the Kyrgyz Republic.

The agreements were sealed with bilateral documents related to military co-operation, signed In June 2002.

Formation of a collective security system in the post-Soviet area began with the break-up of the Soviet Union and creation of the CIS. Thus on 14 February, 1992 it was decided to establish the Council of Defence Ministers and the Main Command of the CIS Joint Armed Forces (JAF) and on 20 March, 1992, an agreement on the JAF, for a transition period, was signed. So an attempt was made to preserve a unified defence area and to reform the former Soviet military as a unified CIS military. Nonetheless many FSU republics at the same time began to form their own national militaries.

Thus by May 1992 it became clear that a centralized CIS military under single command could not be preserved. At the same time the leadership of the majority of the republics was increasingly aware of the need for new, more effective forms and mechanisms of integration in the military-political sphere that would help put in place a more viable security system at far lower economic, scientific and technical costs and stop escalation of armed conflicts in the post-Soviet area. It was these considerations in mind that, on 15 May, 1992, representatives of Armenia, Kazakhstan, Kyrgyzstan, Russia, Tajikistan and Uzbekistan, in Tashkent signed the Collective Security Treaty (CST); an example of a regional security organization formed in full Compliance with the provisions of Article 52 of the UN Charter. Subsequently, it was joined by Azerbaijan, Georgia, and Belarus (1993-1994).

The efforts to put in place a common security system within the CST framework appears to be far more effective. Thus, on 10 February, 1995, the Collective Security Council, its supreme political body, approved a collective security concept, laying down the main principles for interaction between the member states in the military-political sphere. In November of the same year, The Collective Security Treaty was officially registered at the UN Secretariat. The Treaty has been repeatedly invoked since 1996, in connection with threats by Islamic terrorists in Central Asia. By the late 1990 s, however, CST member states came to the conclusion that it does not fully meet their security interests, citing contradictions between certain countries — say Russia and Georgia, Armenia and Azerbaijan, and Uzbekistan and Tajikistan. In this context, in 1999, Georgia, Azerbaijan and Uzbekistan refused to prolong the CST.

The Bishkek (October 2000), Erevan (May 2001) and Jubilee Moscow (May 2002) sessions of the Collective Security Council were key to the future of the CST. In the course of the Bishkek meeting the CST heads of states decided to establish three regional security sub-systems within the CST (European, Caucasian and Central Asian), also signing an agreement of the legal status of collective security forces.

The Erevan session of the Collective Security Council became a landmark in the advancement of military integration with the CST. For the first time in CST history it was decided to form, on a multilateral basis, collective rapid reaction forces in Central Asia with the participation of Russia, Tajik, Kazakh and Kyrgyz military units. Furthermore, it was agreed that collective rapid reaction forces headquarters would be based in Bishkek and that regional groups of forces would be formed in other sectors — Eastern Europe and Caucasus — on a bilateral basis.

In May 2002, a jubilee session of the Collective Security Council was held in Moscow, timed for the 10th anniversary of the CST, which decided to reform the CST as an international regional organization: Organization of the Collective Security Treaty.

It is impossible either to asses the situation or predict its further development outside a very careful analysis of the Russian and Chinese factors, their role in antiterrorist struggle, the way Beijing and Moscow perceive the threats to their security, their interests and their Central Asian Policies. The 9.11 events and the antiterrorist operations in Afghanistan aimed against Al-Qaeda and Taliban completely changed the local situation and confronted both states with a lot of problems. Another important rival, the United States, has come to the area where both China and Russia has already had definite interests.

At the same time new worldwide developments force Beijing to promote its plans more vigorously in Central Asia China is stepping up its military-technical cooperation with the local Countries. In March 2002, during a Central Asian trip of General Liang Guanglie, Army Chief of Staff of the Chinese Peoples Liberation Army, it was announced that China would extend $3 million-worth free military-technical aid to Kazakhstan, to Kyrgyzstan $1.6 m, Uzbekistan-$1m. Later in May 2002, President of Tajikistan Emomali Rakhmonov received from Beijing $1.2m during his visit to China[1].

Today China has all the necessary conditions to pay more attention to Central Asian republics. Beijing's economic interests there are vast. It needs Central Asian energy resources, its capacious market and transport and communication possibilities. Politics, the American factor and Xinjiang separatists remain absolute priorities.

The new stage of Chinese politics will transform its present, mainly political, interests into specific economic aims. In the mid-term perspective China will be able to considerably strengthen its positions there and successfully compete with Russia, the United States, Iran,Turkey and other countries.

The post 9/11 situation in the region was not conducive to resolving the tasks the Chinese leaders had posed themselves and created more threats to China's security. The current situation may push China toward a more active strategy in Central Asia and turn the region into one of the policy priorities. In this way China will work toward greater security in the vitally important western sector and toward closer co-operation with the Central Asian countries[2].

To contain the mounting American influence and to strengthen its relations with China Moscow, will tap the SCO (Shanghai Co-operation Organization) to the full.

The development of the Shanghai Five Shanghai Co-operation Organization (SCO) has made it possible for the first time in history to involve China, Russia, Central Asia states in a multilateral mechanism of regional security and economic co-operation.

Since 1996, this mechanism has played a very important role in the confidence building in Central Asia, and prevented the conflicts like the civil war in Afghanistan from proliferating as seen in the Balkans and the Middle East. Within its framework, China and her SCO partners have resolved, in a matter of several years, their border issues left over from the past two centuries impeding the development of good relationships.

The Shanghai Five was after all the first international community that called for co-operation in countering terrorist groups in Central Asia. Since 1996, the Shanghai Five (SCO) has always been the high-profile organization against-the three evil forces-of terrorism, extremism and separatism in Central Asia. On 15 June, 2001 three months before 9/11 the six member states of SCO signed the Shanghai Convention, which foresaw the necessity of anti terror co-operation in Central Asia and laid down a solid legal base for combating terrorism. After 9/11 SCO members stepped up their co-ordination and consultations. The foreign ministers and law enforcement leaders of the SCO states held consultation meetings to discuss the situation in Central Asia following the US military operations in Afghanistan, and subsequent measures were also taken to accommodate the changes. In addition in their face to face meetings President Jiang Zemin and President Vladimir Putin kept hotline contacts.

After the terrorist attacks on the US, the SCO prime ministers attending the Prime Minister Level Conference at the Almaty, Kazakhstan issued a joint communiqué on 14 September denouncing the terrorist attacks while expressing sympathy for the American people and the victims. The joint communiqué declared that SCO was ready to closely unite with all countries and international organizations, and that effective measures would be taken to wage an unremitting struggle against all forms of terrorism around the world. Chinese Prime Minister Zhu Junzii made two points at the conference. (1) the drafting of the Chapter of the Shanghai Cooperation Organization should be sped up, and (2) the proposed antiterrorist centre in Bishkek should began to operate as soon as possible[3].

The emergence of an international coalition against terrorism, after 9/11, made all the SCO members appreciate the urgency in upgrading the security co-operation and establishing the counter-terror institution. With the all the doubts and differences cleared up, a consensus was soon reached among all the SCO members. In fact since 9/11 more and more bilateral and multilateral co-operation mechanisms have been initiated and established among the SCO members and between the members and other non-members. For example China has so far established bilateral counter-terror mechanisms or dialogues with Russia, America, India, Pakistan France, Britain and Germany. In addition to its interest in conducting bilateral anti-terror co-operation with SCO members, the US has also expressed its readiness to cooperate with SCO's regional counter-terror institution. All these developments have created a favourable atmosphere for SCO to further its security co-operation and carry out its regional anti-terror mission.

On 7 June, 2002, leaders of the six SCO members met in ST.Peterburg holding in depth wide ranging discussions on the major international and regional issues. Based on a review of the work of SCO in the past year, the summer meeting worked out further steps to be taken by the organization. Very significantly, the Charter for Shanghai Cooperation Organization and an Agreement on the Anti-terrorism Agency in the Region were signed by the six leaders, as two major strategic steps to speed up institutional building, raise the level of anti-terror co-operation and bring the organization into mature shape. According to the documents signed, a permanent body and a regional anti-terror agency would formally start to operate in both, Beijing and Bishkek, respectively.

The strategic importance of an Agreement of Anti-terrorism Agency in the Region lies in the fact that it has provided an effective legal basis for initiating the substantial co-operation in the security field. Thus the Bishkek counter-terror mechanism, talked about for more than three years after 1999, would be finally established. With this development the overall co-ordination and rapid response capabilities of the SCO against terrorism and cross-border crimes would be enhanced. On 10 and 11 October, 2002, China and Kyrgyzstan successfully conducted joint military counter-terror manoeuvres in their border area following the SCO anti-terrorism guidelines. It was the first bilateral joint military operation within the SCO framework signifying the formal start-up of the SCO anti terror mission. It can be predicted that against the background of the security situation in the region, SCO and its mechanism for combating terrorism will play an increasingly active role in the future.

It should be noted that this mechanism does not exclude or reject any other states or groups. It is meant to become an important terror-combating force in co-operation with the CIS counter-terror centres in Minsk and Erevan, and in co-operation with the US, Japan, Europe, India, Iran, Pakistan or any other country. Interim Scheme of relations between the Shanghai Cooperation Organization and other International Organizations and States signed at a meeting of the Foreign Ministers Council of the SCO on 23 November, 2002 in Moscow will promote this kind of cooperation.

To conclude, the SCO process has made this Sino-Russia-Central-Asian group integrate into a stabilizing multilateral institution that will help to promote the stability and cooperation in the region. The US military entry into Central Asia for the first time, the possible expansion of the US, war on terrorism, the post-war development in Afghanistan, the internal situation in Pakistan, and the relations between two nuclear powers in the continent, will certainly have a great influence on the future trend of the development of SCO. After the summit meeting in St. Petersburg, SCO with its dedication to counter-terrorism and economic co-operation, will prove to be an increasingly important and effective institution of action, regionally and hopefully, globally as well[4] .

Co-operation with the United States, the largest would power, is of no less importance for our Country. The United States was one of the first countries that recognized our independence.

Diplomatic relations between them were established on 27 December, 1991. In February 1992, the United States opened their embassy in Bishkek. Kyrgyzstan, opened its embassy in Washington in the same year.

Their bilateral relations rest on over 20 agreements negotiated during visits at various levels, the most important of them being an Agreement on Stimulating Investments signed in Washington on 8 May, 1992 and an Agreement on Encouraging Capital Investments and on Their Mutual Protection signed on 19 January 1993. Their bilateral relations rest on the Memorandum of Mutual Assistance between the Government of the Kyrgyzstan and US Government signed on 26 August, 1992.

To correctly assess political relationships between the two capitals one should bear in mind the following. The United States Administration regards Kyrgyzstan as a state that has travelled far along the road of economic and political reforms. Their bilateral cooperation is designed, in particular, to consolidate democratic developments in our republic.

Kyrgyzstan received technical aid through the US Agency for International development (USAID) in 1994-1999 its volume exceeds $170 m. There are 38 American organizations and companies working in Kyrgyzstan within this programme. They closely cooperate with the US embassy in Bishkek. In 2000 the USAID related programmes were designed to reform economy, develop democracy, the social sector, and special initiatives.

Since 1992 Kyrgyzstan has been on the list of countries receiving humanitarian aid within The Food for Progress programme carried out by the US Department of Agriculture. Between 1992 and 1998 the republic had received foodstuffs to the total sum of about $210m, in 1999 alone it got 70 thou. tons of grain worth $18m. In 2000 grain supplies dropped to 60 thou. tons (worth $10 m)

(See Kaana Aidarkul, Mels Omarov. Cooperation between Russia, the US and Kyrgyzstan in new geopolitical context. Central Asia and Caucasus, N1 (19), 2003, P121).

Military bilateral cooperation and cooperation within the Partnership for Peace programme is another important sphere that envisages joint training exercises of the Central Asian Battalion alone with peacekeeping forces of the United States and other countries, exchange of military delegations, and organization of all sorts of courses and on-the-job training. In 1996 the National Guard of Kyrgyzstan established partner relationships with the similar structures in Montana.

Both countries are working toward regional security and both agree that they should continue working in this sphere.

Kyrgyzstan has funded the Military Actions in Mountainous Areas Program launched in 1999 realized together with the American Mountain Warfare School in Alaska to be very useful.

There is also a programme for special forces, defence ministries of both countries are establishing closer cooperation. In 2000 the Defence Ministry of Kyrgyzstan received from the United States over $3m to fight international terrorists. The money was mainly spent on radio stations, night video-devices and ammunition.

The events of 11 September opened a new page in the relations between Kyrgyzstan and the United States. The Counter-terrorist Operation Enduring Freedom brought Americans to Central Asia. In November-December 2001 American units were deployed in Kyrgyzstan and Uzbekistan in full conformity with the special agreements between these republics and US.

There are several agreements on mutually advantageous partnership between the United States and Kyrgyzstan that can serve as an example of closer cooperation between them. Under an Agreement signed during a visit of a governmental delegation of Kyrgyzstan to the United States. In February 2002 Bishkek was to receive $49,9m to carry on democratic, market, and humanitarian reforms. There is a decision on allocating $42m more to Kyrgyzstan to help it realize a number of security-related projects.

President Akaev's visit to the US late in September 2002 played a special role in promoting Bilateral relations. On 23 September he met the President of United States. This was a key event that produced a joint statement designed to help them reach common goals-security and stability in region, continued democratic developments in Kyrgyzstan and the United States support of its Economic advance. The main result of the meeting was consolidating the new format of bilateral relations that had taken shape after 11 September, 2001. This means that in the past years Kyrgyzstan covered a difficult stretch of the road leading to new relations with the United States.

The relations between Moscow and Washington are gradually moving away from confrontation to cooperation that will take into account their mutual interests in the region.

It is obviously important that cooperation between Russia and United States is caused by the need to fight international terrorism, organized crime and drug trafficking that are gaining momentum in Central Asia. The past demonstrated that the local countries could not rebuff the threats on their own, and on a wider scale global, security single handedly. It is a long-term interests of both Moscow and Washington to shoulder the greater share of the burden. This explains, to a great extent, a fairly balanced response from the Kremlin to the deployment of the Forces of the international counter-terrorist coalition in Uzbekistan and Kyrgyzstan.

In their turn, the regional countries expressed their opinion in a fairly balanced interview President of Kyrgyzstan Akaev gave to Nezavisimaya gazeta "In the international sphere we attach primary importance to stronger ties with our CIS partners, the leading place among which undoubtedly belongs to Russia.... All decisions about American military-political presence in Central Asia during the counter-terrorist operation in Afghanistan were taken and are taken on a the basis of agreements between Russia and the regional countries as agreed upon. I have no reasons to expect any negative repercussions there."

This approach alone that recognizes the equality of partners and their need for each other will allow them to realize the national interests of the Central Asian countries and Eurasia as a whole. (See Nezavisimaya gazeta, 10 November, 2001).

Later in May 2002 speaking before the republican parliament President Akaev confirmed his devotion to the foreign policy principles of sovereign Kyrgyzstan and pointed the main directions of diplomatic efforts — opposition to global threats, international terrorism in the first place, stronger partner relations with the regional neighbours and with the world leading powers and international organizations.

CONCLUSIONS

One can say that each of the sides in the RF-US-PRC triangle will try to exploit the contradictions between the other sides in its interests. The post 9/11 period has shown more active Moscow-Washington cooperation in the sphere of global security. The Russia-NATO Council-NATO at 20 and a cooperation agreement between NATO and Russia signed in May 2002 left Beijing in an unfavorable situation.

Meanwhile the United States cannot ignore the Chinese factor even if it wants to do this. Beijing s share in peaceful and sustainable development of the APR is growing, China supports the US led antiterrorist effort while an alliance between China and Russia is a weighty political force.

This curbs Washington and prompts vacillations between harsher and milder courses in relation to Beijing between the talk about the Chinese menace and close partnership. China has became resolved to steadily develop its Central Asian policies to deal with the threats to its own security and to promote economic growth especially in its northwestern corner.

However, despite all this it should be recognized that SCO did not work out an effective, comprehensive speedy and coordinated strategy of response, which may be termed a serious lapse in the wake of the unprecedented terrorist attacks and the consequent war on terrorism.

REFERENCES

1. See. Sergey Minasian. CIS. Building a Collective Security system. *Central Asia and the Caucasus.* N 1(19), 2003, p. 132-34.
2. See: V. Kindalov, O. Limanov, Russia and China in Central Asia: Geopolitical changes.//*Central Asia and Caucasus.* 13(21), 2003. pp. 73-74.
3. See: Pan Guang. Shanghai Cooperation Organization in the context of international antiterrorist Campaign.//*Central Asia and Caucasus,* N3(21) 2003, pp. 49-50.
4. See: Pan Guang. Shanghai Cooperation Organization in the context of international antiterrorist Campaign.//*Central Asia and Caucasus,* N3(21) 2003, pp. 53-54.

27

Mongolia's Security Concerns in the Post-Cold War Period

Sharad K. Soni

Although the end of the Cold War succeeded in eliminating the threat of a global war with the involvement of big powers, the world has yet to become a secured place to live in. There have been cataclysmic developments, particularly the rise of religious extremism and global terrorism, ethnic and sectarian conflicts, civil wars as well as territorial disputes, which have manifested in various parts of the world. Asia, in particular, has experienced some of the most horrendous violence in its soil and, therefore, "Building A New Asia" has become the most sought after theme of the day. This is more so because "if Asia were at peace, more than half the people of the world would be at peace."[1] Nevertheless, in the post-Cold War period, several countries in Asia, both big and small, have carried out drastic changes in their policies and planning so as to make positive contributions towards ensuring peace, stability and development in the continent. Mongolia, too, has could not remain a silent spectator and has tried its best to raise its profile on the Asian map. However, this endeavour of a small country, like Mongolia, is a result of the redefining of the priority directions in its domestic and foreign policies which could ensure national security, not only in terms of preserving independence, sovereignty and territorial integrity, but also achieving a sustainable socio-economic development. From Mongolia's point of view, in today's context, "security is defined not by a country's self-defence capacity but by its capacity to survive and compete."[2]

It is in this context that this study seeks to analyse Mongolia's security concerns in the post-Cold War period on the basis of three key documents adopted by the government, besides highlighting Mongolia's efforts to find a place in regional cooperation for her security and development.

Mongolia,[3] formerly known as the Mongolian People's Republic, and also often referred to as Outer Mongolia, to distinguish itself from Inner Mongolia, an autonomous region of China, has the locational disadvantage of being directly associated with countries other than Russia and China. Bordered by Russia in the north, Inner Mongolia Autonomous Region (IMAR) of China in the south, Xinjiang Uighur Autonomous Region (XUAR) of China in the west and rest of China in the east, Mongolia is a land-locked country sandwiched between its two great neighbours — Russia and China. It stands at the cross junction of Central Asia, North-East Asia, Far East, China and Russia which signifies the geo-strategic importance of Mongolia. It is to be noted here that after centuries of being cut off from the international mainstream, first because of its remote location and then by Chinese and Russian domination, Mongolia has now come a long way since it opted for democracy and market reforms in 1989, under the influence of the then Soviet leader Mikhail Gorbachev's policy of *glasnost and perestroika*. The turning point, however, was Gorbachev's 1986 Vladivostok initiative for removing tension and conflict in the Asia-Pacific region, which also altered the current political status of Mongolia as a "buffer" in the Sino-Soviet relations.[4]

Once having distinction of being the second communist state of the world after the erstwhile Soviet Union, Mongolia's transition to a democratic state structure has not been an easy task; since arguably it remained isolated from the outside world except the Soviet Union for almost seven decades. Even though, the emergence of new situation, under the impact of domestic political reforms and economic restructuring particularly during 1990-92, brought Mongolia at a cross-road where it had to consider its future development and security issues in the framework of new geopolitical realities. As such, a major review of its foreign and security policy was undertaken which resulted in the formulation of three key documents, in June 1994, namely, Concept of National Security, Concept of Foreign Policy and Military Doctrine. These three documents are interlinked so far as basic objectives are concerned, i.e., safeguarding the country's national interests, both internal as well as external, in order to ensure overall advancement of its people. The perceived threats, however, from specific internal and external situations have been the main considerations while defining the national goals in these documents. One striking feature is that the previously made commitments to strengthen international communist order went into oblivion and instead the pursuit of fundamental national interests described as "pragmatic realism" came into focus. As such, National Security of Mongolia was termed as being "multifaceted" by the Mongolian President N. Bagabandi, during his speech delivered on 6 April 1998 to the opening session of the *State Great Hural* (Mongolian Parliament). He stressed that "within the framework of activities aimed at ensuring the national security, it is a pressing task to create favourable external conditions for the existence of Mongolia, strengthen friendly relations with influential countries and carry out a multi-pillared foreign policy".[5]

NEW SECURITY CONCERNS

The adoption of the National Security Concept marked a fundamental change in Mongolia's post-Cold War security thinking. According to the provisions laid down in the Concept paper, "the vital national interests of Mongolia consist in the existence of the Mongolian people and their civilization, in the country's independence, sovereignty, territorial integrity, inviolability of State frontiers, relative economic independence, sustainable ecological development and national unity."[6] In this sense, Mongolia's national security has been defined on quite a new basis in terms of a number of primary areas of concern such as security of the existence of Mongolia, security of the social order and state system, security of citizens' rights and freedoms, economic security, scientific and technological security, security of information, security of Mongolian civilization, security of the population and its gene pool, and ecological security. So, any policy with regard to Mongolia's security concerns revolve around its national interests in the first place, depending upon how constructively the policy and strategy can achieve the defined goals.

However, while highlighting external factors affecting national security, the Concept paper says, "the national security of Mongolia constitutes a part of the international security and as such is directly dependent on the latter. In terms of political spatial security, it is divided into global, regional and subregional."[7] The document further suggests that in its foreign relations Mongolia shall exercise "political realism and consistently principled approach, accord top priority to vital national interests and other national considerations, seek to secure many partners in its international relations and promote a non-aligned policy so long as it does not threaten the country's vital interests."[8] Following this comprehensive approach Mongolia is now pursuing an open foreign policy with a commitment to "promote the policy of consultation with influential countries on issues of strengthening world peace and security, of developing international cooperation, of enhancing the country's strategic significance and fostering strategic interests of major powers in Mongolia." Furthermore, in its relations with developing and land locked countries, Mongolia follows the line of jointly defending and promoting the shared interests in the international field.

As mentioned in its National Security Concept, Mongolia is committed to ensure the security of its existence by strictly observing the policy of not allowing the use of the country's territory against other States; ensuring its Nuclear-Weapon-Free status at the international level and making it an important element of strengthening the country's security by political means. In fact, Mongolia's declaration of Nuclear-Weapon-Free status came in 1992 with the last Russian troops deployed since 1966 during Soviet days leaving the country. It was on 25 September 1992, when speaking at the 47th session of the UN General Assembly, the then Mongolian President P. Ochirbat announced that Mongolia had declared its territory to be a nuclear-weapon-free zone and would work to bring that status recognised internationally.[9] However, the newly adorned status of Mongolia, of being a Nuclear-Weapon-Free Zone (NWFZ), was not only aimed at ensuring its own security by political means but also to make a contribution to regional stability and predictability. As such the declaration included provisions of banning the deployment and transit of foreign troops, of nuclear weapons and of other weapon of mass destruction on its territory. This kind of initiative has essentially the potential to serve as an important confidence building measures for promoting non-proliferation both at the regional as well as global levels. Later on, Mongolia also became a party to the Nuclear Non-Proliferation Treaty (NPT) and other relevant international conventions and treaties including Conventions on Destruction of Chemical and Bacteriological Weapons and the Comprehensive Nuclear Weapons Test Ban Treaty (CTBT).

But the major breakthrough on Mongolia's nuclear-weapon-free policy came on 4 December 1998, when the 53rd session of the United Nations General Assembly adopted a resolution 53/77D, entitled "Mongolia's International Security and Nuclear-Weapon-Free Status." In accordance with paragraph 3 of the resolution, Member States, including the five nuclear-weapon states (P5), were invited to "cooperate with Mongolia in taking the necessary measures to consolidate and strengthen Mongolia's independence, sovereignty and territorial integrity, the inviolability of its borders, its economic security, its ecological balance and its nuclear-weapon-free status as well as its independent foreign policy."[10] This clearly shows that Mongolia's security concerns had already been recognised by the world community. A definite stride on the part of the Mongolian leadership was made on 3 February 2000, when a National Law defining and regulating Nuclear-Weapon-Free status of Mongolia was adopted and passed by the country's Parliament, thereby taking a concrete step towards promoting the aims and objectives of nuclear non-proliferation. A few months later, on 5 October 2000, as a contribution to implementing the UN resolution 53/77D, a joint statement was issued by the P5 countries providing security assurances to Mongolia, which was further transmitted to the UN Security

Council. At present, Mongolia continues to receive assistance and support to promote its international security and nuclear-weapon-free status from various quarters including the relevant UN bodies, the five nuclear-weapon states (P5), the Non Aligned Movement, various regional disarmament meetings etc.[11]

As a follow up of the previous resolution, further on 20 November 2000, the 55th session of the United Nations General Assembly in its another resolution 55/33S on "Mongolia's International Security and Nuclear-Weapon-Free Status" appealed to "the Member States of the Asia and Pacific region to support Mongolia's efforts to join the relevant regional security and economic arrangements."[12] Since then Mongolia has been moving on the right direction with such efforts. In this regard, what is worth to be noted here is that addressing the 58th session of the UN General Assembly on 29 September 2003, Mongolian President Bagabandi reaffirmed his country's support to the establishment of Nuclear-Weapon-Free Zones in other parts of the world, while at the same time also emphasised that "nuclear-weapon states should provide security to non-nuclear-weapon states...[hence stressed on] the conclusion of a multilateral treaty to that effect."[13] That is how Mongolia has been demonstrating its commitment towards promoting transparency and confidence building for ensuring not only its own security but also the world over, particularly in the Asia-Pacific region.

So far as the second document is concerned, it appears that Mongolia's security concerns further depend on its active foreign policy which, too, revolve around its national interests. It has been clearly mentioned in the Foreign Policy Concept that "the priority of Mongolia's foreign policy shall be safeguarding of its security and vital national interests by political and diplomatic means, and creating a favourable external environment for its economic, scientific and technological development."[14] While trying to achieve this objective Mongolia's approach has been to secure maximum benefits offered by international and regional multilateral cooperation. By adopting what is termed as a "multi-pillar" foreign policy Mongolia not only discarded the lopsided attitude of the Cold War period but also opted for a non-aligned policy in order to make its presence in the world felt as a developing country. During the past decade it has broadened its diplomatic outlook and the scope of its international activities by adhering to the principle of flexible priorities in foreign policy implementation. At the same time considering "pragmatism" as being one of the main characteristics of Mongolia's foreign policy, the country relies on ongoing international political reality as well as on the international legal system besides following the trends of international economic developments. However, the key issue involving Mongolia's foreign policy priorities is to ensure the security and prosperity of the country both internally and externally by "forming with influential countries in the region and in the world a network of relationships based on the interdependence of political, economic and other interests."[15] Therefore, within the framework of its multi-pillared and multi-dimensional foreign policy Mongolia has already established new partnership with global and regional powers, and is currently trying to have their support especially in speeding up economic rebuilding of the country.

The third document related to Mongolia's security concerns which became the guiding principles of the country's defence policy is the Military Doctrine. It was adopted at a time when Mongolian leadership acknowledged that although the prospects for mutual understanding, trust and partnership came to be prevailed in international relations with the end of the Cold War, the danger of war and armed conflicts had not been fully eliminated and a collective security system had not yet been formed either at the global or regional level. As such, to avert any kind of danger militarily, Mongolia needed a guiding principle, which has been enshrined in this military doctrine. Significantly, the document asserted that Mongolia's international relations had "shifted from predominantly political and military fields to economic, scientific-technological and informational fields, in other words, from geopolitics to geoeconomics."[16] The document stated that Mongolia would never engage in a conflict except if invaded and that the country would never enter into any military bloc so long as its independence and sovereignty were not threatened.[17] In totality, the military doctrine was formulated on the basis of broader security issues particularly in the Asia-Pacific region, and hence the objective of Mongolia's defence policy aimed at participating in the creation of collective security systems. Now Mongolia has engaged itself in various dialogues on broader regional security issues, thus trying to find a worthy place in the regional cooperation.

REGIONAL COOPERATION FOR SECURITY AND DEVELOPMENT

While maintaining 'complete equality' in its relations with Russia and China, Mongolia also focussed its attention towards developing political and economic cooperation with the United States, Japan, European Union especially Germany, Britain, France as well as Australia, Canada and other western countries. Besides, in order to strengthen its position in Asia, Mongolia attaches great importance towards expanding its relations with India, the Republic of Korea, Turkey, Thailand, Singapore and other ASEAN member countries. Japan was one of the first countries to support Mongolia's move to democracy, both through bilateral and multilateral links, and has been rendering all forms of assistance including loan, aid and technical cooperation. As regards US, since the establishment of diplomatic relations between the two countries in 1987, the bilateral relationship has been developing to the satisfaction of both sides. Mongolia values partnership with US at a great deal especially due to the fact that in recent years the latter has reiterated its support for Mongolia's active participation in the multilateral process of economic and security cooperation taking place in the Asia Pacific region. On the other hand, US interests in Mongolia centre largely on the following considerations:[18] (a) Mongolia's strategic location which could prove to be of vital importance for moderating Asian politics; (b) Mongolia provides a significant, though fragile, example of democratic reforms and economic restructuring in a potentially unstable part of the world; and (c) Mongolia consistently lends its strong support to the US stand on several international issues including those concerning ongoing war on terrorism.

However, Mongolia still accords top priority to the question of relations with its two neighbouring countries — Russia and China and adheres to the principle of a balanced relationship with them.

Russia

Despite initial hiccups, the 1990s saw the emergence of good neighbourly, equal and mutually beneficial ties between Mongolia and Russia, particularly after the signing of the Treaty of Friendly Relations and Cooperation in 1993.[19] The Treaty which was concluded on the basis of equal terms stipulated that Russia would respect Mongolia's policy of denying foreign troops to be stationed or pass through its territory, besides making it clear that neither party would participate in any military or political alliance that would be detriment to the interests of the other. Unlike the 1966 Treaty, the 1993 Treaty was more democratic as although it envisaged wide ranging collaboration, it did not "provide for any form of military alliance and allowed both states to develop relations in accordance with their own national interests."[20]

Significantly, the visit of Mongolian President N. Bagabandi to Russia in 1999 and the return visit by the Russian President Vladimir Putin to Mongolia in 2000 constitute yet another example of their all out efforts to cooperate on several key issues. The significance of Putin's visit on November 13-14, 2000 lies in the fact that it resulted in signing of a 25-point memorandum of cooperation; termed as Ulaanbaatar Declaration. It was a document which determined the principles of directions of extending and developing Mongolia-Russia relations in the 21st century. The declaration displayed that "in many cases both countries see eye to eye on the most important aspects of the global situation, and sets forth the willingness of Moscow and Ulaanbaatar to closely coordinate their policy in international affairs, on a wide range of issues."[21]

This visit also marked by endorsing a military pact committed to a peaceful future between the two sides.[22] The pact, among other things, also signifies impending closer security relationship between Ulaanbaatar and Moscow. Recently, on 13-14 January 2004, Russia's Minister of Foreign Affairs Igor Ivanov paid an official visit to Mongolia. During this visit a joint Russia-Mongolia statement was issued in which both sides advocated reinforcing security and cooperation in the Asia-Pacific Region, particularly, in North East Asia and reaffirmed their commitment to the development of multilateral cooperative approaches towards resolution of existing problems in the interest of safeguarding regional stability and security by politico-diplomatic means.[23] Nonetheless, Russian interest in Mongolia now seems to be influenced by not only political-strategic concerns but also by the economic and trade considerations.

China

Following the establishment of a multi-party political system in Mongolia in 1990, the new Mongolian President P. Ochirbat visited China for the Sino-Mongolian summit. Ochirbat's visit was a historic milestone in Mongolia's difficult relationship with China. But it was in 1994 that the two sides put a seal on their commitments towards restoration of normalised relations, when a new Treaty of Friendship and Cooperation was signed on quite a new basis during Chinese Premier Li Peng's visit to Mongolia.[24] The most important clause of this Treaty was their understanding that neither of them "will take part in any military-political alliance directed against each other and will not conclude any treaty and agreement with a third country that may adversely affect the state sovereignty and security of the other Party." Mongolia and China also decided that they will not "allow a third country to use its territory which may adversely affect the state sovereignty and security of the other Party."

A landmark event in the post-Cold War period of Sino-Mongolian relations was marked by the visit of the then Chinese President Jiang Zemin to Mongolia in July 1999. It signifies that China now respects Mongolia's independence and sovereignty, besides carrying out mutually beneficial cooperation in political and economic spheres. In 2001, an economic agreement was concluded in Beijing between China and Mongolia, which guarantees that the former will become not only Mongolia's most important trading partner, but also remain its largest direct foreign investor. The agreement has undoubtedly paved the way for "Beijing's gradual reassimilation of Mongolia."[25] China is now Mongolia's biggest trading partner, buying 40 per cent of latter's exports. Last year, in June 2003, during the visit of Chinese President Hu Jintao to Mongolia, both sides agreed to "strengthen their cooperation in international and regional affairs in joint efforts to maintain peace and stability in the region."[26] It seems that today China is very much required in Mongolia to fill its economic and strategic vacuum, created a decade or so back by the collapse of the former Soviet Union.

It may also be noted here that changes in the Sino-Soviet/Russian relations as well as the political and economic transformations in both the Russian Federation and China, starting in the 1990s, created a brand new environment and factors affecting Mongolia's security positively. Both China and Russia have agreed not to use or threaten to use force against each other, or use of territory, water and air space of a third country, particularly Mongolia, for this purpose. This provides a powerful impetus to altering the security environment of Mongolia. Even a 20-year term agreement signed in Moscow between China and Russia, in July 2001, alludes that "China will not attempt to take Mongolia outright during this period, but will instead limit herself to economic penetration."[27] But at the same time it is also true that the close connection between Russia-China and Mongolia-China relations would remain a part of the new international order, particularly in North-East Asia.[28] Moreover, as it is also becoming clear that the ability of Russia-China relations to alter Mongolia's relations with China is diminishing, it would, therefore, be in the best interests of both Mongolia and China to take freely their future course of action, as far as cooperation in various fields is concerned.[29] From the Mongolian point of view, so far there is no controversial issue between Mongolia and China, which could spark military conflict between the two countries.[30]

Asia-Pacific Region

The post-Cold War period witnessed the Asia-Pacific region as one of the key areas of Mongolia's security and foreign policy objectives. It is evident from the fact that Mongolia learnt a lot from the economic dynamism of the Asia-Pacific region, which is still required to be followed at the domestic front. In order to find a place in this vast region, Mongolia formally joined in 1993 the Asia Pacific Economic Cooperation (APEC) and in 1998 the ASEAN Regional Forum (ARF), as a full member. Since then Mongolia has been taking part with guest status in some of the APEC working groups, such as energy, trade promotion, transportation, tourism and human resources development.[31] Mongolia has also developed her own Individual Action Plan of trade and investment liberalisation in accordance with the APEC model. More importantly, membership in the PECC, that Mongolia acquired in 2000, is being considered as yet another step towards achieving the ultimate goal of employing the interests of regional countries in contributing to Mongolia's efforts for stability in terms of economic development, thus ensuring the overall security of the country.

Moreover, Mongolia's desire of promoting cooperation among the countries of North East Asia stems from giving due importance to the region as "a key component of the broader Asia-Pacific economic structure and a pivot of the world power equation with the increasing interaction of China, Japan, Russia and the United States."[32] With regard to the Asia-Pacific region, Mongolia's security strategy aims at building a multi-pillar framework of security by adhering to the following:[33]

(a) maintaining friendly and good-neighbourly relations with neighbours;
(b) developing closer bilateral ties with other regional countries;
(c) working within the ARF multilateral process;
(d) contributing towards restoring peace and stability in North East Asia;
(e) developing military-to-military contacts;
(f) implementing global non-proliferation and arms control regimes; and
(g) encouraging "Track II" dialogues on security issues.

During the past few years encouraging signs have emerged in Mongolia's international relations as a result of pursuing a policy of active participation in regional cooperation especially with North East Asia, Asia Pacific and Central Asia as well as involving itself into global economic-political integration. It is to be pointed out that, Mongolia now identifies itself more as a North East Asian country and, therefore, it can not escape from the developments taking place on the Korean peninsula. It is where Mongolia can play a role towards contributing to the consolidation of peace and stability as it enjoys stable and good neighbourly relations with both North and South Korea. Although North East Asia is the only sub-region having no organisational structure of its own, the countries belonging to this area meet time and again on an informal basis and exchange views on the current situation as well as on ways and means of forging regional cooperation in various fields.[34] As part of this effort some large-scale 21st century oriented projects have been undertaken, particularly the construction of main gas and oil pipelines as well as power lines. The Tuman River Area Development Project (TRADP), in which a number of North East Asian countries including Mongolia are participating, is yet another example of promoting wider regional cooperation. This is an ambitious project which aims at creating a trans-border free trade zone by transforming the Tumen River area into the transportation and trading hub for North East Asia. It will help the region's trade to prosper besides attracting investment from outside.

So far as Mongolia's relations with the Central Asian States are concerned, the importance lies in the fact that the latter can serve as the new land bridge to promote Mongolia's overland trade, besides being partners in its economic rebuilding.[35] Even the Mongolian government action plan, of 1996-2000 and 2000-04, reiterated the need for developing cooperation and expanding relations with Central Asia and the Near East. Further, developing ties with international and regional organisations constitutes one of the basic tenants of Mongolia's security and foreign policy priorities. The fact that Mongolia acquired membership of the IMF, the World Bank, the ADB and the WTO testifies Mongolia's endeavour to strike a right balance between its politics and economy. Meanwhile, Mongolia has also shown keen interest in the activities of the Shanghai Cooperation Organisation (SCO) and, for the first time, recently on 15 January 2004, Mongolian Foreign Minister L. Eredenechuluun participated as an observer at the SCO's ministerial meeting held in Beijing. As the experts believe that economic cooperation will be the most promising aspect of the SCO's future,[36] it would also prove to be beneficial for Mongolia in terms of creating a favourable environment for its own development. But it all depends on how quickly Mongolia finds the opportunity to become a full-fledged member of the SCO.

CONCLUSION

Keeping in view the developments since Mongolia opted for democracy, it appears that the fulfilment of much of its security concerns depends on political and diplomatic means. It would always be in the best interests of Mongolia to maintain good neighbourly and balanced relations with Russia and China so as to harness maximum benefits for ensuring its overall security. It is more so because it seems unlikely that either Russia or China would ever think of going back to the Cold War period and exert pressure on Mongolia to once again choose its ally between the two immediate neighbours. There have also been talks about a "third neighbour" which could be a country juxtaposed vis-à-vis Russia and China. But that does not seem to be a feasible idea, and if at all a third neighbour is required, it can be visualised not in terms of a single country rather a group of countries, especially those supported consistently the democratic changes in Mongolia.[37] Perhaps such an idea might have developed on the premise that unlike the Cold War period "isolation" would not be a viable option for a small country like Mongolia if it wants to raise its profile at the regional and global levels. For that matter, it does not require to involve itself in a military or political alliance but can go ahead with developing mutually beneficial relations with all the countries. As such in the past decade Mongolia has broadened its presence in the world by strengthening its bilateral and multilateral ties. But still there is much to be done, both at the domestic as well as external levels. It is vital for Mongolia to be updated with developments taking place in the regional and global affairs and accordingly try to influence as many countries as it can to be partners on mutually advantageous basis. However, due to the problem of having landlocked geographical situation, relations with Russia and China are of paramount and equal importance. In any case, for the foreseeable future Mongolia will have to rely much on its diplomatic initiatives to ensure its security and foreign policy initiatives for maintaining the country's sovereignty and territorial integrity, besides achieving economic security.

NOTES AND REFERENCES

1. Jasjit Singh, "Towards a Safer Asia: An Indian Perspective", *Strategic Analysis* (New Delhi), Vol. XXIII, No. 1, April 1999, p. 5.
2. R. Bold, *The Security of Small State: Option for Mongolia* (Ulaanbaatar: The Institute for Strategic Studies, 2000), p. 36.
3. In order to distance itself from its Communist past, the country changed its new name to Mongolia as of 12 February 1992 under the new Constitution, which was adopted on 13 January 1992. See, *Summary of World Broadcasts*, FE/1303, 13 February 1992. For the full text of the 1992 Constitution, see *The Constitution of Mongolia* (Taipei: Mongolia and Tibetan Foundation, 1992), pp.1-31. The adoption of the 1992 Constitution replaced the last Constitution of 1960. The key elements in the new Constitution emphasised the "establishment of democracy" contrary to the previous Constitutions, which had stressed "building the State through socialism".
4. For more details on Vladivostok initiative which has had direct bearing on Mongolia, see Sharad K. Soni, *Mongolia-Russia Relations: Kiakhta to Vladivostok* (Delhi: Shipra 2002), pp. 218-21.
5. *Collection of the Public Statements and Addresses of the President of Mongolia related to National Security and Defence Policies* (Ulaanbaatar, 2000), p. 14. For the full text of the speech see, pp. 4-17.
6. See, "Concept of National Security of Mongolia", in *National Security Council: Concept, Law and Regulations* (Ulaanbaatar, 2000), second edition, p. 82.
7. *Ibid.*, p. 83.
8. *Ibid.*, p. 89.
9. United Nations General Assembly, 47th Session, 13th Meeting, Verbatim Records, document No. A/47/PV. 13, 1992, p. 11.
10. See, *Report of the Secretary-General on Mongolia's International Security and Nuclear-Weapon-Free Status*, United Nations General Assembly, 55th Session, A/55/166 dated 20 July 2000.
11. *Ibid.*
12. See, *Resolution 55/33S of the United Nations General Assembly*, 55th Session, 69th Plenary Meeting, A/RES/55/33 dated 12 January 2001.
13. For the full text of President Bagabandi's address to the 58th session of the UN General Assembly, see http://www.extmin.mn/2003_UNGA58_President StamtEng.htm
14. "Concept of Mongolia's Foreign Policy", *The Mongolian Journal of International Affairs* (Ulaanbaatar), No. 2, 1995, p. 71.
15. *Ibid.*

16. J. Enkhsaikhan, "Mongolia's Security Policy: Regional and International Aspects," *The Mongol Messenger*, Vol. 18, No. 210, 14 July 1995 at http://www.indiana.edu/~mongsoc/mong/security.htm
17. See, "The Fundamentals of the Military Doctrine of Mongolia", *Strategic Digest* (New Delhi), Vol. 26, No. 2, February 1996, pp. 193-95.
18. See, "Mongolia" at www.usaid.gov/regions/ane/newpages/one_pagers/mong01a.htm
19. For the full text of the Russo-Mongolia 1993 Treaty see, *Mongolian Defence White Paper, 1997-1998*, Ministry of Defence of Mongolia, Ulaanbaatar, pp. 87-92.
20. Galina Yaskina, "Russian-Mongolian Relations: Reality and Outlook", *Far Eastern Affairs*, No. 5, 1998, p. 37.
21. Leonid Moiseev, "Relations Between Russia and Mongolia Are Warming", *Far Eastern Affairs*, No.1, January-February 2001, p. 12.
22. *Independent* (Dhaka), 15 November 2000.
23. See, *The Joint Russian-Mongolian Statement*, 14 January 2004 at http://www.extmin.mn/UBTunhaglaleng.htm
24. For the full text of the China-Mongolia 1994 Treaty see, *Mongolian Defence White Paper, 1997-1998*, n. 19, pp. 93-95.
25. See, Bruce A. Elleman and Sarah C.M. Paine, "Security Pact with Russia Bolsters China's Power", *International Herald Tribune*, 6 August 2001.
26. See, "President Hu Jintao Holds a Formal Talk with Mongolian President", 4 June, 2003, Website of the Ministry of Foreign Affairs of the People's Republic of China at www.fmprc.gov.cn
27. Elleman and Paine, n. 25.
28. R. Bold, "The Changing International Order and Mongolia's Security," *The Mongolian Journal of International Affairs* (Ulaanbaatar), No. 1, 1994, p. 11.
29. *Ibid.*
30. *Mongolian Defence White Paper 1997-1998*, n. 19, p. 21.
31. Oidov Nyamdavaa, *Mongolia-India Relations* (New Delhi: Bhavana Books & Prints and Himalayan Research and Cultural Foundation), p. 50.
32. D. Bayarkhuu, "A New World Order in the Asia-Pacific Region: A Mongolian Perspective," *World Affairs* (New Delhi), Vol. 3, No. 4, Oct-Dec. 1999, p. 101.
33. Ts. Batbayar, "The Development of Mongolia's External Relations in the 1990s", T.S. Batbayar (ed.), *Renovation of Mongolia on the Eve of the XXI Century and Future Development Patterns* (Ulaanbaatar: Mongolian Development Research Centre, 2000), p. 86.
34. Bayarkhuu, n. 32, p. 101.
35. Sharad K. Soni, "Perspectives on Mongolia-Central Asia Relations," *Jadavpur Journal of International Relations* (Calcutta), Vol. 2, 1996, p. 178.
36. "SCO Confronts Security, Economic Concerns" at http:// www.cctv.com/english/news/TV News/Morning News/20030530/100223.html
37. See, Panidjunai Khaliun, "Mongolian Foreign Policy, Past and Present", *Turkish Daily News*, 12 July 2003, at http://www.turkishdailynews.com/old_editions/07_12_03/feature.htm

28

Regional Experiences in Solving Water Resources Problems in Tajikistan

I. SH. NORMATOV

The principal spheres of water resources in Central Asia are irrigated agriculture and hydroelectric engineering.

Problem of mutual relations between irrigation and hydroelectric engineering in the region is determined by the fact that the countries of upper stream-Kyrgyzstan and Tajikistan are interested in the energy regime of river flowing use, and the countries of the lower stream-Kazakhstan, Turkmenistan and Uzbekistan are interested in the irrigative regime.

One of the main resources of Central Asian region is water. It is not without reason that the year 2003 was announced as "International Year of Fresh Water" at the UNO General Assembly, at the initiative of Tajikistan — the country, where more than 50 per cent of all water resources of the region are formed. In August 2003 the International Water Forum was to be held in Dushanbe, the capital of Tajikistan.

Total water resources of the Aral Sea basin surface waters are 115.6km^3/year (Table 1). According to approximate evaluation underground water resources in the Aral Sea basin are 43.7km^3/year, 15.8km^3/year (36.2%) of them being the approved exploitation stores. Moreover, a large quantity of return waters are formed in the Aral Sea basin — 45.8km^3/year, only a small part of which is used anew for irrigation — 6.0km^3/year, and a great part of water is led to rivers (23.5km^3/year) and natural reduction (16.3km^3/year).

Table 1: Surface Water Resources of the Aral Sea basin

Country	*The Amudarya River basin, km^3/year*	*The Syrdarya River basin, km^3/year*	*The Aral Sea basin*	
			km^3/year	*per cent*
1	*2*	*3*	*4*	*5*
Kazakhstan	—	4.50	4.50	3.9
Kyrgyzstan	1.90	27.40	29.30	25.3
Tajikistan	62.90	1.10	64.00	55.4
Turkmenistan	2.78	—	2.78	2.4
Uzbekistan	4.70	4.14	8.84	7.6
Afghanistan	6.18	—	6.18	5.4
CA	78.46	37.14	115.60	100.0

The principal spheres of water resources use in Central Asia today are irrigated agriculture and hydropower engineering.

Irrigated agriculture appearance in Central Asia refers to the 6th –7th century B.C. Since then up to the present times its role has been constantly growing, irrigated areas have increased. By the beginning of the 20th century, about 3.5 mln ha have been already irrigated in the region. Intensive development of irrigation in the region especially began during existence of the USSR (mainly from the 60's up to the 90's of the past century).

As a result by 1990 total area of irrigated lands in the region has increased to 8.8 mln ha, including:

-in Kazakhstan -up to 2.8 mln. ha
-in Kyrgyzstan -up to 1.1 mln. ha
-in Tajikistan -up to 0.7 mln. ha
-in Uzbekistan -up to 4.2 mln. ha

Similar sharp growth in the soviet period was observed in power engineering, too. We can say that beginning from the 30's of the past century the whole generation could observe the foundation of modern basic branch of economy — electropower engineering, that was quite new for it. Total established capacity of all electric power stations in the region by the middle of the 90's grew to 37.8 mln. kW, including:

-in Kazakhstan -18.5 mln. kW
-in Kyrgyzstan -3.8 mln. kW
-in Tajikistan -4.4 mln. kW
-in Uzbekistan -11.3 mln. kW

At that time the capacity of hydropower stations in the region reached 11.31 mln. kW, including:

-in Kazakhstan	-2.22 mln. kW
-in Kyrgyzstan	-2.95 mln. kW
-in Tajikistan	-4.40 mln. kW
-in Uzbekistan	-1.74 mln. kW

Unfortunately all these impressive results led to some negative consequences. Intensity of processes of ecological equilibrium violations in the region, which especially became apparent in the Aral Sea zone, has sharply increased; lands salting and their desertification has grown; the quality of water especially in the lower stream of rivers has worsened. And by the 1970's water resources of the Syrdarya River basin were almost completely exhausted. All this practically turned into a global ecological problem of the region, and regarding the Aral Sea — into ecological disaster.

One of the reasons of this situation was that the programmes of development of both, irrigation and power engineering, laid down at the times of the USSR were not accomplished.

First of all according to ecological, and in the first place according to economic reasons, the project of Siberian rivers transference into the region, which could cardinally solve all the problems of irrigation development and saving the Aral Sea, even under the preservation of existing conditions of management, was fully stopped.

Practically the programme of hydroelectric engineering development in the region has just been started. Construction of new hydroelectric power stations with total capacity of 7,7 mln. KW and putting them into operation was provided for Tajikistan by "Conception of the USSR power engineering development for the period 1991 — 2005".

The problems became even more acute after the collapse of the USSR and formation of new independent states when they obtained intergovernmental status.

One of such problems is connected with the contradiction between irrigation and hydroelectric engineering.

Irrigated agriculture demands maximum use of water during the vegetative period from April to October. And hydroelectric engineering is concerned with the paramount use of river flowing in winter, the coldest period of a year when rivers contain little water, from October to April. Thus by the irrigative regime filling reservoirs is necessary in winter and their use — in summer, and for the energy regime it is vice versa, filling reservoirs is necessary in summer and their use — in winter. It is impossible to combine their interests within one reservoir.

But such a situation just takes place in the Aral Sea basin today. The number of reservoirs is quite limited in the zone of flowing formation, where the principal regulation of flowing has to be carried out. There is only one such reservoir in Tajikistan, in the Amudarya River upper reaches — the Nurek reservoir. In the Syrdarya River basin there are three such reservoirs: the Tocktogul reservoir in Kyrgyzstan, the Kayrakkum reservoir in Tajikistan and the Andijan reservoir in Uzbekistan. But from the latter three the Tocktogul reservoir can only carry out long-term regulation of flowing. Besides, all of them are located in different states, and co-ordination of their work is in itself a problem.

The common problem of mutual relations between irrigation and hydroelectric engineering in the region is determined by the fact that the countries of the upper stream — Kyrgyzstan and Tajikistan, are interested in the energy regime of river flowing use, and the countries of the lower stream — Kazakhstan, Turkmenistan and Uzbekistan, are interested in the irrigative regime.

Present-day scheme of interrelations, between Central Asian republics, began to in 1994. In March 17,1998 it was registered officially by signing Bishkek "Agreement on use of the Syrdarya River basin water and energy resources between the Government of the Republic of Kazakhstan, the Government of the Republic of Kyrgyzstan and the Government of the Republic of Uzbekistan", which was joined by the Republic of Tajikistan in 17 June, 1999.

According to fig.1 and 2 the Tocktogul reservoir does not carry out seasonal regulation of flow in irrigative purposes. It can be well seen that during the last years without exception the Tocktogul reservoir is filled in the vegetative period and used in the winter period, i.e. it works in the pure energy regime. The Tocktogul reservoir does not carry a long-term regulation of flow either. As a consequence, from 1994 to 2002, the reservoir was nearly exhausted, although according to Table 2 depth of the river during all this period was above the norm.

Table 2: Inflowing to the Tocktogul Reservoir

Inflowing km^3/year	*Year*								
	1994	1995	1996	1997	1998	1999	2000	2001	Aver
Annual	15,24	10,9	13,7	10,8	14,5	14,5	12,6	11,4	12,96
Average long-term	11,4								

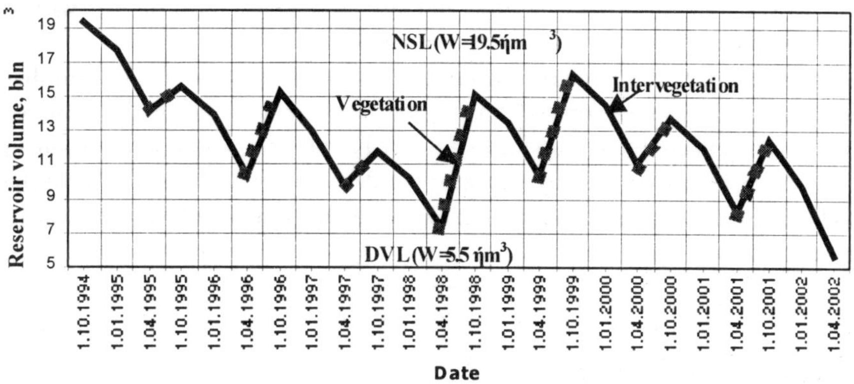

Fig. 1: Tocktogul Reservoir Diagram of Seasonal Filling and Use

Increased winter removals from the Tocktogul reservoir is in addition to the reason of creating an unfavourable situation in the middle stream of the Syrdarya River that is lower than the hydro unit of Chardarya. As a result of the river's insufficient carrying capacity, deluging of developed territories in Kzyl-Orda take place and the water flows into Arnasay cavity, by which the problem of the Aral Sea aggravates. And although the reason of such a situation is erection by Kazakhstan of partitioned off constructions in the Syrdarya riverbed, which is a violation of the acting norms and regulations of CNAR, this only corroborates the thesis that now-a-days-ecological problems in the water energy complex are to a considerable extent connected with the administrative organizational decisions.

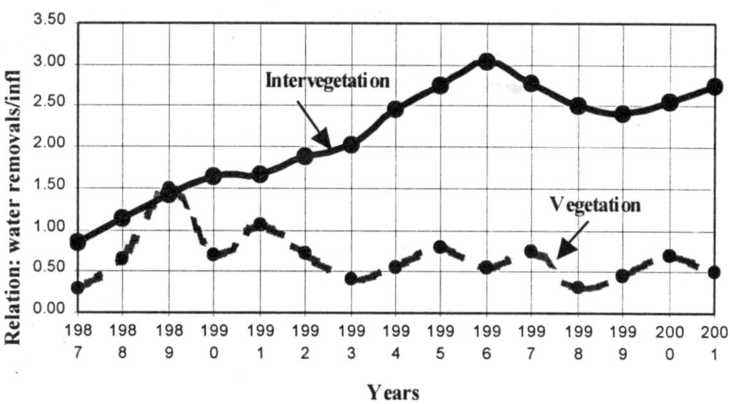

Fig. 2: Regime of Tocktogul Reservoir Work

Until recent times Tajikistan improved the situation, to some extent, by changing the regulation of river flowing by the Kayrakkum reservoir in the interests of the irrigative complex of Kazakhstan and Uzbekistan. This is shown in diagrams on fig. 3 and 4. However, in contrast to the Tocktogul reservoir the Kayrakkum reservoir can only carry out a seasonal but not a long-term regulation of flow that is insufficient in a long-term section. Second, as it is shown below that without getting sufficient compensation for its delivered services Tajikistan makes changes of a flowing regulation just by virtue of the developed tradition, displaying its good will. Such a scheme cannot work long in the existing market conditions.

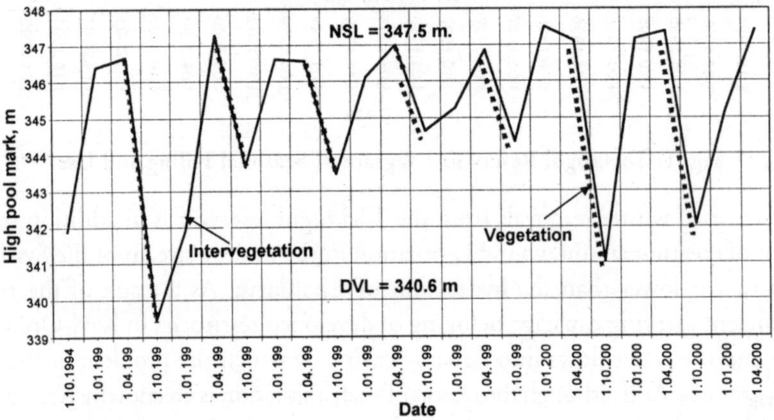

Fig. 3: Kayrakkum Reservoir Diagram of Seasonal Filling and Work

Payment to Kyrgyzstan for its services is carried out according to the following scheme. At the same time with the additional water removals during a vegetative period in the volume of 2,2 bln m^3 Kyrgyzstan also annually supplies Uzbekistan and Kazakhstan with electrical energy surplus in total volume of 2,2 bln KW/h. The energy is distributed in equal parts between the countries-recipients.

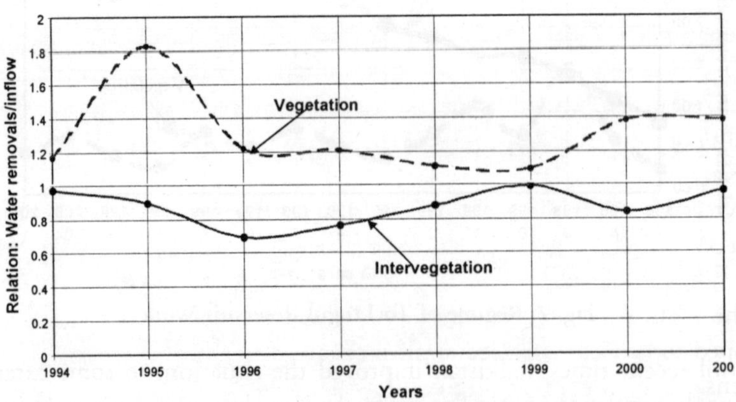

Fig. 4: Regime of Kayrakkum Reservoir Work

- Supplies Kyrgyzstan with 600mln KW/h of natural gas that is equivalent to 3,22 bln KW/h of electric energy at the work of HPS with thermo- and electric energy at 60 per cent of coefficient of efficiency.
- supplies Kyrgyzstan with 20t of turbine oil and 500t of transformer oil. At their price making correspondingly $400/t and $300/t their total cost is equal to $230 thousand that is equivalent to 11,5 mln KW/h of electric energy at its price of 2 cents per KW/h.
- delivers services of railway transportations for the sum equal to $500 thousand that is equivalent to 25 mln KW/h of electric energy at its price of 2 cents per KW/h. Thus, in total Uzbekistan returns Kyrgyzstan in the equivalent 3,25 bln KW/h of electric energy Kazakhstan supplies Kyrgyzstan by the same way of compensation:
- 566,7 t of Karaganda coal, that is equivalent, at its use in TPS for generation of thermo-and electric energy at 60 per cent of coefficient of efficiency, to 2,97 bln KW/h of electric energy even at the low calorific value of coal equal to 4500 kcal/kg.

Consequently as a result of all this Kyrgyzstan has for itself a direct economic profit in the volume of 4,02 bln KW/h of extra electric energy.

The volume of the extra-received electric energy is considerable for Kyrgyzstan. It makes one third of the total electrical energy production in the republic and only a little less than its annual generation in the biggest in the republic, the Tocktogul HPS.

At the same time, together with water removals in a vegetative period, Tajikistan annually supplies Uzbekistan with 300 mln KW/h of electrical energy.

By way of compensation, the republic only received 200mln KW/h of electrical energy from Uzbekistan. Moreover, according to the agreement during three months, when Tajikistan receives electrical energy from Uzbekistan, it does not present payment to the latter for the services on the regulation of frequency. In usual conditions such a payment makes about $250 thousand per month that makes $750 per three months. At the rate of 2 cents per KW/h it is equivalent to 337 mln KW/h of electrical energy. At that price Tajikistan gets no compensation from Kazakhstan at all.

So receiving 200 mln KW/h of electrical energy from Uzbekistan Tajikistan gives it 337 mln KW/h, i.e. unlike Kyrgyzstan Tajikistan which simply works at a loss.

The main reason of this perplexed situation is the absence of a clearly developed and coordinated economic mechanism of calculations of services and compensations for the regulation of flowing. Solution of this problem is a top-priority question for the republics of the Aral Sea basin today.

In principle different schemes are possible here. Apparently one of the best variants for this is the version of joint ownership. It could not only smoothly solve itself the question of the complex use of water flowing, but also serve the purposes of unification, integration of the states. Absence of such problems, in the former USSR, is explained by the existence of common ownership then. It is just this joint ownership, but not ideology, politics and others that united the peoples of the USSR then, and it is just the division of this property and, as a consequence, breakup of economic ties that is the reason of today's economic difficulties of the CIS countries.

In a general way this version looks like in the following manner. The countries with zones of flowing formation, as the base for calculation of the compensations, work out a national regime of their hydro units work (Kyrgyzstan — for the Tocktogul, Tajikistan — for the Kayrakkum) without taking into account the interests of the countries located lower. Then they work out the second version of the same hydro units work, but this time taking into account the interests of the countries located lower. Economic differences between these two versions, losses and damages, connected with transition from the first version to the second one in a pecuniary or physical expression, determine the necessary volume of the compensations.

In conclusion it can be noted that there are also more cardinal settlements of this problem — concordance of the irrigation and energy interests. No matter how paradoxical it is, it lies in greater development of hydroelectric engineering. The point is that today's contradictions between them are connected with the fact that there is only one great reservoir in every republic of upper stream: the Tocktogul in Kyrgyzstan and the Kayrakkum in Tajikistan. It is natural that they cannot work in energy and irrigative regimes at the same time. And if there are more reservoirs then it will be quite possible to distribute their functions.

Another very significant problem of water-energy resources use in Central Asia is the problem of water division. It is the very problem that causes the sharpest arguments, and frequently, mutual suspicions between the republics. This problem is rooted in the Soviet past. Especially the most important thing is the necessity of its open discussion and working out common principles of settlement.

Today the positions of Uzbekistan, Kazakhstan and Turkmenistan in this question consists in the request to preserve the existing limits of water division and allocation of additional limits for the Aral Sea and the Aral Shore. The positions of Kyrgyzstan and Tajikistan consist in reconsideration of these limits with increase of their shares (not for today, but in the perspective). At the same time Kyrgyzstan and Tajikistan demonstratively ground their requests on the increase of water resources limits by the fact that they were deprived of water division and did not get any compensation for this during the times of the USSR. As a consequence they now possess the least specific area of irrigated land per man in comparison with other republics, and they cannot even provide their population with the minimal level of consumption owing to their own agricultural production. Fairness of the requirements of the countries of lower stream on the necessity to increase water resources limits for the Aral Sea raises no doubts. Apropos Kyrgyzstan and Tajikistan were always concordant with them in this regard, as today's situation in the Aral Sea zone negatively impacts on them too. It is connected with dusty and salty winds from the territory of the former sea, which are spread upto the glaciers and cause their intensive thawing. Separation of the Aral Shore as additional water use together with the Aral Sea itself causes objection. It is apparently simply as an effort to increase its own limits. In order to exclude this and, besides, taking into consideration the fact that today there is no reliable and objective control of water use, inside separate republics, it may have sense not only to exclude the Aral Shore but also the Aral Sea itself from the number of water users, and instead if this to set limits to the use by Uzbekistan and Kazakhstan. And one certainly cannot agree with the equal responsibility of all the states for the Aral Sea destruction and with their equal participation in allocation of water limits. Such limits must be created first of all at the expense of the republics, which sharply reduced flowing into the Aral Sea in the 60's–90's due to sharp increase of irrigated lands on their territory, i.e. owing to Kazakhstan, Turkmenistan and Uzbekistan. Both Kyrgyzstan and Tajikistan bear minimal relation to this.

And finally reconsideration of water division limits between Central-Asian states is simply necessary if only because they are not legally assigned till present at all. Today's acting limits are established by protocols of scientific-technical councils of the USSR Ministry of Melioration and Water Economy in the 80's of the past year. Even at that time they bore, not governmental but only departmental, character. Nowadays when there is neither the USSR Ministry of Melioration and Water Economy nor the USSR, they have no juridical force. Of course we should realize that the reconsideration of limits is a complicated question that needs a very carefully approach. But on the other hand any attempt to cover it up will aggravate the situation more, and can finally lead to conflicts between the republics. And moreover requests on reconsideration of water resources limits from the part of Tajikistan, Kyrgyzstan and especially Afghanistan refer, as it has already been noted, not to the present time but to a distant perspective. Therefore there is still time for analysis of the situation, consultations and talks, for preparation and conclusion of appropriate agreements between them.

We can also offer a relatively smooth mechanism of reconsideration of the existing water division for the gains of earlier deprived countries of Tajikistan and Kyrgyzstan. Additional limits of water for them can be received not at the expense of directly reducing the limits for other countries (Kazakhstan, Turkmenistan and Uzbekistan), but owing to economy of water by implementation of more efficient technology in these countries, and at the same time preservation of former irrigated areas.

The above-performed analysis of Central-Asian water-energy complex problems shows that on the whole the region possesses necessary resources and potential for normal sustainable development.

The main obstacle for their efficient use is not economic crisis, from which all the republics of the region suffer now, than from the existing interrelations between them. The reason of all this consists in the breakup of traditional ties and euphoria of independence of young states and well-known populism of politicians.

Therefore the top-priority objective today is overcoming all this and forming good neighbourly mutually beneficial relations between the republics of the region.

29

India and Asia

The Administrational Linkages for Security and Development

HOSHIAR SINGH

At the mid-point of the twentieth century, India gained freedom from an imperial yoke which extended far and wide into the east as well as west. Although the geographical location and political orientations of the paramount powers varied from a highly democratised UK to dyed-in-the wool imperialists in Spain and Portugal with the French fifth Republic adopting postures insensitive to the aspirations of the people of its colonies for democracy and modernity. Resultantly, while India got its freedom after an unprecedented peaceful struggle, led by Mahatma Gandhi for nearly three decades, many countries in Asia had to resort to destructive armed struggles. With the advent of Japanese armies introducing another dimension of violence which, besides causing a lot of material causalities, disrupted the smooth flow of cultural traditions. The disruption being maximal in case of the People's Republic of China which, although it was never fully under the legal-formal imperial control of any foreign country, could acquire sovereign state-hood only after several military conflicts with the victor being an army-like political party whose political control was under-written by a large army which remained on high alert to counter what it saw as the US designs to roll-back the ideology of the Mao-led Communist Party of China.

Unlike India most countries in its east and west, thus, underwent de-colonization amidst major military engagements with most of the new states in Asia finding military, vital organ of the state even after they had acquired sovereign state-hood.

In sharp contrast, immediately after its freedom, eminent persons including members of Parliament were advocating dismemberment of India's military forces, which had acquitted with great honour in both the world wars in Europe, Africa as well as many parts of Asia. It must be admitted that such calls for disarmament were not taken very seriously in free India but the euphoria generated by the success of Gandhi-led non-violent campaigns certainly resulted in de-prioritization of not only armed forces but even neglect of the security dimensions of foreign affairs.

While free India was basking in the glory of non-violence, which compelled the British to withdraw from the Indian sub-continent, it not only retained but even re-inforced the administrative steel-frame which the British Governor-Generals had welded during the eighteenth and nineteenth centuries with a great deal of ingenuity and innovative skills, many of these innovations being tried and tested in British India much before they were introduced in Great Britain, the recruitment and training of the Apex Civil services being one such institutional innovation which has not only survived the "transfer of power" in 1947 but also resulted in a significant diminution in the horrors and atrocities, which erupted on a mass-scale on account of formation of two dominions out of British India. The "Partition" blood bath was, of course, too massive to be checked by the administrative apparatus of either India or Pakistan, but the fact remains that the administrative mechanisms, devised over 2 to 3 centuries, did dampen the killings and mass frenzy and quickly ensured successful rehabilitation of millions of people who had not only been uprooted but travelled hundreds of miles in their quest for new homes, almost without any material possessions; they were also carrying a heavy load of acrimony, animosity and hostility which could have resulted in several more rounds of killings but did not, mainly because the Indian administrative system was well-oiled to handle such eruptions.

The embers of the Partition riots had hardly begun to cool down when the Indian administrative system was clothed with an entirely new role-set viz. extension of new technologies and techniques for agricultural and rural development, in a vast country inhabited by millions of impoverished, illiterate farmers ignorant of scientific methods for raising production and productivity of food crops. In its long life spanning several centuries, the Indian administrative system had handled a lot of welfare agendas, but it had never before acted as an instrument of dissemination of techniques and tools for rural development which necessitated changes in the life styles of millions of men, women and children steeped in age-old customs and traditions. Even in the hey-days of district-oriented "guardians" viz. the famed Indian Civil Service, no administrative functionary in India had acted as extension workers or change-agents as per the evolving canons of Development Administration institutionalized in the entire rural India on October 2, 1952 under the title of Community Development Projects and National Extension Service which made its presence felt in not only in every village but in every individual house-hold in India's half million villages most of which had a resident population of less than 1,000 and many of which are even today not connected by modern means of telecommunications and transport.

The administrational strengths of Post-1947 India were revealed further by the establishment of the Planning Commission in 1950, which adopted a Soviet-style matrix for Planned Development designed to raise the GNP as well as the per capita GNP of India's massive population. This was a totally new phenomenon for the world as a whole, but the administrative system of India responded with the requisite efficiency of this radical transition from an "imperial" model of bureaucracy to a developmental agent of techno-economic modernization based on gigantic multi-purpose capital-intensive industrial projects, never before implemented by a Third World administrative system.

The administrative capabilities of India's administrative system were/are evident in the periodical mega-events like (decennial) census and (quinquennial) elections, in which a majority of the people are involved, the elections rather than being quinquennial almost becoming annual on account of the federal nature of the Indian Union with the union and state level polls taking place on the heels of one another with local-level Panchayats taking place in between: Take the case of Rajasthan which went to the polls for the Lok Sabha in 1998, Vidhan Sabha in 1999, Panchayats in 2000-2001, Vidhan Sabha in 2003; and the Lok Sabha polls are due in May 2004 with the Panchayat elections scheduled for December 2004. While such political mega-events generate only electoral *hectivity*, the Indian administrators have to regularly handle millions of people in several mega-religious activities, besides handling multitude of mini-religious events like processions and mass worship which impede daily life almost every month (if not every week) in every small town and with even large cities experiencing severe inconveniences on this account regularly, placing a huge stress upon the administrators time, energy, funds and, above all, mental tranquility.

The state and its million-strong team of administrative functionaries constitute a very important resource-social capita-which can be a role-model for the rest of Asia, specially those with whom India's cultural linkages are more than two millennia old but some of which have advanced farther than India on the growth path towards economic development. The economic flight of many Asian "tigers" was severely jolted in 1998, while many others were caught in the quagmire of political and administrative instability which were till recently, papered over by their higher overall growth-rates. But with the Indian economy galloping towards a double-digit GNP growth-rate, the Indian record of administrative stability with economic growth would surely provide a replicable model for Asia. India, as it approaches the second decade of the twenty first century, may still be short on physical infrastructure, but its public institutions for regulating market forces would surely constitute a model for other countries of Asia, where the market is exposing many chinks in the moral codes of the people, specially people in power. With electoral democracy still being a rarity in Asia, outside the small club of Japan, Sri Lanka and Israel.

India's adherence to multiparty elections, which have regularly unseated apex power-holders who take the ups and dips in their political fortunes with great equnanimity and continue to pursue their political careers as if nothing has happened is not merely a "Political" artefact: "It is as much a testimony to the people's electoral maturity as to the political neutrality of India's bureaucracy for most of whom "politics" is taboo even though many of them are always closeted with power-holders." No doubt, some administrators do dabble in partisan politics and some even embark upon political careers, but India's success in sanitizing its vast bureaucracy from politics is a major contribution to statecraft which other countries in Asia can profitably emulate.

Over the last five decades India has maintained strong external links with Asia but the linkages have rarely encompassed India's administrational resources whose powers and performance have been rarely appreciated (let alone being exported) outside India. True, the Indian administrative system has borrowed heavily from the White hall-Westminster model, but, during the last five decades, it has made so many innovations that it is now almost a new institutional network, performing a multiplicity of roles amidst scarcities practically unknown in UK but widely prevalent in the rest of Asia, not excluding People's Republic of China but for rather unknown reasons, its administrational resources are never evaluated as a potential input into India's relations with Asia which, all said and done, is firmly located in the Third World as far as the bulk of the people are concerned.

The Indian administrative system has, thus, handled "security:" crises as well as "development" challenges with exemplary success amidst glaring poverty, explosive inequalities and acrimonious diversities, although it may have lagged behind the so-called Asian tigers and mini-tigers in terms of GNP growth-rates. The stability and efficiency of its institutional network has finally placed it in an enviable economic orbit from where it can only go upwards, given the exceptionally large economic mass of the world's fourth largest economy in PPP terms. No doubt, the state-market mix of this institutional network is undergoing changes on account of LPG reforms, but even so India's basic administrational skills and structures do constitute a deployable resources in Asia which is not only geographically proximate but also more culturally compatible than the

Anglo-American world which is skimming-off only India's in-experienced youth and not its skilled administrators and managers mainly because the later group would hardly like to re-locate in the first world despite all the economic bonanzas it offers but would be, surely, available for even longish stints in most countries of Asia even if they are not remunerated on MNC scales.

30

About Roots of Religious and Political Extremism and Dissemination of Terrorism

Askar Shomanov

Among all varieties of terrorism that had a wide extension in the 20th century, religious terrorism, having undergone considerable changes, has developed in the most noticeable way. In its scales and organizational depth, it can compete with such not less powerful social and political phenomena, as ideological, nationalistic, state and international terrorism. To all appearances, this is conditioned by the fact that religious terrorism relying on religious slogans and using the fitting religious doctrines, is eventually directed at achievement of concrete political goals. In other words, religious terrorism arises when religious extremism resorts to the methods of political violence in realization of its slogans.

This implies that religious extremism is one of the directions of modern religious trends aspiring to influence the process of social development proceeding from its own norms and doctrines.

As to religious terrorism, it is the strategy and tactics of extremist groups consisting in systematic, organized, ideologically justified and secretly prepared use of violence for the achievement of political goals.

In its general appearance the purpose of religious terrorism is: (1) demonstration of the inability of authorities of secular countries in the person of the western powers to control the situation; (2) provoking of the ruling regime to apply tough retaliatory measures and (3) creation of the atmosphere of fear and nervousness in society.

As any other widespread social and political phenomenon, religious terrorism has its own carriers in the person of national-extremist or religious-political organizations of different confessional affiliations that in their activity frequently use a certain symbiosis of nationalistic and religious slogans. This concerns not only the methods but also the purposes of these activities as well as personal purposes of the people participating in them.

Possessing a certain mentality, representatives of national-extremist or religious-political groupings may belong to the left as well as to the right part of the political spectrum. In other words, despite the differences in the political orientations, their mental principles have a certain similarity that is expressed in the universality of their extremist and terrorist activities.

The lessons of the 20th century, especially of its second half, quite graphically testify that the bulk of religious-political terrorism is dominated, by virtue of quite objective historical reasons, by extremist structures acting on the basis of Islamic fundamentalism. It is to be borne in mind that "fundamentalism is an idea and Islamism is an action, i.e. an attempt to realize ideas of fundamentalism that is radicalized under the influence of exterior factors and turns into aversion of the diverse, into extremism, and, in a number of cases, into unconcealed terrorisms"[1].

However, at the same time, speaking about the presence of a definite connection between modern terrorism and Islamic religion one should be very delicate and correct, since the ideology of terrorism by itself always performs in veiled, and uses as a cover theories, ideology and slogans of particular varieties[2]. In this case, many politicians and analysts after them, directly or indirectly consider Islam as one of terrorism's sources for a number of reasons[3]. Here are the main ones.

First, Islam is indirectly recognized as one of the factors of terrorism because dynamically developing Muslim Arab countries, demanding their participation in the world policy and failing to play a desirable role in it, directly or indirectly are included into the number of terrorism sponsors.

Secondly, Islam is sometimes directly or indirectly accused of support of terrorist moods, due to non-differentiation of terrorism and the national liberation movement, the distinction the Muslim countries insist on.

Thirdly, sometimes Islam is considered as the source of terrorism because some Islamic fundamentalists appeal to the first centuries of dissemination of Islam by military means throughout the territory of the Arab Peninsula and further, when the peaceful essence of this world religion was distorted.

And fourthly and finally, the reason of linking of Islam religion with terrorism is the presence of a significant number of the natives of Muslim countries among modern terrorists.

In the ramified system of modern terrorist structures that number more than 150 organizations and operate in different regions of the world, the terrorist groups of the pro-Islamic trend are the dominating ones. It is also not accidental that practically half of the most known terrorist groups today are openly pro-Islamic. The 20th century has become the time when such well organized players as the Armed Islamic Group, Islamic Jihad, Hizb-ullah, Al-Qaeda, Palestinian Islamic Jihad, Hamaz, etc. appeared on the geopolitical scene. The majority of them were formed as political unions fighting for independence, freedom and political rights. However, in a number of countries, the victory of the opposition, assistance and granting of the free regime to the groups that got used to active illegal functioning and resistance by force have transferred them to the level of anti-state terrorist activity[4].

Of course, the circle of religious and political organizations in the 20th century enlarged not only because of extremist organizations that acted on the basis of Islamic fundamentalism. In the different parts of the world, terrorist organizations of other religious trend appeared sporadically. As an example we can take such organizations as the "The Church of the Aryan Christian Nation" (CACN) and "Aryan Nations" operating in the United States, "The Irish Republican Army" (IRA) in Northern Ireland, and the Jewish extremist organization "Kakh" in Israel[5]. Or let us take various totalitarian sects like Om Shinrikyo that strived to establish a total control of Japan over the whole world.

However, in the scope of their active functioning and ideological, financial replenishment they certainly concede to pro-Islamic extremist groups. An important factor here is that "Islamic terrorism is directed at realization of the Islamic monotheistic idea, that is at creation (or recreation) of the Islamic empire. On the one hand, this object is utopian, and utopias, as is known, live long. On the other hand, the territorial principle of an empire consists in boundless expansion. It means that establishment of an Islamic order in one country cannot be the final purpose of Islamic ideocracy. It requires unceasing continuation of this activity on new grounds".

Besides, a feature of terrorism on the basis of Islamic fundamentalism is its significant social base both in the countries of traditional Islam, and in the states with large Islamic diasporas. The reason it is that "the first gleams of the ideology of terrorism emerge at its political level. Political terrorism is inspired, at times very indistinctly, at the lowest level by narrowly treated interests of an ethnos (tribe, nation), racial group, etc."[7].

Apart, from a substantially enough social base, a large-scale development of Islamic extremism and terrorism also has global and ideological roots. It is quite obvious that the roots are closely interwoven and spring up in a uniform complex fashion. The globalization process is a certain ideological mechanism that, by and large, renders significant influence on the political awareness of the population practically of all the countries of the globe.

* * *

The experience of the 20th century testifies that ideology is one of the main driving forces of globalization processes. Therefore, within the framework of the two-aspect uniform system "Islamic extremism and globalization", the former should be considered, first of all, from the point of view of its ideological opportunities and potential. The point is that "the emergence of the Islamic factor, as well as formation of the fundamentalist currents in Islam, is connected to changes of the political and economic situations on the regional and international scales..."[8].

Taking into account that the radicalization of the Islamic fundamentalism in the last century, to a certain extent, can be considered as some kind of reaction to the idea of globalization, the rise of the Islamic extremism and terrorism as the answer to the "westernized" globalization lies in the field of ideology, first of all. In this connection, there are no grounds to seriously speak about the Islamic alternative in the economy or state construction, and, more so, in the military sphere. But it is impossible to ignore the fact that the followers of Islamic extremism and terrorism work toughly and consistently within the framework of counteraction to globalization. Moreover, in their understanding the personified image of the global rival competing to them is not limited, in a broad sense, only by the USA or Western Europe.

Quite remarkable here looks the opinion that "non-uniformity of development of different countries putting the underdeveloped country in the conditions of overtaking", with the tendency of a growing gap in the standard of well-being of the advanced and less developed countries... — all this is the background in which terrorism grows"[9].

To all appearances, the present widely stretched branches of Islamic extremism and terrorism spring from the shoots of national liberation movements that resulted in the emergence of the Islamic world of new independent states in the place of former colonies of capitalist countries in the 50-60's of the 20th century. The first shoots of Islamic extremism and terrorism in these countries were fed not only by the internal ideological, social and cultural resources, but also by external ones by the world centers of geopolitical influence. This process received a new impetus in 1970-80's, when the geopolitical struggle for a number of Middle Eastern countries sometimes indirectly acquired a unilateral Islamic ideological rhetoric. In other words, the Islamic ideology was harnessed by the world's centers of influence as a convenient tool for upholding as their geopolitical interests.

Besides this, earlier, "the 'Islamic factor' was used by various political forces, including particular states, proceeding from their purposes, and was carried out multidimensionally both inside concrete countries, and at the regional and international levels for destabilization of the situation and in struggle with political opponents"[10].

Here again it is quite possible to agree with the opinion that the roots of Islamic extremism and terrorism in the 20th century were fed not only by ideological doctrines like Wahabism or Taliban that used Islamic attributes, not only by natural aspiration of the peoples of the Muslim world for fair distribution of the boons of the modern civilization, not only the strivings of the Muslim elite for authority and establishment of independence of their countries. What is not to be overlooked is that these roots of Islamic extremism and terrorism were covertly enough fed through such artificial channels as close interrelation with special services of the world centers of geopolitical influence working with silent approval of their political management.

Thus, Islamic extremism and terrorism as the ideological tool became a product (progeny) not only of the national elites of the Islamic states that successfully appealed to the population, but also from the very beginning of its emergence it received rather appreciable external impulses. Therefore, indirectly, the responsibility for all negative and pernicious consequences of the Islamic extremism and terrorism lies not only on the pro-Islamic national elites of the countries of the Near and Middle East.

Gradual amplification of the influence of internal and external tendencies on the development of Islamic extremism and terrorism in the Muslim world resulted at the beginning of the 21st century in a global ideological opposition of two "religious worlds" that have taken place of the secular bipolar world of the 20th century. The Islamic ideology professed by the developing countries of Arab East began increasingly often to be indirectly projected as the ideology of terrorism in a counterbalance to any forms of "non-Muslim" ideology.

In many respects, this is caused by the fact that "for achievement of the purposes, the new social-political forces, apart from the traditional methods of struggle, started to actively use the terrorist ones as the basis of their activity. The disintegration of the USSR coincided with an aggravation of the situation in the world. The positions of Russia, USA and Israel came closer, and the Judaic-Christian ideology became more active. Now the Judaic-Christian ideology is confronted by Islam, very close in its form to the ideology of the Soviet political authority. The Muslim world now differs from the Islamic world that existed during the existence of two camps — capitalist and socialist. In these conditions, politicization of Islam has taken place in concrete countries at the regional and global levels. Islam's influence is not limited only by political or ideological frames, in all spheres of life and activity of the Muslim peoples and Muslim states it has started to play a role of the political factor. The striving to use Islam actively and comprehensively in achievement of one's political or economic goals has become a major tendency of political forces on the international arena"[11].

On the whole, the main causes of global ideological confrontation between the two "religious worlds" that received a constant replenishment during dissemination of Islamic extremism and terrorism were conditioned by the following conditions:

Firstly, one of the causes of Islamic terrorism's dissemination is that the modernization influence of the advanced western world on undeveloped "new" countries of the Islamic world disregarded deep ethnic and cultural features of these communities. And here lies the main cost of widespread process of modernization that covered the majority of the world's countries in the 20th century. Paradoxically, the fact is "that now instead of Pushtuns and Arabs wearing exotic clothes — children of deserts, mountains and steppes, intellectuals that travelled all over the world and studied in the best American and European universities, have appeared on the scene. In their words and writings terror appears as a legal, consecrated by God weapon against the "infidels"[12].

Secondly, gradual dissemination of Islamic extremism and terrorism was also conditioned in many respects by historical succession of traditional and liberal-democratic values which are typical for the entire non-Muslim world and which has developed into confrontation of these values in the traditional Muslim World. Such a confrontation was often accompanied by origination of political, religious and military conflicts. Because of this, traditional Muslim countries faced the problem of formation of a hybrid system of values that would provide coexistence of traditional and liberal-democratic system of values.

Thirdly, in Muslim countries dissemination of Islamic extremism and terrorism was followed by strengthening of authoritarian tendencies under the guise of the dawn of Islamic ideology. This ideology opportunely appeared in the time for national elites with radical moods. Thus, strengthening of authoritarian tendencies under the guise of religion in a number of countries of the Near and Middle East has become a natural reaction to the invasion (but not perception) of Western values.

Fourthly, significant preconditions for dissemination of Islamic extremism and terrorism have been created also by the same unavoidable costs that appeared during the conduct of social and economic modernization in a number of Muslim countries. "Religious extremism is an objective consequence of the development of modernization processes in society. A close correlation existing between the processes of cardinal modernization of society's vital functioning and the growth of radical moods under the banner of restitution of religious values"[13]. Unpredictable economic development, absence of considerable social returns from modernization reforms, and lack of faith in the capability of ruling elite to overcome social and economic obstacles caused effective preconditions for the appeal to Islamic ideals of social justice, and to the true form of Islamic government, return to the so-called "golden past".

Fifthly, dissemination of Islamic extremism and terrorism in a number of Muslim countries received an additional impulse under the influence of the archaization tendency, which created an absolute precondition for strengthening of the role of Islamic tradition as the regulator of social relations and its influence on the ruling elites. The ruling elites of some countries of the Muslim world, proclaiming removal of the Islam religion from politics, actually used it as an instrument of political struggle, striving to deprive their competitors of monopoly on Islam. New role of Islam in modern policy became apparent.

* * *

Speaking about the specificity of the dissemination of Islamic extremism and terrorism in the 20th century, it is possible to establish a whole number of conditions whose existence gives no rise to doubts and in which the process took place. These conditions of dissemination of Islamic extremism and terrorism could not arise beyond the frames of globalization.

Firstly, development of social and political activity of broad masses of the population under Islamic banners in the frames of dissemination of Islamic extremism and terrorism dissemination in a significant or probably in the major part of Muslim countries had a spontaneous character that has had its own internal (social, economic, ethnic, etc.) causes. In some regions this activity was conditioned by ethnic separatist movements, struggle for power and in others it was an attempt to consolidate one's own state model. In different parts of the world international Muslim organizations based on the radical doctrine started to emerge. They declared the world *Jihad* in the name of creation of an Islamic mega-state and stood on the positions of religious expansionism.

Secondly, in the final analysis, a unified centre in the person of a "Green International" never stood behind the activity of followers of Islamic extremism and terrorism that could give reasons to speak about existence of some common Muslim charisma. "Pointing out the complexity and diversity of various forms of Islamic fundamentalism, it is necessary to note that this phenomenon has a dissimilar character in different regions. Therefore, comments about the existence of some unified worldwide international Islamic extremism are far from reality. From the scientific point of view it would be more correct to speak about different forms of extremism under Islamic banners, taking into consideration a local specificity"[14]. In practice, the homogenous or almost homogenous in its ideological aspect Islamic terrorism and extremism is pluralistic in its organizational basis. Its separate movements and organizations act independently, compete and sometimes confront one another pursuing local ethnic, political, and parochial interests, and goals of inter-clan struggle.

Thirdly, despite the absence of a unified center in its classical understanding, a number of extremist and terrorist groups integrated by the end of the 20th century into global, ramified and well organized conspiratorial network that is supported by the commonality of ideology. In respect of its goals, this network was created in the image and likeness of drug rings and is very effective and has its own efficient logistics. Classical structures of vertical integration, where structure of any state could be referred to, in many respects are powerless against such network structures that are closely related to criminal groupings of the international scale.

Fourthly, the developed model of social and political structure, as well as cultural tradition that were formed during the dissemination of Islamic extremism and terrorism, pretend to the absolute and sacred truth. Instead of the Western variant of globalization, the politicized radical Islam has suggested its own "Islamic order" to whose establishment the whole world should come by virtue of Islamic eschatological tradition. However, creation of the Islamic world order was nothing more than an 'ideologemae' in which religious zealots believed and continues to believe. The major masses of Islamic radicals, to all appearances, deep in their minds acknowledge that the establishment of the Islamic world order is utopian as well as total islamization of the humanity.

Fifthly, from the classical point of understanding, already by the end of the 20th century ideology of the most well-known terrorist structures of Islamic doctrine started to rely on nonstandard and paradoxical basic foundations and axioms on the base of which projects of terrorist acts were planned and carried out. A new nontraditional value-mental toolkit that due to its principal irrationality is beyond the frames of commonly accepted rational logic began to be incorporated in the actions of these structures. In other words, on the verge of the 20th and 21st centuries, the dissemination of Islamic terrorism and extremism was fed by completely new axiomatics that had never emerged in the world practice –a system of values that gradually turns into a completely new, untraditional, irrational and absurdly-paradoxical weapon of a mass-destruction.

On the whole, analyzing the ideological basis of dissemination of religious-political extremism and terrorism it would be more correct to use the term "extremism" rather than "terrorism", since the accent on the terrorist methods is not usually placed. The matter is that extremist theories often justify any means for an achievement of their objectives, even terrorism. Terrorism, in its turn, is usually based exactly on the extremist ideology[15].

* * *

In the beginning of the 21st century, escalation of violence in particular regions of the world under the ideological influence of politicized Islam of the radical kind, its multidimensional character, and combination in it of legal and illegal methods testify to gradual growth of its ideological potential and transformation into one of the most important elements dissemination of the of mechanism of religious-political extremism and terrorism.

Moreover, "Islamic extremism, whose activity quite recently showed up only episodically and rarely crossed the borders of separate regions of the Muslim world, in the last decade turned into the constant factor in political life of many countries, including the Western ones, exerting a strong influence on the whole system of interstate relations"[16].

Building of reliable system of global security, in this situation is the only functioning and effective hindrance for further dissemination of various forms of religious extremism and terrorism in different parts of the world. And obviously the statement that the modern unipolar world will hardly manage to deal with this task is not far from the truth.

Today, when under the influence of globalization, the network of international terrorism and extremism starts to cover almost the whole territory of the world, humanity can develop and realize a reliable system of global security only if, the world will become multipolar. The time will show whether it will manage with it.

REFERENCES

1. Bagliev M. Uroki borby s extremistckim islamizmom // Azia i Afrika segodnya. — 2002. - # 12. — S. 2.
2. Zaichenko V.M. "Ideologiya terrorizma // Tadjikistan i sovremennyi mir. — 2002. - # 1. — S. 104.
3. Nurmuhamedov B.Zh. Podkhody k izucheniu sushnosti sovremennogo terrorizma // ANALYTIC. — 2002. — # 3. — S. 14.
4. Seli naibolee izvestnyh radikalnyh terroristicheskih grup mira // Sayasat. — 2001. — # 9. — S. 6-7.
5. Zhihor U. "Religioznyi extremizm" problemy identifikasii // Kazakhstan-Spektr. — 2002. — # 3. — S. 32-33.
6. Kadyrzhanov R.K. Islamskaya ideokratia i nasionalnaya bezopasnost gosudarstv Sentralnoi Azii // Kazakhstan-Spektr. — 2002. — # 3. — S. 8.
7. Zaichenko V.M. "Ideologiya terrorizma // Tadjikistan i sovremennyi mir. — 2002. - # 1. — S. 102.

8. Dzhalilov K. Islamskii faktor // Tadjikistan i sovremennyi mir. — 2002. - # 1. — S. 91.
9. Nurmuhamedov B.Zh. Podkhody k izucheniu sushnosti sovremennogo terrorizma // ANALYTIC. — 2002. — # 3. — Ś. 14.
10. Dzhalilov K. Islamskii faktor // Tadjikistan i sovremennyi mir. — 2002. - # 1. — S. 91.
11. Tam zhe. — S. 95.
12. Zaichenko V.M. "Ideologiya terrorizma // Tadjikistan i sovremennyi mir. — 2002. - # 1. — S. 102-103.
13. Zhihor U. "Religioznyi extremizm" problemy identifikasii // Kazakhstan-Spektr. — 2002. — # 3. — S. 29.
14. Bagliev M. Uroki borby s extremistckim islamizmom // Azia i Afrika segodnya. — 2002. - # 12. — S. 2.
15. Tam zhe. — S. 2.
16. Sukiyainen L. Islam protiv islamskogo extremizma // Azia i Afrika segodnya. — 2003. - # 2. — S. 8.

31

From Shanghai Five to Shanghai Cooperation Organisation

*An Emerging Mechanism of Regional Security in Eurasia**

Nalin Kumar Mohapatra

Shanghai Cooperation Organisation consisting of five Asian states — China, Kazakhstan, Uzbekistan, Tajikistan, Kyrgyzstan and one Eurasian state Russia — is emerging in recent years as an important regional security mechanism in the whole of Eurasia. This regional Organisation covers a vast landmass with a population of 1.51 billion, GDP of 1.57 trillion US dollars and a total trade turnover of 800 billion US dollars.[1] A mere glance at these above-mentioned facts reflects the vast potential of this organisation and the role it can play in the emerging security scenario in Eurasia. The process of formation of the SCO began in May 1989, when the Soviet President Mikhail Gorbachev visited Beijing and met Li Peng, the Prime Minister of China. During the visit of Gorbachev, both the sides agreed to initiate confidence-building measures to solve the complex border disputes. As a fallout of the talks between the two leaders, in November 1989, the first round of consultation between diplomatic and military experts of the two countries was held in Moscow. Subsequently, experts of both the

* A revised and enlarged version of the paper presented at the International Conference on "Building A New Asia: Problems and Prospects of Regional and Pan-Asian Cooperation for Security and Development", (29-31 March 2004)

sides agreed to draft an interim document on mutual force reduction and confidence-building measures in the border region.[2]

After the disintegration of the Soviet Union, China recognised Russia as the successor of the former and also maintained diplomatic relations with the Central Asian republics as well. The border negotiation process that started in 1989 was later transformed into talks on Confidence Building Measures and Armed Forces Reductions among the countries of Central Asia and Russia on the one hand and China on the other. It may be noted that the process of Confidence Building Measures among the five countries helped to create a conducive environment for strengthening peace and security in this part of the world and laid the base for carrying out further constructive cooperation among them on a number of issues.[3]

In April 1996 the five countries met at Shanghai and signed an Agreement on Strengthening "Military Confidence Building Measures in Border Areas". The second meeting that took place in Moscow in 1997 discussed issues confronting them and signed an "Agreement on Mutual Reduction of Military Forces in the Border Areas". By these agreements signed both at Beijing and Moscow, the contracting parties agreed that "the military forces deployed in the border areas would remain defence-oriented and the countries concerned would not use force" against each other and that "no party to the agreement seeks unilateral military superiority".[4]

These agreements signed in 1996 and 1997 reflected the sincere desire of the Shanghai Five to solve regional territorial disputes in a peaceful manner without mediation of a third party. As the then Chinese President Jiang Zemin said, "The two documents would be inscribed into the history of state-to-state relations among our five countries and would have a positive impact on the rest of the world".[5]

With the border disputes among the five countries resolved to a large extent, they started discussing other pressing problems that confronted them after 1991. The third summit of the Shanghai Five in Almaty in 1998 took note of the situation prevailing at that time. The joint statement signed in Almaty at the end of the summit clearly stated that "any form of national separatism, ethnic exclusion and religious extremism is unacceptable". The summit meeting also discussed the situation prevailing in Afghanistan and observed, "Greater efforts should be made to promote a peaceful settlement of the conflicts in that country under the auspices of the United Nations and with the participation of the countries concerned. At the same time consideration should be given to the interests of all the national and religious groups and political forces involved in the conflict".[6]

The concern showed by member countries of the Shanghai Five proved true, when Islamic fundamentalism, aided and abetted by the Taliban, started expanding into whole of Central Asia. Russia also felt its impact in its Chechnya region as also China in its Xinjiang province bordering three Central Asian republics– Kazakhstan, Kyrgyzstan and Tajikistan. These countries not only faced the problem from radical Islamist terrorists but also from the proliferation of small arms, narcotics and large scale cross-border migration, jeopardizing the security of this region. The surge in Islamic fundamentalist activities in Central Asia resulted in a series of explosions, in Tashkent during February 1999 in which more than 16 people were killed and more than a hundred injured. After the Tashkent explosions, a group of armed militants comprising mostly ethnic Uzbeks crossed over to Batken situated in the southern region of Kyrgyzstan and took four hostages. At the same time close linkages between the Islamist militants of Central Asia and Chechnya came to surface when in May 1999 in Uzbekistan the Islamist militants trained in Chechnya hijacked a bus taking 26 passengers as hostages. In the Dagestan province similar incursions took place during the same period.[7] The members of Eastern Turkestan Liberation Movement (ETM) carried out similar activities after in the Xinjiang province of China after receiving training in Afghanistan. They subsequently established 15 secret cells to train the Uighur youths in making explosives. In early 1999 Bin Laden met the members of the ETM and urged them to coordinate their activities with the Islamic Movement of Uzbekistan and the Taliban.[8] It is reported that the Uighur militants were trained by and fought along with the Afghan Mujhahidin starting from 1986. Chinese officials reported that arms and explosive used against the Chinese government in Xinjiang originated in Afghanistan.[9] Not only Uighur militants got training in Afghanistan for carrying out subversive activities but also got support from terrorist organisations in Pakistan. It was reported that the Pakistani Jehadi groups such as Jamat-I-Islami, Jamat-e-Tablighi and Lashkar-e-Taiba gave support to the insurgent groups of Xinjiang. The Uighur militants also received training at the Al-Badr camp at Ooji, near the Afghan-Pakistani border. These militant groups enjoyed wide support of the Pakistani intelligence — ISI.[10]

It was reported that the radical militants wanted to create instability in this part of the world to facilitate transportation of drugs and narcotics from Afghanistan to Russia and Europe. Ralf Mutschek, Assistant Director, of Interpol's Criminal Intelligence Directorate, reported to the US Congress, "Sixty per cent of Afghan opium export passed through Central Asia and that IMU might be responsible for seventy per cent of heroin and opium transiting through this area". Similarly, Pakistani analyst on Central Asia, Ahmed Rashid, wrote, "IMU and other drug dealers had built a stock-pile of opium in Mazar and Kunduz that the ODCCP officials estimated at more than 240 tons". Quoting Tajik officials Ahmed Rashid further writes, "Juma Namangani, the head of IMU and other drug traffickers had set-up laboratories in Tajikistan to refine the heroin."[11] The United Nations Drugs Control Programme in its 1999 report, pointed out, "There is now substantial evidence that countries in Central Asia are being used as a transit point to transport illicit consignment of opiates and cannabis originating in Afghanistan and the chemicals used for the illicit manufactures of heroin are being transported in the opposite direction".[12] So also, the Tajik authorities during an operation in 1998-99 detained over 480 drug peddlers and confiscated 1,949 kg of narcotics from them.[13] The threat to the security of this region from drug trafficking was highlighted in the statement of Rashid Alimov, the UN representative to Tajikistan on Drug Control Programme. Alimov observed that his country was a victim of an "opium tsunami" and "narcotics aggression". During 1998 and 1999 it was reported that drug trafficking has increased to the extent of 250 per cent in Tajikistan. The Uzbek representative on UN Drug Programme also gave similar data. According to him during the same period the drug trafficking through Uzbekistan increased to a staggering high of 600 per cent. The Kyrgyz Interior Ministry reported 1,600 per cent increase in illicit drug seizure between 1999 and 2000 including an 800 per cent increase in heroin alone. The drug traffickers used three routes, Tajikistan, Uzbekistan and Turkmenistan to transport heroin and opium to Russia, from where it is transported to other Western countries. It is alleged that the reopening of the Quetta-Kandahar-Herat-Ashgabat road during the Taliban regime helped to a great extent the trafficking of drug through Turkmenistan.[14] Kazakhstan is also not immune to the threat of drug trafficking. B. Baibulov, Chairman of Kazakhstan's Committee for the Fight Against Drug Abuse and Illicit Drug Trafficking under the Ministry of Justice wrote that over the last ten years the drug related crime in Kazakhstan increased to a considerable extent. It was not only confined to the southern parts of the country, but was also widely reported in the cities like Almaty, Karaganda and Zhambul.[15] The Interior Ministry of Kazakhstan in its report in 2001 stated that during the last 9 months they confiscated 12 tons and 981 kg of various kinds of drugs, out of which 65.1 kg of heroin. The report further pointed out that apart from drug trafficking, the numbers of drug addicts have also increased to a great extent in the Republic. In 2001, 45,208 drug abuses were reported in Kazakhstan alone.[16] Apart from Kazakhstan and Tajikistan, the Chinese province of Xinjiang and Yunnan are also engulfed by this evil. The new trafficking routes to Central Asia through China are also aggravating the region's problem.[17] It has been reported that in the Xinjiang province of China the number of intravenous drug users in 2000 was around 80,000 to 1,00,000. So also the HIV-infection rate among drug abusers was around 45 per cent in Urumchi, while in Yining, a much higher percentage got infected with the deadly virus.[18]

Another problem the SCO member countries are confronting is the proliferation of illegal small arms and their use by terrorist groups. The problem is more particularly acute in the Central Asian states of Tajikistan, Uzbekistan as well as Kyrgyzstan. One need to mention here the fact that the end of the Afghan crisis and the inter-Tajik civil conflict resulted in weakening of the governments as well as growth of radical Islamist forces in this part of the world. This gave impetus to the proliferation of small arms in Central Asia. The study conducted by S. Neil MacFarlane and Stina Torjesen on small arms in Kyrgyzstan found that the law enforcement agency confiscated 5,000 small arms since 1996 and the Tajik security agency seized 23,000 guns during the same period.[19] According to this study the Kyrgyz National Security Service found 10 weapon caches in the mountains near Batken during June 2000. The majority of arms discovered in the 10 caches were of Soviet production and others were of Chinese and Belgian origin. Similarly, in June 2003 the Kyrgyz army discovered some 200 Chinese-made rifle bullets.[20] Ahmed Rashid writes that in the winter of 1999 the IMU leader Namangani and Tahir Yuldashev visited Kandahar where they met Osama bin Laden and Mullah Omar and discussed the plan to supply arms, ammunitions and money for help in their further expansion.[21] Quoting Western diplomats and intelligence officials, Rashid mentions that Namangani also acquired two Russian built Mi-8 transport helicopters from the Taliban. Several Saudi-Uzbek backers in Saudi Arabia provided another $15-million worth hi-tech equipment like sniper rifles, communication equipment and night-vision goggles which could have been procured from arms dealers in Pakistan and the Gulf.[22] Various studies show that a close nexus exists between the drug trade and small arms proliferation. In the Afghan-Tajik border area drug traffickers are heavily armed and fight between Russian 201 infantry division or Tajik troops guarding the Tajik border and the drug traders is a usual affair. In the border regions of Moskovsky and Shurovad up to Kalayikum and then further East to Vach valley of Tajikistan the Russian border guards found arms in 2002. One need to highlight here the fact that the problem of small arms proliferation is not only confined to Central Asian countries but also to other SCO countries like Xinjiang province of China and Russia. This is evident from the operations the militant groups carried out against the governments of the respective countries.[23]

The subsequent meeting of the Shanghai Five, which was held in August 1999 in Bishkek, discussed all the above-mentioned challenges confronting the region. As border dispute was solved to a large extent, they realized the necessity of evolving a common approach to combat the problem of Islamist fundamentalism, drug trafficking, etc. The joint statements issued at the end of the summit stated, "To effectively crackdown on international terrorism, illegal dealing in drug trafficking, arms smuggling, illegal migration and other forms of cross-border crimes of significance, the responsible departments of the five countries will adopt measures to launch practical cooperation including the consultation and working out of programme of joint-action during the period 1999-2000".[24]

As per the decision of the Bishkek Summit, the heads of the Law Enforcement agencies of the "Shanghai-five" countries met in Bishkek in the month of December 1999. At the meeting the participants agreed that the "law enforcement agencies of the Shanghai Five would apply forms and methods of cooperation including joint operations". In order to carry out joint operation they decided to set up the so called "Bishkek Group" consisting of the chiefs of the law enforcement agencies, which will meet once in a year.[25]

Slowly but steadily, the Shanghai Five regional security mechanism apart from discussing common problems, which confronted them, also took interest in discussing global problems and their implications for them. Their common approach towards international problems was evident in the Dushanbe summit in 2000. In this meeting Russia under its new President Vladimir Putin attended the summit and Uzbekistan's President Islam Karimov took part in the summit as an observer. The five countries supported the Anti-Ballistic Missile Treaty (ABM) treaty signed in 1972 and opposed deployment of the Theatre Missile Defence System in the Asia-Pacific region, as it will disrupt stability and security in this region. They also pledged their total support to the United Nations and opposed those countries that use "humanitarianism" and "protecting human rights" as pretexts to intervene in others' internal affairs. They extended support to each other in their efforts to preserve national independence, sovereignty, territorial integrity and social stability.[26]

After five years of its existence and with the joining of Uzbekistan, the Shanghai Five renamed as Shanghai Cooperation Organisation in June 2001 at the summit meeting in Shanghai. The joint declaration after the summit appreciated the role it played during the last five years of its existence in promoting and deepening the good neighbourly relations, mutual confidence and friendship among the member countries apart from strengthening stability and security in the region. The participant countries also expressed their desire to evolve a common approach towards the global problems and with regard to security and economic development of the area. The conference also emphasized the mutually beneficial cooperation among the participating countries in trade and economic field, efforts to promote cooperation and diversify its forms between the participating states on a bilateral and multilateral basis. It also took note of the need to strengthen the mechanism of consultations and coordination of their actions on regional issues. The declaration also emphasised that the organisation adheres to the goals and principles of the Charter of the United Nations, the principles of mutual respect for independence, sovereignty and territorial integrity, equality and mutual benefit, the solution of all issues through mutual consultations, non-interference in the internal affairs, non-use of military force or threat of force and renunciation of unilateral military superiority in contiguous areas.[27]

SCO'S PERCEPTIONS OF SHIFTING GEO-STRATEGIC SITUATION IN EURASIA AFTER 9/11

Although, the 11 September incident took place in America its effect was clearly felt in the whole of Eurasia. Soon after the 9/11 incident, America sought help from the Central Asian countries to carry out its operation against al-Qaida and the Taliban — the very forces which were "created and nurtured during the cold war period in the name of fighting the Soviet Union".

Realising the gravity of the situation, member states of SCO also expressed their readiness to give support to America in its war against the radical forces. In fact Russian President Vladimir Putin was first to call up President Bush and offer Russian support to America in its fight against terrorism.[28] Similarly, many SCO members from Central Asian states like Uzbekistan, Kyrgyzstan, Tajikistan and Kazakhstan also gave their support to America. Through an agreement with Uzbekistan the United States stationed its troops in Khanabad to carry out its offensive against the Taliban. The Kyrgyz Parliament in December 2001 also agreed to allow the United States to set-up a military base at Manas International Airport, 30 kilometers from Bishkek. During the visit of US Defence Secretary Donald Rumsfeld to Tajikistan, Dushanbe offered three of the country's airfield namely, Kulyab, Khojent and Kurgan-Tyube. Apart from offer of air bases it also assisted in the shipment of humanitarian aid to Afghanistan.[29]

Although the US came to Central Asia to fight the radical militants based in Afghanistan, it soon showed keenness to promote its geo-political objectives in this region. This is evident from the testimony given by Elizabeth Jones, Assistant Secretary of State for European and Eurasian Affairs before the Foreign Affairs committee in December 2001. Just two months after the 11 September incident, during the US Senate sub-committee hearing, Elizabeth Jones outlined the US position, which went beyond the anti- terrorist operation in Afghanistan for which the United States secured the bases in Uzbekistan and Kyrgyzstan. She stated, "We will not leave Central Asia after resolving the conflict [in Afghanistan]. We want to support the Central Asian countries in their desire to reform their societies as they supported us in the war against terrorism. These are not only new but long-term relations." The other objectives of America in this region as outlined by Jones are "combating terrorism; reform; the rule of law; Caspian Sea energy resources".[30] Similarly while addressing a press conference in December 2001 at Tashkent, Secretary of State Collin Powell declared: "The US interests in the Central Asian region stretched beyond the current crisis in Afghanistan", maintaining that these interests were "long-term in Uzbekistan and should be permanent in the region as a whole."[31] The geo-political objective of America in Central Asia has been succinctly brought out by American political scientist, S. Cohen, who, in an interview to the Russian newspaper *Komsomolskaya Pravda,* admitted that "while the Romanticists can derive satisfaction from the victory over the al-Qaida and the Taliban terrorists, the United States has in fact more enduring goals to achieve military hegemony, widening its sphere of influence at the expense of Russia and China, and access to the rich oil resources not under the OPEC control".[32]

It was against the backdrop of these developments that the Foreign Ministers of the Shanghai Cooperation Organisation met at Beijing in January 2002. The joint-statement issued after the meeting emphsised that they would like to see Afghanistan "a peaceful and neutral state" and that the "international forces maintaining security in this country should work according to the mandate of the UN Security Council and with an agreement of lawful authorities". The SCO Foreign Ministers' meeting also took note of the fact that the "global anti–terrorism system should rely on regional, sub-regional and national structures". This highlights the keenness on part of the SCO member countries to ensure a solution to the problem of Afghanistan by employing other existing mechanism rather than through unilateralist measures of America.[33] Similarly, at the meeting of member countries' Defence Ministers in May 2002, a decision was taken regarding the need to set-up permanently a standing working group within the SCO for joint cooperation on regional defence and security issues which may arise from time to time in this region.[34]

The second summit of the Shanghai Cooperation Organisation, which met at St. Petersburg in June 2002, discussed at length the significant geo-political developments that took place in this region after the 11 September incident. One significant feature of this summit was the signing of the Charter by six member countries which laid the legal foundation of the organisation. Under article 1 of the Charter the Organisation called upon member states to "to strengthen mutual trust, friendship and good neighborliness between the member States; to consolidate multidisciplinary cooperation in the maintenance and strengthening of peace, security and stability in the region and promotion of a new democratic, fair and rational political and economic international order; to jointly counteract terrorism, separatism and extremism in all their manifestations, to fight against illicit narcotics and arms trafficking and other types of criminal activity of a transnational character, and also illegal migration; to encourage the efficient regional cooperation in such spheres as politics, trade and economy, defense, law enforcement, environment protection, culture, science and technology, education, energy, transport, credit and finance, and also other spheres of common interest; to facilitate comprehensive and balanced economic growth, social and cultural development in the region through joint action on the basis of equal partnership for the purpose of a steady increase of living standards and improvement of living conditions of the peoples of the member States; to coordinate approaches to integration into the global economy; to promote human rights and fundamental freedoms in accordance with the international obligations of the member States and their national legislation; to maintain and develop relations with other States and international organizations; to cooperate in the prevention of international conflicts and in their peaceful settlement; to jointly search for solutions to the problems that would arise in the 21st century".[35]

Apart from Article1, the Charter contains 23 other Articles dealing with such issues as principles and institutional structure of the organisation, mechanism to administer the organisation, admitting new members to the organisation. Article 3 of the Charter identifies areas of cooperation for the member states. Article 4 of the Charter outlines the institutional structure of the organisation. Article 5 says that "the Council of Heads of state will be the highest decision-making body, which will meet once in a year". Article 10 of Charter emphasizes the creation of a Regional Anti-Terrorist Structure and Article 11 of the organisation deals with the administrative mechanism of the organisation, i.e., the Secretariat of the organisation. An interesting aspect of this article is that it envisages equality of member states with regards to appointment to key positions in the organisation. As the article notes, "the Executive Secretary shall be appointed from among the nationals of member states on a rotational basis in the Russian alphabetical order of the member states' names for a period of three years without a right to be appointed for another period". To make the organisation a truly international one and to maintain its interaction with other organisations, Article 14 says, "SCO may interact and maintain dialogue in particular in certain areas of cooperation, with other states and international organisations". The same article also deals with the mechanism through which the "organisation may grant to the state or international organisation concerned the status of a dialogue partner or observer."[36]

The Declaration issued after the end of the summit closely resembles the Charter of the organisation adopted at the same summit. It call upon the member states to support the efforts of each other to wipe out the menace of terrorism, separatism and extremism, as well as, the steps of the international community aimed at closing the channel of financing terrorist activity and build up efforts to prevent on their territories the preparation and financing of acts of terrorism. It also reaffirmed the intention of member states to strengthen the role of the United Nations Security Council in bearing the main responsibility for maintenance of international peace and security. One hallmark of the declaration signed at the summit was that it laid emphasis on creating a favourable condition for boosting trade and investment in this region on the basis of elaborating a long-term programme of multilateral trade and investment cooperation in accordance with the Memorandum between the governments of the SCO member states held in September 2001. The declaration also identified the priority areas of cooperation among the member states in such areas as the construction of transport, communications and power supply projects, water use, the extraction and transportation of energy resources as well as in other fields of mutual interest.[37]

The regional security situation around this area has not improved much after the 11 September incident. In fact one can notice the proliferation of drug trade, and Islamist fundamentalism, proliferation of small arms in this part of the world. Another important problem which confront the region's security is the reemergence of the problem of Islamist fundamentalism after 9/11 incident. As Kali Imankulov, the head of the Kyrgyz National Security Service pointed out, the Islamic Movement of Uzbekistan, Hizbut Tahrir al Islami, Uighur separatists from Xinjiang province of China are uniting themselves under the banner of Islamic Movement of Turkestan. He further stated that the aim of the new organisation is to create an Islamic Caliphate that will begin in Uzbekistan before extending to Tajikistan and Kyrgyzstan and moving on to the rest of Central Asia and Xinjiang province of China.[38] Similarly, the Pakistani analyst Ahmad Rashid believes that though the IMU has of late become weak, its underground activity remains intact.[39] Russia is also not immune to the danger from radical Islamist groups based in Chechnya. In January 2002 the Dagestani Islamic militants carried out a blast killing seven soldiers. In May 2002 during the victory festival in Kaspisk, the Chechen militants exploded a bomb killing 42 people and injuring over 100.[40] These radical forces carried out two explosions in 2003, one on 5 December 2003 in a train not far from Yessentuki in the Stavropol Region in which 45 people were killed and over 200 wounded. Similarly, on 9 December, a woman suicide bomber blew herself in a hotel in Moscow.[41] The Beslan crisis of Russia which happened in September 2004 in the North Ossetian town of Beslan involving the taking of more than 1,200 adults and children as hostages resulting in the death of 326 people and injuring of 700 (just a week after the downing of two civil aircrafts) reflects the barbaric acts of the terrorists and the extent they can go to achieve their narrow-sectarian objective.[42]

Another issue in which the Shanghai Cooperation Organisation has of late stated taking interest is related to environmental disaster and its long-term implication for the security of this region. There are several environmental hazardous zones in Central Asia. The largest one is the Aral Sea disaster zone which covers part of Uzbekistan, Kazakhstan and Turkmenistan. Apart from this zone the other area where the environmental situation is quite grave is in Uzbekistan's Karakalpak Autonomous Region and in Kazakhstan the Kyzl Orda and Akhtyubinsk oblasts and Dashauz region of Turkmenistan. The environmental degradation puts a serious strain on human health. It also causes economic losses ranging from U.S$1.345 to2.5 billion annually.[43] Apart from environmental degradation the issue of distribution of scarce-water resources between Tajikistan and Kyrgyzstan on the one hand and the Uzbekistan, Kazakhstan and Turkmenistan on the other has the potential to cause a conflict situation. It was reported that in the year 2000 the production of agriculture declined by somewhat 30 per cent. The Xinjiang region of China is also facing this problem of water scarcity and environmental degradation. It has been observed that in the Yining County to increase production, the farmers uses too much pesticides and which leads to water pollution as well as soil salinity. The water shortages have also affected many urban and industrial cities, which include Urumchi, the capital city of Xinjiang province of China.[44]

Besides combating Islamist fundamentalism in which members of SCO have a common interest, the other objective which binds them is the establishment of a multipolar world order and faith in the UN as a mechanism to resolve international conflicts. To checkmate the "hegemonistic policy" of the United States, Russia under its leadership set up the Collective Security Treaty Organisation (CSTO) and established an air base in Kant in Kyrgyzstan for operation of the rapid action force of the CSTO. During the opening ceremony both President Vladimir Putin and President Askar Akaev made it clear that the American air base at Manas was temporarily established for executing the mission in Afghanistan while the Russian base in Kant is a permanent one.[45] This reflected the desire of both the governments to get rid of American presence. The growing resentment against the American presence in this part of the world is evident from newspaper articles published in various Russian and Chinese newspapers. An article published in *Nezavisimaya Gazette* on 29 September 2003, stated that the United States and the NATO want to expand their influence in Central Asia on the pretext of the "worsening situation in Afghanistan". Through NATO, as the article stated, the Americans would like in the future "to gradually take control of the entire military structure in the majority of the CIS countries". It further mentioned that "it would be easy for Russia to blunt the US efforts to expand its strategic influence". To do so, "Russia was advised to boost arms sales to the Central Asian states and expand the officers' training programme"[46]. China is also cagey of American military presence in Central Asia. The American effort to obtain a military base in Semipalatinsk in Kazakhstan, the old Soviet nuclear testing site and the one already established at Manas just 300 miles from its border are indication of American interest in this region. During the visit of a Chinese delegation to Central Asia in January 2002, Beijing announced an aid package worth 600 million dollars to Uzbekistan, (the US pledged only 162 million dollars).[47] Apart from Uzbekistan, China has also provided aid worth three million dollars to Kazakhstan's Ministry of Defence for upgrading the latter's equipment and communication infrastructure for Kazakhstan's special forces.[48] Besides the Russian newspaper many Chinese and Central Asian analysts also do not see the American moves in this part of the world favourably. Thus for example *The People's Daily* in its 22 March 2002 issue carried an article titled "The United States Seeks Global Hegemony under the Pretext of Fighting Terrorism", in which a Chinese analyst Ren Yujun compared the current presence of the United States in the Central Asian region with that of American presence in the Middle East after the 1991 Gulf War, "The new U.S presence in the NIS makes one think of how the US did not ... pullout from the Gulf region after the 1991 Gulf War but instead built military bases in six countries... and decided to keep troops there for a long time".[49] The same daily in its 6 September 2002 issue titled "Strategic Significance of Central Asia Stands Out", Chinese analyst Wang Bin examining the fall out of the "Great Game" observed, "The United States has cleverly and preemptively positioned a chess piece on the Grand Chessboard of the Asian continent".[50] Similar fear was also raised by the Director of the Centre for Foreign Policy and Analysis of Kazakhstan, Bulat Sultanov. According to him, "the United States is going, under the banner of eradicating international terrorism, to take advantage of the prevailing situation, to realize its own geopolitical interests in Central Asia, to consolidate its military presence and take control of real and potential routes of hydrocarbon raw materials".[51] Kazakh analyst M. Laumulin also made a similar observation regarding the move of China in Central Asia. According to Laumulin: "China thinks that big American military presence in Kyrgyzstan and Uzbekistan and American interest in Central Asia are threats to its security. To meet this threat China tries to expand its cooperation with the Central Asian states both bilaterally as well as through the framework of SCO".[52]

The unilateralist approach of the US to solve the Afghan problem, growing menace of terrorism and drug trafficking and closer cooperation among Central Asia, Russia and China, both at bilateral and multilateral level provided the backdrop to the Foreign Ministers meeting of the SCO countries held in April 2003. The statement issued after the end of the ministerial meeting noted, "The drug trafficking is the main source of financial assistance to transnational crime and international terrorism". The meeting also called for "peaceful settlement of international conflicts provoked by ethnic, confessional, territorial and political and other contradictions in strict compliance with the UN Charter and norms of international law".[53]

The meeting of Heads of SCO states in Moscow in May 2003 followed the SCO Foreign Ministers' meeting. The summit meeting decided to set-up a permanent secretariat and regional anti-terrorist structure at Bishkek. At this summit the flag and emblem of the SCO was adopted and Ẓhang Deguang, Ambassador of China to Russia, was appointed as SCO Executive Secretary. The summit also decided to take up the development of the North-South Transport Corridor Project which is constructed to ensure continuous transit of containers cargos from Asia to Europe.[54] After the summit at Moscow, the SCO countries conducted their first ever military exercises named as *Coalition 2003* in which all the SCO countries minus Uzbekistan participated. The major objective of this exercise was to boost SCO's capability to coordinate their fight against terrorism and to ensure stability and regional security.[55]

The subsequent Prime Ministers' meeting which was held in Beijing in September 2003 also discussed commonality of issues affecting the member countries of SCO. One important aspect of the meeting was its discussion of measure to boost regional cooperation among member countries in the economic field to ensure cohesiveness and economic development of this region. It identified the potential areas like energy, information, telecommunication as well as environmental problems. The meeting also laid down the long-term objective of this Organisation as creation of a SCO free trade area. In this meeting the shifting of anti terrorist structure of SCO from Bishkek to Tashkent was also taken up.[56]

The SCO'S efforts to establish an important mechanism to ensure security in this region got added impetus by the establishment of its own Secretariat in Beijing in January 2004. The importance of SCO Secretariat has been aptly described by the United Nations Secretary General who in a congratulatory message said, "An institutionally strengthened SCO has been evolving into an increasingly important Regional Security Organisation". He further pointed out that the establishment of the Secretariat was "the logical extension of that progress" and assured that the "United Nations looks forward to multi-faceted cooperation with our new regional partner".[57]

The shared objective of all the six Eurasian countries in eliminating common threats like narcotic trade, religious extremism and cross-border terrorism also provides an additional leverage to the Shanghai Cooperation Organisation to pursue common objectives through mutual consultations both at the bilateral level as well as at their annual meetings of the heads of states and prime ministers' meetings of SCO. According to Basil Polemitis, the founding President of East Mediterranean Institute for Scientific Research and Studies of Cyprus, "through SCO the Central Asian states will benefit immensely, as they will get financial assistance both from Russia and China in order to counter the influence of the USA in this region".[58]

The latest meeting of the heads of states which took place at Tashkent on 17 June, 2004 in its joint declaration issued after the end of the meeting gave priority to the economic cooperation among the member countries. As the declaration stated, "To strengthen SCO in general, and to develop the long-term Programme of multilateral trade and economic cooperation of SCO member states, approved by the Council of Heads of the Governments (Prime Ministers) in Beijing in September 2003, the document has not only pointed out common understanding of business partnership reference points, goals and tasks of six countries for the perspective up to 2020, but also outlined ways and methods of their realization."[59] Apart from the issues of cross-border terrorism, proliferation of small arms, as well as drugs, the meeting also for the first time raised one important issue, i.e., the water issue that is of relevance for all the member countries as mentioned above. The Tashkent conference also discussed the environmental protection. As the summit noted, "Matters of environmental protection, rational and effective utilization of water resources have to be included into the agenda of developing cooperation within the Organisation's framework. Corresponding ministries and services, as well as scientific institutions could begin this year joint work to prepare SCO strategy in these areas". The summit meeting also repeated the "central role of the United Nations in fighting important global problems like cross-border terrorism, narco-trade as well as maintaining peace and tranquility and also creating necessary conditions for peaceful reconstruction of Afghanistan". The declaration also praised the "initiative of Uzbekistan with regard to holding of regular meetings of Security Council secretariat of the member states of the organisation to face new challenges". The Tashkent Declaration of Heads of SCO States also expressed the "further institutionalistion of the organisation". The organisation also evaluated the "development of cooperation in various fields such as external economic and foreign trade activity, transport, defence, and culture." To achieve success in these areas it called upon member states to "coordinate their activities at various levels of the Shanghai Cooperation Organisation". The Tashkent declaration of the Shanghai Cooperation Organisation also stressed on "constructive cooperation with all the regional associations of the Asia-Pacific Region as this would promote peace and stability in this part of the world."[60]

The Shanghai Cooperation Organisation's Foreign Ministers' who met at Astana in February 2005 in preparation for the June Heads of States Summit meeting which is going to take place in Kazakhstan's capital in the month of June 2005 discussed wide range of issues confronting the organisation and developments that took place in the region since the Tashkent Summit of SCO.[61]

The growing resentment among the Central Asian political elite against the efforts of the external actors to change the regimes through the so-called "revolution" and "rose revolution" as happened in Ukraine and Georgia has to some extent helped in changing the geo-political situation in the Eurasian region. This is evident from the rejection by Bishkek of the US request to deploy the AWACS reconnaissance planes at the US airbase, and the growing trend towards military cooperation with Russia. Many observers think Akaev regime's decision not to deploy the AWACS planes at Ganci was basically done to please Russia.[62] The efforts to forge a closer relationship with Russia was also evident from the Tajik President Rakhmonov's statement about, Russia and Tajikistan as "strategic allies". In fact, Tajikistan is hosting Russia's biggest overseas military base. [63] Similarly Russian President Vladimir Putin has also in March 2005 signed the federal law on ratification of the agreement between the Russian Federation and the Republic of Kazakhstan on joint military planning reflecting common security interests of the two countries. The growing warmth in the Russo-Central Asian, Russo-Chinese as well as Chinese-Central Asian relations at the bilateral level (both economic and political relations) will certainly have an impact on the functioning of the Shanghai Cooperation Organisation and the overall security of this region.[64]

The criticism often heard that the SCO has failed to provide "security" and only added to "a long line of abortive attempts to reorganise Central Asia under Russian leadership"[65] is not justified. In this connection one should not forget that that the Charter of SCO was signed in 2002 only after the 9/11 incident and its permanent secretariat was established in 2004. It is thus inconceivable that the SCO should have ensured security before its creation. It may be pointed out that even before SCO's formation the Shanghai Five countries in their third summit meeting at Almaty had raised the issue of cross-border terrorism, and taken steps to check this menace. Apart from the Shanghai Five level, the member countries through bilateral relations made significant efforts to enhance each other's security. For example the Russian 201st Motorized Infantry Division was guarding Tajikistan's border. At the conference of Shanghai Five in 1998 the member states raised the issue of fighting terrorism, which the United States took up only after the 9/11 incident. The massive anti-terrorist exercises conducted successfully by the SCO forces as noted above demonstrated their preparedness to carry out operation against the Islamist militants.[66]

The institutionalistion process which is currently underway after the formation of its Secretariat and regional anti-terrorist centre in Tashkent as mentioned above will certainly give impetus to the organisation's effectiveness. The SCO's success will, however, ultimately depend on how best it promotes the course of regional economic cooperation among the member countries, which alone, will banish the multitude of threats to the security of the region.

REFERENCES

1. Li Fenglin, "SCO Forges Ahead on new journey", *International Strategic Studies* 1. Issue, 2004. p. 37.
2. G. Kirev, "The Serpentine Path to the Shanghai G-5", *International Affairs,* Vol. 49, No. 3, 2003, (Moscow) pp. 86-87.
3. Yevgeny Kozhokin, "Shanghai Five: Present Realities and Future Prospects", *Strategic Digest,* IDSA, (New Delhi) July 2001, p. 883.
4. Xu Tao, "Promoting "Shanghai Five" Spirit for Regional Cooperation", *Contemporary International Relations,* 11(5), May 2001, p. 15.
5. *Ibid.*
6. Xu Tao, "On the SCO Under New Situation", *Contemporary International Relation,* Vol. 12, No. 6, June 2002, pp. 9-10.
7. Devendra Kaushik, "Islamic Fundamentalism in Central Asia", *Himalayan and Central Asian Studies,* Vol. 4, No. 3-4, July-December2000, pp. 14-15.
8. *Beijing Review,* 31 January 2003, p. 19; for details on ethno-religious conflict in the Xinjiang province of China see, Nalin Kumar Mohapatra, "Ethno-Religious Conflict in a Multi-Cultural Society: A Study of China's North West Frontier Province of Xinjiang", Azad Institute Paper-25, Maulana Abul Kalam Azad Institute of Asian Studies, Kolkata, 2004.
9. Yitzhak Shichor, "The Great Wall of Steel: Military and Strategy in Xinjiang" in S. Frederic Starr (ed.), *Xinjiang: China's Muslim Borderland,* M.E. Sharpe, Armonk, New York, 2004, p. 158.
10. *Ibid.*, p. 145.
11. Ahmed Rashid, *Jihad: The Rise of Militant Islam in Central Asia,* Orient Longman, Hyderabad, 2002, p. 165.
12. Mahendra Ved "When Silk Routes Becomes Destructive Drug Routes," *Asian-Eurasian Commentary,* Vol. 111, No. 5-7, April-December, 2000, (New Delhi) p. 52.
13. *Summary of World Broadcasts*/SU/3665/G/2, 14. October 1999.
14. Pierre Arnaud Chouvey, "Opiates Smuggling routes from Afghanistan to Europe and Asia", *Jane's Intelligence Review,* March 2003, p. 31; see also Yury Yegorov, "How Heroin Enters Russia" *New Time,* December 2002, pp. 48-50.
15. B. Baibulov, "Illegal drug Trafficking as a Threat to National Security", *Central Asia's Affairs,* (Almaty), No. 1, Jan-March 2003, p. 6.
16. Asel Berimjarov, "Afghan Drugs: Right now they are the main threats", *The Times of Central Asia, 29* December 2001, p. 4.

17. Niklas Swanstrom "The South East Asian and Chinese Connection to Drug Trade in Central Asia" *Central Asia and Caucuses Analyst*, www.cacianalyst.org, 27 August 2003, pp. 1-3.
18. Jay Dautcher, "Public Health and Social Pathologies" in S. Frederic Starr, (ed.), op. cit, p. 289.
19. S. Neil MacFarlane and Stina Torjesen, *Kyrgyzstan: A Small Arms Anomaly in Central Asia*? February 2004, *Small Arms Survey*, Graduate Institute of International Studies, Geneva, pp. IX and 11.
20. *Ibid.*, pp. 12-13.
21. Ahmed Rashid, *op. cit.*, p. 165.
22. *Ibid.*, p. 166.
23. S. Neil MacFarlane and Stina Torjesen, *op. cit.*, p. 24.
24. Xu Tao, *op. cit.*, p. 11.
25. Ibid;" Police, security Chiefs of Shanghai Five states sign memorandum" *Interfax News Agency*, 2. Dec. 1999 reproduced in *Contemporary Central Asia*, Vol. 111, No, 3, 1999, p. 59.
26. Ren Xin, "Fruitful Dushanbe Summit", http://www.china.org.cn/Beijing-Review/2000Jul/bjr2000-29e-4.htm
27. "Declaration of the Shanghai Cooperation Organisation", Shanghai, 15 June, 2001, *China Report*, 37: 4, 2001, pp. 553-56.
28. A. Lukin, "Russia, China and Iraqi Conflict", *International Affairs*, (Moscow), Vol. 49, No. 3, 2003, p. 9.
29. Devendra Kaushik "Central Asia: Changing Geo-Political Alignment in the aftermath of 11 September", *Dialogue*, Vol. 3, No. 4, April-June 2002, pp. 43-56.
30. "USA Pledges Not To Abandon Central Asia After Afghan War ", BBC, originally from Interfax-Kazakhstan news agency, 19 December 2001, from Internet.
31. *The Times of Central Asia*, Vol. 3, No. 50, 13 December 2001, p. 4.
32. *Komsomolskaya Pravda*, 30 January 2002, cited in Devendra Kaushik, *Dialogue, op. cit.*, p. 54.
33. Ibid, pp. 52-53; "Shanghai 6 vow to fight "three vices", *The Times of Central Asia*, 10 January 2002; A. Lukin, "Russia, China and the Iraqi conflict", *op. cit.*, p. 16
34. Murad Esenov, "The Anti-Terrorist Campaign and the Regional Security System", in *Russian Regional Perspectives, Russia's New Southern Border: Western Siberia-Central Asia, IISS Quarterly*, London, issue 2, 2003, p. 27
35. http://www.sectsco.org/news_detail.asp?id=96&LanguageID=2
36. *Ibid.*
37. For details of declaration see Publication of the Ministry of Foreign Affairs of the Russian Federation. http://russia.shaps.hawaii.edu/fp/russia/sco_20020610_4.html
38. ttp;//www.dailytimes.com.pk/default.asp?Page=story ;http://English.Pravda.ru/main/2002/09/16/36647.html.
39. Central Asia: Is the IMU Still A Threat to Regional Security?, 1/24/04, http://www.eurasianet.org/departments/ insight/articles/pp012404.shtml
40. Xu Tao, *op. cit.*, 2002, p. 13.

41. Vladimir Vornov, The "Pacification of Chechnya" *New Times,* January 2004, pp. 16-17.
42. Mark Galeotti," Beslan shows growing Islamist influence in Chechen War", *Jane's Intelligence Review,* October 2004, p. 12.
43. Amanda Wooden, "The Nexus Between Environmental Policy and Human Rights in Central Asia", *Harvard Asia Quarterly,* Spring, 2004, pp. 14-15.
44. Stanley W. Toops, "The Ecology of Xinjiang: A Focus on Water", in S. Frederic Starr (ed),, op. cit, pp. 273-274; Randa M. Slim, "The Ferghana Valley: In the Midst of a Host of Crises", in Monique Mekenkamp, Paul van Tongeren and Hans van de Veen(eds.), *Searching for Peace in Central and South Asia,* Lynne Rienner, Boulder/London, 2003, p. 147.
45. http://www.eurasianet.org/resource/kyrgyzstan/hypermail/2003 10/0040.shtml
46. Cited in Todd Diamond, "US Unilateralism Fuels Great power rivalry in Central Asia", 10/01/03 http://www.eurasianet.org/index.shtml
47. Alec Rasizade, "Entering the Old Great Game in Central Asia", *Orbis,* Winter, 2003, p. 56.
48. Michael Dhillon, "China and the U.S base in Central Asia" *The World Today,* July, 2002, p. 15
49. Ren Yujun, "The United States seeks Global Hegemony under the pretext of Fighting Terrorism", *Renmin Ribao,* 22 March 2002, cited in Lyle J. Godstein, "Beyond the Steppe: Projecting Power into the New Central Asian States", *Journal of Slavic Military Studies,* 17, 2004, p. 200.
50. Wang Bin "The Strategic Significance of Central Asia Stands Out", *Renmin Riabo,* 06 September 2002, cited in *Ibid.*
51. Situation in Central Asia and the Shanghai Cooperation Organisation, Collection of the conference materials, Shanghai Institute of International Relations, Shanghai, 2003, pp. 292-293 cited in A. Lukin, "Shanghai Cooperation Organisation: Problems and Prospects", *International Affairs* (Moscow), Vol. 50, No. 3, 2004, p. 36.
52. M. Laumulin, "Current Strategies and International Relations in Central Asia", *Central Asia's Affairs,* Jan-March, 2003, p. 25.
53. *Krasnaya Zvezda,* 91 in full, reproduced in *RIA Novosti Daily Review,* 27 May 2003.
54. Devendra Kaushik, "The Eurasian Perspective of an Emerging Asian Security Structure", Mahavir Singh (ed.), *Asia Annual, 2003,* Shipra Publications, New Delhi, p. 75.
55. *China Daily,* 7 August 2003, p. 5.
56. LI Fenglin, *op. cit,* p. 36; http://www.chinadaily.com, 23.09.03
57. http://www.i.chinadaily.com.en/doc/2004-01/15/content299277.htm
58. Basil Polemitis, "How Can Central Asian Republics Benefit from the Shanghai Cooperation Organisation", *Harvard Asia Quarterly,* Spring, 2004, p. 64; Xu Tao, "On the SCO under New Situation", 2002, op. cit.
59. "The Tashkent Declaration of the Heads of the States Participating in the Shanghai Cooperation Organisation" http://www.sectsco.org/news_detail.asp?id=119&LanguageID=2, 17 June 2004.

60 *Ibid.*

61. Transcript of Russia, Kazakhstan, Kyrgyzstan, China, Uzbekistan Foreign Ministers Press Conference Following Shanghai Cooperation Organization Foreign Ministers Council Session (Astana, 25, February) 377-25-02-200, http://www.ln.mid.ru/brp_4.nsf/0/076849c5e4019c59c3256fb600422a0e?Open Document

62. http://www.rferl-org/features article/2005/02/059615a/4237-4861-b9d9-197855075814.html

63. "Russia and Tajikistan Strategic Allies: President Rakhmonov", *News from Russia,* No. 3, No. 1 March, 2005.

64. "Putin signs security agreements with Kazakhstan and Kyrgyzstan" News *from Russia,* 11 March, 2005; many ardent eurasianists also hold similar views and this can be evident in their writings.

65. Stephen Blank, "The Shanghai Cooperation Organisation: A Post Mortem". *Nordic Newsletter of Asian Studies,* No. 3, 2002, cited in Devendra Kaushik, in Mahavir Singh (ed), *op. cit.*, p. 75

66. *Ibid.*, p. 76; see also A. Lukin, "Shanghai Cooperation Organisation: Problems and Prospects", *op. cit.*, p. 35.

Contributors

Ainur Elebaeva is Director, Institute of Ethnology, International University of Kyrgyzstan, Bishkek, Kyrgyzstan.

Ajay Patnaik is Professor in the Centre for Russian, Central Asian and East European Studies at Jawaharlal Nehru University, New Delhi.

Askar Shomanov is First Deputy Director, Kazakhstan Institute of Strategic Studies, Almaty, Republic of Kazakhstan.

C.P. Bhambhri is Professor of Eminence in Political Studies, Jawaharlal Nehru University, New Delhi.

D.R. Goyal is a veteran journalist and author and a Fellow of MAKAIAS.

Devendra Kaushik is the Chairman of the Executive-Council of Maulana Abul Kalam Azad Institute of Asian Studies, Kolkata.

Du Yanling is the Deputy Director-General, China Center for Contemporary World Studies, Beijing, Peoples' Republic of China.

F.G. Teshabaev (Late) was Ambassador of Uzbekistan in the USA and the UK.

Felix N. Yurlov is the Head, Modern Studies Department, Department of Indian Studies, Institute of Oriental Studies, Russian Academy of Sciences, Moscow, Russia.

Hari Vasudevan is the Head of the Academy of Third World Studies, Jamia Millia Islamia, New Delhi.

Hoshiar Singh is Vice-Chancellor, University of Bikaner, Bikaner, Rajasthan.

I. Sh. Normatov, is Director, Institute of Water Problems, Hydropower and Ecology, Tajik Academy of Sciences,. Dushanbe, Republic of Tajikistan.

Meena Singh Roy is an Associate Fellow of the Institute of Defence Studies & Analyses, New Delhi.

Nalin Kumar Mohapatra is Project Fellow, MAKAIAS, Kolkata.

P.L. Dash is Professor in the Centre for Central Eurasian Studies, University of Mumbai, Mumbai.

R.R. Sharma is the Dean, School of International Studies, Jawaharlal Nehru University, New Delhi.

R.R. Subramanian is Research Scholar in the Institute for Defence Studies and Analyses, New Delhi.

R.S. Yadav is Professor in the Department of Political Science, Kurukshetra University, Haryana.

S.P. Singh is Head of the Department of History, L.N. Mithila University, Darbhanga, Bihar.

Sanjana Joshi is a Project Fellow, Maulana Abul Kalam Azad Institute of Asian Studies (MAKAIAS), Kolkata.

Saradindu Mukherji is Reader in the Deptt. of History, Hansraj College, University of Delhi.

Sergei Lounev is Professor in the Institute of World Economy and International Relations, Russian Academy of Sciences, Moscow, Russia.

Shankari Sundararaman is an Associate Professor in the Centre for South, Central, South-East Asian and South-West Pacific Studies, School of International Studies, Jawaharlal Nehru University, New Delhi.

Sharad K. Soni is a Project Fellow, MAKAIAS, and Assistant Editor, Himalayan and Central Asian Studies, published from New Delhi.

Surat Mirkasymov is presently in the Academy of State Construction and the Institute of Oriental Studies, Tashkent, Republic of Uzbekistan and was first Ambassador of Uzbekistan to India.

Surendra Gopal is former Professor of History, Patna University, Bihar and also a Fellow of MAKAIAS.

V. Suryanarayan is Professor of Maritime Studies and Research, Calicut University, Kerala.

Vasundhara Mohan is Director Centre for Central Eurasian Studies, University of Bombay, Mumbai.

Xu Yongquan is Associate Fellow of the China Center for Contemporary World Studies, Beijing, Peoples' Republic of China.

Zhang Jianwei is an Associate Research Fellow of the China Center for Contemporary World Studies, Beijing, Peoples' Republic of China.

Zhou Yuyun is Research Fellow of the China Center for Contemporary World Studies, Beijing, Peoples' Republic of China.

Index

N

O

P

V

W

X

Y

Z